MW01672583

From The Beginning - Unity

Volume One

By Arthur Zebley

FROM THE BEGINNING - UNITY

Copyright © 1995
by Arthur Zebley
All Rights Reserved.

Printed in the
United States of America by:
Morris Publishing
P.O. Box 2110
3312 E. Hwy 30
Kearney, NE 68848
(800) 650-7888

Library of Congress Catalog Card Number: 97-90484

ISBN 0-9655411-0-X

Contents

FORWARD

Arthur Zebley and I share many memories of growing up at Unity Village. His book reminds me of my wonderful childhood and of the people and activities that were a part of those days when both Unity Farm, as it was then called, and I were young.

Anyone who is interested in the growth and development of Unity will find in Arthur's book information that has never before been compiled in such detailed, chronological order. Through years of research Arthur has captured the spirit of the people who joined with the Fillmores in creating Unity Village.

It has always seemed to me that those who were working here in the early years realized that they were part of something more than building buildings, farming, landscaping, or whatever other work they were doing. It was as if everyone realized that they had come to be a part of the creation of a special place on earth--a place of beauty, a place of peace, a place of God. And each person who lived and worked here contributed a special soul gift that has created the consciousness that makes Unity Village a unique place.

Arthur has done a remarkable job in detailing the history of Unity. He has brought to life the dedication, the love, the integrity, the very spirit of those special people who joined together to bring to fruition the beautiful vision that began with Charles and Myrtle Fillmore some hundred years ago.

By Rosemary Fillmore Rhea

PROLOGUE

The purpose of this book is to relate the history, dates, records and the pertinent facts pertaining to the Fillmore Family, The Unity School of Christianity, the physical growth of its facilities and the inclusion of the dedicated Unity employees in this special book that combines these four elements in a historical review.

Myrtle Page and Charles Fillmore married and their three sons became their family. Personal healing came to Myrtle through her own prayers and faith. Charles saw Myrtle's healing and applied the same principles for his own healing. Their religious movement began with concerted study of all religions by Charles. The five Fillmores emerged from the nineteenth century with their own religious philosophy and a determined dedication to follow the teaching of Jesus Christ and their use of divine principles. Soon help for others to also find healing, success, happiness, prosperity and of most importance "God Within" became their goal.

A thorough history review of the four generations of the Fillmore family that have given their lifetimes to create, establish and continue the growth of this religious movement is documented throughout this book. Now the grandchildren and great-grandchildren are continuing "on the path" with the same constant divinely guided determination!

Throughout this book are special articles by Unity ministers, authors and employees that continue the teachings of Jesus Christ, Charles Fillmore and the Unity School of Christianity.

Additionally there is a rhythm throughout this book that relates the physical growth of the Unity movement from its meager beginnings, through its building of its headquarters on Tracy Avenue from 9th to10th in Kansas City, Missouri. Then to follow the dream of Charles Fillmore for a "Unity City" where the Unity Training School would be housed on a farm that could supply provisions for the Unity Inn in Kansas City and have recreational facilities for its employees and families. Rather than "Unity City" the new area was named "Unity

Farm" and many years later incorporated into a municipality that is now "Unity Village."

Much of the information gathered for this book came from a publication that was geared towards the Unity worker to advise them of the happenings in the daily life and growth of Unity. Publication began in 1916, survived several name changes and in 1919 became the Unity News and was printed weekly. From this "in house organ" was found much of the humor, interaction between workers and the human interest facts that happened in the daily work. Most of all it detailed how people from every walk in life came to work at Unity, at just the right time, with just the right talent to fill the needs of this fantastic organization that is known and loved by millions of people!

Each and every one discussed in the book has their own story about Unity and the affects on his or her life after becoming a part of the Unity movement. Such is my personal story: My name is Arthur Zebley. At the assembly of this information for publication, I am in my seventy-second year. Seventy of those years I have been a small part of Unity, but Unity has been a very large part of my life!

At my age of two years in 1925, my family moved to Unity Farm. My father, Arthur Carey Zebley, was a blacksmith and came to Unity Farm looking for work. When he was interviewed, in the Spring, he was told that there was a need for a life guard for the swimming pool more than a need for a blacksmith. He took the job offered and our family of four was given a house on the grounds to live in as part of father's salary. This is a prime example of a typical situation that can be related over and over of how one person came to Unity and his life's work had an undeniable effect on some part of the Unity growth. As far as my father was concerned, his skills concerned Unity Farm's beauty!

When the swimming season ended in 1926, my father was sent to the power house. There he set up a blacksmith shop and started construction of the many ornamental pieces of iron work and plaster casts that became part of the lasting beauty that still remains at Unity Village today. Rick Fillmore, the second son of Charles and Myrtle, and my father worked together as a team. Mr. Fillmore was the designer and manager and my father was the craftsman and producer. Every piece of wrought iron that was fashioned into a hanging indoor or outdoor lamp fixture, every swinging gate, beautiful multiple flower pot holders, many other decorative pieces plus the hundreds of metal frame benches with wooden slats that first went into the Amphitheater were fashioned by these two people.

Rick Fillmore was so pleased with the results of my father's efforts that he found many places around the farm to have special iron work and plaster casts made and installed. Mr. Fillmore loved designing stone enclosures with arch tops where he would have my father make special fixtures to fit each arch perfectly and give just the right touch of ornamentation. Mr. Fillmore designed plaster casts that adorned the support columns in the Terrace Tea Room and smaller lineal feet of castings for decorative rail around the walls in his mother and father's private offices. All of my father's work was accomplished between 1926 and 1939, when he passed away. This also was the last of the ornamental iron work and plaster casts to be made at Unity Farm.

To be a young person and to have had the wonderful experience of living at Unity Farm and personally seeing its growth and development gave me a true insiders opportunity to tell this revealing story about Unity. I, too, worked at Unity. In our youth the farm worker's children could work in the berry patches after we were ten years old. We looked forward to Spring when we could pick berries and receive a little spending money for our efforts. At the age of fourteen I went to work at the Terrace Tea Room. This was after school, week-ends and then full time in the summer. There I first worked as the pot scrubber, then moved to dishwasher, bus boy, waiter and soda fountain "jerk," as that job was referred to in the thirties. Here in this most beautiful Tea Room and on the lower and upper outside terraces I was blessed to see and serve the thousands of people that came to Unity for classes, training, conventions and especially to serve the Unity ministers and members of the Fillmore family throughout my teen years. During my school years I attended Unity Sunday school and church. In 1940 I was privileged to serve as President of the Unity Village Chapel Youth of Unity. Since 1989 I have been blessed to serve as an officer of the Unity Village Chapel Men of Unity.

In 1942 at the age of nineteen, I joined the Marine Corps and spent thirty-two months in the Pacific war. What a different world I found when I left the close confines of Unity Farm and ventured away to serve my country! My Unity training carried me safely through the Pacific war years as a Marine Corps Raider and always on the initial landings. My being here to write this story is a true documentary of what blessings one can receive when he carries the Unity affirmations inside the top of his helmet and Christ in his heart!

It was of most importance that I verify the accuracy of the information I have been gathering about Unity for most of my life. The research began at the Unity Village Library on January 3, 1995. Little did I realize the journey that was awaiting me. The library and Heritage rooms contain vast volumes of Unity history. Much of which I found I knew little or nothing about. Not only was I on a research mission, but also I found myself on a most fantastic journey of 150 years of Unity history!

At the Unity Village library I was graciously received, and eagerly directed in finding the information needed. Priscilla Richards, Library Director, Carolyn Stewart, Archivist and David Jackson, Assistant Archivist are commended for their dedication, knowledge and their genuine effort to help every visitor and those doing research. During many months spent in research Carolyn and David became friends and their suggestions and help were appreciated.

Also personal "thanks" go to my granddaughter, Kelly Nelson, and my youngest son, Chris, for the many many hours spent transcribing my notes as the full book was being assembled and prepared for publication.

With the preparation of this book completed and ready for publishing my prayer now is that you, the reader, will enjoy reading this book as much as I have enjoyed preparing it "Just For You"!

With Much Love,

Arthur Zebley

From the Beginning - Unity

The Story of the Fillmore Family - The Unity School of Christianity - Unity in Kansas City, Missouri - Unity Farm - Unity Village and the historical facts - and physical growth of facilities.

1845 - Mary Caroline Page was born August 6th in Pagetown, Ohio, the eighth of nine children born to Marcus and Lucy Page. The Page children in order of their births: Jane, November 22, 1830 - Henrietta, May 17, 1832 - Sarah, April 27, 1834 - Thomas August 11, 1836 - Sophronia, June 29, 1838 - David, July 26, 1840 - Daniel, December 16, 1842 - Mary Caroline, August 6, 1845 - Frances (also known as Buena), July 16, 1848. Sophronia and Frances died in infancy, Thomas at the age of twenty-nine. Two of the children, Jane and Henrietta, lived into their nineties.

Marcus Page was the founding father of Pagetown. The parents were deeply religious and faithful members of the Methodist church. Mary Caroline attended church with her parents, but never joined the church as she found much of the Methodist doctrine unacceptable. Marcus Page was very fond of his small daughter and often danced with her in her childhood years and called her "Myrtlee" as they danced. Later he called her "Myrtle", but Lucy continued to call her Mary Caroline. Her name was never legally changed to Myrtle, but she accepted the name and used it for the remainder of her life. At an early age she was diagnosed as having tuberculosis and considered to be an invalid. Myrtle completed High School during the Civil War.

1854 - Charles Sherlock Fillmore was born on August 22nd on an Indian reservation near St. Cloud, Minnesota. His father, Henry Fillmore, was a second cousin of Millard Fillmore, a United States President. His mother, Mary Georgiana Stone, of Welch and English ancestry, was born in Nova Scotia.

1861 - Henry Fillmore left his family and built a hut in the forest to live alone. His leaving left Mary, his wife, with Charles and second son Norton. Charles had very little formal education.

1864 - Charles suffered a dislocated hip while ice skating. An infection formed in the hip joint and in the ensuing two years duration left him with a withered leg at the age of twelve. His right leg then was about three inches shorter than the left.

1865 - Myrtle's father passed away on August 23rd. With Marcus Pages' passing much of the responsibilities to help her mother fell to Myrtle, as many of the older children were gone from home.

1866 - Myrtle went to Columbus, Ohio and was employed as a writer for a newspaper. Charles Fillmore was twelve years old, his younger brother Norton was ten, Norton ran away from home.

1867 - Myrtle enrolled in "The literary course for ladies" at Oberlin College in Oberlin, Ohio. It was a one year course and she was licensed as a school teacher.

1868 - Myrtle secured a position as a school teacher in Clinton, Missouri. Her brother, David, and his family followed her to Clinton, later in the year, and Myrtle lived with them. Myrtle loved the little town of Clinton, but her illness in the damp Midwest area continued to sap her strength. Doctors in Clinton advised her to move to Dennison, Texas where the weather would be more helpful for her health.

1869 - Charles Fillmore went to work as a printer's helper. He was tutored by the wife of an Army officer whose son was a close friend of Charles. His tutor was Mrs. Edgar Taylor and was greatly influenced by the writings of Shakespeare, Tennyson, Emerson and Lowell. He later worked as a grocery clerk and in a bank in St. Cloud, Minnesota.

1874 - Charles left Minnesota by train at the age of twenty for Caddo, just north of the Texas border in the Indian Territory that is now Oklahoma. Later that year he left Caddo for Dennison, Texas, twenty miles to the south, and secured work as a clerk for the M.K.& T. Railroad. Later Charles was appointed chief clerk and when he was settled into his job of authority he sent for his mother to come to Dennison and live with him.

1876 - Myrtle moved to Dennison, Texas and on the advise of her doctor in Clinton did not continue her public school teaching. She did private tutoring and joined the local Literary club. Another member of that club was Charles Fillmore, they soon became attracted to each other. One evening when Myrtle was delivering an original reading Charles was looking at her and something within him said, "There's your wife, Charles."

1878 - The weather was good for Myrtle and she was feeling better and decided to resume her teaching career. She opened a private school which was very successful. Later she made the decision to return to Clinton, Missouri and resume her public school teaching. She taught there for three years and was paid the highest salary on the school staff.

1879 - Charles Fillmore left Dennison, Texas moving to Colorado and became a mule team driver. He later took a course to become an assayer and sold real estate.

1881 - Charles wrote Myrtle a letter in which he proposed marriage and she accepted. They were married in Clinton, Missouri on March 29th and later that night left for their home together in Gunnison, Colorado. They first traveled by train, then stage coach and finally on sleigh runners to go over the Rocky Mountains. By July of that year they moved, going back over the mountains, to settle in Pueblo, Colorado. Charles set himself up in the real estate and insurance business. He was very successful as Pueblo was growing rapidly.

1882 - On January 4th Charles and Myrtle's first son was born. He was named Lowell Page Fillmore.

1883 - Pueblo was still growing and Charles and a friend developed a suburb to be known as Pueblo Gardens through their business, Small, Fillmore and Company.

1884 - The Fillmore's second son was born on June 1st and was named Waldo Rickert Fillmore. As both of the parents were lovers of literature the two sons names reflected those of popular writers; James Russell Lowell and Ralph Waldo Emerson. The real estate boom in

Pueblo had passed in 1883 and continued to worsen. Charles sent for his mother to come from Dennison, Texas to help Myrtle with the children. Charles was beginning to lose the sight in his right eye and hearing in his right ear. Later that year the decision was made to pack and move again. They went to Omaha, Nebraska, but were there only a few months and moved on to Kansas City, Missouri. Charles again opened a real estate company and in a short period was doing well and was prospering. He acquired land in the northeast section of Kansas City where he laid out the subdivision Gladstone Heights. Streets in Kansas City still bear the names given them by Charles. Myrtle Avenue, in honor of his wife, Norton Avenue, named for his brother and also Cypress and Elmwood.

1885 - Myrtle's health, which had improved when in Dennison, Texas and in the mountain air of Colorado was worsening again in the moist air of the Midwest. Charles and Myrtle discussed moving back to Colorado. It was then that Charles had an inspiring dream that convinced him that they should stay in Kansas City.

1886 - By Spring Myrtle's condition was continuing to deteriorate. She too had a dream about her future. Soon after this experience Myrtle and Charles attended a lecture featuring Dr. E.B. Weeks, from the Illinois Metaphysical College. He had been a pupil of Emma Curtis Hopkins who was an apostle pupil of Mary Baker Eddy. At the New Thought lecture Myrtle heard these words, "I am a child of God and therefore I do not inherit sickness." This simple statement continued in her thoughts through that night. She let this statement illumine the depth of her soul. She used this as an affirmation and also talked to her body. Months went by and she began feeling an improvement in her health. She turned to her Bible during these months and studied the words of Jesus Christ applying them to her own health and healing. Myrtle had healed herself at the end of a year. She accepted her healing and shared it with Charles, her family and friends in an article she wrote entitled:

How I Found Health

> "I have made what seems to me a discovery. I was fearfully sick; I had all the ills of mind and body that I could bear. Medicine and doctors ceased to give me relief and I was in

despair, when I found practical Christianity. I took it up and I was healed. I did most of the healing myself, because I wanted the understanding for future use. This is how I made what I call my discovery: I was thinking about life. Life is everywhere - in worm and in man. 'Then why does not the life in the worm make a body like mans?' I asked. Then I thought, 'The worm has not as much sense as man.' Ah! Intelligence, as well as life, is needed to make a body. Here is the key to my discovery. Life has to be guided by intelligence in making all forms. The same law works in my own body. Life is simply a form of energy and has to be guided and directed in man's body by his intelligence. How do we communicate intelligence? By thinking and talking, of course. Then it flashed upon me that I might talk to the life in every part of my body and have it do just what I wanted. I began to teach my body and got marvelous results. I told the life in my liver that it was not torpid or inert, but full of energy. I told the life in my stomach that it was not weak or inefficient, but energetic, strong and intelligent. I told the life in my abdomen that it was no longer infested with ignorant ideas of disease, put there by myself and by doctors, but it was all athrill with the sweet, pure, wholesome energy of God. I told my limbs that they were active and strong. I told my eyes that they did not see of themselves, but that they expressed the sight of Spirit and that they were drawing on an unlimited source. I told them that they were young eyes, clear bright eyes, because the light of God shone right through them.

I told my heart that the pure love of Jesus Christ flowed in and through its' beatings and that all the world felt its joyous pulsation. I went to all the life centers in my body and spoke words of Truth to them - words of strength and power. I asked for their forgiveness for the foolish, ignorant course that I had pursued in the past, when I had condemned them and called them weak, inefficient and diseased. I did not become discouraged at their being slow to wake up, but kept right on both silently and aloud, declaring the words of Truth, until the organs responded. And neither did I forget to tell them that they were free, unlimited Spirit. I told them that they were no longer in bondage to the carnal mind; that they were not corruptible flesh, but centers of life and energy omnipresent.

Then I asked the Father to forgive me for taking His life into my organism and there using it so meanly. I promised Him that I would never, never again retard the free flow of that life through my mind and body by any false word or thought; that I would always bless it and encourage it with true thoughts and words in its' wise work of building up my body temple; that I would use all diligence and wisdom in telling it just what I wanted it to do. I also saw that I was using the life of the Father in thinking thoughts and speaking words and I became very watchful as to what I thought and said. I did not let any worried or anxious thoughts into my mind and I stopped gossipy, frivolous, petulant angry words. I let a little prayer go up every hour that Jesus Christ would be with me and help me to think and speak only kind, loving, true words and I am sure that He is with me, because I am so peaceful and happy now. I want everybody to know about this beautiful, true law and to use it. It is not a new discovery, but when you use it and get the fruits of health and harmony it will seem new to you and you will feel that it is your own discovery."

1886 - Charles and Myrtle felt the need for more study and religious information. They went to Chicago, Illinois to attend classes conducted by Emma Curtis Hopkins. After their class work they were each presented with certificates dated December 10, 1886 from the Theological Seminary - Chicago. The certificates read as follows: Theological Seminary for the preparation of Students for the Christian Science Ministry Healing from sickness is an essential part of true Christian Ministry. First Course - Let this certify that Charles Fillmore has completed the First Course, at the Theological Seminary under my supervision and is sent forth to the healing ministry, Emma Curtis Hopkins. We have not shown that we are in full fellowship with pure Christian Doctrine till we have preached salvation from, sin, and, death, as well as sickness. Second Course - From this course of Study to the Perfect Ministry you are ordained in the name of the Father, Son and Holy Spirit, Emma Curtis Hopkins. Charles and Myrtle continued their study at home through correspondence courses.

1887 - When Charles and Myrtle completed the correspondence courses they were each presented with certificates dated July 1887 from the Normal Class Graduate of the Massachusetts Metaphysical College, Boston. The certificates read as follows: This It To Certify That Mr. Charles Fillmore has received from me a course of instructions in the Principles of Christian Science, as taught by Mrs. Eddy in her book entitled Science and Health, at present date, we see no reason why he is not about to demonstrate the same in the cure of sin and sickness, and the various forms of moral evil, Joseph Adams.

1888 - Neighbors and friends heard of Myrtle's healing and came asking for her prayers for their healing. She prayed with and for many and each resulted in healing. It was then that Charles reached a turning point in his life. He had watched his wife's healing and saw friends coming to her for prayer and their leaving with a new attitude toward healing. Charles made the decision to take charge in his life also and go directly to God. He took up his interest in the "New Thought" ideas and studied religions and philosophies. His withered leg began to grow, his eye and ear were healing and in a few years he was able to discard the iron leg brace. He saw that he was being healed by his own prayers. He cast off the anxieties and doubts and devoted himself to more and more spiritual research. The Fillmore's lived in a large dwelling on Wabash Avenue in Kansas City, Missouri. Lowell was enrolled in grade school.

1889 - With economic conditions in real estate sales and the economy in Kansas City weakening Charles and Myrtle decided to start a religious publishing venture. With the recent healing of each they felt it was the right and proper time to share the Truth they had learned. With many of the Fillmore's new friends and those that Myrtle had led in their own healing, a round table of prayer became the first group meeting to be held at the Fillmore home.

The first publication from the Fillmore's was named Modern Thought and its' first issue carried the date of April 1889. Modern Thought was a compendium of contemporary, Metaphysics, New Thought, Christian Science, Occultism and Theosophy. The publication contained sixteen pages and sold for ten cents per copy. The Fillmore's hand delivered each copy hanging them on the buyers door knob. Modern Thought had this statement as a motto on the title page, "Devoted to the Spiritualization of Humanity from an Independent Standpoint." On July 16, 1889 the third Fillmore son, John Royal was born. The first location where the Unity work in publishing was prepared was in the Journal Building on the northwest corner of 10th and Main in downtown Kansas City, Missouri. Quarters there were occupied for five months. Then moved for more space to the Deardorff Building on the Southeast corner of 11th and Main.

1890 - January marked ten months of the new publication. So many people were writing in and those in Kansas City were asking for prayer and personal counseling that Charles and Myrtle were teaching, editing, publishing and practicing Spiritual healing through prayer at the same time. In April the name of the Fillmore publication was changed from Modern Thought to Christian Science Thought. More office space was needed for their publication so again it was moved to the Hall Building at 9th and Walnut. By September the magazine was successfully edited, printed and delivered on time. "The Society of Silent Help" was formed in 1890. The Fillmore's oldest son Lowell was now of the age of eight and did help with the publishing when not in school. Emma Curtis Hopkins came to Kansas City to lecture and teach. The clarity of her teaching completely won over the Fillmore's and their friendship with her was a true blessing throughout their lives. The words of Emma Curtis Hopkins were a revelation to Charles because she spoke of Christ. When Charles had found Christ he found himself. Rick was enrolled in Oakley Grade School.

1891 - Charles Fillmore was still in the real estate business and his associates ridiculed his new activities. So he wrote articles for the magazine under the pen name of Leo Virgo. The title was fitting as he was born on August 22nd when the sun was leaving the sign of Leo and entering the sign of Virgo. At a meeting in the Spring Charles and Myrtle were with other Truth students. Charles suddenly shouted "That's it! Unity, that's the name of our work!" The name Unity reflected the best parts of the many religions they had studied and that all religions should work together for a common purpose of oneness with God. Also, in 1891 the "Society of Silent Help" was renamed the "Society of Silent Unity". The first issue of Unity magazine was published in June 1891 to be a semi-monthly publication, with the winged globe emblem on the cover which became the well known symbol of Unity. Charles explained that the winged globe represents the relation between Spirit, soul and body. Back of the soul is Spirit, which quickens and energizes the soul, that is, gives the soul wings. Also, 1891 was the year that Charles announced his belief in reincarnation.

After Unity magazine was published he changed the Unity Book Company name to the "Unity Tract Society". He said, "We have adopted the word 'tract' because it is a synonym of religious literature issued without the idea of gain. This is not a business, but a ministry!" When the Fillmore's moved their growing publishing to the Hall building they hired their first printer, Harry Church. He was a Seventh Day Adventist and a vegetarian. His presence became a major influence in the Fillmore's lives and his abilities as a printer allowed their time for writing and editing. On June 1, 1891 both Charles and Myrtle were ordained in the Christian Science Ministry. A protest was raised by Mary Baker Eddy of the use of "her words" Christian Science. In September 1891 the Fillmore's changed the name of their publication from Christian Science Thought to the single word Thought.

1892 - Dr. H. Emilie Cady's first article appeared in Unity magazine on December 7th soon after Charles and Myrtle's ordination in the Christian Science ministry and the name of their work was revealed to Charles, a very special event happened that sealed their commitment to Truth. Charles wrote what was called Dedication and Covenant. He and Myrtle signed it and lived by it the remainder of their lives;

Dedication and Covenant

> "We, Charles Fillmore and Myrtle Fillmore, husband and wife, hereby dedicate ourselves, our time, our money, all we have and all we expect to have, to the Spirit of Truth and through it, to the Society of Silent Unity. It being understood and agreed that the said Spirit of Truth shall render unto us an equivalent for this dedication, in peace of mind, health of body, wisdom, understanding, love, life and an abundant supply of all things necessary to meet every want without our making any of these things the object of our existence. In the

presence of the Conscious Mind of Christ Jesus this 7th day of December A.D. 1892."

1893 - Myrtle Fillmore was divinely guided to address the needs of children. First she was responsible for the beginning of Sunday school for the children. Then came a magazine as a ministry directed to the children, on a national bases. Wee Wisdom magazine containing eight pages in its' first issue was dated August 1893. It contained Mrs. Fillmore's intent with the following mission statement:

> "The mission of Wee Wisdom is not to entertain the children, but to call them out. To be always entertained is to be dwarfed and independent. To be called out is to follow the harmonious law of the soul's unfoldment. Who meddles with the rosebud? What fingers are deft enough to pry open that marvel of folded beauty? We are wise enough to leave it alone to follow the glad law of it's own unfolding. But our children! Have we dealt as wisely with these bits of marvelous possibilities? Have we always remembered that they, too, must quicken and unfold through the innate law of their own genius?"

Myrtle began a serial in Wee Wisdom called "Wee Wisdom Way" basically for her sons, they were her critics and also the ones to press her to continue the serial. After a year she told the boys, "If there is to be a continuation of the serial you will be the ones that write it." The serial was so popular that it finally was put in book form and published. "Aunt Joy", in the story was from the personal life of Myrtle. Trixy and Ned were the two main characters in the long running story, they represented her sons.

1894 - The first Lessons In Truth was published in the Unity magazine. Lessons In Truth became the first book published by Unity.

1895 - Because of financial problems Wee Wisdom was discontinued in 1895 and became a small feature in Unity magazine. The success of Unity's Thought magazine had grown from subscriptions in the hundreds to in the thousands. Thought was combined with Unity in October and the Unity name was used.

1896 - The Fillmore's were hosts for the "International New Thought Alliance", which held a meeting in Kansas City, Missouri. The Fillmore's were associated with this group until 1906 when the relationship ended, to be resumed in 1919 and finally to be terminated in 1922. Lowell entered Central High School in Kansas City, Missouri.

1897 - Myrtle Fillmore wrote an article entitled, How I Found Health, in 1886. The full text was published in the Unity magazine in 1897.

1898 - The printing operation was moved from the Hall building to a large house at 1315 McGee Street on May 15th. Two women were employed joining Mr. Church, the printer, Charles, Myrtle and Lowell Fillmore. The Fillmore family moved into their second house in Kansas City at 438 Elmwood. In July of 1898 Unity magazine became a monthly publication. In August of 1898 the Wee Wisdom magazine was again published. Myrtle's young readers ask and ask for a picture of her and finally on the front cover of the December 1898 Wee Wisdom appeared the picture of Myrtle and her three sons. She wrote of the occasion as follows, "On Earth peace and good will to every living creature, is our Christmas salutation. We are glad to visit you, one and all and meet you face to face in your homes and Sabbath schools. It seems quite an undertaking when we planned this numerous visit. Part of a precious Saturday was cheerfully given to its' preparation, though these boys do feel that it requires more courage to face a camera than a cannon, especially when the camera is pointed toward them and the cannon is not. But all obstacles are met and vanquished and here we are. As this roguist-eye boy (Rick) at our right states it, 'The funny part of it is, mama, we'll be everywhere at once.' And so we are, which proves our omnipresence. We've had great times talking over this wonderful tour and what it means to visit all the way from the Northern seas to the Southern oceans, to find ourselves entertained in homes from Denmark to Australia, from Alaska to South America, to become guest in every state, country and clime, even to far off Japan and the islands of the sea. The everywhereness of our visit means that in the joy of Christmas, we are one." Myrtle's son Rickert was a talented artist and his fine artwork appeared on many Wee Wisdom covers and illustrated stories for many years.

1900 - With the new year the Unity movement showed good signs of growth. Charles Fillmore returned to Colorado in the Summer to hold church services in Pueblo and Denver. Lowell graduated from Central High School and then entered the K. C. Business college for one year.

WEE WISDOM
Stands For

The unwarped faith that believeth and hopeth all things.
"All things are possible to them that believe."

The freshness and purity that beholdeth Good Always.
"Blessed are the pure in heart, for they shall see God."

The joy and gladness that are fullness of life and health.
"In Thy presence is fullness of joy . . . .
. . . . Thou wilt show me the path of life."

The truth that frees from the clutches of race heredity.
"One is your Father, even God."

The knowledge that Jesus Christ is the subjective spirit of every child.
"The kingdom of God is within you."

The understanding that our word is the builder of our environment.
"For without the Word was not anything made that was made."

"Be ye therefore perfect,
Even as your Father in heaven is perfect."
--Jesus.

Wee Wisdom poem selected from Lilliput Lectures.

Great Wide World

Great, wide, beautiful, wonderful world,
With the wonderful water round you curled,
And the wonderful grass upon your breast.
World, you are beautifully dressed!

The wonderful air is over me,
And the wonderful wind is shaking the tree;
It walks on the water, and whirls the mill,
And talks to itself on the top of the hill.

You friendly earth, how far do you go
With the wheat fields that nod and the rivers that flow,
With cities and gardens and cliffs and isles,
And people upon you for thousands of miles?

Ah! you are so great, and I am so small,
I tremble to think of you, world, at all,
And yet, when I said my prayers today,
A whisper inside me seemed to say--

"You are more than the earth, though you are such a dot,
You can love and think, and the earth cannot."

Epistles from Wee Wisdom.

"Dear Mrs. Fillmore -- I will be six this month and I want to send you fifty of my pennies and you can send Wee Wisdom for a year to some little child as a birthday present from me. I have been treating Mabel Wilson, a young lady who thinks she cannot see. I wish that all the Wee Wisdoms and their mammas would help me treat that God is Mable's sight. Mable is so sweet, I know you would love her if you could see her. That's all. Tessie Evelyn Wallace - Kansas City, MO.

Dear Wee Wisdom -- You will please find enclosed a pillow verse to publish in your bright and happy columns if you can easily find space. With love to Mother Sparr and all the little readers, I remain for this time. Belle Poteet - Alaculsy, GA.

Dear Wee Wisdom -- I have never written to you before, and I thought I would write you a few lines now while I have time. I am a little girl eleven years young. I am the president of the Band of Mercy, and mamma is the superintendent. I have a little kitten for my pet and its name is Tabby. I have five dolls, a pickaninny and two rag cats. I take Wee Wisdom and like it very much. Papa and mamma take Unity,

Harmony, Life, and Light. We are having a new school house built, so we will have about six months vacation. I am in the fifth grade. I think this is all I can write this time. Yours in love and truth. Violet Hellikson - Mable, MN.

Dear Wee Wisdom -- I will take the pleasure to write you a few lines. I am twelve years old. I go to Sunday School every Sunday if I can. I have one sister and four brothers. I take Wee Wisdom and I like to read them. I save my Wee Wisdom papers, and after while I am going to make a book out of them. I would like one of Mother Sparr's moss cards. This is a little verse I made up: God is good, God is true, And that is, What we ought to do. I will close in love. Anna Vogt - Pender, NE.

Dear Mrs. Fillmore -- My mother has taken your paper for some time. I like it very much. I will take it this year. I enclosed $1.00 for a new subscriber and myself. I would like one of your moss cards. My love to Wee Wisdom. Miss Jennie Cuthbert - Viola, ID."

1901 - The Fillmore's again went to Colorado for the "Colorado Summer School of Metaphysics" in August. It was an outdoor school held in a large tent. The Fillmore's, teachers and students stayed in smaller tents nearby. The event was held in Manitou. Lowell, age 19, became a full time employee at Unity.

Wee Wisdom Kansas City, Missouri September 1901. How Morlena Was Healed (A True Story) by Lucy C. Kellerhouse.

> "Morlena lay very still in her little bed. Every morning the sun, peeping over the roof of the neighboring house, found her there; and again in the evening, when he looked in through the front window, he found her lying just the same, straight and still. The children next door romped and played, but Morlena had never joined their sport. The wind was lively in the branches of the trees, the leaves danced, the birds hopped on the ground, or pierced the air with swift motion; the water, the clouds, all things moved, but Morlena lay still. Yes, the brook lay just so when winter came and locked it up with chains of

ice. But underneath the brook's icy bonds is moving water -- that is life.

The doctors came -- one, two, three, four. But Morlena's mother only cried harder, and Morlena's father looked more tender and sad when in the evening he came home and stooped and kissed his child. "It is October, isn't it, papa?" asked Morlena one evening, looking out at the falling mellow leaves. "Yes, darling." "Christmas will soon be here." "Yes, my child." "It will be two years then, since you laid me just so in my bed. It will be very lazy for me to lie in bed two whole years. I really must be well for Christmas." "Yes, Morlena." He turned his face away, as if to look at the crimson sunset through the golden trees. "Were you easy today, Morlena?" he asked presently. "Perhaps I didn't feel so very good today, papa. But I am a big girl now -- twelve years old -- and I do not mind so when my back hurts as I did when I was little. I never cry, but I am trusting in God to heal me." The father did not speak, but looked again through the window. The bright trees and sky were very pretty, but he did not see them.

The doctors had said that Morlena would never be well -- never, what a cruel word; never romp and play, never walk, never move her feet again! Yet her mother and father would have given all the world for the glad sound of her footsteps.

One day somebody sent Morlena a story to read -- a true story. A woman had been sick a long, long time. Her doctors, just like Morlena's doctors, had said that she would always be so; but she had prayed to the dear Lord, and He had made her whole.

Morlena did not read any more stories that day, but thought very hard of this one; it was so good and beautiful, if it were really true; and Morlena believed that it was true. And then the words, "The Lord is my shepherd," came to her. "The Lord is my shepherd" -- mine, too, and will take up this lamb in His arms. Morlena had prayed before, saying each morn and night her little prayer, but now she prayed earnestly, feeling that God was really listening to her and would make her well.

Morlena did begin to get well the very day that she began to pray earnestly. One evening her father, bending to kiss her, noted a soft color in her cheeks, always so white before. She saw his look of pleased surprised. "Yes, mamma told me that there was a little, just a little color in my cheeks; and I said that it was the tiny rosebud of His promise which God had sent me that He would heal me -- just a little flower; but it means, Oh, so much!" "Yes, Morlena," he said, but Morlena saw doubt in his dear eyes. He was going away for a whole week, and she hated to have him go with that look on his face. She put her arms around his neck and drew his face to hers. "Oh, papa, papa," she cried, "if only you could feel as I do -- that God is going to make me well!" "I will try, Morlena; I will believe it, my darling." "Yes, believe it all -- that by-and-by I shall be able to walk and run about, like Bessie and Ray and Mabel."

Then the doubt came back into his eyes. Her two little white feet lay so still on the pillow, so still. For nearly two years they had not moved. But the next day Morlena called her mother to her side. "What is it, my child?" Morlena laughed. "See, mamma, see; my naughty little foot is moving from its place! And the other moves too! Little truants!" How golden the sunshine seemed; how bright were the red leaves; what sweet music the little brown sparrows made to the ears of Morlena's mother! "They are all true -- God's promises," she said. "My child will be well again."

Every day Morlena was a little better. One bright morning she said, "Mamma, if you will help me I think I can get up." Then Morlena saw doubt looking from her mother's eyes. "The doctor said you ought not be moved," said her mother hesitatingly. "Mamma, God is my doctor. He told me I could sit up." Her face was so earnest that her mother stooped and put her arms about her, gently lifting her. Morlena drew a deep happy breath as she sat up. "Help me a little more mamma, so that I can sit on the side of the bed." For nearly two years her head had lain lower than her motionless feet, to help her suffering back; but now Morlena sat up as proud as a little queen. She put up her gentle little hand and smoothed away the look of anxiety which would come to her mother's brow. "It is all right, mamma; God has made me well."

The next day her mother helped Morlena from her bed; and the little white feet, which had been paralyzed so long, took one step, two, three. "Mamma," said Morlena, her eyes dancing as she rested from her first triumphal walk, "I feel as though I had traveled around the world!" The third day Morlena spent seated in a great chair.

Now Morlena's father did not know all about this getting up and sitting up and walking. Morlena was getting well as fast as she could; that he might see, when he returned home, that the sun had melted the ice that bound the brook, and the little stream now flowed free and happy. What a great, joyful surprise it would be for him! "Papa did not think that God could or would heal me, but now I can show him that he has healed the little sick lamb in His flock."

What a long, long day that last day was, with the big hand creeping so slowly around the clock, so many, many times. Then sounded the opening of the door, steps, and the father's never-omitted question, "How is Morlena?" "She is better today," replied the mother. She felt that her father sighed; for "better" had always meant so very, very little. The door of the room opened, with his dear, kind, sad face at the door; and Morlena, her eyes bright with happy excitement, arose and walked bravely to him. Her father opened his arms to enfold her, and held her close to his heart, weeping insuppressible tears upon her dear head. She lifted her glad face to his. "Oh, papa, God does not know what incurable means."

Every day Morlena was stronger and better. The good, the learned -- everybody came to see her, marveling, and speaking of her healing as a miracle; because they could not explain it any other way. But Morlena knew naught of miracle; she only knew God's beautiful law, through which the faith of a little child is mighty in its power. So she did not wonder, as the others did; because she said it was God's way, and Morlena knew.

Go forth, go forth with an earnest heart,
And do the best you can;
'Tis the little deeds and the willing hand
That sows the seed in every land.

And each one doing his little part,
He render all with a loving heart,
To the God who guides the toil and strife,
And rewards each one with a crown of life.

--L.C.M.

If you want to be happy and make others happy never say anything unkind."

1902 - There are now six workers at Unity headquarters to help Charles and Myrtle answer letters written to Silent Unity for prayer and advice. "The Christian Business Men's Federation" held it's annual meeting in Kansas City, Missouri on October 21st and 22nd. The Kansas City chapter was established at that meeting. Charles Fillmore and Robert L. Gross were in attendance. Rick Fillmore graduated from Manuel Training High School in Kansas City, Missouri and then entered the Chicago Art Institute.

Wee Wisdom Kansas City, Missouri January 1902. A Happy New Year by Mabel Porter.

"A little girl named Ethel went to her brother one day and said: 'Oh dear, I just saw a real poor little girl on the street. She seemed to be looking for something, and I asked her what was the matter. She said, 'Mamma gave me a nickel and sent me to the store to buy a loaf of bread, and a big dog came by and knocked me over, and I dropped it.' I told her that I would help her find it. After we got it, she thanked me, and I told her to take a quarter that papa had given me that morning and get something else for her mamma.'

'What did she buy?' asked Edward, her brother. 'I don't know,' said Ethel, 'but I mean to ask mamma if we may buy a dinner for them on New Year's day -- a turkey, you know, and some nice potatoes, and some cranberries.' 'How do you know they won't have one?' said Edward. 'Why, I was talking to her, you know, and her mamma is sick, and they have a baby four years old, and Bessie, (that's the little girl's name,) has to get the dinners. And I guess they don't get big dinners, either,' said Ethel sadly. 'And she told me that she never had a New Year's dinner.' 'Well,' said Edward, 'I'll help you out on it.' 'Will you?' said Ethel, happily. 'Well, then, I'll go and ask mamma.' 'And I'll go too,' said Edward.

Then they both went to mamma, who was sitting in the parlor, and laid their whole plan before her. 'Why, certainly, my children,' said mamma, 'but let us sit down now and send some good thoughts to Bessie's mamma.' Ethel sat down, and then all three sent good, true thoughts to the poor lady. Afterwards Ethel and Edward went out of doors and had a good play. That night when their papa came home they told him about the little girl, and he thought it would be a good plan to help little Bessie.

So the day before New Year's papa and mamma each gave the children some money, and Ethel and Edward opened their banks and each took out a part of their savings, and they went to the store with their mother and bought a nice turkey, a peck of potatoes, some cranberries, and a few vegetables. But when they paid the bill they found they had quite a little money left. So they decided to buy something for Bessie and her mamma and baby brother to wear. They bought a nice warm bonnet for Bessie, and a cap for her brother, some mittens and stockings for both of them, and a shawl for Bessie's mamma. They found that this used up all of their money, so they took up their bundles and went home.

That night Edward and Ethel went to bed early, so they might get up early and fix their bundles in good order. Their mother and father were sitting in the parlor reading when suddenly Mr. Williams, Ethel's father, got up and put on his overcoat and hat. Mrs. Williams asked him where he was going, and he told her he was going to buy some wood for 'Ethel's poor people,' as he called them. He also said that a gentleman friend of his told him about these same people, and that they did not have a fire hardly ever, unless Bessie could find coal or wood lying on the street and make a fire with that.

So Mr. Williams went out and bought some wood, and ordered a man to take it to No. 45 B--- street. The man looked at Mr. Williams rather curiously, but Mr. Williams laughed and said, 'Never mind, my man; only have that wood there before seven o'clock, and I will be much obliged to you.'

The next morning Ethel and Edward took their bundles down to Bessie's house, and knocked at the door. Bessie opened it, and asked them to come in, and asked Ethel if she wanted something. Ethel smiled as she and Edward deposited their bundles on the table and answered, 'No, Bessie, but please take these things.' 'Oh, my!' said Bessie. 'Are they for us?' 'Yes,' said Ethel. 'O mamma, come here quick!' said Bessie. 'What's the matter, Bessie?' said her mother, coming in.

Then Bessie told her mother about the bundles, and she turned to the children with tears in her eyes, and said brokenly, 'God bless you.' Then she sat down and put her head in her hands and sat for a long time. Ethel and Edward sat looking out the window, blinking hard to keep the tears back. Soon Bessie nodded to the brother and sister, and they followed her into a tumbled old kitchen, but it was as clean, or cleaner, than some kitchens belonging to very fine houses. Bessie pointed to a great pile of wood, and said, 'Some one else has been good to us, too.' Ethel and her brother did not know what their father had done. 'Mamma got up yesterday for the first time in four weeks, and Oh, it seems so nice to have her around again,' said Bessie.

Ethel and Edward looked at each other and smiled. They had treated Bessie's mamma every day since Ethel met Bessie. Ethel and Edward thought they had better go, so they said good-bye to Bessie's mother, who told them her name was Mrs. Jordan, and then they went to see the little boy, who was lying in bed under a ragged old quilt. He was clasping a wooden head of a horse, which Mrs. Jordan said he found in the alley.

Ethel kissed Bessie and her mother, and Edward shook hands with both of them, and they went home. After they had gone Bessie and her mother opened the packages. The first that they opened was the turkey. Then came the rest of the things. When they had opened them all, Bessie sighed and said, 'O mamma, was there ever any one so good as those dear children?'

When Ethel went to bed that night she kissed her mamma and said, 'I always thought that I had the happiest New Year's days I had ever heard of, but I guess I was mistaken.'

'Keep thy heart with all diligence, for out of it are the issues of life.'"

1903 - On the Sunday School program, for the Easter service on April 12, the last page had the following article entitled:

What is practical Christianity?

"Practical Christianity is the application in all the affairs of life of the doctrine of Jesus Christ. It explains how men may come into conscious relation with the Father and what Jesus meant when he said, 'God is spirit and they that worship him must worship in spirit and truth.' John 4:25 R.V. It explains the Spiritual Being of man and his relation to soul and body. It explains the action of the mind and how it is the connecting link between God and man. Also, how mind action affects the body, producing discord or harmony, sickness or health. It shows what the faculties of man are, their relation and how to develop them as symbolized by the type-man, Jesus Christ, and his twelve apostles were. 'We have the mind of Christ.' I. Corinthians 2:16.

It explains why a failure to bring forth these faculties or there misuse, is a falling short of the God-idea, the image and likeness and which falling short is sin. It explains how man has thus fallen short and brought upon himself sin, sickness, poverty, sorrow and death. It shows how all these conditions can be overcome and a new relation established between the Creator and the created. It explains in a rational, comprehensive way the mission of Jesus Christ, the atonement he made for us and how we may take advantage of it. It interprets the Scripture as a whole and shows them to be a wonderful revelation to man, explaining his origin, his development and his destiny. It bridges the gulf between science and religion and shows the New Testament to be an acronym of the subtle forces underlying all manifest life and which are now being discovered by the advanced schools of physical science.

It solves all problems of existence and brings man into the understanding of Divine Law, harmony, health and peace, here and now. It is pure Christianity and proves itself to be such by the signs which follow its' exposition, as promised in Mark 16, 17, 18, 20. It admits and accepts the truth that is expressed in any system of religion, but does not confine itself to any set creed or dogma, or to any fixed name of organization. It accepts the Gospel of Jesus Christ as the highest given to man and recognizes, but one source of revelation for that Gospel: 'Even the Spirit of Truth which is the Holy Ghost, whom the Father will send in my name, he shall teach you all things and bring all things to your remembrance whatsoever I have said unto you.' John 14:26.

Its' disciples seek to fulfill all the commands of Christ. 'Preach the Gospel and Heal the sick, cleanse the leper, raise the dead, cast out devils; freely you have received, freely give.' Matthew 10:18 because they accept literally his prophesy and promise, 'He that believith on me, the things that I do shall he do also, and greater works than these shall he do.' John 14:12. This great truth is being applied in a practical way by thousands and they are getting the results in newness of understanding, strength and health. You are cordially invited to join in the work of revealing this transforming truth to humanity and through it reap the great benefits in mind, body and affairs with those who are putting it into practical use."

A small group of Unity students applied in Jackson County, Missouri for articles of incorporation for the Unity Society of Practical Christianity. Thus the first Unity Center was formed in Kansas City, Missouri. From the efforts of those few charter members has grown a thriving organization whose program includes not only regular worship services, but also study classes, Sunday school, young people's groups and auxiliaries, all emphasizing the value of right thinking as the key to the Christ way of abundant living. July 29, 1903 Unity Society of Practical Christianity was incorporated as a society for scientific and educational purposes, "The study and demonstration of universal law."

Royal Fillmore graduated from Thacher grade school in Kansas City, Missouri and enrolled in Manual Training High School.

1905 - A building committee, formed in 1901, had been discussing and searching for a proper location where the Unity organization could build, grow and expand. They found an eight room house with a large lot for sale at 913 Tracy Avenue in Kansas City, Missouri. Charles Fillmore said, "let's buy" all though the building fund was only $601.00. Myrtle was especially pleased that the location was near the family home and close to the street car line. Within a few weeks the house had been moved to the back of the lot and excavation for a new building in front of the house was started. God worked through one member of the Unity Society to mortgage his assets and loan the proceeds to the Unity building program. Many Unity supporters and readers of Unity literature responded with love offerings for Unity's expansion, plus friends and students in Kansas City were very generous.

When the first Unity youth group was organized by Myrtle Fillmore it was called the "Joyful Circle". Lowell was one of its' first members and was the club's secretary. In the records that he kept the first meeting was held on July 12th and the last book entry was in 1906.

After the house at 913 Tracy was moved to the back of the lot the lower front part of the house was remodeled for a Unity Inn and it became the first vegetarian cafeteria in Kansas City. A new building, on the front of the lot, was soon under construction.

A personal letter to Sir W. Rickert Fillmore, dated January 1, 1905. "When you came into the Fillmore family twenty-one years ago, from the point of observation, you were 'small potatoes and few in a hill.' You were reticent as to your past and brought neither name or wardrobe with you. The family bestowed upon you the above name, but finding it unwilly for daily use have handled you by the arephonioris name of Rick. The wardrobe had been a matter of your seniors considerations in as much as it has involved change and expense from the period of swaddling clothes to the timing of swallow tail coats. So today as you mount the guns of your infantry and count yourself 'big potatoes and plenty in the hill.' With our blessings and congratulations we enclose you more wardrobe. With our untied love. Your Pa and Ma Fillmore."

1906 - In 1906 Rick Fillmore had completed four years of study at the Chicago Art Institute in Illinois. He returned to Kansas City and opened a studio on Tracy Avenue in the Orchestra Hall which was across the street from Unity's headquarters. For two years he made architectural renderings and did commercial art work.

On July 26th the first services were conducted in the new Unity building on the corner of 9th and Tracy. Dedication services were held August 19th through 25th. It had been twenty years since Myrtle had been blessed to start her journey toward total healing. She and Charles could now look around and see much evidence of God's good. Their Truth magazines were being sent all over the country and to foreign lands. Silent Unity was serving countless thousands, they had a new building with a chapel that could seat two-hundred and a loyal following, but something wasn't quite right. Both Charles and Myrtle were ordained Christian Science Ministers, shouldn't they be Unity ordained? On August 31st a special ordination meeting was conducted, W.G. Haseltine, President of the board of the Unity Society of Practical Christianity announced that seventeen Unity students had taken the Unity ordination examination and twelve had passed. Those twelve committed themselves to becoming full time ministers. Included in the twelve were Charles and Myrtle.

The free will offering of Unity students and friends plus the income from the sales of the Unity publications were always the supporting factors of the Unity movement. Often the question was asked, "How is Unity supported?" Always the Fillmore answer was, 'through prayer'. More often than not money was not on hand when needed. Once an office worker, knowing that the expenses were heavy and the money supply low said, "Let us pray that the money will hold out." "Oh no!" Myrtle replied, "Let us pray that our faith will hold out."

1907 - In 1907 Myrtle turned over the primary responsibilities of the editing of Wee Wisdom to her assistant, Blanche Sage Haseltine.

During the early 1900's, receipts on file indicated that Unity paid for everything for the Fillmore family including clothing, food, transportation (cars) repairs, cleaning, etc. There was every indication that the Fillmore's, during this period of time, were not paid a salary. Also, from the files every indication shows that the Fillmore's were not extravagant in their dress. Nor were there expenses for frivolous items. They were so dedicated to their work that they did very little other than work long hours and full weeks. They did have automobiles and lots of repair bills. The cars were used, in the early days, for transporting out of town guests back and forth to the train or bus station.

Certificate of membership, "This is to certify that John Royal Fillmore has this 28th day of January 1907 been duly elected a member of the Unity Society of Practical Christianity and is entitled to such privileges as provided in the by-laws of this society. Souvenir Program Unity Building Dedication and Mid-continent Convention of Practical Christians August 19-22, 1906 at the Unity building 913-15 Tracy Ave."

A letter dated September 22, 1907 to Mary G. Fillmore 428 Elmwood Avenue Kansas City, Missouri from her second son Norton's wife Jennie from Austin, Nevada as follows: "Dear Mother I hope you will pardon our long silence. Norton and I don't mean to neglect you, but Norton dislikes letter writing worse than I do and that is saying a great deal. Only yesterday he remarked how careless he was getting about writing to you. That made me think I ought to answer your letter. We have been away from Austin the greater part of the summer. We were touring Nevada with our horses and a camp wagon. We camped, hunted, fished and enjoyed outdoor life in general. Since our return to Austin about three weeks ago I have been busy getting straightened out and settled down to house keeping again.

We are enjoying beautiful fall weather, but expect to see snow very soon. The winters are horrid here in the mountains. They come early and they stay late. I am going to try to persuade Norton, that a trip east this summer would be beneficial to our health. I do want to see you and know you all so much. I am also anxious to visit my relatives in the east who I have not seen in ten years. They live in Boston and vicinity. Perhaps it will give you some pleasure to know that Norton and I have been very happy in our married life. He is the dearest kindest husband in the world and I try to be a good wife. We received your letter and photo a few days after our return home. I know you will be generous and not keep us waiting as long as we kept you waiting for a letter. I will promise to be more prompt in the future. Love and best wishes for all from Norton and Jennie"

1908 - Royal Fillmore attended Manual Training High School in Kansas City, Missouri. He graduated in 1908 at the age of nineteen. He was a member and officer in the men's glee club, member of the debate team and editor-in-chief of the Nautilus school annual of 1908. In 1908 Royal enrolled in the University of Missouri at Columbia.

1909 - In May of 1909 a new Unity publication was introduced, Weekly Unity, with Lowell as the editor. It was for purchase by anyone that wished to be kept up with the happenings at Unity and in particular the articles by its' editor. A feature that became very popular was an article entitled Things to be remembered, by Lowell.

The first Weekly Unity May 15, 1909, "What the Weekly Unity is for. As the local Unity Society continues to grow and prosper the need of a local organ has become more and more apparent. The members and attendants of the society need to keep in close touch with the work and all of its phases in order that they can cooperate and bring about the best results for themselves as well as for the cause. We have been printing programs of the services from time to time. The committee now thinks it wise to enlarge this program and make it a little weekly paper; the official organ of the local Unity Society. All news items of the Society, meetings, entertainments, reports, etc., will be printed in it. We ask the cooperation of all members and attendants in making this paper a success and true representative of the Society.

Weekly Unity May 22, 1909, "The Woman's Auxiliary was organized in April 1905 for the purpose of sustaining and advancing, so far as woman's work would permit, the efforts of the Unity Society of Practical Christianity, and the organization has been called the right hand of the Society which has achieved such greatness in establishing this flourishing center of Truth. The Auxiliary has devoted its energies principally to the furnishings and beautifying of Unity buildings, and some statistics of what has been accomplished may prove of interest.

First, we will note that in the early days of the organization various methods were resorted to, to gain money for the purposes of the Auxiliary. Bazaars, supers, lectures, etc. were given, but as the Principles of Truth were put into practical application, it was seen that there was a better way to obtain the same result, and the members resolved to depend absolutely upon the power of the Word for their prosperity. The Woman's Auxiliary meets the last Friday in the month, at 3:00 p.m. in the parlor of the Unity building."

The Unity Guild, a band of the young people of Unity Society, organized for the purpose of assisting in every movement of the whole center for the extension of the principles upon which the Society is founded. The Guild started the movement which resulted in the gift of our beautiful Aeolean Orchestral.

The Unity Society of Practical Christianity was incorporated under the laws of the state of Missouri July 24, 1903 for scientific and educational purposes. The business of the Society is carried forward by a board of twelve directors which meet regularly the last Monday evening of each month. The members of the board are elected, four each year, by the members of the Society on the first Sunday of each year. Unity Society had its inception when Mr. and Mrs. Charles Fillmore began this religious movement. In 1900 an executive committee of three; Mr. H.E. Marshall, Mr. E.C. Prather, and Mrs. Jennie H. Croft, were chosen to further the interests of the Society.

The Unity Library. Here may be found all of the standard metaphysical books, also a Circulating Library for the use of the members of the local Society and city friends. Our librarian will be glad to confer with anyone desiring information about reading material suited to individual needs, or in relation to any special line of study. The establishment of Branch Unity Libraries in other cities is under the supervision of Mrs. Croft and information relative to this subject will be cheerfully furnished upon application. The Unity Information Bureau is also conducted by the librarian, who will answer all questions concerning the work, workers, books, publications, etc., in this or other locations.

Lowell Fillmore is the editor of this new Unity publication. It is for purchase by anyone that wishes to be kept up with the happening at Unity Society."

Weekly Unity May 29, 1909, "Royal Fillmore is returning from Columbia, Missouri where he has been attending college. One-hundred ninety pounds of him came Wednesday evening. We bade adieu to two-hundred thirty pounds last fall. We are expecting another shipment soon. He will remain in the city during his summer vacation."

Weekly Unity June 12, 1909, "Incidental expenses. The incidental expenses of the Unity Society, consisting of janitor's wages, lights, water, heat, repairs, offerings to organist, etc., averaged $17.66 per week for the year 1908. The average envelope collection for defraying these expenses amounted to $4.68 a week for the same period of time. Thus, it will be seen that some of the building fund will have to be used. Every cent in the building fund should be used in paying the obligation against the Unity buildings. It may be that many do not use the envelopes because they feel that the small amount they can afford to give would not be worthwhile. There are seldom fewer than 150 persons at the Sunday morning service and not less than 50 at the evening meeting. Now, if each person present would put 10 cents in the envelope each Sunday the total would be $20.00. No one need be ashamed to put his mite in, even though it be but a nickel or a penny. It all helps swell the grand total and prospers the good work. It is a privilege of every attendant at Unity to cooperate in defraying the little expenses that are contracted in making the building a pleasant and comfortable place in which to meet."

Weekly Unity June 26, 1909, "New literature. Charles Fillmore's Book of Lessons is out. The long looked for Book of Lessons in Christian Healing by Charles Fillmore is now ready for delivery in neat paper cover. The cloth edition will be out in a few weeks. Besides the regular twelve lessons there are two auxiliary lessons and several interesting and instructive articles, together with statements and instructions for giving treatment in special cases. The book contains 200 pages and sells for 60 cents in the paper cover. Another department was created at Unity, the Correspondence School. Two-thousand were enrolled within two years and it taught many thousands of students until that department was closed in 1972."

Weekly Unity December 25, 1909, "The origin of Christmas by Royal Fillmore. The Christians were not the first to celebrate Christmas. Long years before Christ came to bless this world with precious Christianity, Christmas was observed, not as a birthday, of course, but as a time for rejoicing. Every nation on the earth, which is recorded in history, kept this day for feasting and praising their gods. But why especially this day December 25th? Would not any day in the calendar do? No, they gave thanks, and had good cause, for on this day the sun started north to bless them with wealth and plenty again. The Egyptians first observed this in their astronomical pursuits. They noticed that the sun went south and drought and famine followed in its path, but on December 17th it stopped and on the 25th started back again to smile once more upon the poor mortals, and give them rain and flood the Nile and make their borders produce an abundance of grain.

So it was with good reason that they feasted and rejoiced on this day and welcomed the sun back again. In time all nations observed the action of the sun and rejoiced. The holiday went by different names. In Greece the people named the day 'The Feast of Dionysia.' Then when Rome rose from her barbarism and put out her powerful hand and grasped the world, she called this happy time of the year, 'Saturnalia,' and gave thanks to her god of harvest Saturn. When the warm sun went south intense cold descended on the poor inhabitants and killed many, for they had not learned to erect warm dwellings, so the Celts called this day, when the welcome sun started back to smile on them, the 'Yuletide,' and the hardy Norseman called it the 'Twelve Nights.'

Thus it was when Christianity bloomed forth it found this pagan holiday being observed everywhere by feasting, drinking and devoutly thanking their gods; something like we celebrate Thanksgiving of today. The Christian emperors tried to strike this holiday from the pagan calendar, but as it was impossible they wisely compromised and adopted it as a day for celebrating the birth of Christ in 89 A.D., and as it did not make much difference to the pagan what he celebrated so he had a good time, he accepted the compromise. It is a well known fact that Christ was not born on December 25th, because the Bible speaks of the shepherds tending their flocks out of doors, and at this time of year it was so rainy that it was impossible to herd sheep or stay out doors at all. Some argue that Christ was born in May, but the exact date does not matter.

Though his coming has been mixed with the old pagan idea somewhat; it was the turning point of religion, for Christianity was born with Jesus Christ to enlighten the world. England denounced Christmas in 1647 and prohibited its celebration, because it said it was a pagan holiday, and to this day many Scotch do not recognize it. But where did the idea of Santa Claus come from and what was its origin? Santa Claus is the Dutch pet name for St. Nicholas whom it is said lived in Myra and was a great friend of the children. He had them hang up their stockings and at night he would steal from house to house and give them little presents; but this old myth goes farther back than St. Nick. The Greeks had a jolly old satyr Silenus, the god of the drunkards who presided over their festival of Dionysia. The Romans had Saturn to preside over their Saturnalia and the Germans their god Thor as the object of their festivals.

All these gods were represented to be old and to symbolize the dying year. When we see Christmas trees all be-spangled with presents and candles, we might stop to wonder why it has become a custom and that this delight of the little child is all borrowed from the ancient pagans. Virgil mentions the Christmas tree in his works. Emperor Drusus brought the tree custom into Germany and there it has its strongest hold today. The Germans claim that their ancestors brought the tree into their houses to entice the gods of the forest to enter and leave some gifts. One thing is certain that they all used the fir and pine, because they represent eternal life and knowledge. The Yule custom used in England to celebrate Christmas was originated by the Scandinavians, who had large bonfires at Yuletide to please the god of the sun and the wood sprites and to represent renewed life.

The Druids considered the oak a sacred tree, and as the mistletoe grew on it and had berries which generally came in bunches of three representing the Trinity and ripened in December, they considered the plant a symbol of their god of the sun and hung it over their doors to entice the wood sprites to enter. If a friend met a friend under such a bunch of mistletoe it was a sign of eternal love and friendship and Oden, father of Bolden, the sun god, took note of all their good wishes. The human race has become more and more affectionate and today seals such friendship under the mistletoe with a kiss. Thus we find all our holiday customs have their origin in the semi-civilized pagan of yesterday and the old saying is revived, 'There is nothing new under the sun.'"

1910 - An insurance policy for the coverage of a Welch automobile, four cylinders, 1910 model produced by Welch-Pontiac with the title in the names of Charles or Lowell Fillmore, plus a long list of garage bills and parts.

A new department of Unity was formed and named Silent Seventy. Its' purpose was to furnish and distribute free Unity literature to prisons, hospitals, schools, libraries and such other institutions.

The Prosperity Bank plan was conceived by Lowell Fillmore to encourage savings and investing that thousands have learned to use and profit by.

Construction began on a new Unity School headquarters building at 917 Tracy, the adjacent lot to 913 Tracy. The printing plant was moved to the new building on its' completion. The magazines Unity and Wee Wisdom were printed there. Over the next four years the 917 Tracy building was remodeled and enlarged twice.

Weekly Unity March 12, 1910, "Lowell Fillmore's column Things To Be Remembered first appeared and continued as one of Lowell's most popular Weekly Unity features throughout the years that this organ was published. 'Remember to smile as if you really felt that way.' 'Remember that you become like what you think about.' 'Remember that the man worth while is the man who can smile when everything goes dead wrong.'"

The first time that the Things To Be Remembered column was listed in Weekly Unity magazine with a bold heading was in the issue of April 2, 1910.

Weekly Unity published weekly by Unity Tract Society Unity Building 913 Tracy Avenue Kansas City, Missouri Lowell Fillmore, managing editor. Official organ of the Unity Society June 26, 1910, "Do you live in your purse? Last Tuesday afternoon, Charles Fillmore in his Health and Harmony class took up the subject of Prosperity from a standpoint entirely new. He referred to the sending forth a standpoint entirely new. He referred to the sending forth of the Seventy and called attention to that part of their instructions which forbade the use of a purse. Then he went on to show that many people limit their supply to the amount there contained. By way of illustration he told of one woman who went for a car ride with the man to whom she was engaged. He drew from his pocket a small purse and fumbled around in it, hunting for a dime for the fares and all at once it came over her with a rush what it would be to live year after year with a man like that and she broke the engagement. Her woman's intuition told her he was not free and generous in money matters. The lesson of the afternoon was, get away from all financial limitations and make connection with the great Universal Source of supply.

Almost unconsciously the purse idea becomes fixed in the mind as the storehouse of supply and when it is empty one thinks the resource is not in existence for him. Jesus said, 'Judge not according to the appearances.' When the purse appears to be empty, be wise and know that back of it is the Great Unlimited Resource. By finding your purse with that sort of thought-substance you make it a magnet for plenty and supply will come in new ways to fill it. Again, if you are in the habit of living financially in your purse, and counting your resources by what it contains, it is better that you have no purse at all, so Jesus said to those whom he set forth at the last, 'Take neither purse nor script.'"

Weekly Unity June 30, 1910, "Some necessary repairs will be made on the old Inn during the next few days and it will be reopened under the management of Mr. E.V. Ingraham. We are looking forward to a new Inn which is sure to materialize before long, but in the meantime we must make the best of the old one."

Things To Be Remembered. "Remember when you concentrate upon a statement of truth to think just the statement and not think what you think you ought to think about it." "Remember that you should be sure you want a thing before you pray for it."

Weekly Unity August 4, 1910, "New Unity Building Fund. Up to date the New Unity Building Fund contains $2,349.25. This fund is being raised for the purpose of erecting a suitable Unity Inn. About $50,000.00 will be needed to complete the building which is planned."

"The Unity Guild. Frank Lynch told what the Unity Guild is thankful for. The Unity Guild, as an auxiliary of the Unity Society of Practical Christianity has been working during the past years in the interest of the new building fund. The members of the Guild are the grown-up young people of Unity Society, whose object is to spread the teachings of this center and to assist the work in any way they can. The Guild was organized four years ago, with a membership of sixteen. Today they have a membership of about fifty. From the various entertainments they have been able to turn over $300.00 to the new building fund and still have a balance in their treasury of $80.00."

Things To Be Remembered "Remember that nothing comes to you but that which you have invited." "Remember to forget everything unpleasant."

Weekly Unity December 29, 1910, "Annual election. The by-laws of the Unity Society provides that four directors shall be elected each year on the first Sunday in January for a term of three years. Next Sunday morning after the regular services the meeting will be called to order and ballots distributed; J.I. Wallace, David Hoagland, Mrs. Emma Hay, Lowell Fillmore, Carl Glesser, Edwin Clyde Curtis, Frank B. Lynch, Mrs. F.L. Jones. The first four are the present directors, whose term now expires. The votes are to elect any four of the eight for a three year term ending January 1914, by drawing a line through four and leaving the four which are the voters choice."

Things To Be Remembered "Remember that a smile brings sunshine to the face and joy to the heart." "Remember to turn your smile inside as well as outside.'"

1911 - At the end of Royal's third year of college he left school to work at Unity. He was twenty-two years old. His first job was as a "printers devil" year 1911.

Weekly Unity May 10, 1911, "Weekly Unity begins its third year. Two years ago Weekly Unity was begun as an aid to the work of the Local Unity Society of Practical Christianity. It contained announcements, responsive services and items of interest to the local members and attendants. The little paper has been blessed and prospered and has constantly grown in interest and favor. Not long after it was started the list of officers and committees had to be omitted from its pages, in order to allow more room for reading matter. A little later a new feature was added; extracts from the various addresses delivered in the Unity Auditorium were printed in each issue. Quite often an issue appeared with eight pages instead of four in order to accommodate the increasing number of good things. Thus it has gradually outgrown its original size and purpose. We begin the third volume with a large page and larger aim.

While we will take the same interest in the local work as heretofore, we will also endeavor to reach Truth students everywhere as well and will devote a portion of the paper to reports and matters of interest to Unity centers and libraries in other places. In view of the past growth it is easy to foresee a flourishing paper of thirty-two pages devoted to the organization and spread of the good work. We earnestly ask all friends to help in bringing this idea into reality. This can be done by sending us subscriptions and offering suggestions and items of interest. As the popularity of Weekly Unity increased each issue carried the text of the previous Sunday morning address by Mr. Charles Fillmore and with the large paper reprints from other periodicals. Also added was a report on the mid-week meetings, responsive readings and a weekly column, The Vegetarian. During this period the Unity Pure Food store stocked and sold vegetarian products nationally."

Weekly Unity June 28, 1911, "God be praised for the fulfillment of His bounty in Unity. This statement has proved to be a literal fact. On Sunday June 25th, the treasury seemingly lacked about $2,000.00 of having enough to pay the obligation on the Unity building which was to fall due on the following day. After a Prosperity Talk by Charles Fillmore and short earnest speeches by other members, the Spirit of enthusiasm, good will, and consciousness of abundance in pledges was realized. One man said, 'I have four in my family and I will give $25.00 for each of them.' Another, not to be outdone, said, 'I have six in my family and will give $25.00 for each.' Still another said, 'I will give $50.00 if nine others present will agree to give $50.00 each.' Ten persons immediately responded. Pledges and money came from all parts of the room.

The total amount of pledges reaches $2,040.00 which when paid in will more than cover the obligation. On Monday afternoon, June 26th, the president, treasurer and secretary of the Society went to see the man who holds the note for $5,500.00. He received the $3,700.00 which the Society had raised in cash and said he would allow ninety days in which to collect the pledges for payment of the balance of $1,800.00. He also pledged $100.00 himself. The Unity people have great cause for rejoicing! The paying for the Unity building has been a beautiful demonstration of what faith and the power of the Word will do."

Weekly Unity October 25, 1911, "Benjamin Fay Mills at Unity headquarters. The lessons and lectures which have been given at Unity Auditorium by Benjamin Fay Mills, the noted New Thought evangelist, have proved most uplifting and beneficial. No matter upon what subject Mr. Mills talks, he brings out the redeeming and recreating power of the Spirit when it is allowed to act through the human consciousness. The practical healing lessons were a feature of the course which were indeed helpful and many gave testimony to that effect. Kansas City and Unity congregations especially will always welcome Mr. Mills."

Weekly Unity November 29, 1911, "Auxiliary notes. The Woman's Auxiliary will give its usual 'Thanksgiving Shower' for Unity Inn Wednesday, November 29th. This notice did not get in last weeks Weekly Unity and that no one may be denied the privilege of helping on the good work at the Inn, the shower will last for a week. Contributions of eatables, supplies, table and bed linen, etc., will be acceptable. At the monthly meeting of the Auxiliary held Friday, November 24th, different committees were appointed to look after the Christmas needs of the Sunday school and church, which the women of this organization usually attend to.

The membership of the Auxiliary is increasing, new members coming in and old members returning. Mrs. Walter M. Davis, an active worker in every branch of Unity Society before her removal to Texas, has returned to Kansas City to live and the Auxiliary is happy in having her again to aid with her good counsels and service. The Prosperity Thought which the Woman's Auxiliary is to hold through this month is; 'the rich substance of Spirit is now abundantly poured out upon me, expressing itself in every avenue of my life."

Things To Be Remembered "Remember to speak only true words." "Remember if at first you don't succeed, smile and try again." "Remember that god helps those that help themselves."

1912 - Royal had assumed the title of managing editor for Wee Wisdom magazine. Two new departments were created for the magazine. Because of more adults reading the magazine Home was added and for the young adults Youth was added.

Royal served Unity as its' purchasing agent, but he also continued to be involved with the editing of Wee Wisdom. Royal was active in the Kansas City, Missouri business community, member of YMCA, Rotary club, Chamber of Commerce, Shrine, Law enforcement association, University of Missouri club and a member of the Board of Directors of the University extension. Additionally, he took great interest in the Boosters clubs for young people that his mother promoted in the new Unity centers opening. He served as Secretary of the Boosters club. His mother encouraged him to travel for Unity to help establish Booster clubs. On one of his trips east he met a young lady Booster club member, Frances Sleater at Merchantville, New Jersey.

Weekly Unity March 31, 1912, "The Golden Rule" extract from an address by Lowell Fillmore, in Unity auditorium, Kansas City, Sunday evening, March 31, 1912.

> "Therefore all things whatsoever ye would that men should do to you, do ye even so to them.' This rule comes to us commonly in the following words, 'Do unto others as you would have others do to you.' We often hear this quotation; in fact we have become so accustomed to it that we are apt to think only of the sound of the words, or of its application to the other fellow and seldom of its true meaning as applied to our own selves. Nor are we quick to grasp in a practical way the idea that this teaching can govern our every-day actions. It is a very simple rule, and yet if it were used universally by men and women in their week day transactions as well as their Sunday worshiping, it would remedy a large number of complex troubles, and make the world pretty nearly over in many ways.
>
> For example, armies and battleships would melt away as does the snow before the March sun, and in their places would appear skilled bands of men who would transform the barren wastes into beautiful garden spots and palaces of learning. Men would bend their energies toward inventing machinery that would help their fellows to more truly live, instead of concentrating their efforts upon the building of engines for their destruction. Enemies would be friends, and friends would become closer friends. This great simple teaching was given to men 2,000 years ago to help them then, but to this day no better rule of action has been found.
>
> Christ was not the first to teach it, but he emphasized it and gave it simplicity of language in his wonderful Sermon on the Mount. He also lived it to the fullest extend himself. A living example of this kind is a great addition to the work teaching. But the spoken word has its place, for by it the

listener forms a little image or thought of loving kindness deep down in his consciousness, to which he will be able later to make his every action conform. Christ might have spread this same teaching out into rules of many words, specifying just how man should use his fellows under certain conditions, but by giving it as he did in this simple thought he has covered every condition, and has done it in language that every one may understand and accept. We each know how we would like to be treated.

Therefore, by exchanging place, in our imaginations, with our neighbors it will become easy to judge what they would wish us to do. By carefully observing our relations with others we will find that this rule can be applied very often. In fact, just about all the time. We can use it very nicely at home, on the street-car, at the party, while making a call, or even while walking down the street. Wherever we meet living creatures we can make use of this rule. Yes, even when we are alone, opportunity for its use presents itself. No one is near us, but we are thinking and our thoughts are of others. Let us stop to analyze these thoughts. Are we thinking of them as we would like them to think of us? Are we seeing them strong and well and good and kind? Are we thinking of them as sons and daughters of God?

If we are holding them in our thoughts in any less degree than the highest good of which we know, we are falling short of the rule, for we would want others to hold us in their highest thoughts. Some may ask how anyone who has not learned of the Truth could possibly desire to be thought of as perfect in the absolute sense. In answer to this I would call attention to the fact that high within each individual's consciousness there is a Divine Self, which is constantly working toward the end that perfection may be expressed in every part of his being. This is taking place often unknown to the conscious mind of the individual, although it is right in his midst, as it were.

In fact, few people in the world realize what is going on in their thought realms. This true self in us would wish to be recognized and helped by the thoughts of others. Doing unto others as we would have them do to us means that we must do everything for them according to our highest understanding of good. If, therefore, we are growing in understanding, we will be able to do more for others today than we were able to do yesterday. So it behooves us to do unto ourselves, as well as to others, as we would have others do to us, in order that we may improve, since by that same improvement we are more able to do for others. This means that we must stop all self-condemnation, and all unhealthy thinking, all habits of mind and body that do not improve our wits, our joys, our understanding and our health.

We should not make any statements about ourselves that are not absolutely true, if we would do unto ourselves as we would have others do to us. We must not say, 'I am sick; I am tired; I am weak,' or make any negative statement. But we must claim as our own the conditions which we wish to manifest in our bodies and affairs and which we know to be true in the absolute. It is not kindness to cause others to listen to our troubles and growlings. Other people do not enjoy hearing of how many times we were operated upon, or how our tooth caused us untold pain, or how someone snubbed us, or how we caught cold. Neither do we care to hear of our neighbor's troubles. What really pleases and helps our associates is our happiness and our optimistic conversation.

Everyone likes to be lifted up out of sorrow into joy. Say 'I am well; I am strong; I am happy.' We need not say these things in so many words, but we can think them so strong that our every word and action will radiate health, happiness and helpfulness. These conditions are contagious. We would like to have others make us happy and therefore, by radiating these good conditions we are following Christ's teachings of doing unto others as we would have them do to us. To really do unto others in all respects as we would have them do to us, we should not tell of calamities, or fill our listener's ears with gossip. These things are unkind to the ones of whom we speak, unkind to the ones who listen, and disheartening to our own spirit of high standard.

Doing unto others as we would have them do unto us is the very foundation of politeness. One who has had no schooling in society can be polite if he has ingrained this rule deep in his thoughts and actions. True politeness consists of making others feel at ease and happy. He who understands the art of doing unto others as he would be done by will naturally do this, and will consequently be at ease himself at all times. No matter if he does not know the forms and customs of polite society, he will soon drop easily into them, if they be based upon true politeness. He will always be a welcome visitor among all people, whether they be of humble circumstances or whether they live in palaces. It is sometimes laughable to see people crowd onto a street car during the rush hours. They jostle and push one another, men crushing and rushing past women and children by using their superior strength, and each person seemingly possessed of an insane desire to get ahead of someone else at whatever cost.

These same people will, on that same evening, bow and most insistently offer vacant chairs to each other, with sweet words and smiles. This simply shows that the Golden Rule is not deeply seated in the consciousness of these people, but is looked upon by them as a sort of thing outside of themselves, and to be used only upon certain special occasions. One moved by the rule of doing unto others as he would have others do to him will always be polite. Going a step farther, we can apply this rule to our relations with all living creatures. You may say, surely you would not have us waste our time and 'golden rule' upon dumb beasts? Why not? Are they not animated by God's life, which is in every thing? Do they not suffer when we hurt them? Do they not become hungry and thirsty? Do they not breathe the same air that we do? Do they not have brain cells, and are not these cells for the purpose of thinking? They surely do understand and appreciate man's application of the 'golden rule' in his treatment of them.

How can we be kind to dumb creatures and show them the 'golden rule'? By not eating them; by not wearing them; by not causing them to suffer through our own actions or the actions of others in our behalf; by giving them their freedom, and by recognizing in them the working of the Divine Law. We have considered this rule of doing unto others as we would have them do to us in the light of each act of this kind as unselfish, yet upon second thought, each act of unselfishness in its ultimate brings great returns of increased good to us. For whatever we do for the good of others, whether in thought, word or act, is also done for ourselves. Every good thought must come home to roost, and it must bring other thoughts of a like kind with it in a flock. Really if we were to measure the selfishness of an act by the increase we were to receive as a result of it, instead of considering our motive for doing it, it would seem that the most selfish thing we could do would be to do unto others as we would have others do to us, because it would bring the largest returns in the end."

Weekly Unity May 8, 1912, The Healing Word by Cora Dedrick.

"Through the power of the Lord Jesus Christ we can send forth the healing word to the one desiring to be healed, no matter where he may be, and know that it does accomplish that where-unto it is sent. We are all one in Spirit. The Power of Omnipotence is established in us. The first healing is always the mental realm. It consists in turning away from former beliefs in the reality and power of sickness and coming into the knowledge that life and health only are possible, because life and health are of God, the Omnipotent One, and through the Lord Jesus Christ we are one with God. The body is the child of the mind, and through the power of true words we can nourish it with the living bread which comes down from heaven and give it to drink out of the wells of salvation and thus the outer manifestation corresponds with the inner realization."

Weekly Unity May 29, 1912, "Building Fund. It has been some time since anything has been said about the Building Fund, so we are going to bring it to your attention now to keep you from entirely forgetting that there is such a thing. The pledges are being paid slowly, but surely and money is coming in to meet the general expenses, but as a number of bonds will be due the first of July and some borrowed money should be paid soon, the Finance Committee will welcome donations at all times with grateful hearts. If anyone who has made a pledge desires to know how much he still owes on the pledge, he may ask the secretary who will be glad to tell him. Those who have not made pledges and are desirous of making donations to a good cause are invited to help. All money must be sent freely and with no thought of lack or grudging."

1913 - Rick Fillmore had not as yet joined his family in full time work at Unity. However, he had been doing the art work for his mother's Wee Wisdom magazine and was the artist for the front cover art work for Unity magazine. Over several years his art work for Unity magazine revealed the changing philosophy of the Unity movement in a very subtle way. [In a film slide presentation showing the front covers of the Unity magazine, from the early years, the changes in philosophy were pointed out and discussed by the presenter, Philip White, the editor of Unity magazine at a meeting of the Men of Unity in February 1991.]

Weekly Unity February 12, 1913, "Practical Christianity for Practical Christians. Practical Christianity is growing in popularity as a good name for those who are making practical application in all ways of the Christian religion. At present not many societies in this country have adopted the name, but it will eventually cover the whole earth, because it is in Divine Order. These various societies are not branches of the original Unity Society of Practical Christianity of Kansas City, but stand as independent organizations, bringing forth the fruits of the Christian religion under the guidance of the Spirit, and fulfilling the promise, 'When the Spirit of Truth is come, he will lead you into all Truth.'"

1914 - Charles Fillmore merged the various departments, the Unity Tract Society (formally the Unity Book Company), the Society of Silent Unity, the Unity Correspondence School and Silent Seventy into a new corporation, The Unity School of Christianity. The term "school", Charles felt, described the fundamental work of the Unity movement.

The name of the Wee Wisdom magazine was changed to Wisdom on the urging of Royal Fillmore. The change lasted one year and Myrtle resumed the Wee Wisdom name.

From a Sunday school lesson of January 1914, an article of Myrtle Fillmore was entitled The Truth Child's Rosary, by Aunt Myrtle. (Hannah Moore Kahaus poem The Prayer of Faith).

> "God is my help in every need: God does my every hunger feed. God walks beside me, guides my way, through every moment of the day. I now am wise, I now am true, patient, kind and loving, too. All things I am, can do and be. Through Christ the truth that is in me. God is my health, I can't be sick. God is my strength, unfailing quick. God is my all, I know no fear. Since God and Love and Truth are here. The six little verses given above are for you to put on your memory-string, like beads that some little children are given to count so as to help them remember good things. Every one of these six rhymes is a little prayer that will help you to remember how to be wise and brave and true and well."

This is ideal for showing the beautiful compassion Myrtle had for the children she loved. The poem was first published in August 1898 in the Wee Wisdom magazine.

The following blessing, hand written on the Unity School of Christianity letterhead listing Unity building 917 Tracy Avenue Kansas City, Missouri, Silent Unity Department August 12, 1914. "A Blessing: This building is dedicated to God, the Father of all. Omnipresence, Omnipotence, Omniscience be then in the minds of all who congregate here. And the blessings of Health, Love, Peace, and Prosperity be upon all the world in the name of Jesus Christ. Judson Raymond Rude, Society of Silent Unity."

1915 - The Foundation and Object of the Unity Work, by Charles Fillmore. Excerpts from an address delivered at the Dedication of the Unity building, 917 Tracy, Kansas City, Missouri, January 1, 1915.

"Every great work must have as its foundation a great idea. If the great idea is not present, the work will fail in attaining the object for which it stands. The great idea upon which the Unity work is founded is a right concept of God. Our God is not an enlarged man, but the one great principle of Being. God is Spirit, the direct opposite of matter. God is supreme mind, the storehouse of perfect ideas. God is the one Spirit-Mind, in whom all ideas of life, love, substance, intelligence, power originate. Spirit-Mind is the indwelling idea at the center of everything that has real existence.

Under the divine law, all the great ideas of Spirit-Mind are gathered together and epitomized in God's supreme creation Spiritual Man. This man-idea is the 'only begotten Son' of God. He is the one creative idea of Divine Mind. All other ideas are parts, man is the whole. Through His man-idea, God creates His universe. Christ is the manifest name of this supreme God-Idea, and through Him the worlds come into existence.

Jesus demonstrated the capacity of man to received the inspiration and power of Divine Mind. He restored to our consciousness the man-idea conceived in us by Divine Mind in the beginning, which conception we had lost sight of through sin, a disregard of the divine law. The great work of spiritual man is to restore this divine consciousness to the whole race. This is our work, and this dedication of another workshop is evidence that there is demand for the teaching that we set forth; also that we are going forward in our efforts to meet that demand.

One of the fundamentals of Truth is that whatever God has revealed to man in one age He will continue to reveal to him in all ages. Spirit-Mind is omnipresent, immanent in all creation. It is the logical truth of these premises, and the inspiration that follows the worship of God as the one omnipotent, omniscient, and omnipresent Spirit, that has moved us to plant here these temporal structures, from which this Truth shall be taught.

Paul did not hesitate to tell that Jesus had talked with him as he journeyed to Damascus, or that He stood by his couch at night and encouraged him when he was in great peril in Jerusalem. Why should we, in this day of religious skepticism, be afraid to proclaim that God has again and again told us of the work that we are to do? Over forty years ago, the Lord in a dream prophesied this work and directed us to this locality. His guiding Spirit has ever since been with us in dreams and visions, inspirations, and spiritual quickenings.

The object of this school is the redemption of the human race. It is a link in the great educational movement inaugurated by Jesus, which not only taught the Truth but demonstrated it also. This school intends to discern the Truth in Christianity and prove it. We do not bind ourselves to precedents in our study of Truth or in its demonstrations.

We know, however, that what has been done by man can be done again, under like relations, it is merely a matter of finding the law.

This school is an open door to the heretofore secret things of Spirit. Although we are not a financially endowed institution, we are inviting students everywhere to take our lessons and literature and give in return what seems to them just and right. 'Ho, every one that thirsteth, come ye to the water, come ye, buy, and eat, without money and without price.'

The 'signs' that follow prove that we are teaching the doctrine taught by Jesus. The evils (devils) are cast out; a right use of words is inculcated ('speak with new tongues'); the subtleties of sense consciousness are taken up ('shall take up serpents')' destructive thoughts are rendered harmless ('if they drink any deadly thing, it shall in no wise hurt them')' and the power of the Spirit is exercised in healing ('they shall lay hands on the sick, and they shall recover'). But these 'signs' do not constitute all the proof we have that the Truth is being promulgated. Thousands testify that their minds have been illuminated with a new understanding of God, man, and the universe, and from nearly every part of the world men and women are writing us letters of thanksgiving for the light that has come into their souls through the study of our literature.

We thank you, dear friends, not only here present, but wherever you may be, for the help you have extended toward the erection of this new Unity building. The Lord has assured us again and again that those who give to the furtherance of His work shall receive again with increase.

This is but the beginning of a work that will in due season encircle the earth. The vision of the future that the Lord has shown us is of magnitude beyond present description. The new Jerusalem is not to be in Palestine but in the heart of the American continent."

1916 - The Kansas City Daily Sun January 3, "The Kansas City Daily Sun begins to shine today. It will rise and shine six times a week for the purpose of brightening the members of the Unity Community. It will not get hot enough to roast, but just enough to keep hearts from freezing up. The object of the Sun, primarily is the creation of a Unity Spirit, and a closer relationship between the workers. We want you to make this your Sun, on bright days and on dark days. Another object of the paper will be the immediate announcement of important matters of interest which you might not otherwise hear about. The Sun begins to rise each morning at about 8:00. It will be visible to all at 11:40 a.m. No subscription price will be charged for the Sun, but a box for free will offerings will be placed in the book keeping department on the second floor near the dummy elevator on Saturdays and Mondays. The present editorial staff, consisting of eight members, has been appointed for a period of six months. This staff, however, is not entirely responsible for the paper, its up to the readers to help make it a success. Send matters for publication to the attention of Lowell Fillmore."

The Kansas City Daily Sun January 6th, 1916, "There was quite a large attendance at the meeting of the Unity Guild. The year just past has been quite prosperous for the Guild and several donations from the surplus funds have been made to the Unity Society. Ah yes, the Guild's reputation for doing things is being sustained. Just watch the Guild! Don't forget about the play to be presented within a few weeks."

The Kansas City Daily Sun January 31, 1916, "The Circus. While it is not certain just what day the circus will be given, it is quite certain that the circus committee has begun its work, and plans for even a larger and more entertaining circus than the one given last year. A number of acts and booths have already been arranged for, but the committee will gladly receive any offers of assistance or suggestions that anyone at Unity has to offer. Of course we will have a country store, a refreshment stand, etc., there will also be a magician, a bucking bronco, a zobo band, a Charlie Chaplin, clowns, etc. Someone has all ready asked for the exclusive vegetarian hot dog concession. The committee wants names of anyone who can put on a good 'stunt'. Committee: Grace Kraft, Mattie Saunders, Lowell Fillmore."

The Kansas City Daily Sun February 8, 1916, "Mr. Xavier Boillot, who is superintending the building of the Unity Auditorium, has quite a record as a builder and Unity is fortunate in having him. Some of the big buildings which he has built are; Old Convention Hall, The Garden Theatre and Elsmere Hotel and the Globe Theater. Our tennis court. During the coming month, the Unity Tennis Club will organize. The members will build their own court in the rear of the garden. By active cooperation in this work, we can have as good a tennis court as any in the city. A notice will be inserted in the Sun when this club is ready to organize and plans will be discussed pertaining to the same."

The Kansas City Daily Sun February 11, 1916, "On next Sunday evening the Right Honorable, Reverendus, Esquires, Royaloo Filmorey will deliver an address in the Unity Auditorium. This is a rare opportunity to hear one of the coming speakers of the age and all Unity employees should take advantage of this opportunity. We know it will be a very interesting address, and those who know him as the quiet, unassuming young man during the week, will be surprised at how he can blossom out. Silent Unity now conducts a continuous Silent Prayer for the ushering in of the New Race and the New Earth. Each member is given thirty minutes in the Silence Room, and in this way the prayer is carried forward from 8:00 in the morning until 9:00 in the evening. This includes Sunday also, as several of the members have volunteered their services for that day. The increase of spiritual power is very noticeable, since this plan has been adopted."

The Kansas City Daily Sun February 14, 1916, "To those that have been asleep for the last few days, we wish to say that Mr. Royal Fillmore delivered the address at Unity last night, and also delivered the goods. If you didn't have ambition enough to come down, we are not going to tell you what he said. After the meeting he was surrounded and congratulated by his friends. We hope Mr. Fillmore, Jr. will soon become a regular speaker at Unity, for he speaks in our native tongue and does not try to hand us any yard-long adjectives, like some other lecturers we have heard."

The Kansas City Daily Sun March 23, 1916, "All about the Silent Seventy. The Silent Seventy department is organized for the distribution of free literature tracts and sample copies. It is founded on the incident in the 10th chapter of Luke, when the 'seventy others' were sent out. The members are divided into bands of seventy and we have a membership of nearly 3,000. The members of each band containing a number of members in foreign countries. So the office force of two (generally one) with the assistance of the stock clerk handles these 3,000 workers in the field. We have twelve regular assortments of literature, each consisting of four each of about ten different tracts, Unities, weeklies and Wee Wisdom. Upon being enrolled, a member is sent one of these assortments and a letter containing instructions regarding the work and distribution of the literature. He is then supposed to report once a month, and when the literature is exhausted another assortment is sent. These assortments are carefully compiled as to subject."

<u>The Kansas City Daily Sun</u> April 24, 1916, "Two-hundred turned away! The new auditorium dedicated yesterday was entirely too small for the attendance. Long before 11:00 the Auditorium and balcony were filed to overflowing and even the aisles in the balcony were so filled that there was no getting in or out. The least that can be said of the service is that it was beautiful. A spirit of peace and harmony and rest pervaded the Auditorium, that is seldom found and the speaker seemed especially inspired. His words made us feel that if we had not all ready dedicated ourselves and our lives to God and this great work, we must do so at once. Mrs. Croft gave a splendid talk about the finances of the Unity Society of Practical Christianity, telling us how one little penny, with all its possibilities of increase, started the building fund, for this great home of Truth. Nine other pennies were added to this one and they were put away and blessed and increased until a sufficient amount was on hand to start the first Unity building.

Judging by the attendance yesterday, it will not be long until we will need a larger Auditorium than the one we now have, and it will only be a short time until Unity will occupy the entire block. The evening services were well attended also. Mrs. Croft conducted the meeting and there were talks by the heads of the various auxiliaries of the Unity Society, each one giving an idea of the work and the purpose of the department or club. Mr. D.W. Pye, of New York, was with us yesterday, and he too gave a most interesting little talk in the evening, on giving and receiving. We were all glad to hear from him and trust he will be with us some time."

The new Unity headquarters building at 917 Tracy was partially completed and those areas occupied. The new auditorium was completed and a souvenir booklet announced that dedication week for the New Unity auditorium would be held on April 23rd through 29th, 1916 at 917 Tracy Kansas City, Missouri of the Unity Society of Practical Christianity.

The Kansas City Daily Sun June 2, 1916, "To all Unity friends. Mr. & Mrs. Daniel Hoagland request your presence at the marriage of their daughter Clara May to Frank Blenlarry Whitney Monday June 12, 1916 Unity Auditorium, 8:00."

June 20, 1916, "This is the last issue of this paper under the name of the Kansas City Daily Sun, as we have learned that there is another Kansas City paper using that name. The Kansas City Daily Sun began January 1916 and was replaced on July 1, 1916 with the Daily Unity. In search of another name, the management decided that no better one could be found than Daily Unity. Accordingly, Daily Unity comes to you today in place of the Daily Sun. The paper will be managed in the same manner as before. The July 1st menu for the Unity Vegetarian Inn. Lunch 12:00 to 1:00 Vegetable Broth - Nut Loaf - Boiled Potatoes - Beet Greens - Lima Beans - Mixed Salad - Cucumber Salad - Rice Peach Pudding - Rhubarb Sauce - Fruits. Dinner 5:45 to 7:00 Soup - Fried Eggplant - Browned Potatoes - Cabbage - Stewed Tomatoes - Salads - Desserts."

Daily Unity Sun June 21, 1916, "Mr. Royal Fillmore leaves tomorrow for New York City, accompanied by his grandmother. Royal speaks at Unity Center, New York, Sunday night. From New York they will go to Plainfield, New Jersey to visit with Mr. Howard Colby. The following letter tells what will happen then better than we can tell it. 'Dear Royal, Great! Bring your dear grandmother direct to Plainfield. We will be here to receive you both. I think she would enjoy a few days here resting and roaming around the country in the automobile. Then, in a few days, we will motor down to Mantoloking, and see how she likes it there. It is really a unique little place. As you may have seen on the map it is only a strip of sand about as wide as a nail file, between the ocean and Barnegat Bay. I have taken a fancy to it on account of its simplicity. there are only about ten houses and they are all within twenty yards of the ocean, so we put our bathing suits on in the house and with a good jump from the roof you can dive into the sea. No duds of any kind. Just flannel trousers and an old shirt. We are going to keep both houses open and just migrate back and forth as we please. Affectionately Howard.'"

Daily Unity July 11, 1916, "Some of the Silent Unity members, in a meeting, began telling their boyhood ambitions. Charles Fillmore wanted to tell his first, 'He wanted to go out on the wild prairie, wear leather breeches, break wild broncos, sing "Joe Bowers" until the natives all cried, and be an honest to goodness cowboy.' Real dignified, wasn't he? Miss Cora Dedrick of Silent Unity left Sunday visiting friends and sight seeing. Miss Dedrick expects to cross the lake and to visit the Israelites at Benton Harbor. We sincerely wish her a pleasant vacation and will gladly welcome her home again."

Daily Unity July 17, 1916, "There's only one way to acquire wisdom, but when it comes to making a fool of yourself you have your choice of a million different ways. Responsibilities gravitate to the person who can shoulder them and power and success flow to the man who knows how and who exercises his know how. The following written by C.A. Peters;

> "When we enter the silence and come into conscious union with God, the source of all life, our conscious mind and body is merged into the one Universal Spirit-Substance. It is then quite easy to see and know there is only one Spirit, one life, one substance, one power. When in this state of consciousnes the personal man is lost sight of, together with all objective things; then when we speak living words of Truth, it is not the personal man that speaks, but our impersonal universal God - Self - Words of Truth spoken when in conscious union with God, go forth alive with power to heal and bless.
>
> "When we have entered the 'secret place of the most high,' we are then in a state of consciousness that knows no evil. We then see and know that so called evil has no foundation in Truth, none whatever. All inharmonious conditions of whatever name or nature, are the results of wrong thinking and wrong acting. They are self inflicted, man made, and will pass away just as soon as we know the Truth and live it. Sin, sickness, sorrow, poverty and death have no place in the mind, body or affairs of one who is living in conscious union with God. I am redeemed out of all nations, all races, all people into the great God life that is in all, through all and over all."

Daily Unity July 22, 1916, "Letter to Mr. Lowell Fillmore. 'Dear Friend, It is such a pleasure to express my gratitude for the Unity Center being established in Omaha. My great desire for a long time is now realized. Miss Nevill is presenting the Truth in such an earnest and clear way, we cannot thank her enough. Many new faces are joining each meeting. I cannot refrain from thanking the dear workers at Unity for the new understandings and many blessings I have received, also for the wonderful opening we are having here. I am very thankful. Most sincerely, Josephine W. Shipman."

Daily Unity July 25, 1916, "Did you have some of the excellent corn at the Unity Inn last night? It was raised in the Unity gardens. Some day Unity will be able to raise all of their own vegetables and fruits. When good thoughts are given the seeds to grow on and they are tended with the loving care of Unity gardeners, think how much bigger and better their products will be." [This statement was certainly an unknown prophesy that would be realized in just a few years!]

Daily Unity August 1, 1916, "Another shipment of Good Words Club pins has been received, but will no doubt be exhausted by the time you read this. The orders are coming in faster than the pins can be made. These pins are available in solid gold at a dollar, in sterling silver at seventy-five cents and in gold plate for forty cents. There are two styles, one for a gentlemen's coat lapel with a screw button back and the other, a pin with safely clasp. Safety clasps are on all priced pins. If you wish one of these emblems of membership in this worthy organization, you may place your order with Mr. Lowell Fillmore."

Daily Unity August 2, 1916, "Unity Irrigation Project. You have all no doubt heard of the Salt River Project and the Roosevelt Dam, but how many have heard of the Unity Irrigation Project? As yet it is only in its infancy, and its fame has yet to be known to the world. The project was planned by Mr. Royal Fillmore, a well known civil engineer. In the Unity garden is the reservoir, which is also used as a fish pond. Water is constantly flowing into the reservoir and is kept from overflowing by an outlet pipe. This pipe carries off into the Unity vegetable garden, irrigating it so that the vegetables grow quite rapidly. The vast work of building this was carried out by Kreigh & Peters

Construction Company, who do many large contracts drawn up by Mr. Fillmore."

Daily Unity August 28, 1916, "A committee is working on plans to form regular daily classes to be held in the other building. As this work grows and enlarges it will become a regular college. This work is being started to meet the growing demand from people who wish to come here and take regular courses of study in the Unity teachings. The day is not far off when Unity headquarters will have great dormitories, mess rooms and lecture halls, with thousands of students from all parts of the globe, studying and preparing to spread this great teaching over the whole earth."

Daily Unity September 4, 1916, "A Four Years Increase. The September issue of Unity magazine for 1912 was 30,000. The same issue for 1916 is 50,000 copies. The issue for Weekly Unity for September 7, 1912 was 8,700. For September 9, 1916 it is 22,000. The September 1912 issue of Wee Wisdom was 3,700 copies. For September 1916 it was 4,800."

Daily Unity September 8, 1916, "This morning the office had their Joy Day. An entertainment committee had prepared a program. Was it a success? The laughter that issued from the room must have been heard for a block. Volunteers for funny stories were secured before hand. Then the fun began. As a story was told, Royal, as interlocutor, failed to see the point and demanded an explanation. Mrs. De Voss was the first victim, but saved the day with witticism. Virgil and Mrs. Croft also proved a match for Royal. Then a game was played, the object being to see who could eat fifteen peanuts then whistle first. Earl won the first prize, Mrs. De Voss the booby prize. Their prize consisted of being' dubbed' Squirrel and Nut which they were required to emulate."

Daily Unity September 12, 1916, "The Unity Life Expression Club announcement of great importance. A meeting of all departments of the Unity Life Expression Club is called tomorrow night in the Lecture Hall at 5:15. Plans for the season of 1916-17 will be formed. Classes in studies which the members wish to take up will be considered and directors and teachers voted upon. Bring your plans and ideas to this meeting."

Daily Unity September 13, 1916, "The Unity Mechanical Department is now equipped with a Kellogg Air Blowing machine. By means of an electric motor, compressed air is stored up in a tank and this air may be used to blow dust from machinery by a hose and nozzle attached to the tank. At pressure of 120 pounds the nozzle will take off dust, grease and everything but the paint. The machine is portable and power to run it may be taken from any light socket. If your cerebral department is dusty this is your chance. Winter is coming. Dallas Kreigh is white-washing his boiler room and cleaning out the boilers. Soon we will see him with monkey wrench in hand adjusting radiators."

Daily Unity September 29, 1916, "Fireman Fires First Fire. Dallas Kreigh is firing up his boilers this morning and it will soon be summer again. All offering and votes of thanks may be addressed simply: D.M. Kreigh, 1st floor. This insures immediate delivery. Kreigh likes cakes."

Daily Unity October 2, 1916, "Mr. Waldo Rickert Fillmore is designing the cover for a new folder which will advertise the new booklet, Miscellaneous Writings. It will be embossed in the Unity printing department. Miscellaneous Writings has had a tremendous sale in the last month."

Daily Unity October 3, 1916, "The Unity School will publish shortly new editions of H. Emilie Cady's booklets, Oneness With God, Trusting and Resting and All Sufficiency in All Things. The books have proved so popular and the demand for them so great that the present supply is about exhausted. Christian Dietetics, a class in this subject was started last night under the tutelage of Mr. Royal Fillmore. There were a goodly number present and the work promises much interesting and profitable study. Mr. Fillmore will tell you what the different values of food are, what and how much you should eat and how to prepare your food. If you intend to join this class you should start by the next meeting, as a regular course is being taken up and late comers will not derive as much as they otherwise would.

The class meets regularly every Monday evening at 7:00 p.m. The new India paper editions of Christian Healing and Lessons in Truth are being printed now. When completed these editions will have limp Keratol covers. The entire book, Christian Healing, will not be more than half an inch thick. The present paper bound volume is an inch and a quarter thick. The oil contract has been let to the Kansas City Refineries. There will be two tanks, holding a total of 6,500 gallons. The Unity Inn will be an entirely different looking place after its remodeling, when it is reopened to the public next Sunday. Three new lanterns will be placed in the ceiling, lending much more light. There will be some appropriate mottos painted on the chimney places. The Inn also has a fine new five gallon coffee urn for cereal coffee."

Daily Unity October 4, 1916, "Todays classes at Unity School of Christianity.
10:30 a.m. - Christian Healing, Ida M. Palmer
12:00 - High Noon Silence, Myrtle Fillmore
2:30 p.m. - Med-week Meeting of Unity Society of Practical Christianity
4:00 p.m. - Prosperity Class, Edith Haseltine
7:30 p.m. - The Way of Silence, Jennie H. Croft
8:00 p.m. - Healing Meeting, Charles and Myrtle Fillmore

Daily Unity October 16, 1916, "Mr. Waldo Rickert Fillmore has just finished the design of a very beautiful cover for the Beaux Art booklets. The new covers will be embossed with the Printing Department's new embossing machine."

Daily Unity October 21, 1916, "Society News. Silent Unity had a 'popcorn party' at 12:30 Friday. Frank Whitney was the 'popper' and we all marveled at the dexterity in which he handled the popper and think him an artist in the culinary art. The corn was popped over the large fire place and we watched with delight the corn transformed into a mass of white by the expansion of the heat. The kernel multiplied in size reminded us that we too are a kernel of God's divine life and that by applying the consuming fire of Truth we too can be transformed into a white living presence of the angelic purity."

Daily Unity October 25, 1916, "A record crowd attended the Joyful Circle dance last night. The great hall was filled and there was hardly room to dance. Fully two thirds of the visitors were new people, which shows that the Joyful Circle's mission in bringing new young people to Unity is being fulfilled. The Joyful Circle faces a new era of success. We extend best wishes to President Eckert."

Daily Unity November 7, 1916, "We burn oil, no smoke, no cinders. The oil burners were started in the Unity boilers at 9:15 last night. Mr. Royal Fillmore struck the match that lighted the first burner to be put in operation. Dallas Kreigh, our valiant fireman, is going to sell his jumper and buy a dinner coat. As soon as he gets the place all cleaned up he is going to invite you all down to see him."

Daily Unity November 8, 1916, "Woodrow Wilson is Re-elected. All of the votes have not yet been counted, but it is assured fact that President Wilson has won. Of the electoral votes 266 are needed and President Wilson received over 288."

Daily Unity December 1, 1916, "He Was Surprised. At the public speaking class entertainment last night, something happened not on the program. Practically every seat was taken and all of the speakers were well received. Mr. Earl Miller and Mrs. January favored us with selections on the violin and Hawaiian guitar. The part not on the program was the presentation to Mr. Lowell Fillmore, the teacher of the class, with a beautiful potted azalea. This was the gift of the members of the class to show their appreciation of what he has done for them.

A resume of ten years. Ten years ago the Unity Tract Society had just moved into its new building at 913 Tracy, which is the front part of the Auditorium building now. The Silent Unity Department was on the third floor, where Mrs. Fillmore, Mrs. Parrish and Miss Carpenter have their offices now. The second floor, of course, was the lecture room or meeting room. On the first floor was the Library, the business office, and the printing office. Instead of the modern addressograph mailing system in use now, the mailing list was printed on galley proofs and hung up on the wall. The mailing list was set up in type in the printing office, and when the galley proofs had been struck, the names were cut apart and pasted on the wrappers.

There were but about three typewriters in the entire office.The printing machinery consisted of a foot-power job press, a hand power stitcher, and a hand-power stock cutter. A few cases of type and a gasoline can would just about complete the inventory. Today we have over fifty typewriters, about eighty desks, a complete addressograph plant, a linotype, two cylinder presses, one with an automatic feeder attachment, an automatic feed job press, an automatic clamp stock cuter, an autopress, four folding machines, an automatic clamp book trimmer, two power stitchers, and many other small labor saving machines.

The present Unity Administration building has more than eight times the amount of floor space than was in the original building. As compared with ten workers then, there are about a hundred and thirty now. Mention must also be made of the chemical laboratory which is located on the fifth floor of the Administration building. At the present time we are cramped for room and will soon need a building for the printing and bindery departments alone. Unity headquarters is growing rapidly and at an ever increasing rate of speed."

Daily Unity December 5, 1916, "What Do You Think. It has been suggested that a Christian Diet 'squad' be formed, under the direction of Mr. Royal Fillmore, to show that one can live most economically, most healthily and most cleanly on a strictly vegetarian diet. Such a test would put the one in Chicago in the shade from the standpoint of economy and the participants would be ever so much more healthy. If you would like to try such a stunt for two weeks, give your name to the editor today. To save embarrassment, it would not be necessary to say who was doing it."

Daily Unity December 11, 1916, "Diet Squad Starts Today. Lunch; lima bean soup, dried whole wheat bread, salad with olive oil, black figs, new water. Dinner; 1 oz nuts (preferably pecans), and acid fruits. If possible, Mr. Royal Fillmore would like to have you all eat at the same table. He will officiate behind the steam table to see that you get what is coming to you. Everyone should go down to Mr. Garrison's office some time today and weigh as exactly as possible. Send your weight to Diet Squad secretary, c/o Daily Unity. Nuts and fruits for your evening meal will not be eaten by the squad assembly."

Daily Unity December 18, 1916, "Diet Squad Notes. Today we eat whole-wheat and maple syrup, tomato soup, slaw, and bread, if we want it. All of the members of the squad were at the Inn yesterday for a hot dinner, rather than eat dried fruits. Get weighed today, and see how much you have gained."

Daily Unity December 26, 1916, "Squad Continues To Diet. The Diet Squad was so successful that it will be continued on a larger scale. Anyone may eat a diet meal by just selecting the articles on the menu that are starred. There will be no separate table for dieters. Everyone on the Diet Squad ate what was prescribed and all say they have been benefited."

The Unity benefactor that mortgaged his assets and loaned the proceeds to Unity was David Hoagland and he was ultimately repaid. In 1916 his daughter, Clara May Rowland became director of Silent Unity.

1917 - Daily Unity February 7, 1917, "Good Words Club Gains 100%. The membership roll of the Good Words Club is climbing. On January 26, 1916 the membership was 3,200. On February 5, 1917 membership totaled 6,501. A club with such a worthy purpose cannot help but grow. There are no dues or fees."

Daily Unity February 22, 1917, "Inn Gets New Equipment. The Unity Inn is being equipped to care for an increase in business. A magnificent new Born stove has been purchased as well as new plates, dishes, and silver service have been added. Miss Higgins, manager, says that the Inn will soon need more tables too."

Daily Unity February 23, 1917, "Unity to Build in the Spring. The Unity School of Christianity will build a two story annex to the south of the present structure which will extend southward to the end of the lot on which the Unity Inn is situated. It will be forty feet wide and the walls will be made of glass as much as possible. The fountain in the garden will be moved forward. A separate heating plant will be built on the opposite side of the alley and the space occupied by the present one will be given over to a stock room for printing paper. More particulars will be printed later."

Daily Unity February 24, 1917, "A New Inn Manager. Beginning the 1st of March Mrs. Reca Shaffer will assume active management of the Inn, as Miss Higgins has announced her resignation effective on that date. Mrs. Shaffer will begin Monday to become acquainted with her new duties. Mrs. Shaffer was the founder of the embryonic Unity Inn when the entire plant of the Unity Tract Society was in a little frame house down on McGee Street. She lived in the house and cooked lunch for the workers. Mr. Shaffer was the first worker in the Silent Unity besides Mr. & Mrs. Fillmore, which then consisted of these three people. So once again the cycle turns and once again Mrs. Shaffer is getting lunch for the Unity workers, figuratively speaking."

Daily Unity February 26, 1917, "Royal Fillmore went shopping last Saturday and purchased a brand new Buick. He is all wrapped up in it."

Daily Unity February 27, 1917, "A five minute silence. Starting tomorrow morning the workers in all departments will start the days work with a five minute silence, to be held just as the 8:00 bell rings. At five minutes after eight another bell will ring to announce the end of the silence. Workers coming in late must remain in the vestibule until the silence is over. The following is the thought to be held: 'There is only one presence in this room. This one presence is the presence of God or Good. No evil can enter here. There is no evil in God. God, the Good, dwells here. Whoever enters here will be conscious of the one divine presence of Good.' This silence should be of great benefit to all in helping to start the day right, especially if you happened to get up on the wrong side of the bed. The music we have been hearing at the Inn the last few days has been a real treat. The Grafonola certainly is a wonderful instrument. Good things to eat and good music are nice, and when you have good music in the presence of good eats, well, just ask Whitty.

Board Meeting Business. At the board meeting last night it was decided to purchase an Austin Pipe Organ for the new Auditorium having three manuals, a movable keyboard, and costing $2,100.00. $1,600.00 for the organ has already been subscribed. The matter of decorating the new Auditorium was turned over to the Woman's Auxiliary. When these two features have been finished it will then be time to consider another Auditorium. Very good silence. The silence which is now held by all departments at 8:00 a.m. was found to be very beneficial and will no doubt prove more so as time goes on. The entire building was so still that Mr. Garrison could have heard George Huston chewing gum if he had been."

Daily Unity March 5, 1917, "Having finished arrangements for all night work Silent Unity last week took up the matter of continuing the work on Sunday and found a number of willing volunteers. Good reports are beginning to come in from the all night plan. It is now over a year since the plan was adopted to have one of the healers in the Silence Room all the time during the day."

Daily Unity March 6, 1917, "Decorating Has Commenced. Scaffolding is being placed today in the new Auditorium preparatory to decorating it, which will be done under the personal direction of Mr. Waldo Rickert Fillmore. New building to start soon. As soon as some people evacuate the apartment on Tenth Street and the goods stored in the garage can be moved into it, the garage will be torn down and work begun on the new addition."

Daily Unity March 9, 1917, "A Four Story Addition. The new addition to be built to the Unity building will go four stories instead of two, as originally planned. It will be 98 feet long and 35 feet wide. This will make a building very near as large as the present one. The work will be started Monday. The garage will be torn down first and the fountain and fish pond will be moved forward to about the center of the garden. Trees and benches will be grouped about it, making a sort of lovers paradise."

Daily Unity March 19, 1917, "Mr. Royal Fillmore is experimenting with making peanut milk. No doubt in a year or so we'll have rutabaga cordial, radish eclair and lima bean brandy."

Daily Unity March 20, 1917, "Spring Time is Here. Today is the first day of spring, officially. Perhaps, then it is quite appropriate that we have a vocal recital in the Auditorium this evening. Also, quite appropriate that the building be begun in earnest. Mr. Boillot expects to have it finished by the 1st of June. When the new building is completed the bindery and printing departments will be located on the first floor. Much new and more efficient composing room equipment has been ordered."

Daily Unity March 23, 1917, "Everything Is Going Up. The glorious springtime is upon us and everything is going up. Also, prices of food at the Inn are going up April 1st. All dishes will go up to six cents, except prunes and apple sauce.   No vibrations in new building. The first floor of the new building, on which the presses will be located, will be laid independent of the rest of the structure. A crack two inches wide will be left all around the edges and this crack will be filled with tar. This will do away with all vibrations from machinery."

Daily Unity April 27, 1917, "A New Office In The Unity Building. Waldo Rickert Fillmore, artist and oil and real estate magnate, has taken a suite of offices on the fifth floor of the Unity building. His furniture and effects were moved in yesterday. Welcome to our city.

Inn Will Bake Its Own Bread. The basement of the Inn has been fitted up for baking bread and Mrs. Shaffer will soon start baking her own bread. That will be great.

An Extension To Silent Seventy. A beautiful new office table has been installed in Silent 70 to accommodate the assistant, Mrs. Lois Coldren, and we wish to express to the management our appreciation. Mrs. Coldren is an assistant of more than material help to the department, for she radiates a fine spiritual influence which is felt by all with whom she comes in contact. She is with us three half days a week and for her this is a 'labor of love.'

Daily Unity May 4, 1917, "Keratol Bound Books Are Popular. Five-hundred more copies of the new edition of Christian Healing have just been sent to St. Louis to be bound in Keratol. The original supply of 500 is almost exhausted. Keratol is a purely vegetable product brought out to take the place of leather for book-binding and making traveling bags and suitcases, etc. It looks better than leather and is said to wear longer.

Brick Work Goes Forward. With the clearing of the skies yesterday, the bricks began to fly into their places to make the walls of the new addition. That second frame you see on the east side will be the doorway to the receiving dock. There will be no stairway on the first floor, but there will be on the three floors above.

A Case Of Divine Protection. Several months ago a Unity bond held by Lily Stack, our friend in London, fell due. Mr. Lowell Fillmore obtained a London draft, wrote her a letter and sent the letter and draft on its way. About three months afterwards Mr. Fillmore had a letter from her, telling the following story. The ship on which the letter was sent to England was torpedoed and sent to the bottom, but one lone mail sack floated and was picked up by another ship. When the letter was received there was hardly anything left to it. The sea water had eaten away the letter so that it was hardly recognizable, but the draft itself was in perfect condition. Lily Stack was very thankful to receive the money, as it was quite a neat little sum."

Daily Unity May 19, 1917, "Work All Night On Building. The concrete for the second floor of the wing to the Unity building was laid last night, and the men were still working on it this morning. A great number of them worked all night. Mr. Boillot hopes to have one floor a week laid from now until the building is finished."

Daily Unity May 29, 1917, "Everyone Must Register. The Unity School received a letter from the Mayor of the city this morning concerning the new registration law, which requires all male persons between the age prescribed to register June 5, no matter what their creed, nationality, or color. The letter is posted on the bulletin board. If you are more than 21 and not yet 31 on June 5 you must register or answer to the government."

Daily Unity May 31, 1917, "A Boy's Meeting Today. Mr. Charles Fillmore desired to meet all of the boys who come under the requirements of the United States government's registration law in the addressograph department at 4:00 today. Many from Unity register. Alex Alberg, Herbert McCurry, Herbert Swope, Elmer Grinnell, George Grinnell, Lloyd Deyes, Ralph Bello, Herald Landon, Arthur Hicks, Royal Fillmore, Arthur Martin, William Waschke, Frank Richard Synch, Victor Goode, F.B. Whitney, and George Huston."

Daily Unity June 6, 1917, " Something new in beads is a string of them worn by Mrs. Fillmore. They were sent to her by a friend in California. The beads were made by winding strips of paper around a pin and then putting shellac on them. The strips of paper in these beads were made from old Unity magazine covers. They were made by a Unity Booster in a California school."

Daily Unity June 15, 1917, "The Unity School has recently been equipped with an electric lightning letter opener. This has been made necessary on account of the increase in letters. Opening with a knife is now too slow."

Charles Fillmore began discussing with his sons that he could envision the time drawing near when Unity would outgrow their block long location on Tracy avenue. He talked about going into the country, not far from Kansas City and building a "Unity City". They discussed that its' beginning could be a place in the country where the Unity workers in Kansas City could go to relax on the week ends, have a place to stay and have recreational facilities.

The building of additional space for Unity between 9th and 10th on Tracy avenue continued. A letter from Flora B. Miller of Lancaster, PA sent to Unity contained a $1.00 bill for the purchase of one brick for the new South wing and suggested that all Unity supporters do the same. These bricks to face the buildings interior and to have the persons name, city and state listed. At $1.00 each she suggested the brick interior would be low maintenance and a memorial to those that helped in the building's cost.

Weekly Unity December 1, 1917, "Brick Blessings. We thank you, our dear friends and co-workers for your blessings upon the new building. We have not yet begun the names on the walls, but the painters have marked the bricks on the two floors allotted to the blessings. Little panels with winged globes at the top, have been put on the four sides of the supporting columns. These are to contain some of the blessings. Others will be paneled and others, framed and unframed, will make the walls most unique and interesting. The Unity building belongs to the Unity people everywhere. If you are one of us, put a little money into the Society's real estate. This will be one of the blessings;

Bless the four corners of this house,
And be the lintel blest;
And bless the hearth, and bless the board,
And bless each place of rest;
And bless the door that opens wide
To stranger as to kin;
And bless each crystal windowpane
that lets the starlight in;

And bless the rooftree overhead
And every sturdy wall;
The Peace of Man the Peace of God,
The Peace of Love on all!

Also, during the year this article appeared, titled Unity a good investment. The building projects that Unity is involved in gives the opportunity to offer Unity people more Unity bonds to invest in. Each bond is issued for $100.00 for any length of time up to five years. By the purchase it helps Unity's expansion and at the same time it is a good place your money can earn good interest.

From June 30, 1917 until January 31, 1919 there are no records of any news publication in the archives, except the paper edited by Lowell Fillmore, which basically contained articles of religious nature. The January 31, 1919 edition was the last, in this period, to be published under the name of Daily Unity. The publication name The Unity News first appeared on February 14, 1919. There was a news publication gap from November 21, 1919, until January 9, 1920. "The" was dropped from the masthead and the name became Unity News on May 20, 1922. The next change was made in January 10, 1924 in the masthead banner with the winged globe printed over the name Unity News.

1918 - Weekly Unity January 12, 1918, "The church and new cults by Edith Armstrong Talbot and published in the Congregationalist. The following was printed in the issue dated October 11, 1917:

> What of New Thought, Christian Science and the other new cults? Shall we fear and condemn them, or believe in them? Our neighbors seem to derive from them a comfort and satisfaction which their church life has never given them. What should be our attitude toward them and their new faith? And what should the church do about them? Without attempting to answer fully these questions, it is the aim of these papers to furnish some data in the way of facts and personal observations.
>
> These sects, as a whole, have a common origin. They began in America, with the teachings of one of those original geniuses, largely self-taught, to whom we are indebted for

many fertile ideas. Among the many branches which have developed from the leadership of individuals in New Thought, the most important is the Unity Society, Kansas City, Missouri, which, under Mr. Charles Fillmore, has become both large and well known. It has an efficient organization, monthly and weekly organs, with respective circulations of 100,000 and a plant in Kansas City worth $200,000. All funds have been contributed voluntarily, without solicitation. No bookkeeping is done. The Society of Silent Unity is a group of about forty people who spend their time in a room devoted to their uses, in given 'absent treatment', not only for sickness, but for every ill which flesh is heir to, poverty, misfortune, unhappiness and sin. They, too make no charge for their services, aiding thousands of people in all parts of the world on the voluntary offering plan.

An idea of Mr. Charles Fillmore and his work can be gathered from the following letter written by a Congregational minister in Kansas City, Missouri: 'The greatest reaction of Unity is, perhaps, the tremendous interest in the study of the Bible and spiritual meditation which it seems to arouse, also in the transfer of the thought of the people whom it touches from the material to the spiritual, no to asceticism, but to the sanctifying the material as the medium for higher spiritual attainment.

I called on one of my former parishioners, who used to suffer much and cause others to suffer from a recital of her grievances. She has recently joined the Unity Society. There was a wonderful contrast. No word was dropped by her which was not kind and loving. The devil has been cast out of her; she is well, sleeps peacefully as a child, and is happy. Her influence is radically different. There are many others like her. These changes come about, of course, whenever the Gospel has a fair chance, but I am inclined to think that the lesson which our churches should learn from all this is that they should be so organized and administered that the main issue, which is to know God and practice his Presence, should not be obscured.

It is the practical result of an implicit acceptance of the Savior's teaching which attracts people to these sects; not their philosophy. There is no reason why our churches should not incorporate this good in their own lives; I cherish the hope that this may be the sequel.

There are no financial demands, but the purse strings are loosened with an adroitness which discounts the 'Every Member Canvass.' I attended a little gathering at Unity Church a short time ago and the way in which the offering was fondled and glorified for about eight minutes made me understand that 'begging' is no way to get money. A man came to Unity for treatment for rheumatism during the year and received constant treatment extending over some months, living in Mr. Fillmore's own house. No bill was sent him and he left without speaking of payment. Shortly afterward, he sent a check for $1,500, saying that he had never received treatment so much in the spirit of Christ and that he was convinced that the society was genuine. So much for 'Faith methods!"

With World War I and the United States becoming involved Rick Fillmore joined the Army. After basic training he was placed in the Tank Corps. By mid 1918 he was in England, had attained the rank of Sergeant and later his unit went to Europe in Normandy. A letter dated October 25, 1918, "To Rick, our brave 'Tank Boy'; Even though you have gone from our midst, remember that our thoughts, hopes, and aspirations are for a safe and triumphant return. May God's loving care guide, guard and protect you in all your ways. With love and blessing, Mother, Father, Lowell and Unity Friends."

Royal Fillmore registered at the draft board. He received his draft card dated March 6th placing him in class one. He joined the National Guard of the State of Missouri on April 25, 1918. He was appointed as Regimental Supply Sergeant for the 7th Infantry. He became a Second Lieutenant in the Officers Reserve Corps on December 6th.

Lowell Fillmore received a certificate of ordination as a Unity minister dated September 8, 1918.

1919 - The Unity News June 13, 1919, "At Unity Men's Extension Club, Monday evening at 8:00 Richard Lynch will speak on 'Man's Right Place in the Universal Plan.' Meeting is for men only and is held in the Unity Lecture Hall."

Frank Whitney came to work at Unity after World War I. He became dean of the Correspondence School.

Rick and Royal were home from the military service. Charles and his three sons decided to look for a sight for "Unity City". They watched real estate adds in the Kansas City Star for property in Jackson County. In a Sunday paper they saw an add for a thirty-eight acre farm. They called the realtor and were told that the property had all ready been sold. They were asked what their need was and the kind of property they were wanting. After their answer the realtor said, "I believe we have exactly what you are looking for," and suggested that he drive them out to see the property. The sight was fifty-eight acres of rolling, timber stand, grass meadows and with two creeks. Rick was especially pleased with the sight, its' location, seventeen miles from 9th and Tracy, and then they discussed the price. Charles said, "we will buy it" and a down payment was given.

The Unity News, dated July 4, 1919, it was announced, "The Unity School has purchased a farm of fifty eight acres from Mr. W.W. Thruston, R.R. 2 Lee's Summit, Missouri. This farm is seventeen miles from Kansas City with good roads all the way. The idea of the farm is to furnish a clean, quiet place for Unity workers to spend weekends and vacations." The deed was dated June 27, 1919.

A camp committee was appointed and recommended a Camp club be formed of all workers that are interested in the camp. "There will be a meeting soon of all interested workers to organize and elect officers and appoint committees who will have charge of the management of the camp. The camp is for the use of Unity workers primarily with the privilege to take immediate family at the discretion of the committee and to the capacity of the equipment. The camp at the present has the following equipment: 4 - 16' x 16' Army tents which will accommodate thirty-two, one wall dining tent 18' x 20' with equipment for twenty-four, one 9' x 9' kitchen tent and one wood burning cook stove and three outdoor cooking furnaces."

The Unity News, July 11, 1919, "After a delay in clearing the title to Unity Farm the deal is finally closed. The tents and tent cottages are taking form and it begins to look like a real retreat!"

The Unity News July 18, 1919, "The man who is to build the electric line to Lee's Summit was in to see Lowell Fillmore this week. This line will pass Unity Farm and the round trip will be only 25 cents. The first mile of track will be in this fall. In addition there is to be a wide boulevard along this line, making the distance by automobile much shorter."

The Unity News July 25, 1919, "Grandma Fillmore is spending her vacation at Unity Farm. She is very comfortable located in a new five room tent-cottage. There is a large porch across one end and half way down one side, all screened in and overlooking the little stream that leads down to the canyon and woods. This week water from a spring is to be piped to her cottage and it will have all the comforts of home, with the advantage of country air, cool nights, honest to goodness water, clear as crystal and right out of the rocks. Also, the water is to be piped to the garden with beans, corn, onions, tomatoes, cucumbers, watermelon and everything right there and country cream, butter and eggs at the near by neighbors. Is that the life? We say it is!"

The Unity News August 8, 1919, "The distinguished young lady in western attire who visited Unity on Monday afternoon is Miss Cleo Berlin of Haileyville, Oklahoma who is traveling through the country on horseback. She has parked her blooded Hambleonian in the vacant lot opposite Unity for about three weeks, and finally decided to come across and investigate us. She joined the Silent-70 and will distribute our literature during her travels. Her mother is a Chactaw Indian. The marriage epidemic has now spread to the Fillmore family so it is hard to tell who it will catch next. Rick Fillmore and Harriet Collins were married about 6:00 and then left that night, August 4th, for New York on their honeymoon. The ceremony was performed by Mr. Charles Fillmore. Rick thought to keep it all a secret, but the newspapers are no respecters of persons. Consequently old shoes, rice and other things too numerous to mention followed him through the day and well into the night."

The Unity News August 15, 1919, "Harriet seems to have difficulty in remembering who she is these days. A letter received by Miss Christal was signed, Harriet Collins, then 'scratched' and resigned Mrs. W. Rickert Fillmore. They report a splendid time in New York. New

York is not so big. The other day Mrs. Croft was standing on 5th avenue. Her attention was attracted to one of the large buses which was passing, and who do you think she saw? Rick and Harriet, of course, but a rather unexpected coincidence. As a result of the Silent-70 page in the August Unity magazine, many readers are taking special interest in our work with prisons. They send us contributions to cover subscriptions for the prisoner referred to, also for others in the same condition, and some subscribe for Unity to be sent to the prison in their own home state. We greatly appreciate the cooperation."

The Unity News August 29, 1919, "Mr. and Mrs. W. Rickert Fillmore are playing house over in the Oberlin Apartments 1328 E. 10th Street these days."

The Unity News September 12, 1919, "Unity has bought a new 1 3/4 ton Garford truck to be delivered about the first of October. This will help solve the high cost of drayage. In the last month 16,136 pounds of printed matter was hauled from Unity besides books, papers and letters that went through the regular mail and express channels."

The Unity News October 3, 1919, "Now is the time to spend an evening at Unity Farm, and as this good weather is not expected to continue. You are advised to take advantage of it right away. It would take a poet to describe the gentle breeze, the soft moonlight, the millions of stars, the grass and the trees that are enjoyed by the parties at the farm these evenings.

Both Mr. Lowell and Mr. Royal Fillmore are spending a few days in Chicago and up in the Great Lakes region buying supplies and machinery. Silent-70 sent out 24,217 pieces of literature during the month of September."

The Unity News October 10, 1919, "Mr. Ingraham and Mr. Royal Fillmore were elected members of the New Thought Alliance and will attend a meeting of the executive officers in New York City next week. Mr. Fillmore will probably spend a month in the east.

Mr. Arthur Hicks is now decorating the wall on the second floor of the new building. He is stenciling the names of those who gave love offerings to the Building Fund, on the bricks. Did you buy a brick? If so, your name will be in the writing on the wall."

The Unity News November 14, 1919, "Royal Fillmore has started a library on agriculture and has twelve large volumes already. Wonder what he expects to raise? (Shades of Unity Farm)

Mr. Boillot is out on the farm now and has eight farmers working on the roads. It might be interesting to mention here that we will start work on the orchards soon and expect to have one of the finest orchards in this part of the country when completed."

Charles Fillmore was in his sixty-fifth year in 1919 and his thirty plus years of working every day and often far into the nights began to take its toll on him. He passed through a physical crisis, though his illness was severe he never wavered. There were times when he had to hold fast to life, much as he had to do when he was eleven. He had fought the battle then and he was determined to fight it again. Charles felt the support of his family, the prayers for him from Silent Unity and most of all the support from his wife, Myrtle. In the end, affirming his divinity as he had taught others to do, Charles won the battle. By 1920 he was stronger and he immerged with new vigor!

There was an employee at Unity that worked in the furnace-boiler room at 917 Tracy, his name was Dallas Kreigh. He was the first person to live and work at the new Unity Farm. He went there, lived in a tent, was a caretaker of the new Unity property and planted and cared for the early vegetables. He was a true handyman and had a determined dedication to Unity and his studies and practice of Unity Truth principles. In the historical files a picture was found of the log cabin that was on the grounds when purchased. Dallas Kreigh was in the picture standing at the doorway. It is believed that this cabin, which remains today, was on the original fifty-eight acres purchased.

1920 - The Unity News, Kansas City, Missouri January 9, 1920, "The Unity News is a paper published each week by the workers at Unity headquarters and is not for outside circulation. Farm News. Louis Wamsley and his mother are living out on the farm now and seem to be having the time of their lives. Louis is fixing up our new orchard which is going to be one of the best in this part of the country when it is finished. The following is a letter received by one of our Silent-70 workers from the warden at San Quentin State Prison, California; San Quentin, California December 12, 1919. Mrs. Kramer, Dear Madam, I am receiving regularly a supply of pamphlets and the periodicals, and wish to thank you heartily on behalf of the inmates of this institution, for there are a number of men here who have become deeply interested in the study of Unity. I saw your name in the Unity magazine and I have no one else whom I can thank; therefore, I am thanking you. I hope that you can put me in touch with some of the Unity readers. Trusting to hear more of your Unity work, I am. Yours, a Unity reader, E.M. McKnight, San Quentin, California State Prison."

The Unity News January 23, 1920, "Latest Farm news; There are to be four acres of Irish potatoes planted and it is expected this will furnish the Kansas City Unity Inn for the summer.

At the Thursday morning silence held by the business office, it was decided to hold classes every Thursday morning for the purpose of learning more about Unity teachings, so that all may be more efficient in the work. First, Lessons in Truth will be studied, reading and discussing its points until they are thoroughly understood.

Within the next thirty days work will begin on the new Inn at 9th and Tracy. This project requires a good many thousands of dollars, and if any of the Unity workers would like to buy bonds to help pay for it, they will receive six percent on their money. Arrangements will be made for paying for bonds on the installment plan."

Letter to Royal dated February 17, 1920 with estimated costs on furniture for the new Unity apartments that are to be built on the second floor of the new planned building. Items covered are beds, mattresses, dressers, rockers, chairs, tables and pillows. 917 Tracy Kansas City, Missouri.

Letter announcement from Unity that the new Unity Inn will be formally dedicated on Thanksgiving Day at 8:00 P.M. in the ballroom above the cafeteria on November 25, 1920 at 913 Tracy Avenue Kansas City, Missouri.

The Unity News March 22, 1920, "Farm news; the duck pond up near the house is going to be made into a swimming pool, the reference to the house was the tent-cottage that had been prepared for Mother Fillmore on the hill overlooking the canyon. The pool will be one-hundred fifty feet long, so you can see that it is going to be some ole' swimming hole."

The Unity News March 29, 1920, "A new Ford truck has been purchased for the farm.

On account of the rising costs of material and labor a special meeting was held by the trustees of Unity School to determine whether the prices of our publications should be increased. Figures shown indicated that the publications were costing as much as the subscription price. However, after talking the situation over it was decided that more people could be reached and greater work done in Truth if prices of the three publications be left at $1.00 each. It was suggested that an article be put in both Unity and Weekly explaining that $1.00 per year would be the minimum price, but that if the periodical was worth more to this subscriber he could send enough more to bring the price up to valuation. It was also decided that the prices of books and booklets would be raised from time to time to meet the increased cost."

The Unity News April 12, 1920, "Owning to the recent rains an elegant new spring was discovered up in the orchard. There is great speculation whether the spring will continue throughout the summer. A new road scraper has been purchased which will be used to keep the road smooth and all the bumps sheared off. Several hundred trees have been set out and also two or three-hundred berry bushes.

Unity Cafeteria. Mr. Boillot is casting footings for the steel work and the steel trusses have arrived. The skeleton work will soon be up and we can get a better idea of what the new cafeteria will look like."

The Unity News April 17, 1920, "Farm notes. Lewis Wamsley, farm manager, has seven brown leghorn hens and three dozen tiny little chickens."

The Unity News May 15, 1920, "Lowell Fillmore and several Unity employees have garden lots at the new farm. Lowell reports that he has topless radishes, headless lettuce and odorless onions blooming abundantly in his garden spot."

Letter from Royal Fillmore dated May 10, 1920 to "Dear Friend, your inquiry concerning Unity Farm is received. The farm was purchased with the idea of furnishing a recreation spot for the Unity workers in Kansas City. However it is hopeful that in the course of a few years we will be able to develop it into a spot where Unity people from all parts of the world may come and commune with nature and study Unity principles. As the work develops it will probably be announced in the Unity magazine."

The Unity News May 29, 1920, "Farm notes; five trips have been made to the Farm this week. Modernizing improvements are being made every day, so that in the next several years every convenience possible will be installed. Unity is doing this for the employees. Thousands of dollars are being spent to fix up the farm. Rustic bridges are being built, pumps are being installed, roads are being made around the entire fifty-eight acres. A swimming pool, tennis court, fruit and other trees and many additional things are contemplated. A store stocked with staples, such as sugar, flour, potatoes, eggs, etc will open June 1st. The store will be in the farm house, on the grounds when the farm was purchased. Fresh vegetables from the farm, will be sold. The latest plan for the swimming pool is to have it near the present pond, moving it down the creek about one-hundred feet, and Rick Fillmore said 'damit!'

The Unity News June 12, 1920, "Lowell says that there are ten tons of alfalfa on the farm about ready to be cut, so we will have no salad shortage this summer!"

Official notice from the state of Missouri dated June 17, 1920, "It is ordered by the court that the Superintendent of Road Oiling be directed to oil the following road to wit: A thirty foot road about one half mile in length north from Lee's Summit Raytown road to Unity Farm. Said road beginning East of the Hazel Grove School House. Keeping an accurate account of expense incurred and render account of same to Royal Fillmore of 913 Tracy Avenue Kansas City, Missouri to the end that Jackson Country be reimbursed for such oiling done. By Peter J. Kelly, clerk of the County Court."

The Unity News June 19, 1920, "One hundred eighty three crates (quart boxes) of strawberries have been sold off of the farm this season."

The Unity News June 26, 1920, "The watermelons and cantaloupe are growing at the farm. There are going to be dew berries soon."

Letter from Royal Fillmore dated July 29, 1920 to Carl R. Sechler, Lee's Summit, Missouri concerning carpenter work to be done on Unity Farm, "We are planning to build a rough frame structure to use as a cannery. Our superintendent will be at the farm Saturday July 31st and you may drop by and talk matters over with him if you wish."

Letter from Royal to Green Light and Power Company Lee's Summit, Missouri dated August 10, 1920 concerning the running of electrical power to Unity Farm.

Royal's letter of August 18, 1920 to the Kansas City Telephone Co. asking for phone service at the farm and stating that Unity will pay for the three quarters of a mile to the existing line.

Unity placed an advertisement in the newspaper, The Kansas City Star, on October 2, 1920 accompanied by a picture of the building housing the Unity Inn, with the following copy, "The most beautiful cafeteria in the city. Located at the corner of 9th and Tracy. The largest and finest cafeteria in the world where meatless home cooking is served. Every taste of the inner and outer man is satisfied by palatable food and artistic surroundings. Sunday night supper a speciality. Plenty of room to park cars. Breakfast 7 to 10 A.M., lunch 11 to 2, dinner 5:30 to 7:30. Soda fountain service continuous from 11:00 A.M. to 11:00 P.M."

Letter to a friend from Royal dated October 5, 1920, "We have acquired more farm land, now have two-hundred forty acres, about two-hundred which is the best farm land in Missouri." Letter to Royal asking about the oil well casing that is needed on the farm and questions concerning an order for materials. A letter from Royal in answer, "Our well was started in September 1918 at our Kansas City, Missouri location at 917 Tracy, not on the farm, and proceed with delivery of said order to the Kansas City address."

A letter from Unity dated October 1920, "To whom it may concern, Cora Page has been employed at the Unity Inn for the past fifteen months as head salad woman. We found her resourceful, industrious and reliable."

The Unity News October 9, 1920, "The trips to Unity Farm are becoming more popular than ever, in spite of a slight fall of temperature. This is really the best time of the year to enjoy the woods."

The Unity News October 16, 1920, "Those who now go to Unity Farm will eat off of china dishes! These were used at the old Unity Inn. The farm is also lighted with electricity, so we guess that all we need out there at present to make it ultra modern is a roof garden and some indoor beds! Lewis Wamsley is preparing to set out several hundred more fruit trees! The Unity cannery, also at the farm, has just put up two barrels of mince meat to be used at the Unity Inn this winter."

A letter to Unity asking about "vegetarian shoes" was received and answered November 2, 1920, "We regret to say that up to the present time, a satisfactory imitation leather for shoes has not been produced. However, the U.S. Rubber Company is now making a canvas shoe with composition sole which does fairly well." Where to write the shoe company was enclosed.

The Unity News November 13, 1920, "Royal has signed up for apartment P. at the Oberlin. Mrs. Anthony will occupy the apartment until Royal's return in December. Royal is leaving tomorrow for his journey to his fair one and we all wish him a bon voyage. He will stop in Chicago for a few days on his way east and will visit Portland, Maine to fix up some of our mill business. He will also visit Boston for a few days and New York City and finally end up at the end of the rainbow."

On November 27, 1920 Royal Fillmore was married to Miss Frances Eulalie Sleater, the daughter of Mr. and Mrs. John Cooper Sleater of Merchantville, New Jersey. The marriage took place in Merchantville. After a wedding trip to Atlantic City the newlyweds came by train to Kansas City. Royal and Fran went to work in the Wee Wisdom editorial department and in a short time took over a large share of the responsibility for the magazine. Together they brought about many changes in Wee Wisdom.

A letter dated December 1, 1920 from Lowell, in answer to Charles Harris requesting the opportunity to lease some of Unity Farm land, "Your request will be considered for leasing some of the Unity Farm ground provided that we receive a clear title to the land before March 1, 1921."

1921 - Letter to Lowell and Royal dated January 2, 1921 reads as follows, "There are a great many things to be decided upon and prepared for, in regard to the work here for the coming season in order to minimize confusion and wasted efforts. There has never been a real business meeting here between us where details of the phases of the work could be gone into and definite decisions reached. Can't you arrange for just the two of you to come spend at least an afternoon on the farm for this purpose? Sincerely, Lewis A Wamsley."

[At the very early stages of the emergence of Unity Farm, Mr. Wamsley had been given the responsibility of overseeing the work at the farm. His note indicates that he needed guidance and direction. This was obviously a trying time for Lowell and Royal the growth at Unity headquarters in Kansas City was also growing at a rapid pace and needed their attention. It was about this period of time when W. Rickert Fillmore took control of Unity Farm, prepared building plans, was the overseer and counseled with architect and engineers for the layout of the new Unity City. Just as Charles and Myrtle Fillmore were the two visionary people that were responsible for the Unity religious movement, Rick was the visionary principle for the development of physical Unity Farm that became Unity Village many years later.]

Letter dated January 4, 1921 from Henrici-Lowry consulting engineers, "We are enclosing herewith a white print of the proposed dam for the Unity Farm." signed W.M. Lowry. [This was the dam to be built in the canyon to impound water for the proposed swimming pool.]

The Unity News January 7, 1921, "We have on hand at the farm for the Unity Inn the following: About five dozen quarts chili sauce, about 12 1/2 gallons chili sauce, about 2 dozen quarts catsup, about 2 dozen quarts yellow tomato preserves, sour and dill pickles, sour kraut, pumpkins, turnips, apples-5, peaches-3, plums-2, cherries-3, pears and grapes-3, black raspberries-2, strawberries, nuts-5, rhubarb, asparagus, potatoes, onions, sweet pepper, tomatoes, pole beans, beets, carrots, parsnips and corn."

The Unity News January 8, 1921, "Almost an entire orchard has been added at Unity Farm. Several hundred fruit and nut trees have been planted recently."

The Unity News March 5, 1921, "Negotiations for an additional one-hundred seventy-five acres to Unity Farm have been completed. We now have 235 acres. This latest purchase lies northwest of the existing ground."

March 16, 1921 information concerning the purchase of a tractor and implements for Unity Farm.

A letter to Royal dated March 22, 1921 from a Mr. King who had written offering cattle for sale. Royal's answer, "It is not our intention to have cattle on this farm as it will be devoted to fruit and gardening."

[By Spring of 1921 Royal's wife Fran was pregnant, very frail and ill. She was no longer able to work and was virtually bedfast. She was told by her doctor she might loose the baby and also her life. She made the decision to carry the baby full term.]

The Unity News March 26, 1921, "The first crop on the farm this year was rhubarb. Louis Wamsley has purchased three-thousand raspberry plants for the farm."

The Unity News May 21, 1921, "Mr. Boillot is staying on Unity Farm while he is directing construction work. His men have already started to work on the pump house at the well, from which water will be pumped to the new structures. The old mess tent has evolved into a better name and location, the new building will be known as the Unity Club House. Also, under construction is a home at the farm for Rick Fillmore."

[Mr. Boillot was a partner in a Kansas City architecture and engineering firm that Rick Fillmore had hired to prepare plans and oversee work for the first permanent structures at Unity Farm. When the Fillmore's purchased the first fifty-eight acres for Unity Farm Rick was much impressed with the lay of the land. One of the two creeks on the grounds was in a perfect location for the recreational areas that the Fillmore's desired for the Kansas City Unity workers to use as a retreat. There was an area, referred to as a "canyon", which ran from high ground on the south to the north where the creek bed was quite deep. This was the area Rick choose for the swimming pools and to have a bridge dam. Adjacent to the pool on the east side of the creek was Rick's location for the club house. West of the creek on the hill to the south Rick chose a location for his home, spaces for other homes were chosen and just northwest of the pool the area for tennis courts. To the West of the areas for homes and tennis courts the open rolling meadow area was perfect for a golf course. Farther north from the club house was a wooded area planned for a large picnic area and places for cottages to be built to rent for the Kansas City visitors on vacation or weekends.]

The Unity News May 27, 1921, "A two hole golf course is all ready to play on, but it isn't very good as yet. It will be a dandy in time. Some day this will be the most unique country club in the world."

The Unity News June 4, 1921, "The Unity baseball team will play today on Unity's diamond at Unity Farm. A small irrigation system is being installed from the creek, to furnish water for a few acres."

June 5, 1921 letter from insurance company with policy to cover one dwelling and two barns on Unity Farm.

Letter from consulting engineers Henrici-Lowry concerning an authorization to tap into a Lee's Summit, Missouri water line and purchase of necessary water for Unity Farm.

The Unity News June 11, 1921, "Mr. Moreland has been hired to supervise the Unity Farm gardens. The excavation and foundations for Rick's house and club house are nearing completion. The railroad ties which were purchased to be used in the interior of the two new structures have arrived on the site."

The Unity News July 2, 1921, "A sample cottage for renting purposes is finished. Others will be built to be rented to the Unity workers for week ends and vacations. Electric lights and running water will be put in all the cottages and other conveniences have been planned. The golf course is being mowed and is being used more than expected."

The Unity News August 20, 1921, "Many of the vegetables now being served at the Unity Inn are coming from the farm. Cantaloupes, squash, parsnips, cucumbers, carrots, beets, potatoes, peppers and vegetable oysters."

The Unity News August 27, 1921, "Things at Unity Farm are growing and not just crops! There are now six cottages or houses under construction. Rick's house is nearing completion with just some interior work remaining. The club house is framed in, but as this structure will be larger and have more conveniences than the others construction will take longer."

The Unity News September 24, 1921,"Water hydrants have arrived and soon the farm water works system will be connected up. All the big beams in the living room of the club house are finished and now work is being done on the 'Romeo and Juliet' balcony leading from the girls sleeping porch and overlooking the main club room."

The Unity News October 1, 1921, "Rick and his wife Harriet and son Charles Rickert are now moving into there new home at Unity Farm!"

[A baby girl was born October 1, 1921 to Frances and Royal Fillmore. They named the child after their mothers, Myrtle and Innocincia. Frances lived but six weeks after the birth, she passed away November 12, 1921. Royal and his family decided that the baby would live with Myrtle and that the baby's name would be changed to Frances Sleater Fillmore.]

The Unity News October 8, 1921, "Royal and his wife Frances are the proud parents of a daughter born October 1st. The first girl born into the Fillmore family in a century. We saw Charles Fillmore carrying his hat the next day. Wonder if it's too small!

Letter dated October 17, 1921 from the Kansas City Telephone Company advising that they can not furnish long distance telephone service to Unity Farm at this time.

The Unity News October 29, 1921, "An order was placed for 1,200 Jonathan apple trees and 300 cherry trees that will be set out on the farm. Winter wheat is coming up on twenty acres. Eighty percent of the vegetables served at Unity Inn in Kansas City are brought fresh from the farm."

A special flyer sheet dated November 26, 1921 with the heading Unity Country Club. "The purpose of the club is to provide clean constructive amusements such as parties, dances, baseball, golf, tennis, hiking parties, nature study, for the workers of the Unity School of Christianity and their friends. All workers of the school are eligible for membership. Cards will be issued twice yearly, dating from January 1st and July 1st. Dues of $1.00 for each half year or fraction there of. The first cards are to be dated January 1922. As the Unity standard is to be maintained in all of the activities at the farm, meat is not to be served at the club house. As it is desired to protect all wild life and to encourage the wild animals and birds to make their homes at the farm, no hunting will be allowed. On the other hand, steps are to be taken by those interested to make the farm as attractive as possible for wild birds and animals. Nature study is to be encouraged. The club house has been erected at a large cost and for the express purpose of serving the workers of the school and it is hoped that all workers will cooperate and become members and enter into the activities."

The Unity News December 3, 1921, a Unity phonograph record, "Here is something new in the methods of presenting Truth teachings. A phonograph record entitled "Practical Christianity" which gives the fundamental principles of Unity Faith on life, health and prosperity has been made by Richard Lynch, speaker and teacher at the Unity Truth Center in New York City. Mr. Lynch treats the subject in a clear concise manner. Price $3.00."

December 19, 1921, letter from Green Light and Power company in Lee's Summit, Missouri about the power line installed to Unity Farm and their invoice for wiring at Unity Farm.

The Unity News December 24, 1921, "Unity Farm has another new building. It is a hen house and will accommodate 600 chickens. The floor in the club house has been finished and is now ready for parties. Make your date with the Farm committee for use of the club house. Royal Fillmore has a close friend, Charles H. Watts, a member of the men's club of the Divine Science association of Philadelphia, PA, affiliated with the International New Thought Alliance. Mr. Watts wrote Royal urging that he organize a club in Kansas City."

1922 - One of the first radio stations in the Midwest has been licensed in Kansas City, Missouri. Its call letters are WOQ.[It was Royal Fillmore that saw the possibilities of radio as another outlet of communication for the Unity message. He convinced his family and the officers of Unity and received their permission to pursue this new channel. He arranged for purchasing time on the radio and then he encouraged Francis J. Gable to broadcast talks on Unity principles. Soon after the talks began calls and letters arrived at Unity telling of hearing the Unity message and how much they appreciated receiving these messages into their homes. Also, the broadcasts brought orders for Unity books and pamphlets as well as letters asking for prayers. WOQ broadcast from a downtown building street level glass front and crowds began to come watch and hear the messages which also brought Unity more exposure in Kansas City!]

Letter dated January 12, 1922 telling of the drilling and striking of low grade oil and a small quantity at two different depths, but nothing of commercial value at Unity Farm.

Letter from Royal dated January 19, 1922 to the Kansas City Telephone Company asking if Unity could run a telephone line to a close neighbors house, Mr. Kinneman, that had their phone service.

A written request from Stanley T. Payne, Unity Farm manager, requesting help at the farm in organization and cost monitoring, dated January 25, 1922. He suggested the firm of Stanley F. Morse, consulting Agricultural Engineer.

A letter dated February 13, 1922 to the Health Department from Royal Fillmore. "Gentlemen, I note that you have registered the name of my daughter as Frances Innocencia Fillmore. Her name has been changed to Frances Sleater Fillmore. I would appreciate it very much if you would change the name on the register to conform with this. Very cordially yours, Royal Fillmore."

The Unity News February 18, 1922, "Corn meal raised, ground and brought in from Unity Farm is now being used to make the corn sticks at our Inn. By getting the corn meal from our mill on the farm the Inn is sure of getting all the good from thc corn. Thc tastc tclls all."

The Unity News February 25, 1922, "At Unity Farm, a well near the Harris house, on the grounds when purchased, is being cleaned out and cemented. A good flow of water is secured from this well, even in the winter."

The Unity News March 4, 1922, "Rick was snowbound at the farm this week. Grandmother Fillmore, Rick's wife and baby and a snug home supplied with food, kept him company! Who would mind being snowbound? The Unity baseball team, which was organized in 1921 with Royal as the manager is raring to go! Practice games with the boys at the Unity Farm bunkhouse will begin soon."

The Unity News March 25, 1922, "The old Harris house at the Farm is to be remodeled for a country home for Charles and Myrtle. The county is furnishing crushed rock and the farm hands are building a rock road into Unity Farm, from the main road, beginning at the big billboard. From now on, no difficultly will be encountered in driving in or through the farm roads to all points of interest, including Rick's chateau! The farm committee is very busy planning for the coming season, which will be the busiest yet. The club house is being readied for parties."

The Unity News April 1, 1922, "Unity Withdraws From The I.N.T.A. On March 7, 1922, a special meeting was called to consider the relationship of the Unity School of Christianity with the International New Thought Alliance. Our directors, department heads and teachers were in attendance. It was unanimously voted that the Unity School of Christianity resign from the Alliance the resignation to take effect at once. This withdrawal from the I.N.T.A was determined upon because of the many protests received from our students against our membership and owing to the fact that the present methods of the Alliance make it virtually another metaphysical school rather than an association of schools, thereby rendering it impractical for the Unity School to give time and support to it.

Some steps and work on the terrace around the club house are being finished. Work will soon begin on the swimming pool. This pool will be built just south of the waterfalls. It will be ten feet deep at the dam and 150 feet long. There are many springs above the pool to the south and these will supply fresh water. The pool will be so constructed that it can be drained and cleaned of dirt and crawdads. The swimming pool will be close to the club house with grass between."

The Unity News April 8, 1922, "The farm committee appointed Mr. Kellogg caretaker of the Unity Club House for one month beginning April 15, 1922. The club house will be open Saturday afternoon and Sundays and on those days parties will have to register, unless they wish to stay overnight. In a few days the club will be organized and fully equipped for parties."

Eggs - Actly don't be afraid!

"They won't do you harm. The little red hens at Unity Farm. That frightful report you should not heed, that Unity's chicks are 'fighting cock breed!' They are not spur legs, but ruddy Leghorns. Signed Charles Fillmore."

Letter to Royal, dated April 17, 1922, from Stanley Payne, farm manager, in which he discussed the needs of the crew at Unity Farm that has now grown to nineteen men. That the cook is threatening to quit if he does not get help and a raise in wages. Also, that Mr. Rafael has three men besides himself and intends to get at least two more men. He suggests that Royal should come to the Farm and talk with Mr. Kestner the cook.

The Unity News April 29, 1922, "The swimming pool is nearing completion. Plumbing in the club house is almost completed. A large water heater will assure hot water for shower baths, washing dishes, etc."

The Unity News May 6, 1922, "A little thing like night can't bother us, on our visits to the Farm now. What could be nicer than gathering around the fireplace at the club house and listening to the new victrola and player piano records, which have been selected for our enjoyment? Every morning, all the farm inhabitants are awakened about five o'clock by the thousands of birds' songs. Even Rick has to get up! The Harris house has been remodeled and now a water line is being dug to the country home of Charles and Myrtle Fillmore. The farm roads have been graded and several culverts installed. The swimming pools are being finished. The creek bed has been blasted, so that the width of this pool will be at least seventy-five feet. The five acre strawberry patch is covered with little green berries. Garden plots are in readiness for the workers. Anyone wishing a garden plot should register promptly with Alice Lee."

Unity News May 27, 1922, "Mr. Knight and his family are now residing in the old Hoagland house on the farm, that was on the ground when purchased."

Unity News June 3, 1922, "The sunrise prayer meeting of the Business Men's Christian Association at Unity Farm May 27th, 28th, 29th was an exceptionally happy and prosperous beginning of a great movement. The men ate, slept and prayed without the help of a woman in any capacity. Even the cook at the farm house was a man! Four meetings were held Sunday and the men were so pleased that they voted to have the conclave again very soon."

Unity News June 10, 1922, "Unity Farm, we now have a strictly up-to-date farm. Yes, we keep bees! A swarm has been persuaded to take up residence in a dynamite keg. Mr. Raphael is temporarily managing the farm in connection with overseeing the construction work."

Article from The Christian Business Man. July, 1922 Christianity and Commerce by Charles Fillmore.

[For a number of years, Charles Fillmore was actively engaged in business pursuits. Becoming interested in the results obtained by applying some of the high laws in the ordinary activities of life, he left the business world to devote his entire time to an intensive study of Christian principles. Later, he founded the Unity School of Christianity, for the purpose of giving to the world the results of his study and research. His teachings stand very high in the esteem of Christian metaphysicians.]

> "At frequent intervals the question comes up: Has Christianity failed in righting the evils of the world? This question has been discussed, pro and con, generation after generation, and has been answered in various ways. It should be plain to any one familiar with the New Testament, that the principles of Christianity have never been adopted as the governing laws for the actions of business men. A man here and there may have tried divine guidance in his temporal affairs, but no general standard of action, based on Christian principles, has been observed in business.
>
> Does the church believe that the rules which Jesus Christ laid down, are practical in the business world? Do Christian minister preach: 'If any man would go to law with thee, and take away thy coat, let him have thy cloak also'? There are

those who claim to be conducting their business on Christian principles, but their methods do not measure up to the Jesus Christ standard. For instance, a traveling representative of Unity literature called upon a large concern that handles Christian literature exclusively. He talked with the manager, to whom he explained that the Unity books teach the doctrines of Jesus, and that they show how Christianity may be made practical in all living. The manager replied: 'Christianity is not practical in business. Religion and business do not go together.' This is the candid opinion of a business man, who is ostensibly a Christian, and who handles Christian literature exclusively. His opinion may be taken as an index to the thought of Christian business men everywhere.

If you were to go into a bank and say, 'Do you conduct your business on Christian principles?' the answer would undoubtedly be, 'no.' Not because the banker is a dishonest man, but because he does not combine his business with his religion.

We have to admit that Christianity has not been tried in the commercial world. But today, business men are talking about religion as a help, as never before, and it begins to look as though Christianity is going to have a trial. Here and there, business men have been testing the Golden Rule, and their success has been such as to attract unusual public attention. Business managers, like Mr. Nash, of Cincinnati, head of the Nash Manufacturing company, are lecturing, and writing for the magazines about their experiments in applying the Golden Rule in their business.

The Rotary Club, whose members practice the Golden Rule, have for their motto: 'Service.' The Rotarians are known everywhere, although the movement was begun but a few years ago. This club approaches very closely to Christian brotherhood. The members stand together and help one another in all of life's activities, and really practice Christian unity. They even call one another by their Christian names, as the early Christians did. If a Rotary brother gets into financial trouble, the others lend a hand to help him out. The Rotary Club is a wedge for opening up the commercial world to the application of Christian principles.

Jesus taught all this. He illustrated the spirit of unity, even in commerce. When the Pharisees tried to ensnare him in his teaching, and said unto him: 'Teacher, . . .what thinkest thou? Is it lawful to give tribute unto Caesar, or not?' Jesus said unto them: 'Show me the tribute money.' Then said he: 'Whose is this image and superscription?' They answered: 'Caesar's.' He said unto them: 'Render therefore unto Caesar the things that are Caesar's; and unto God the things that are God's.' And so in all his ways, he did not spend any time opposing, but taught the right relation between monetary affairs and God's affairs; that they are inseparable.

Peter said to Jesus: 'Lo, we have left all, and have followed thee.' Jesus replied: 'There is no man that hath left house, or brethren, or sisters, or mother, or father, or children, or lands, for my sake, and for the gospel's sake, but he shall receive a hundredfold now in this time, houses, and brethren, and sisters, and mothers, and children, and lands, . . . and in the world to come eternal life.' This was a strong promise, and may seem to have failed of fulfillment in his disciples. But has it failed? As we study the rise of the disciples of Jesus, from obscure men of small means to teachers of world-wide renown, we see that they not only received riches, but honors as well. Peter's unbroken line of successors, the popes of Rome, have had riches untold, and power the world over. Those who have been faithful in following Jesus, have received fathers and mothers and houses and lands, abundantly. If Jesus' disciples were personally present in the world today, they could have anything that they might ask.

Those who put Christian principles to the test, say that Christianity will work. Justice, honesty, unselfishness, service, always work. A traveling salesman from an eastern printing press company told us, just a few days ago, of a man whom he heard of in the state of Michigan, who, he said, 'had strange business methods, and devoted half of his time to religion.' This man, who has such strange ways of conducting his business, is a manufacturer of printing presses. The salesman said that a customer went to see one of this man's presses; he liked it, and paid $1,000 down on the purchase price, which was $26,000. The next day, he heard of a secondhand press of the same make, for sale for $14,000. He paid $100 down on this press, and made up his mind that he would try to get back the $1,000 which he had paid on the new press. He went to see the manufacturer and told him what he had done, and that he would like the return of the $1,000.

'But,' said the manufacturer, 'I sold you that press, and the transaction is closed. It costs us $2,500 to sell one of those presses, and if I give you back your $1,000 we shall lose $2,500. However, I never decide any important matter without first taking it to the Lord. Come back tomorrow, and I will tell you what the Lord directs me to do.'

The next day, the purchaser went back, and the manufacturer returned the $1,000, and said: 'The Lord tells me to send down two of my best men to help you set your press up.'

The result was that the purchaser, who was an editor, was so well pleased with the way in which he had been treated, that he began recommending that press to his friends, and advertising it in his paper, so that in a little while, four different concerns bought new presses from this manufacturer, through the editor's efforts.

This incident is an illustration of the law that Jesus taught when he said: 'And if any man would go to law with thee, and take away thy coat, let him have thy cloak also.' But, some one asks: 'Would this method work today? Would I not lose all that I have by being too generous?' It will work, if you go about it in the right spirit. If you have faith in God as your resource, the more you give, the more you will receive. As you express generosity, and realize that everything is under Divine Law, your faith sets forces into action, above and beyond your present comprehension. In order to have harmony in business, and to have continuous prosperity, which belong to all departments of life, we must abandon the prevalent methods of competition, and substitute cooperation and mutual helpfulness. The business men of the world are beginning to see that competition eats up a business, while cooperation expands it and makes it grow. A law suit would undoubtedly have followed the transaction above mentioned, had the manufacturer been doing business in the world's way. As it was, he carried out the spirit of the injunction of Jesus: 'If any man would go to law with thee, and take away thy coat, let him have thy cloak also.'

In Europe, we have evidence of the result of grasping, competitive thought, working its way out in the recent great war. Germany is now being penalized because she fired the first gun and lost the war. France is demanding indemnity to the last farthing. All the other nations are struggling for what they claim as their rights, and the commerce of the world is thrown out of balance. It is easy to prophesy the result of this grasping, contentious policy, and further conflict is inevitable, unless there is a change of thought.

The old Hebrews had a law which provided that all debts should be canceled every fifty years. If the nations of Europe would incorporate a similar law into their commercial code, and would heed the advice of Jesus, 'Give, and it shall be given unto you; good measure, pressed down, shaken together, running over,' it would not be long until their industries would be restored, and permanent peace would result.

All kinds of panaceas are being offered for the economic ills of Europe, but no one has dared to suggest the forgiving love of God through Christ. But there will never be lasting peace in Europe, or in any other country, until the law of love is adopted as the principle governing all relations between men and nations. From even an economic standpoint, France would be better off at the end of fifty years, if she would forgive Germany all her debt, and in the meantime, cultivate the neighborly kindness of Christianity. The expense of the standing army of France, considering her great need of man power for reconstruction, will more than equal all that she may be able to compel Germany to pay.

But the most grievous factors to be dealt with, are the thoughts of hate and revenge that are piling up like a thunder cloud over the two nations. These thoughts will destroy them both, unless they recognize that 'God . . . hath made of one blood all nations of men.' the law of love, which Jesus stated, must eventually be worked out by all nations, and the sooner religion is made fundamental in national conferences, the better for the peace of the world.

It is prophesied in the Old Testament, and confirmed in the New, that the stone which has been rejected by the builders shall be made the head of the corner; this stone is Christ. The prophets of this age are pointing out that the present is the fulfillment of that ancient prophecy. The turmoil is so great and the leadership is so weak, that the intervention of a higher power seems necessary if civilization is to continue on the earth. We see spiritual-minded men and women everywhere turning to God for help. They are not only individually, but collectively, forming themselves into societies for mutual protection against the anarchy which seems to be literally destroying undisciplined souls, the world over.

Christ is the savior of the world, and the incorporation into our human affairs of Christian principles will save us, not only individually, but as a whole. The financial world is ripe for the introduction of more successful methods of doing business. Cooperation, instead of competition, is the keynote of the new commercial wave that is sweeping over the land. Business men should organize everywhere, to put these fundamental principles of the new commercial age into quick action.

Organize! Organize! Organize everywhere, under the banner of Christ! Proclaim him as the head of your order, and put his laws into your platform. Do not wait for numbers, but let a few earnest, honest souls band together in every community for the purpose of putting the laws of God, as promulgated in the doctrine of Jesus Christ, into operation in your affairs, no matter how insignificant in numbers your organization may appear. Loyalty to Christian principles in all your dealing, will make your success so phenomenal, that the world will inquire the cause and will follow you. A little group of business men, here in Kansas City, have banded together under the name, 'Business Men's Christian Unity,' for the purpose of demonstrating the practicability of the principles of reciprocity and universal brotherhood. They pledge themselves to do business under the laws of Christ and in his name. They are not afraid to proclaim that Jesus Christ is the invisible head of the movement. The name of their society is notice to the world that their aim is to carry into all business relations, fair dealing, honesty, justice, love, efficiency, and thus inevitably demonstrate the prosperity which will follow the practice of such principles.

And above all, do not be afraid to put Christ into the name of your organization -- 'the name which is above every name.'

Pleasure comes through toil and not by self indulgence and indolence. When one gets to love work, his life is a happy one. --Ruskin."

Article from The Christian Business Man July, 1922. The Truth About Selling by Ralph E. Boileau.

"Editor's Note -- The author of this article has been a successful salesman for a number of years. He was what is called a 'high pressure' man, one who uses a great amount of nervous energy in trying to force sales, and who usually alternates between periods of high exaltation and gloomy depression. For the past three years, he has done all his selling on the principles of practical Christianity, with the result that business has come to him more easily than ever before, his earnings have been greater through what men called a period of business depression, and above all, he has lived in an atmosphere of the utmost security with the constant assurance that God is his unfailing supply.

Prosperity, which always comes from successful selling, is linked with the operation of certain universal laws which can be invoked by all men. When the salesman learns how to put himself into conscious touch with these laws, he cannot fail. The minute the salesman starts to find these laws, he begins to get results, although it may require a great change in his mental practices, and in his ideas of what makes for business success.

The salesman who goes forth with 'hypnotize-the-buyer,' 'make-'em-sign,' 'put-it-over,' 'get-the-money' ideas, may seem to succeed, and for a time may increase his bank roll, but to bend the purchaser to the salesman's will against his own, is not good or successful salesmanship, and in time will impoverish him who persists in such practice.

The Christian business man is aware that it is necessary to break away from many of the traditional business ideas which the race has long held as conducive to success and prosperity. He knows that the successful salesman must lay a foundation as broad as that one laid by him who would live a life of service to humanity, for he who knows the unfailing law of prosperity, finds service as great in selling as in preaching.

Then how shall the salesman knowingly put himself into touch with the universal laws that will make sure his success?

The first step is to seek unity with the first Cause of every good desire within his own soul. In truth, to seek first kingdom of heaven, which lies within him. There in quiet communion, he will find the wisdom that points out the sure road to successful salesmanship and prosperity. There alone will he find the limitless supply of wealth that his Father is ready and anxious to make manifest for him, when he will let Him.

True religion and business success are one and inseparable; spirituality and prosperity are one; love, faith, and wealth, ever go hand in hand.

'I knew a grand Christian gentleman who was a faithful church attendant, gave freely to charity, and was held to be a spiritual giant, yet he failed utterly in business, right in the prime of life.' Nearly all of us have known a man whom the above description fits.

Come now, let us not make a mockery of Truth and let us get our terms straight. Spirituality has not a vague, indefinite, insipid meaning. Spirituality means conscious contact with love, wisdom, power, wealth, peace, happiness, and joy. Spirituality is unity with the Father within, whose creative word goes forth through you, when you pray. Then, when you pray to manifest wealth, which is always found first within, it will be made manifest out where you can see it and use it, by the creative word of God going forth through you.

You say: 'Isn't such preparation for selling, a long road? Who can wait for the development of this higher consciousness, when the needs of life press heavily upon us?'

Be assured that it is the short road and the sure road to prosperity. You may take it upon yourself to go the path of the old race mind, and launch out into the wild selfish struggle, where men burn up the sweet, vitalizing essence of life in the mad pace to possess what is the world's idea of wealth. But what shall it profit a man to climb up the old false way, when the sure way is the Christ path of Truth to wealth? 'He that . . . climbeth up some other way, the same is a thief and a robber;' but he has robbed no other so much as he has robbed himself. What are millions of dollars, without love; millions, without happiness and peace of soul? Know you not that love, faith, and good will, truly awakened in your heart, are the sure, unfailing means of acquiring prosperity and wealth that can manifest as houses and lands, or millions of dollars, if you ask it?

Wealth lies not in the possession of millions. Wealth lies in the right appreciation and use, under the law of love, of whatever is given into your hands, whether it be five dollars or five million dollars.

Never lose sight of the truth that it is your divine birthright to be prosperous; that a beautiful home of stucco, brick, or brown stone, brought forth from the stuff that love and good will are made of, is a proof of sonship. That is letting your light shine, that others may see your good works and glorify your Father in heaven. That is getting down to the business of answering the prayer: 'Thy will be done, as in heaven, so on earth.'

Faith is born of love, and there is no defeat or failure for the man of faith. How does faith work? Faith takes hold of the unseen substance and brings the thing which you desire out where you can see it. Faith is the substance of things you ask for; the proof of the existence of those things as yet not seen. The salesman of faith can go into the field, and in one hundred attempts to sell, even though one hundred say no, he will not cease to rejoice and give thanks. Why? Because faith never fails. Faith always gets results. Faith is God in action in his own wise way. What if it is pouring down rain in torrents, on the day on which you planned to launch a big selling campaign? Will the salesman of faith go pouting about, damning the weather, and fussing himself into a nightmare of gloom? Not a bit of it. He will say, 'I thank God for the unity of life, now operative in all my affairs.' Then he will have the time of his life with his wife and kiddies, and every time he laughs, he has made a sale. His 'cup runneth over,' for he knows that the Christ who awakens faith within, is true to his word. Then when the sun shines and fair weather comes again, what a harvest! It is the law.

But you say, 'How may one have such faith?' Sell yourself on the one big idea that Jesus Christ meant it when he said: 'All things are possible to him that believeth.' Know that the desire in your heart for prosperity has its answer from only one source -- God, your Father. His love and wisdom will lead you into the paths of wealth and happiness, if you will but ask of him, and believe.

What is a definite first step for the growth of this faith consciousness?

That which a man persists in thinking, he ultimately becomes. Before going out for the day's work, go some place where you can be quiet and alone, then think this thought: 'I am love and good will toward all men.' Then when on your way, keep sending out that thought; pray it without ceasing. 'I am love.' Let that thought go forth before every sales talk, when you pause, and after. Some day you will find that this thought has grown into a tender and kindly interest in all men. 'As he thinketh within himself, so is he.'

Well, what has that to do with selling? Love is the key to faith, which cannot fail. Love and good will make up a magnetic force that draws to you prosperity, wealth, and every good thing. Love is the key that will unlock the door to any man's heart, no matter how cold, or how much he may try to hide behind gruff mannerisms and a countenance of stone. Love will not let you sell when it is not good for the purchaser to buy, for love knows that the buyer's loss is the seller's loss. Love will not let you sell a product that you yourself do not believe in. Love will show you how to get into a good business and make it prosperous. Eye has not seen, nor ear heard, neither has entered into the heart of man, what prosperity and wealth await him who will learn the law of love. Prosperity will take on the nature of abundant, happy, convenient, and usable things, here in the manifest world.

Here is a salesman going out into the field who will not know defeat. Study his thought as he prepares for his work:

'This day, I go forth to my task in the confidence and happiness of faith. My success is assured, for love within me casts out all doubt, and clears the way for faith that makes success sure. Though my eyes do not behold the immediate results, they are sure, and I will not cease to give thanks to the Giver of every good thing. I know that whatsoever I ask, if I doubt not, I shall receive. The world without may be dark with doubt and pessimism, but I rejoice, for I dwell in the secret place of the Most High. A thousand may lose courage and fall by the way, and ten thousand fail on every hand, but failure shall not come nigh me, for my trust is in Him who never fails.

What I have, and what I persist in believing I have, that I do have. I am persuaded that neither height nor depth nor personality nor power can keep from me my success and my prosperity. I am master of my own destiny. Not by personal power not ability; not by intellectual attainment, but by intuition of the soul, that learns from the Christ within me, whose wisdom and love now bring forth my abundant life. I know that the universal Spirit of prosperity is now operative in all my affairs; and I shall be prospered in all my ways. I have asked, I believe, and I shall receive.'

'Whatsoever thou shalt ask of God, God will give thee.'

Letter from Royal dated July 5, 1922 to the Lee's Summit Telephone Company asking for phone service to be installed at the Unity Farm club house and the residence of W.R. Fillmore plus listings in the phone book for the club house, Rick's house the Farm managers office and for Royal's home.

Unity News July 8, 1922, "The Farm committee has been very fortunate in securing Mrs. Hayden as caretaker and hostess for the Country Club House. The latch string will always be out for Unity people and Mrs. Hayden will make everyone very welcome. The dam at the pool is being poured, which means we should be able to swim in the new pool sometime this month."

In July 1922 a new Unity magazine, Christian Business Man was introduced.

Letter from the Lee's Summit Phone Co. dated July 11, 1922 stating, "The requested phone lines will be installed soon."

Letter from Royal to the phone company dated July 31, 1922, "The wiring is now in place at the Club House and W.R. Fillmore residence ready for your hook up."

Unity News August 12, 1922, "A new gas well on the farm was opened. Dan Andrews, the new farm manager, began work on August 1st. The farmhouse has been remodeled, painted, papered and readied for Mr. and Mrs. Andrews to move in. The swimming pool dam is finished and the bottom of the pool cleaned and put into shape so that as soon as we get water, we can go swimming."

Unity News August 19, 1922, "Great excitement prevailed this week at Unity Farm! Another gas well was brought in. This well averages a flow of 500,000 cubic feet a day, twice as much as the first well. Gas was found at a depth of 420 feet. The engineers in charge of the drilling operation, states that enough gas is flowing from the two wells to supply a town of 1,500 people. Some oil made its appearances. Hopes are expressed that a gusher may be brought in. The road to the north picnic grounds has been completed. The pool is now finished and the first big rain will furnish water for our swimming and diving friends!"

Unity News September 2, 1922, "There are now four phones installed at Unity Farm. Those are the Club house, Farm manager's house, Rick and Royal's houses. These are long distant calls from Kansas City. The third gas well was brought in and is bigger than either of the first two. The rig is now being moved to the northwest part of the farm where they will try to find water."

Letter to Royal from the consulting geologist, "I am enclosing for your approval a log of gas well #2 at Unity Farm."

Unity News September 9, 1922, "This week Unity made its' fourth attempt to strike water for the swimming pool, they struck a heavy flow of gas. They cased off the gas and proceeded, only to strike twenty-seven feet of oil sand. The news reached the Unity office about 10:30 A.M. and a delegation headed by Charles Fillmore went out to see them "shoot" the well. Twenty-five quarts of nitroglycerin were exploded 425 feet under ground and after the explosion the well did some spouting, belching up enough oil to grease several pigs!

Fresh cider is served at Unity Inn now at five cents per glass. This cider is made on Unity Farm and is brought to the Inn, fresh, three times a week."

Unity News September 16, 1922, "The first to swim in the new pool was a worker to adjust the water gates to conserve the fresh spring water coming in. The derrick is all set over #1 gas well at the farm. The plan is to run it down into the oil sand so that #1 and #4 wells will be oilers. This well is to be shot with fifty quarts of nitroglycerin. If you plan to go to the farm on Saturday, better wear your oilskin coat."

Unity News September 23, 1922, "The fifth oil well will be started this week. It is located 300 feet north of #4. Well #3 has produced about 100 barrels. This oil has been spread over the roads so that they will be in good condition, rain or shine. A new gas furnace will be installed in the Club House soon, our own gas will be used. This has been a productive year on the Farm. Mushrooms are appearing in profusion and the crop of black walnuts and hickory nuts are almost ready for harvesting. Now that cool weather has arrived the swimming pool has filled up with water."

Unity News September 30, 1922, "Three large trees of Gentian apples have been discovered at the farm. These are delicious apples! Also, a number of trees of the largest and most beautiful Ben Davis we have seen. Everyday the pumps work for several hours, forcing oil from the wells into a large storage tank, to be sent to Unity headquarters to keep us warm this winter."

Unity News October 7, 1922, "Approximately 150 workers journeyed out to Unity Farm for a party last Saturday. Royal established a 'spaget' kitchen in the yard of the club house for a big feed. Plates were heaping with spaghetti, bread, butter, doughnuts, like mother used to make and fresh apple cider. Some of the party remained overnight and spent Sunday in hiking and exploring the surrounding country. The woods are a riot of color and the keen Autumn air makes hiking one of the most pleasurable sports of the season.

Gas lines are being run to all of the cottages, homes and buildings at the farm. All will be heated by natural gas in a short time."

Letter from Royal, dated October 11, 1922 to the Kansas City Phone Company, asking again for a direct line phone service to Kansas City.

Unity News October 14, 1922, "This oil has not had the naphtha or gasoline taken out of it and "burns like blazes."

October 21, 1922 letter from Louis Johnson to Royal, "Report of analysis made from your oil sample: Gasoline and Naphtha - 14%, Kerosine - 19%, Gas oil - 20%, wax distillate - 25%, asphalt - 22% = 100%."

A number of letters were being received at the Unity office from nearby and adjoining land owners to Unity Farm advising that their ground is for sale.

Unity News October 28, 1922, "All the houses and the club house have been connected to the gas mains and have gas stoves. This modern and up-to-date convenience will make the dwellers comfortable for the winter. The cider being made at the farm now is from Gentian apples. It has a peculiar, delicious flavor all its' own."

Unity News November 11, 1922, "The celery crop at the farm has been a good one and among the most enthusiastic harvester of the celery is Lowell Fillmore. One-hundred bushels of sweet potatoes were harvested and three tanks, (95 barrels) of oil have been hauled to heat the buildings at 9th to 10th on Tracy in Kansas City."

Unity News December 9, 1922, "Regular church services will be held in the club house at Unity Farm each Sunday morning at 11:00, beginning tomorrow. E.V. Ingraham is to play the role of 'Country Preacher' and conduct these meetings, all the neighbors are to be invited. A bridge over the swimming pool dam has been finished and a new spillway constructed for the dam. The pool is ready for ice skating purposes as soon as freezing weather arrives. In the spring, the early swimmers can break the ice, if they wish."

Unity News December 16, 1922, "A new resource has been discovered at the farm, horse radish. Lowell says, "Gee its' hot stuff!" Plans for four new cottages, to be built this winter, are being drawn up. There is a new promenade or sidewalk by the swimming pool now."

December 28, 1922 letter from Lowell telling a prospective teacher for the planned Wee Wisdom school that it would not be opened this year.

[During the research for this book there was no information found regarding where and when a home was built for Royal Fillmore. The only information found was when a telephone was ordered for his house. By using a process of elimination it is believed that the small house, just East of Rick's home and adjacent to the road to the pool was built for Royal. After Royal's death in 1923 that small structure was referred to, on the farm, as Rick's office. It surely was built at the same time as Rick's home and the club house to have a telephone installed along with the others as listed.]

1923 - Unity News February 17, 1923, "Unity Farm now has twenty employees. A new home for Francis and Jesse Gable is now under construction a short distance to the northwest of Rick Fillmore's house. The well house at the Farm, over the big well, is almost complete."

Unity News February 24, 1923, growth at Unity headquarters, "The following interesting facts concerning the growth of the Unity work were gleaned from Lowell Fillmore's talk before the Intensive Training School February 12, 1923.

> 'The Unity movement made its' start thirty-four years ago in April 1889. At first the publishing and all other work related to getting out the first Unity magazine, Modern Thought, afterward known as Thought and now known as Unity were taken care of in three rooms in a downtown office building. There Charles and Myrtle Fillmore did all the work of answering letters, entering subscriptions and addressing wrappers and carried on their personal healing ministry. Meetings were held in those rooms until the quarters were outgrown. Then the meetings were held in the Arlington building, which formerly stood on the northeast corner of 10th

and Walnut and the publishing work was done at a little brick cottage at 1315 McGee St. It was seen that still larger quarters were needed, so that all the work could be carried on in one place. It was decided to locate at 913 Tracy. In the meantime, in 1903, the Unity School of Practical Christianity was incorporated and a three story brick building was begun on the lot at 913 Tracy. This building, which extended back as far as the present auditorium was finished in 1905 and dedicated in 1906.

In 1909 Unity magazine was enlarged from sixty-eight pages to one-hundred pages in size and the magazine grew in circulation from 11,000 to 16,000 in one year. The idea of the Prosperity Bank came one day in May, 1910, as a helpful plan for Unity workers to use in saving the amount of the Weekly Unity subscription. Later the prosperity bank plan was adopted for all Unity periodicals.

Work on the building which is now known as the Administration building at 917 Tracy, was begun in March 1910. In the summer of that year, the printing department moved into the first floor of that building, which was only the east half of the north wing of the present building. The front was added later. The bindery occupied the second floor and the Society of Silent Unity the third floor. The fourth floor of this wing was added later. After the north wing was completed, the front was added and the fourth floor built, a wing was extended south as far as the present south wing. About one year later, the sub-basement and two floors were constructed on 10th street; they were the beginning of the south wing. As most of you know, the third, fourth and fifth floors were added in the spring of 1922. The new addition, the pressroom, which was built where a sunken garden and the old Unity Inn formerly stood, was completed in July 1922.

A recent count of the publishing department correspondents by the name of Smith revealed that there are more than 5,200 subscription cards in our files bearing this name. The cards occupy about five feet, five inches of space. There are almost three feet, three inches of Browns, or 3,120 of them; 1,760 Millers, 3,440 Johnsons and 2,720 Jones."

"All Aboard! The Unity Country Club committee decided at its' regular meeting last Thursday that the Unity truck would begin regular trips to Unity Farm sometime in April. The trips will be made on Saturday. The truck will leave the Unity buildings at 1:00 P.M. and return at 7:30 P.M. The charge for the round trip will be fifty cents to non-members of the club and twenty-five cents to members. A carload of railroad ties has been ordered to be used in the construction work, in lengths of 10 to 16 feet, on the homes at Unity Farm."

Unity News March 3, 1923, "Unity Farm has natural gas shooting out of four wells at the farm .We are not surprised to find that Royal Fillmore is figuring on the installation of a machine which will take the gasoline properties from natural gas and fit them for use in automobiles. It is claimed as such a machine can be purchased for six-hundred dollars and that the natural gas will still retain its' heating and lighting properties."

Unity News March 10, 1923, "An area north of the swimming pool and next to some of the cottages has been cleaned off for an elegant picnic ground. Comfort stations are being built at convenient places on the farm and Rick is having gas lights installed at the recreation area. Frances Gables house is progressing."

Unity News March 17, 1923, "Unity Farm; 1,000 apple trees are being planted. The main water well is thirty-five feet deep and will hold eighty-thousand gallons. A special pump has been installed for pumping the water from the well to the dwellers on the farm. Four tons of rock phosphate has been purchased for fertilizing some farm ground. Persimmon trees will be planted soon. The new rock crusher is grinding up the rock to finish the tennis courts. Dan Andrews is planting several acres of oats."

In April of 1923 Unity Sunday School Leaflet was first published. The purpose of this leaflet was to be a guideline for Sunday school leaders to use and or to teach from. This was made available to all Unity churches at a nominal cost. It became quite popular and was very helpful, especially to those that were teaching the young and had little or no training for the service to their church that they were performing. First Charles and then later Lowell edited this leaflet.

Letter from Royal dated April 6, 1923, "We have bought the Harris house west of where we were and now have 240 acres. Dan Andrews, a college graduate and practical farmer is the farm manager. We have a fine crew of farmers. There is a club house down pretty well in the woods and a big swimming pool 100 x 150 feet, a water system and we have dug our own gas wells and have gas and oil on the farm."

Unity News April 7, 1923, "Al Osenborg, head carpenter at the farm and Sam Davis are largely responsible for the good work done in making the dam at the swimming pool and 'sea beach'. This new pool is very modern and up to date in every way. It will soon be officially open. The tennis courts are almost finished."

Unity News April 14, 1923, "The first unit of a lighting system has been installed at Unity Farm. This unit is a 40 foot tower with a large light on top which can be seen for many miles. More lights will be installed until the roads on the farm are well illuminated."

Letter to Royal dated April 23, 1923 from the Reliance Brick Co. Vale, Missouri regarding tiles for building roofs. "The 5" x 8" tiling is the only size we are making and is available at our yard."

Unity News May 12, 1923, "Helen Draver and Alice Lee win the plaster of paris bathing suits for being the first to swim in the new pool on April 30th. Tennis courts will be ready for use on May 19th."

Unity News May 19, 1923, "More gas lights are being erected at the Farm. Four of these high lamp poles are being placed near the swimming pool and the bridge which leads over the creek to the baseball diamond. These lights burn Unity Farm gas, day and night. Because turning the lights off and on limits the life of the mantle, it is less expensive to let them burn constantly.

E.V. Ingraham's improved sod cutter worked so efficiently that in four hours one man cuts more sod than ten men can put down in several days. The sod is being used to cover the excavations made for water and pipe lines. A hydrant has been installed located close to the baseball diamond and picnic grounds."

Unity News June 2, 1923, "Decoration Day brought many swimmers to the new pool, which had nine feet of water in it at the deep end. A Spring diving board and a guard rail for the deep end are being installed."

Unity News June 16, 1923, "Gas lights are being installed at each end of the pool, a slide has been ordered, a canopy is being erected over two benches on the east side and two honest to goodness life preservers float about on the water."

Unity News June 23, 1923, "The swimming pool now has a fountain which sprays water fifteen feet in the air, its purpose is to purify the water in the pool. There are twelve new benches on the grounds of Unity Farm and plenty of lights. Black raspberries as well as wild gooseberries are ready for picking. The cherry crop is now ripe. The trees are full of the finest cherry pies you ever saw."

Unity News July 14, 1923, "A large charcoal filter is being installed for the purifying of the water that enters the pool on the farm."

An address by Charles Fillmore, made in 1923 at the opening of a Unity Conference and Healing Revival.

> "This is the first gathering of a conference of the movement called Unity. We here, have for nearly forty years been studying some of the attributes of Spirit. Unity as a religion does not claim to have discovered anything new. We have simply gathered together and unified all that is good in many religions. We do not claim that we have discovered any new truths, nor that we have had any special revelation of Truth. There is Truth in every religion. It is my privilege to take truth from any source, put it into my religion and make it fundamental as a rule of action in my life. This is what Unity students do.
>
> Thirty-eight years ago, Mrs. Fillmore and I began this Unity work and it was a very small beginning. We had studied various religions, but were not satisfied to accept any of them wholly. We said, 'There are so many religions. Let us go ahead for ourselves; let us do what we think is best and ask God to be with us and to lead us and guide us.' People of

every religion under the sun claim that we either belong to them or have borrowed the best part of our teaching from them. We have borrowed the best from all religions; that is the reason why we are called Unity. The name Unity was revealed to us by spirit. Before that we had called ourselves Practical Christians, new Thoughters. In fact we had called ourselves any old thing. We had just wandered about in the wilderness of 'isms'.

When we took the unifying ideas, that all religions are essentially good, that all have some truth and began to see that they all came from one source, we saw that they all fit into what was taught in primitive Christianity. As fast as we worked out an idea and had logically adopted it, our attention was in some way called to the same teaching in the Bible. In this way we found that we were being guided by a higher power.

Unity is not a sect, not a separation of people into an exclusive group of know-it-alls. Unity is the truth that is taught in all religion, simplified and systematized so that anyone can understand and apply it. We have recounted a few points in the religious composite called Unity, but the most important is this: Jesus is in our midst as the visible head and leader of the Unity Society. I say visible head because he is visible to those who have even come partially into, 'the light which lighteth every man coming into the world.' The only visibility is the visibility of Spirit. All people who have not spiritual light are in darkness."

Unity News August 4, 1923, "A new board walk around the back of the basement of the club house to the swimming pool has been built for the bathers at the Farm. Carpenters are again at work on the Francis Gable house."

Letter dated August 14, 1923 from E.W. Bacharach & Co. concerning a proper filtering system for the swimming pool. "The present filter system is not adequate nor does it have a filter washing system. However the equipment you have can be included in a new system that we can furnish at a cost of approximately $1,000.00."

Unity News August 18, 1923, "It's grape time at Unity Farm. The luscious fruit is fast ripening on the laden trellises. Four-hundred bushels of potatoes have been raised this year."

Unity News September 1, 1923, "A hucksters stand has been erected at the main entrance of Unity Farm, from which grapes and apples grown on the farm will be sold."

Unity News September 8, 1923, "The pictures of Unity Farm which appeared in last Sunday's Kansas City Star newspaper, brought out a large number of visitors. Equestrian sport may now be had at Unity Farm. Dan Andrews has several steeds in the farm stable which may be rented at twenty-five cents per hour, and ten cents per hour thereafter. Three tons of grapes have been sold this season."

[By mid-year of 1923 Myrtle Fillmore could see the pain that Royal continued to endure from the loss of his wife. She took time away from Unity and traveled with Royal around the Great lakes area. By late summer Royal's health continued to deteriorate and Myrtle decided that he should go to a special hospital for special care. She arranged for him to go by train to the Battle Creek Sanitarium in Battle Creek, Michigan. He passed away there on September 9, 1923. There was a tremendous outpouring of sympathy cards, letters, telegrams and calls to Unity expressing love in Royal's memory and for the family.

Myrtle Fillmore was appointed as guardian of Royal's baby Frances Sleater Fillmore and Lowell Fillmore, the baby's uncle as curator of the estate of the child by the Probate Court of Jackson County, Missouri dated September 28, 1923.]

Unity News September 29, 1923, "Excavation work for the mushroom cellar has been completed. The cellar is 15' x 30'. The upper part of the structure will be used for a garage. Mushrooms will be cultivated for use in the Unity Inn. At present the vegetable is being plucked wild in the woods, by the early risers. A large apple crop is about ready for harvest."

Unity News October 6, 1923, "Several Farm guests last Sunday proved either that the Summer is not yet gone or that they were gifted with a surplus of nerve or lacked good judgment, by going swimming in the pool. Full of pure rain water that fell recently, the pool was tempting. No problems were reported."

Unity News November 10, 1923, "Unity Farm: One thousand narcissus are being set out above the high rock wall across from the swimming pool. Five-hundred crocuses will be planted on the grass slope around the pool. The mushroom cellar is almost completed and some vegetables have all ready been planted in it. Later on mushrooms will be cultivated. The upper floor will be a tool house and repair shop where the autos and machinery used on the farm can be worked on."

Unity News November 17, 1923, "Concrete stalls are being constructed on Unity Farm for the cattle. This will be a grade A stable. Dan Andrews has two new saddles hanging in the farm stable. Now he is praying for two more horses.   A Packard bus for Unity. Plans for a sixteen seat bus, for transportation between the Unity buildings in Kansas City and Unity Farm have been consummated and will be specially built from Rick Fillmore's design. Rick also designed the Fillmore's 'Winston Six' which had the first specially built body in Kansas City. The new bus will be completed in time for the Auto Show where it will be on exhibition. After that it will buzz to and from the farm."

Unity News December 8, 1923, "The new machine shop that is being erected on the farm, between the barn and the farmhouse is almost completed."

December 15, 1923, "A railroad switch is to be run in Unity Farm from the tracks that now passes through the farm.

The Unity School has recently purchased an additional 111 acres, joining Unity Farm on the east. In completing the transaction it was necessary to send to Washington D.C. to obtain copies of the original government patents issued on the land. When they arrived it was found that they were issued by Millard Fillmore and signed by Millard Fillmore and Zackary Taylor. Millard Fillmore was a second cousin of Charles Fillmore's father.

John Royal Fillmore, the third son of Charles and Myrtle, made his transition on September 9, 1923, he was thirty-four years old. He was in the Battle Creek Sanitarium, Battle Creek, Michigan being treated for diabetes and high blood pressure."

1924 - Unity News January 5, 1924, "A new Crescent Universal woodworking machine is now a part of the Unity Farm equipment. The machine will be used in turning out parts for construction work of various kinds in the carpenter shop."

Unity News January 12, 1924, "Ice skating has been the chief diversion at Unity Farm during the cold weather. The swimming pool made an ideal place for skating. Unity Farm offers more attractions this year than ever before. Among these are swimming, tennis, baseball, horseback riding, picnicking, medicine ball, horseshoe playing, dancing on the new open air floor, gardening, croquet and 110 more acres of beautiful land to roam over."

Unity News January 19, 1924, "Through scientific management Dan Andrews has managed to increase the daily egg production from his chickens from fifteen to one-hundred twenty. Several cases of these eggs go to Unity Inn each week. Unity has signed a contract for the drilling of five more oil wells at the farm. With these additional wells we should have enough oil to supply our fuel."

January 26, 1924 Unity Daily Word new monthly magazine giving daily lessons; "To meet the demand for a monthly manual of daily meditation and instructions the Unity School will publish a new magazine, starting July 1st. It will have a full page for each day, giving the word for meditation, instructions on its' application and practice and passages from the Bible and from Unity textbooks. This monthly periodical will be pocket size. The person that conceived the idea for this new publication was Frank B. Whitney and he will be its' editor. he has been with Unity since 1919 and has served as the Dean of Correspondence School."

Unity News February 2, 1924, "The mushrooms are beginning to "mush", Rick Fillmore says and the first crop of the season will be harvested in the farm cellar next week. A cow and a calf have been purchased for the farm herd. Farm hands have named the bovine Imogene."

Unity News March 29, 1924, "Mr. & Mrs. A.C. Harris have joined our farm family. He will take over the chicken raising. She is a former swimming instructor at Northeast High School in Kansas City. The Harris' are living in the Al Wakeman house. The first of the new oil wells was brought in last week. Work on the next was started immediately. Mr. Grable is taking charge of all of the gas and oil wells."

Unity News April 5, 1924, "Dan Andrews planted a large quantity of potatoes and eight-thousand new grape vines recently. The Unity engineer met a Missouri-Pacific engineer at Unity Farm recently for the purpose of determining the possibility of making a large lake by the railroad tracks. This lake to be used to supply water for general purposes on the farm. They also discussed providing a road through a tunnel culvert under the tracks large enough to drive a car through."

Unity News April 12, 1924, "Apparently the tennis and swimming seasons have begun as players and swimmers have been observed. Dan Andrews has finished the plowing at the farm and has nearly completed the planting."

Unity News April 19, 1924, "Myrtle Fillmore's dream house at Unity Farm is nearing construction. Her son Rick is completing the plans and has made the decision to place the house in the apple orchard. It will be west of the old farm home that was earlier reconstructed and added to for Grandmother Fillmore. A border of old fashion flowers is now being planted on the edge of where the lawn will be around her house.

Apple, pear, cherry and plum trees have been planted at the farm. An aquatic garden is now being made south of the swimming pool. It will add a distinctive charm to the area. It will contain water lilies, willows, cat-tails and other water plants."

Unity News April 26, 1924, "A large quantity of perennial plants will be set out soon at the farm including oriental poppy, phlox, foxglove, day lily, sweet williams, painted daisy, larkspur and many rose bushes."

When Rick was in Europe during World War I he was very impressed with the "Cotswold" cottage designs. He used this basic design in planning his parent's new home. Despite its' being referred to as a cottage the rooms are surprisingly large and it has a front porch that Myrtle especially likes. The house has peaked roof gables, new style casement windows, but one item the house does not have is a kitchen. This was Myrtles idea as she wanted to come here to relax and enjoy. She and Charles will take their meals with Grandmother Fillmore who has a kitchen and has been the family cook for years!" The old Harris house was refurbished for Grandmother and is across the street from the new Fillmore house.

Unity News June 7, 1924, "The drilling of a deep well has started on the farm. It is hoped to avoid gas and oil and to strike water. The new well is just south of the swimming pool. The lily pond, farther south of the swimming pool is now complete."

Unity News June 14, 1924, "Myrtle Fillmore's new home is nearing completion and is certainly under the law of divine protection. Last Saturday, after he had been showing his mother through her new dream home, Rick found himself unexplainably drawn to remain in the vicinity of the house. While standing by and watching the house, trying to analyze his feelings, Rick saw a flash of light and upon going into the house to investigate the source he found that oil rags, used in the finishing, piled in a corner had caused spontaneous combustion. Before any damage he put out the fire. There are splendid prospects for a tremendous fruit crop at the farm this year, judging from the fruit now on the trees."

Unity News June 21, 1924, "The swimming pool is being enlarged and cement work is almost completed. The shallow part is thirty-two inches deep and all the bottom is cement and a new filter is to be installed. We have been having a terrible time the last few days dodging oil. In the new well oil was struck at 285 feet. Digging past this vein oil was struck again at 400 feet. The plan now is to try to hit water at 1,500 feet."

Unity News July 12, 1924, "Sulphur water was reached in the new well being drilled on the farm."

Unity News July 26, 1924, "A wading pool for the children, just south of the big pool is nearing completion. A large crop of alfalfa has been harvested on the farm. An additional tennis court is being built."

On September 3, 1924 Unity purchased the Kansas City radio station WOQ and moved it to the headquarters on Tracy Avenue.

Unity News September 27, 1924, "The cottage that has had several owners and was called Hilltop cabin is being reconstructed into a very nice home for the Ralph Boileau family.

Ralph Edwin Boileau began his career as a singing evangelist. His wife, Maude Kendall Boileau, was a soprano soloist and song leader. They joined Unity in 1924. He served as director of field services for Unity. Also traveled lecturing for Unity in the U.S., Canada and England through 1931. His sister was E. Pharaby Boileau who served Unity as its' Librarian and started the Heritage Room. The Boileau children are sons Vance and Dwight and daughter Pharaby. She became an actress and used the stage name of Lucille Norman."

Wee Wisdom Lessons For Young Students by Imelda Octavia Shanklin. Our Perfect Brother; His Miracles.

> "When we speak of a miracle we mean an occurrence that we cannot account for by our present understanding of the laws of life and expression.
>
> To a man who knew nothing about the radio, a concert coming out of the air would seem a miracle. We know that the ether carries sound waves, but the reason why it carries them is as great a mystery to us as the radio concert would be to the man who knew nothing about the radio. In that sense, the radio concert is a miracle to every one who hears it.
>
> We say that wind and rain and sun and soil acting on a seed produce a plant; we can name the chemical changes that occur in ripening fruit, but what is the cause of the chemical changes, no one knows. We say that nature is their cause, but that statement really does not explain their beginning and their power.
>
> All natural laws are forms of God's mind, which is the only power that is or that ever can be. When God speaks, the thing which he says is accomplished instantly. Those who believe in the mind of God as the only power in life, find that by letting God's mind act freely things take place quickly and

that there are results such as cannot come when they do not give him full power in them.

Our Perfect Brother knew how to let God's mind act through him, and because he was able to do this, he worked miracles. People who call God's mind the law of nature also have had miraculous results, but their results have not been so wonderful as those brought about by our Perfect Brother.

He knew God to be present everywhere as substance. By letting the mind of God act through him without the delays which we have believed necessary as natural law, he increased the food supply that they brought to him in the desert. In this way he fed thousands, from a beginning which naturally would have been sufficient for only a few persons.

He knew that our souls always are alive and intelligent, whether they are acting in a physical body or not. He knew that it is good for every soul to act through a physical body. For these reasons he was able to speak to those who had gone out of their bodies and to persuade them to return. This is what he did for his friend Lazarus, and, as we say, Lazarus was raised from the dead. Our Perfect Brother raised others from the dead, and by using for himself the same law that he had used for them, he resurrected his own body, after his crucifixion.

The miracle works of our Perfect Brother are the most thrilling of all his deeds.

Our Father is bringing to our minds some of the laws by which Jesus worked, so that we are beginning to realize what lies in store for us. Jesus knew that these laws would be revealed to us, for he said: 'He that believeth on me, the works that I do shall he do also.' This is just such a promise as a man who understands the radio might make to a man who knew nothing about it: 'Come to our shop, and there you will be taught how to make and to use the radio.' All that we ever can learn comes out of the mind of God, and one who had studied the methods of our Perfect Brother, tells us: 'If any of you lacketh wisdom, let him ask of God, who giveth to all liberally.'

Our Perfect Brother knew that the Father will teach us more of his laws than have ever knowingly been used by man, for he said of every one who lets God act through him: 'Greater works than these shall he do.'

Our Perfect Brother knew all the laws of God's mind, but he did not perform all the miracles that he had the power to perform. He gave us a hint of this when he said: 'I have yet many things to say unto you, but ye cannot bear them now.' That is like the wise teacher of music who does not give eight-year-old fingers the difficult compositions. Our Perfect Brother gave us lesson enough; we must learn it and use it before we have another and more wonderful lesson assigned.

Let the mind of God think its thoughts in my mind."

Unity News October 18, 1924, "We feel very proud of the Unity chickens. Last month the hens laid over four-thousand eggs. A poultry breeder recently visited the new hen house and said it was the most up-to-date and complete poultry house he has seen."

Unity News November 8, 1924, "The golf course is now in good playable condition. The total yardage in the nine holes is a little over a mile. The fairway is in good shape and the greens are improving with age."

Unity News November 15, 1924, "Charles Rickert Fillmore is the brave man of the Farm. He has the honor of being the last person in the swimming pool this year. The Unity Farm Inn is being dressed up for winter with a new coat of stucco and a basement."

[This is the first mention of an Inn at the Farm. In the first year, the farm had a male cook that provided meals for the farm workers in a house that was on the grounds when the first farm was purchased. Later a bunkhouse was built, just north of the large chicken house, for the unmarried workers to live and have their meals. The kitchen and dining room were on the south end of that building. When the basement was added showers for the men were installed. At this Inn meals were available also for guests at the farm.]

Unity News November 22, 1924, "Charlie Watson has the corn sheller and grinder now in operation, turning corn right from the field into corn chops and corn meal. A new foundation is being built under Floyd Cumming's home, he is the farm electrician. He and his family live in a farm house on Rhinehart Road at the northwest part of Unity Farm, that was just recently purchased. Another oil well has been discovered on the farm and looks quite promising."

Unity News December 13, 1924, "Dallas Kreigh won a blanket at a raffle given by the Hazel Grove school at their party recently. More evidence in regard to his ideas of single blessedness!"

Hazel Grove School is a rural one room grade school that sits directly across the road from the Farm's main front entrance. It is very convenient for the many children of the families moving to Unity Farm at homes provided by the new employer.

In 1924 Rick Fillmore became a member of the Kansas City Rotary club. He was placed on a committee to develop the "Rotary Boys Camp" in Jackson County.

[That camp is a few miles East of Unity Farm on Colbern Road. In the years to come there was a close relationship between the Rotary Camp and Unity Farm. In the late 20's and 30's the Unity Farm Sunday school and Youth of Unity often had outdoor activities at the Rotary Camp.]

1925 - Unity News January 10, 1925, "Al Osenberg has concentrated the whole construction crew at the farm on a new power house building. At the present rate of speed the building will soon be completed. The power house will be another of Rick Fillmore's unusual building designs. The front corner of the building will have a cylinder design and a centered peak roof at a two story height. The interior will house the pumping system for all the oil wells.

The Boileaus have moved into their rebuilt home. It is north of the Gable's house and also on the east edge of the golf course. The music and healing service from Unity's WOQ radio station came in clear and fine over Grandmother Fillmore's radio on Saturday night. Cyrus Kreeger is the man that does all of the painting at the farm now. Twenty-eight thousand copies of the Daily Word were printed for February. One-hundred sixty-five thousand five-hundred copies of the new magazine have been printed to date."

Unity News January 24, 1925, "The oil pumping engine at the farm is now under cover at the new power house. We have thus far this winter been able to obtain all of the oil supply needed for the complex on Tracy Avenue in Kansas City from Unity Farm."

Unity News January 31, 1925, "Myrtle Fillmore is spending a few days in her new little dream home on the farm. She doesn't have one moment in which to be lonesome. Charles Rickert and baby Fran keep her busy with animal puzzle pictures."

Unity News February 7, 1925, "Mrs. Harry Buckley is now the manager of the Unity Farm Inn."

Unity News February 14, 1925, "The addition of a sun parlor is now being made at Gray Gables, the home of Francis and Jessie Gable. The Gables enjoy entertaining guests, before the sun porch was added they often had as many as thirty guests. Jessie says, 'now we can have sixty!'"

Unity News February 28, 1925, "Rick Fillmore says the swimming pool will be ready for swimmers next week. There is always someone that wants to be the first in! The foundation for a 30,000 gallon water tank has been started at the farm. The farms two geologists, Ray Harris and David Webster are daily making valuable discoveries in the stone quarry on the farm. George Cravens is very busy these days trimming apple trees and grape vines."

Unity News March 14, 1925, "Thurman and Ester Carroll are busy gathering eggs, some days they get as many as 525 eggs. Floyd Cummings, farm electrician, has invented an electrical contrivance to keep the water for the chickens in the trough from freezing. At the farm the cardinals in flaming red, the blue birds and many others are decorating the landscape and filling the air with sweet melodies."

Unity News March 21, 1925, "Unity Farm has an addition. The pretty woodland site, east of the railroad tracks on the farm, including some fields of cultivated land has been purchased. There are two springs on this tract of land. Frank Curtis is a new farm worker. Al Kinneman looks after the farm where the old Kinneman home place was that Unity purchased."

Unity News March 28, 1925, "The single farm workers have moved into the new bunk house. It has three rooms and showers in the cellar, quite palatial! Dallas Kreigh, the first Unity worker at the farm, has a single room of his own, guess he deserved that after living in a tent!"

Unity News April 4, 1925, "Myrtle Fillmore has named her dream home at the farm. It is now called Orchard Crest. Fifty-two acres have been added to Unity Farm on the west. There is some discussion about making part of the new addition a picnic ground and a touring camp for the benefit of the public. The Buckleys are having a porch built on the southside of their home."

[Myrtle's dream home had a number of names, but the workers on the farm called it the Arches because of the arches at the front of the house. The name finally stuck and it continues to be referred to as "the Arches" today.]

Unity News April 18, 1925, "At Unity Farm the ingenuity of man's mind, the fashioning power of man's hand and the expending of muscles and brawn are evolving a dream of beauty into a reality. A stone quarry may seem an uninteresting place, but where this stone is placed into rustic walls, into bridges spanning ravines, into steps climbing hillsides, into low inviting seats along footpaths, it becomes a thing of romance. Ground up in small bits the stone makes easier driving over muddy roads or ground into powder it serves as a foundation for the tennis courts. Sam Davis and a squad of from five to ten men under the supervision of Rick Fillmore are constant at this work. At present another lily pond is under construction, a wading pool for children has been built and the creek running into the ravine is being lined with rock. The general effect of all this must be seen to be appreciated. In the stone quarry itself, history is written. Recently fossilized shells were found, a silent message from the dim past of Earth's fancy!"

Unity News April 25, 1925, "There are some workers at the farm who are very little in evidence, who are doing much to make Unity Farm beautiful and to the joy of the city folks. All though they have made no effort to be noticed, we would like to introduce you to them; Charles Acock, the cement man, and John Keller, stone mason have worked on the farm since improvements began. Plus, Clarence Kinneman, Marion Alley and Harrison Blatt during the past two years."

Unity News May 2, 1925, "The new public highway, #12 when completed, will bring Unity Farm within twelve miles of 10th and Tracy and the trip one way can be made in twenty minutes. One-thousand seven-hundred fifty apple trees have been planted at the farm this spring. A pergola is being built in front of the lily pond."

Unity News May 23, 1925, "Harry Herchifield is the contractor drilling the wells. He has four workers, two on days and two at nights. Those are Paul Liebengood, Tom Morrison, Bill Eldredge and Frank Kinster. They have drilled fourteen wells of which ten are now productive. In only one of these wells no oil has been found. That was the last one, on the east side near the railroad tracks. The men are now moving to the west side of the farm to continue their search for oil. Another pergola and dressing room combined is being built beside the children's pool."

Unity News May 29, 1925, "A new chicken house is now going up back of the present one. A water tower is going up behind the club house road. It will be connected with pipes to the spring near the railroad."

Unity News June 13, 1925, "The men who are putting up the water tank are E.M. Render, V.T. Gray and D.H. Donnevan. A 26,000 gallon tank is being erected by the Horton Tank Works of Chicago, Illinois. Menton Elnyre and Hugh Pendergast, surveyors, are making the club house their home for a few weeks. These men are here for the purpose of trying to locate underground water on the farm. Cecil Tippet, who lives near Unity Farm, is serving as an assistant to the surveyors. George Fry says that the farm has distilled 950 gallons of gasoline. Rex Eubank, the engineer, has named it the Unity Special."

Unity News June 27, 1925, "H.G. Nagle and Arthur Zebley are new workers on the farm. Zebley is the first life-guard for the pool and also serves as the policeman for the Club House and pool area. The pond lilies in both ponds are in bloom. George Craven is caring for the lilies."

Unity News July 11, 1925, "Eighty people registered at the farm pool for swimming on Wednesday. This breaks all previous records! Two new motors and two transformers have been purchased for the lighting system on the farm."

Report of Topographic survey for Unity Farm of Little Cedar Creek drainage basin dated July 14, 1925 for a proposed dam one eighth of a mile east of the Missouri-Pacific Railroad Line. The proposed lake area dam site is to be one mile west of the Jefferson Highway; north-south road from Independence to Lee's Summit, Missouri. A good dirt road connects the Doty farm (lake site) with Jefferson Highway. One half mile south of the dam site an improved road runs east and west through the Doundna farm, a farm of two-hundred acres which Unity now owns, as well as part of the Doty farm. The purpose of the survey was to ascertain the best location for the construction of a dam and reservoir or lake for water supply. Little Cedar Creek parallels the railroad line north and south.

The area surveyed has these rock formations; Hertha limestone, Ladore shale, Bethany falls, Galesburg shale, Winterset limestone and a thin mantle composed of the erosional products of the Cherryvale shale. This survey states that only the Winterset limestone is usable for masonry work. Also, that a small quarry has been opened.

On page fifty-one of this report is a notice to contractors for proposal for constructing Little Cedar dam in the northwest quarter of the northwest quarter of Section 30, township 48 north, range 31, West Jackson County, Missouri. Summary and recommendations, dated 1926. Area 17.1 acres, length 2,170 feet, maximum width 790 feet, minimum width 130 feet, average width 390 feet, maximum depth 40.3 feet, capacity 55,744,173 gallons, watershed area 420 acres. Dam 538 feet in length, 45.7 feet high in the center of the channel, at the dam's thickest would measure 118.9 feet at its' base. The top of the dam to be 24 feet wide of which 10 feet occupied for a roadway."

The Unity annual conference was held July14, 1925. At that meeting an organization named the Unity Ministers Association resulted.

Unity News August 29, 1925, "The oat crop this year at the farm was 1,800 bushels. The third crop of alfalfa is now growing. The peach and grape crop were fine. Dallas Kreigh has sold a good deal of products at the produce stand at the entrance to the farm. Will Lux,

George Travis, David Cantor and Virgil and Mary Nonamaker are all new workers on the farm. Floyd Cummings, farm electrician, has put up lights on the tennis courts."

Unity News September 26, 1925, "Frances Fillmore has issued invitations for a birthday party, she will be four years old. Recently she said, 'I'm getting to be a big girl now and we have decided to call me Fran.' Grading has begun on #12 highway, which runs through the southwest corner of Unity Farm. This road is part of the direct highway which goes to St. Louis and will be of concrete."

Unity News October 10, 1925, "A Unity Farm study group has inaugurated a fund for a chapel on the farm. There is a call for a Sunday school on the farm and a new building is needed for religious meetings and classes."

Unity News October 17, 1925, "New Unity radio station opened. Many radio fans attended the dedication service of the new $20,000.00 radio casting station of the Unity School of Christianity, at 9th and Tracy, in Kansas City, Missouri. The new station of 1,000 watts capacity is the most powerful in Kansas City. Charles Fillmore, president and co-founder of Unity, officiated at the dedication which was followed by the initial radio casting program that included speeches and music.

Silent Seventy has received a beautiful necklace to be forwarded to H. Emily Cady in appreciation of Lesson in Truth. This was made for her by a prisoner and is one of the most artistic necklaces ever received. Silent Seventy provides Unity literature free to the inmates in the federal prison at Leavenworth, Kansas."

Unity News October 24, 1925, "When Charles Rickert Fillmore was introduced to the new baby sister, that arrived Wednesday, the baby was exercising her lungs and Charles feeling sympathetic remarked, 'Isn't it too bad the poor little thing has to cry so hard. I know what is the matter with her, the nurse has two hot water bottles up against her.' We wager that Charles will not allow any harm to come to baby sister, Rosemary, born October 21st. Max Mitchell is a new farm employee and is trimming all the trees to make them pretty next spring. The name of the new chicken man is Russell Good. Pretty good name!"

Unity News December 5, 1925, "Little Rosemary Fillmore sends her love to all her friends at Unity. Mrs. C.E. True is at present assisting Harriet to look after the baby's wants. Rosemary is slowly unfolding her petals and is developing as a healthy infant should. The farm gardener is planting 3,000 different varieties of bulbs around the farm."

Unity News December 19, 1925, "Grandmother is very much pleased with the table that Charlie Watson made for her. He also made one for Mrs. Buckley at the bunkhouse. The road to the farm, state highway #12 is expected to be opened soon. It has been closed since October 16th."

Unity News December 31, 1925, "The Unity Farm Sunday school, which is being held in a little unused house on Pederson's farm, north of Unity Farm, is in full swing. We want to especially thank Frances Gable for suppling us with Sunday school papers, Dan Andrews for sending us benches to sit on, Grandmother Fillmore, for a tablecloth and Allen Kinneman for suppling and putting up a stove pipe and for his continued faithful service. We also thank Mrs. Pederson for helping us to secure a meeting place and otherwise offering us her assistance. After the sleet last week the farm was all aglitter and presented a beautiful picture in the sunlight. It seems to be transformed into an enchanted country, where everything scintillated!"

1926 - In January of 1926 the title of the Unity publication, Christian Business Man changed to Christian Business.

Article from Christian Business. Taxes by E. Roe.

> "John Grey was one of those men who believed that the solution to all his problems depended solely upon his personal efforts. Indeed, his success in business had been such that, whereas he naturally was a really pleasant chap to meet, John Grey had acquired an air of arrogance, a 'Look at me, see what I can do' attitude. This had resulted in there being very few whom he could truly call real friends.
>
> But gradually, so gradually as to be almost unnoticeable, John Grey's affairs became less and less prosperous. Deals did

not go through as he had planned, his credit began to suffer, until finally he was faced with the fact that his bank account was a thing of the past. Men upon whom he had formerly counted in an emergency seemed purposely to avoid him. Conditions had become serious. In fact the taxes on his beautiful home must be paid within the next two weeks, and he had not a cent with which to pay them. Nor could he see where or how he could raise the money. His home was already mortgaged to the limit.

One day, while sitting at his desk, trying to see a way out of his difficulty, the door of his office opened and a man entered. The visitor was smiling cheerfully and his hand was outstretched, as he said, 'Well, Grey, how are you?'

John was taken by surprise and for a moment did not recognize his caller. In a few seconds, however, he exclaimed, 'David White, sure as shootin'. Where did you drop from?' While he was speaking, John was puzzled. The last time he had seen David White the latter was just about down and out. Now here he was looking like a very prosperous business man. What could it mean?

'Well, I am in the city for a few hours and I thought that I'd just run in and see if you wouldn't like to have lunch with me,' said David. 'Glad to,' replied John. 'There's a quiet little restaurant around the corner, and the food is excellent.'

After seating themselves at a table in a secluded corner of the restaurant, David asked, 'How's everything, John? Business good? I remember that you always were a hustler.' There was silence for a moment and then John blurted out, 'Business is rotten! Everything is rotten! An honest man can't make a dollar these days!'

For a moment David looked startled, then a smile crept over his face, and he remarked, 'Oh, come now, I shouldn't say that. It's just that you've lost your perspective for a time.' 'That's all right for you to say; you look as if you'd been lucky. But I haven't had a decent break for months.' The resentment that he had been nursing for months was in his voice. 'Why, I don't even know how I'm going to pay my taxes, and they're due in two weeks. Perspective! Bah!'

'So you think I've been lucky, eh?' laughed David. 'Well, I guess I have; but not in the way you mean. Want to hear about it?' 'Sure! Shoot, maybe I'll get an idea,' said John, as he settled back in his chair.

'All right,' was David's reply. 'Here goes. You will remember that when you last saw me I was hardly what you would call prosperous, and my chances for becoming so looked pretty slim. I had reached a point where I didn't know which way to turn. I owed several months' rent, tradespeople had refused to let me have anything more until I paid them for what I had already received.

One day, while sitting on a bench in the park, wondering what to do next, I picked up a small book that some one had left on the bench. I turned the pages idly, until the word 'prosperity' caught my eye. I became interested and began to read. Before long I had read every article in the book and wished there were more. I knew that at last I had found the way out of my troubles. I hurried home, taking the book with me, and told my wife that I felt sure I had found a path that would lead us out of our worries. Together we read the various articles in the book, and when we had finished a great burden had been lifted from our minds. You see, we had begun to realize that one of the first things we had to do was to change our way of thinking; get a new perspective on life, as it were.

The next morning I started out with a very earnest desire to serve. I felt that there must be some one for whom I could do a service. You see, I had determined to go out not with the thought that I must *get*, but that I wanted to *give*.

Instead of walking around the block to avoid the grocer who had supplied us for so long, I walked by the store. Something told me to turn back and see if there were not something that I could do to express my gratitude to the man who had made it possible for me to eat, even though I had no money to offer him. He looked very much surprised and laughingly said, 'No, I guess there isn't anything you can do, unless you want to play errand boy for me for a few hours; my boy is not here today.' He was taken aback when I eagerly offered to deliver his orders, but he said no more.

Well, I spent the forenoon delivering groceries. When I had finished, he insisted that I should be paid, so I asked that he apply the amount to my account. He agreed, but in addition gave me a fine order of groceries. That afternoon I met a man to who I had applied several times for work and who had always been very curt and discouraging. This time, however, he stated that he had a position that he believed I could fill. Needless to say, I accepted it.

From that time on we grew in our understanding of Truth. Through learning where my real supply came from, and how to contact it and bring abundance into my life, I became a changed man. Call it luck if you want to; I call it something different. To me it is God.'

Both men were quiet for a few minutes. At last John said, 'It sounds like a dream, Dave, but if it is I hope that I can learn how to dream in the same way. At any rate I believe I'll do a little investigating on my own account.'

About two weeks later, when Dave entered John's office, he found an altogether different man. It was John all right, but the harassed look had gone from his face, and he greeted David with a broad grin. 'How's everything?' asked David.

'Fine,' replied John. 'After you left I hunted up one of those Truth centers that you told me about, and I've learned what Jesus meant when He said, 'Ask, and ye shall receive.'

"Fine!' exclaimed David. 'How about the taxes?' 'Oh, as soon as I learned where to look for my supply, things began to open up. I was given a deal to handle, the commission on which more than paid the taxes.'

The Business Counselor says: 'When God is permitted to work through man, there is never idleness or lack.'"

Unity News February 13, 1926, "Rex Eubanks reports one oil well producing fifteen barrels a day. It is good to see the oil men on the job again after being away. The newest workers on the farm are Charles McKinley, Leon Clark, Weldon Seckler and Rolla Marquette. No, the building going up west of the pool is not a hotel, but is Miss McMahon's new home."

On Valentine's Day February 14, 1926 Lowell and Alice Lee were married. Alice has been an employee of the Unity School of Christianity for several years.

Unity News March 6, 1926, "Russell Good, who has been in charge of the poultry, has left and was replaced by Mr. Schlabach."

Unity News April 2, 1926, "Many improvements are being planned for the farm. The swimming pool is to have a new floor and sulphosaline water from the deep well. A new shower building for the boys is being constructed, to give the whole basement of the club house to the girls. Another summer cottage will be added making three for the use of club members. The natural bridge area is under contract to be purchased and added to the farm and will make an excellent picnic ground. Two-thousand five-hundred new chicks have been bought for the farm. These are to add to the butter and egg man, Foster Hulse. At present the poultry yields about 900 eggs a day."

Unity News April 10, 1926, "All of the employees on the farm who are eligible to vote went to the school election last Tuesday at the Hazel Grove school. It was voted that Unity might use the school building for meetings and Sunday school without expense. The Sunday school is growing and more interest is shown all the time. A new Ford truck has been purchased for use on the farm, especially on the golf course."

Unity News April 17, 1926, "The road to the farm was closed a week ago yesterday. If you wish to reach the farm you must use the road built by that famous Frenchman M. De Tour. Several rolls of wire were delivered, the farm is going to have new fences."

Unity News June 5, 1926, "The following produce is now for sale at Unity Farm; asparagus, peas, onions, strawberries, cherries, eggs, milk, cream and ice. Cherries and strawberries are available in twenty-four pint crates. New gas lights have been installed around the vacation cottages. Mrs. McMahon has moved into her new home west of the swimming pools. It is reported that the new paving, highway #12 will reach the farm today, from the south!"

Unity News June 26, 1926, "Miss Francis Fillmore has a new pony! It is black and stands about three feet high. It is kept at the farm stables and Fran, the Boileau children and Charles Rickert spend most of their time looking at it. The other day Fran came to town and said that she was going shopping. We asked her what she was going to buy and she said, 'Oh, a bridle and halter at Sears-Roebucks.' When she was told that there was no one to go with her she said, 'On yes there is, uncle Odie will go.' And off Fran and Lowell went shopping."

Unity News July 3, 1926, "You may begin playing on the larger golf course at Unity Farm today. The yardage now totals 4,200 yards with a 72 par for the eighteen holes."

Unity News July 24, 1926, "Work on the Tarvia roads on the farm was started and visitors are requested not to break through the barriers on the roads. The latest report on Highway 50, formerly listed as #12, is that it is open from Lee's Summit to almost Knobtown and that in three weeks part of the road will be open to Kansas City."

Unity News August 28, 1926, "The road is open, by gosh! Francis J. Gable says that this is the best news he has heard. In the honor of the opening of the road, Unity plans a celebration this afternoon and evening. One feature of the celebration will be a parade from the farm to Lee's Summit where the band will play on the streets. The parade will leave the farm at 4:00 P.M. and will consist of fifty cars, each with a banner. In the evening the band and the orchestra will give a program on the new dance floor over the double garage, just east of the lily ponds. The dance floor faces the Unity Farm natural amphitheater. Visitors from the surrounding country are expected in great numbers. Grapes, peaches and ice cream will be served!

Now appearing in the Unity News is an article by a supposed grey mouse. Here is a conversation of the little gray mouse. 'Speaking of the Farm, I was sitting down by the swimming pool talking to Arthur Zebley, he thinks there isn't any other place quite so nice as the farm you know, and suddenly I saw a lady coming across the swimming pool bridge. Arthur, I squeaked, is it - can it be one of the seven Sutherland sisters? No, it can't he said. That's Margaret Norwoods' sister Mrs. Smith of Kansas City. Well, say I, I wish you could have seen her hair. It was hanging down and reached almost to the ground, a golden haze as the breeze gently wafted it about. Oh boy!'"

Unity News September 4, 1926, "Again the little gray mouse. 'Last Saturday as I set by the swimming pool talking to Sandy McNab, Charles Rickert's dog, he said, Look grey mouse isn't this a peaceful picture? And I looked around and saw Zebley, all dressed up ready for the parade, standing near by and over on the sandy beach lay Ed Christman, sound asleep. But the best part of the picture was Ed's little boy in his bathing suit, playing by the edge of the pool. And then as the peace and quietness had just about rendered Sandy and me oblivious to any surroundings, we heard a splash, the baby had fallen in! Well believe me, quicker than a flash, in jumped Arthur and rescued him. He's right on the job that man is. And of course his clothes were no good for the parade after that, but Dick Rowland loaned him trousers, socks and shoes as well. Three cheers for Arthur I say!"

Unity News September 11, 1926, "Dance at the farm. Don't forget the big moonlight dance to be given at the Unity Country Club Tuesday September 21st. This will be the first Unity dance on the new out-of-doors dance floor at the amphitheater pavilion and should be the best dance we've ever had. Come out and make it a wonderful success. $1.00 per couple, dancing from 9:00 to 12:00 P.M. Earl Coleman's Orchestra!

Have you purchased any of the wonderful fruit from the farm this fall? It has been classed by horticulturists as 99% perfect. On Labor Day at the stand on new 50 highway the sales amounted to $203.00. Dallas Kreigh, who has charge of the stand, says that the sales each day have been very good.

Mrs. Parker has charge of the kindergarten at the club house. The hours are from 10:00 to 2:00. The pupils are Charles Rickert, Frances and Pharaby Boileau. Frances and Charles are getting to be experts in the saddle. Charles says he can ride at a gallop now. Mr. & Mrs. Flynn are the Farm's new neighbors. Mr. Flynn is overseeing the construction work at the new dam and lake being built. It is hoped that the work will be completed the first of next year. Mrs. June Adams is at the farm again as May Harris' assistant as hostess at the club house."

Unity News September 18, 1926, "A green house is being built at the farm and is progressing well. Mark Mitchell is overseeing its' construction. He will be in charge of the green house when completed. How is this for poultry production? Mr. Sleigbank reports that three pullets have laid eleven eggs each in ten days. When at Unity Farm one misses some very beautiful scenery if he fails to take a stroll down Lowell's bridle paths. At the end of the swimming season the policeman at the pool and club house, Arthur Zebley, went to the power house, there he set up a blacksmith and repair shop."

Unity News September 25, 1926, "In the future the Sunday school and evening church services will be held at the club house instead of Hazel Grove school. Harriet Fillmore, wife of Rickert, asked her husband for permission to move the church services to the club house. All the children living on the farm and nearby neighbor children were invited to attend. The farm superintendent Earl Ackerman has moved into his new office which has been finished."

Unity News October 9, 1926, "There are one-hundred workers at Unity Farm now."

Unity News October 23, 1926, "A triple birthday dinner was enjoyed when Grandmother, Miss Frances and Miss Rosemary Fillmore celebrated birthdays. Rosemary was one year old, Frances five years and Grandmother?"

Letter from Elmer Boillot, architect, 1202 Scarrit Building Kansas City, Missouri. Buildings for the Unity School of Christianity to W. Rickert Fillmore dated October 26, 1926. Sizes for proposed new buildings at Unity Farm.

Building #1 - 82' x 241' Printing and raw stock, at front three floors and basement, rear part one story and basement total area 63,324 square feet.
Building #2 - 66' x 176' Administration building, two floors and basement, total area 34,848 square feet.
Building #3 - 66' x 176' Bindery and finish stock building, two stories and basement, total area 34,848 square feet.
Building #4 - 66' x 176' and 66' x 100' Silent Unity building, two stories and basement, total area 41, 448 square feet.

Building #5 - 66' x 176' Editorial and art, two stories and basement, total area 34,848 square feet.
Building #6 - 50' x 125' Reception/Information building, two stories and basement, total area 18,750 square feet.
Building #7 - 70' x 80' Heating plant and shops, two stories and basement, total area 16,800 square feet.
Building #8 - 120' x 120' Chapel, one story, balcony and basement, total area 19, 200 square feet.

Construction:

1 - Concrete and stone foundations and basements.
2 - Hollow tile exterior walls, stuccoed on exteriors.
3 - Clay tile roofs over concrete slab.
4 - Steel girders and columns, steel roof trusses.
5 - Reinforced concrete floor slabs and steel joists.
6 - All buildings plastered interiors, except basements.
7 - Vacuum steam heat from central heating plant.
8 - Automatic sprinkler systems, except chapel.
9 - Standard grade of plumbing.
10 - Finish floors will be concrete, wood, tile and marble.
11 - Preliminary estimated cost of the above buildings $1,500,000.00.

[It is important that in the reading of the contents of Mr. Boillot's letter to W. Rickert Fillmore it should be understood that the architect was carrying out Mr. Fillmore's dream, vision, ideas and plans concerning the complex of buildings that might someday be built at Unity Farm. Earlier Charles Fillmore had discussed with his sons that he could envision the day when all of the headquarters facilities at 9th to 10th streets on Tracy Avenue in Kansas City, Missouri would be closed and moved to a new country location. Once the original fifty-eight acres of farm land was purchased Rick Fillmore surely must have had a vision of what the proper use of the ground would be in a long range plan. Proof of this fact lies in these unfolding years of the history of the buildings and activities generated on the farm land and today's realization that no intended permanent building has ever been removed or replaced. This fact even includes such facilities as the club house, swimming pool and golf course which have been used continuously.]

[In the folder where Mr. Boillot's letter was found also was multiple copies of architectural drawings of the buildings, plus the original positioning of the buildings around the Administration building, fountains and the original Silent Unity building and the Tower. All of the buildings in the complex are connected with tunnels from each basement. This is a very far sighted plan for the Unity worker that needs to move from building to building especially in the harsh Missouri winters and summers. Those drawings, rendered in 1926, and the birds-eye view of the complex of buildings are so very nearly the same as what can be seen today. We can realize that Rick Fillmore was truly a visionary genius!]

Unity News November 6, 1926, "Work on the lake and dam is progressing rapidly. The light from the pump tower can be seen for miles. The drillers have just completed a dandy oil and gas well."

Unity News November 13, 1926, "The green house is completed, now that the heating was turned on for the first time last Monday. The Inn will soon have a supply of green stuff from the farm. The green house is heated with steam heat generated from the Unity oil supplies. The boiler heating unit is in a permanent uniquely designed building with a high exhaust stack. That building housed the office for the green houses and storage space for boxes, crates and the supplies used in the green house.

[That attractive building referred to as the Potting Shed, remains today and sits in the east parking lot of the Unity Village chapel. In its' stately position it draws much attention and praise for its' design from all who pass by. It is a true reminder of the early days of Unity Farm when the fuel supply under the farm ground silently supplied the buildings heat. And in addition it is a reminder of the mind set of Rick Fillmore for the design and the method of construction used for the buildings built prior to the 1940's.]

"Building materials are now being delivered to the farm on the recently installed switch line of the Missouri Pacific Railroad. The new road to the dam is nearly finished."

Unity News December 18, 1926, "The workers who have been entertained so delightfully at the farm Club House will be glad to know that a library is being started at the Club House."

Unity News December 24, 1926, "The workers are moving the big rock crusher from the dam site to the farm in preparation for road making."

Unity News December 31, 1926, "Skating was popular at the swimming pool on the farm over the Christmas holidays and several fancy figures were cut. Ralph Boileau says that he wrote his name and only put one period in it. The new garage for the Gables and the Boileaus is finished. With a room above it, affords Francis the seclusion he has needed in a study. Lowell will meet the farm workers again next Wednesday evening in the club house. These get together talks are voted a great success. The first crop of lettuce is now being harvested at the new green house."

Charles Fillmore's third book, Talks on Truth, was published in 1926, fifteen years after his first book Christian Healing.

In Lowell Fillmore's file in the library the following statement was found: "We have been asked why Unity does not carry advertisements in its periodicals. In 1926 Unity School of Christianity was declared exempt from the payment of federal income taxes by the United States Board of Tax Appeals. One of the considerations interring into the decision made by the court was the fact that no paid advertising was accepted in our magazines. Therefore, Unity does not carry paid advertisements in any of its literature."

1927 - Unity launched a new magazine Youth with this heading: "For all young people who find living the most intersting thing in life."

Articles entitled Two Messages To Youth by Charles and Myrtle Fillmore.

> "From Charles Fillmore. God bless the man who first invented youth. The man who first invented youth was Jehovah, Elohim's image and likeness, the superman of every man. Jehovah formed Adam of the 'dust of the ground.' Adam did not succumb to the old age idea until he had lived 930 years.
>
> We are warned to forget Adam and think about Christ. 'For as in Adam all die, so also in Christ shall all be made alive.' When the Jews attempted to bring Jesus under the race bondage of his ancestors he said, 'Before Abraham was born,

I am.' That is a good affirmation for all people who are following Jesus in the regeneration.

Youth is the natural state of man. When Jehovah breathed into man the breath of life there was no thought of old age. Instead of decrepitude years should bring man added vigor, vitality, wisdom, strength, and power. 'Ye who have followed me, in the regeneration . . . ye shall also sit upon twelve thrones, judging the twelve tribes of Israel,' sings the victorious Jesus.

'As he thinketh within himself, so is he.' It is possible always to be youthful. Continuous youth can be attained by conserving the vitality of the organism and directing it intelligently. Feebleness is not the result of years but of depleted vitality. Time does not bring on old age, but unrestrained passion does.

'Remember also thy Creator in the days of thy youth, before the evil days come, and the years draw nigh, when thou shalt say, I have no pleasure in them.' In the vigor of youth man revels in pleasure and repents in pain.

In the allegory of Adam and Eve in the Garden of Eden this is called eating of the tree of the knowledge of good and evil. Do not give yourself over to the sensations of the flesh (serpent). Listen for the still small voice of Jehovah within you. Meditate much and pray often and joy will be yours.

Do not think that religion will rob you of life's thrill. There is no joy that can compare with that of the pure life centered in Christ. Exalted thoughts rejuvenate the body and fill the soul with bliss. Cultivate contact with the kingdom of the heavens within your soul and you will realize what Jesus means when he says, 'That my joy may be in you."

"From Myrtle Fillmore. As I face the subject of youth, there comes to my awakening consciousness, not the definition and limitation of our ordinary use of the term, but an innate spirit of joy and expectation that belongs to life in all its manifestations.

That glorious time of life described in the word, youth, in truth has no beginning and no end. Youth denotes the soul's devotion consciously or unconsciously, to the God-urge within, which is inspiring the individual to unlimited vision; to realization of all with which the soul is endowed; to the attainment of that joyous estate to which we are created.

To you, beloved youth, whether ten years, or one hundred years have marked your progress in our midst, it is given to unfold the plan of God. Time, and years, are not factors in this unfoldment. 'We dwell in the consciousness of eternal youth, now.' The clear vision is yours to catch and to hold the beauty, and power, and life, and love, and light which know no change, no decline, no end. The power is yours to lay hold of the things of heaven and earth, to picture forth and to live the perfect pattern of life which you brought with you from God.

In this new magazine is given to us a blessed privilege, which we cherish. Through its pages, and on the wings of spiritual thought released day by day as we prepare to send forth the printed messages, we are joyously bearing witness with you to the Truth which shall make you immune to the ravages of time and age.

'There is a spirit in man, and the inspiration of the Almighty giveth them understanding.' You need not that any man should teach you the foolishness of limitations. You need not heed nor accept the suggestions of failure. You need not accept race thoughts of flesh heredity, or take as final the decree that man is born to die, or be satisfied with anything less than the fullest measure of success and health and the attainment of your highest ideals. The spirit of youth in you is the Spirit of God in you. You are of the Infinite, and there is no failure for you -- the only apparent failure is your failure to see and to claim as yours this truth of your being. The moment you catch the vision, you let flood your soul and your body that light and life which make you to know that all things are possible with you, now."

Article in Youth magazine. Marion Talley Sends a Real Message Direct to Readers of Youth.

"The editors have asked me to send through the pages of Youth a brief message to young people who are hoping, striving and studying to succeed. I suppose this is because, from their standpoint, the success that has come to me looks very large and imposing and awe-inspiring. Well, I may as well confess that it looks large and imposing and awe-inspiring to me, too. Sometimes I can hardly believe it myself. But it has taught me something -- this thing that you call success; and the best message I can send to other young people is to tell them what that something is.

I think of my voice as the gift of God. Of course it is; it couldn't come to me from any other source, because God is the only source of all that is good. I knew, a long time ago, that it was God's gift -- when I first began to use it, in the days when I first sang at Unity in Kansas City. And the thing that I have found out is that, as I use God's gift, it grows. I know that my voice has grown in beauty and power because I have used it. It has amazed me sometimes.

I am no older now than many of you who will read this. I'm nineteen. I know what you think and what you like and what you do. I think and like and do many of the same things. I believe that each of you, too, like me, has a gift of some kind. Maybe you can't sing as I can; but I can't paint, as perhaps you can -- or carry on a business, or write a book, or build houses, or manage people. I have my gift; but you have yours. You may think yours is a very small one compared with mine; but there was a time when I thought mine was small. And I know that if you will use your gift -- if you will give out what you have -- it will grow into a great one -- simply because that's the way it is with God's gifts. But you must use it, and not waste it. Giving it out doesn't mean throwing it away wantonly. Maybe you will have to make some sacrifices for it; I have made sacrifices that probably you don't even dream of. But oh, it's worth while!

People ask about my courage before audiences, my lack of stage fright! Well, to me it is a very simple thing. When I stood before the huge audience in the Metropolitan Opera House in New York for my debut -- when I faced the famous diamond horse-shoe! -- people said they marveled at my poise. But I was not afraid. Why should I be? I knew that the most sophisticated audience in America, if not in the world, was waiting to hear me, and that maybe they were not all hoping for my success. I knew that the cleverest critics of all the great papers were there to study and pass judgment upon me. I knew that hundreds of real musicians, some of them great, were listening. But I wasn't afraid. Because it seemed to me that if it was God's gift I had to give them I need not be concerned about their opinion of it. I knew that my voice only comes through me after all. It is from God -- and if I just let it come from him through me to them, it must be perfect as everything from him is perfect. I knew that he always takes care of that. So -- I just stood up and sang -- and loved it! And the people seemed pleased. I was happy -- oh, so happy! Not just because it was success for me, but because the sense that the great gift was flowing through me brought with it a joy, an exaltation, quite apart from the applause and the promise of fame and money and all that. It was just that I knew I'd been given something to give to them -- all I had to do was to give it. I did. And it was a beautiful experience. But even that night my voice grew!

Now this is a much longer letter than I planned to write. So, for that reason, I am not going to call it my 'message' at all, because I was asked for a brief message! The letter is the explanation of my message, which I think I can put very briefly indeed now. But it means so much! So I say, because I've found out what it means, to anyone with ambition and a talent there is just one possible, but one sure, road to success, and it is summed up in a word: Give! If you do, you will succeed. Truly, Marion Talley."

Weekly Unity January 29, 1927, "Unity City. Nearly seven years ago Unity School of Christianity acquired the first sixty acres of Unity farm, which is located fifteen miles southeast of Kansas City. The farm now comprises 1,100 acres of unusually fertile land.

Nature has blessed Unity farm in many ways. In addition to a very productive soil, the farm has both oil and gas wells. The oil wells are not 'gushers,' but they furnish sufficient to supply the heating plant at Unity headquarters in Kansas City, to oil the farm's roads, and to furnish enough gasoline for all the trucks and for the other farm machinery that is propelled by gasoline motors. In addition to the oil sands there are two gas sands, at depths of 480 and 550 feet, which supply natural gas of fine quality and in sufficient quantity to meet all needs. The gas heats all buildings (including hothouses) and boilers of drilling rigs on the farm. The gas pool has been explored one mile north and south and one and a half miles east and west.

The water supply at present is from springs and wells, but a dam is being built that will impound a lake of approximately twenty acres, with 75,000,000 gallons of water. The dam, which 100 men are now building, will cost about $100,000. The gorges and the hills in the vicinity of the dam are, in beauty and topography, compared to the Ozarks.

The improvements at the farm to date represent an outlay of more than half a million dollars. Plans for buildings to be erected in 1927-28, costing one and a half million dollars, are now in the hands of architects. Pictures of these buildings may be seen in the directors' room at 917 Tracy avenue, Kansas City, Missouri. It is expected that the Silent Unity department of the school will be moved to the farm this year, and other departments will be transferred as buildings for them are ready.

The building of the coast-to-coast highway from Washington to Los Angeles was a great thing for Unity farm. This highway runs through the farm, and shortens the road to Kansas City by about five miles. The automobile time from Kansas City to Unity farm now is only thirty minutes.

The fruit crop of Unity farm is no small item. There are 150 acres of fruit, which includes 7,500 apple trees, many grapevines, berries, and small fruits in large variety. Two thousand white Leghorn hens on the farm lay about 900 eggs daily. A large dairy has not so far been established. Eight cows supply the farm hands with milk. The Cedar Creek valley, running two miles through the farm, is rich with blue grass, and looks tempting to the dairyman.

Unity farm has a neighbor only two miles distant, the thriving town of Lee's Summit, with 1,500 population.

In addition to its many other resources Unity farm has several large quarries of white and yellow limestone, of which all its buildings and walls are constructed. A clubhouse, an apartment house, a swimming pool, a tennis court, a golf course, and comfortable and artistic residences are already finished at the farm. A well, 1,500 feet deep produces sulphosaline water; the analysis shows it to be identical with the sulphosaline water at Excelsior Springs, twenty-five miles to the north.

The activities of the Unity School of Christianity at its headquarters in Kansas City have crowded the buildings there to capacity. More room is needed, and much more room will be needed as time goes on. Unity's eleven periodicals are rapidly growing in circulation. Greater numbers of lessons and books are printed at each new edition. Each year more letters are received than were received the year before, multitudes are asking for prayers. The work has outgrown its present quarters. The pressroom and the bindery are crowded. The office desks are coming closer and closer together. Stock is being piled in every available corner. It is evident that we need more room. The work must not be hampered by lack of space. At Unity farm there is abundant room for expansion. The farm seems to be the logical place to carry on the enormous world-redeeming work that Unity is doing. There will need to be buildings, many buildings. The architect has planned them with floor space double our present space, and provision is made for additions. Unity farm is to be the location of a Unity city. 'Unity City' may not be the name of the community which the Unity trustees plan, but it will bear the name 'Unity,' with a suffix sufficient to designate it as no mean city. Suggestions for a name will be received gladly.

The question naturally arises in the minds of you who read this: 'Whence has the money come to buy all this land and make these improvements, and where is more money coming from to carry out the plans of the future?' The answer is that the money to carry on this work has come from Unity people all over the world. Many of them have made offerings; others have purchased Unity bonds. Still others have given to the Unity School considerable amounts, under an agreement that they are to receive interest therefrom as long as they live. This explanation of Unity farm and its progress up to the present is an invitation to you to lend a hand in this attempt to develop an educational center based on the principles adopted by the early followers of Jesus, who had all things in common.

All Unity property is held by the corporation, to be used by the community as a whole. The homes at Unity City will be owned by Unity School, and each occupant will be asked to pay for his accommodation, as rental, a certain percentage of the initial cost of his home. Those who spiritually understand the Truth taught by Jesus and who are able to render needed assistance to the cause will be eligible to become residents of Unity City. The industrial activities will be varied; the idea of a self-sustaining body of people will be fundamental.

The paramount ideal of Unity City will be the setting up, on earth, of the kingdom of the heavens, to be established right here in the earth. We look forward to the fulfillment of the vision of John as given in the 21st chapter of Revelation.

Unity City shall be first, last, and always an educational city, a community where all the people will constantly be at school, learning more each day about the law of God and the application of that law to human affairs and broadcasting this knowledge to the world. It will be a community school inculcating spiritual, ethical, and industrial knowledge. All members of the city, regardless of age, will be pupils of the school. Special summer schools will be held as soon as suitable buildings can be furnished for meeting places and as dwellings for students.

If the Lord moves you to help this good work we shall be glad to hear from you. If you are giving your surplus to educational institutions, let us explain to you the advantages of the Unity School of Christianity. If you desire a 6% investment, investigate our coupon notes. If you want an income from your money for the present, with an ultimate gift of the principal to the school, we will guarantee 6% under such an arrangement.

In the bonds of the brotherhood of Jesus Christ we greet you. Trustees of the Unity School of Christianity, Kansas City, Missouri."

Unity News February 19, 1927, "The ladies on the farm always enjoy their trips to Kansas City when Billy Bergen drives. Besides driving carefully he finds time to be helpful in a number of ways. Bill Bergen was a new employee, hired as an auto mechanic and driver for Grandmother and Myrtle Fillmore."

Unity News February 26, 1927, "A new born well turned out to be triplets. It contained oil, gas and coal."

Unity News March 5, 1927, "Francis Gable recently purchased a ten acre farm for an investment, it is near Unity Farm. The plans for a new Silent Unity building at Unity Farm have been completed. Contract and specifications for the new lakes filtration system were signed March 8, 1927. Rick Fillmore collaborated with the architectural firm of Boillot and Lauck in the design work for the new Silent Unity building and the Tower, often referred to as the Campanile."

Unity News March 12, 1927, "Ernest C. Wilson was the leader of the Harmonial Institute of San Diego, California in 1922. He was drawn close to the Unity teachings and has been a Unity student for many years before that. In 1925 he became associated with the Unity Healing Center in Cleveland, Ohio. In April 1926 he took full charge of the Cleveland Unity Center. Now March 1927 he comes to Unity headquarters to be editor of Youth magazine. In Charles Fillmore's writing he discussed the emergence of Unity City."

Unity News March 26, 1927, "The new rock road at Unity Farm from the rock crusher to the green house is finished."

Unity News April 2, 1927, "There are 10,000 tomato plants now at the farm. They will cover five acres this year. There are 15,000 baby chicks at the farm. It is planned to raise 45,000 chickens. There is now a big sign advising motorists of their nearness to Unity Farm now in place."

Unity News April 16, 1927, "The new apartment house at the farm is being referred to as the Silent Unity apartment house, but needs a new name."

Unity News April 30, 1927, "The big red barn which stood near Dan Andrews house at Unity Farm has been razed and in its' place a large garage has been built to shelter some of the farm trucks and cars. The new dwellers in the Chateau de Lac say the view of the new lake is charming. A soda fountain has been installed in the Tea Room on the first floor of the Chateau de Lac."

[The new Silent Unity apartment building, later referred to as the Chateau de Lac, was built just north of the natural amphitheater. It is three stories high including the basement which was called the first floor and housed the Tea Room and soda fountain. In later years this building was simply called the Annex. It remains as one of the original buildings built to house students, visitors and guests.]

Unity News May 7, 1927, "The house built for Mrs. Laura Mac Mahan was occupied by her for less than a year. After her death it was discovered that she had willed the house to Unity. Soon after its' transfer of ownership Rick Fillmore had physical changes made so it could be converted into a hotel. No meals were ever served to guests at the hotel. [That structure, that sets on the hill west of the swimming pool and abutts the golf course, remains today with its' original charm and distinctive design character.]

[From May 10, 1927 there was a constant flow of letters to and from Lowell Fillmore and H. Emily Cady until August 23, 1933. Dr. Cady was a Christian Science Minister and writer. Both Charles and Myrtle were impressed with her writings, communicated with her and she wrote an article for the December 7, 1892 Unity magazine. Later she made trips to Kansas city to meet with the Fillmore's. In most every trip she and Charles argued about religion philosophy and she would leave their meetings and return home. Soon after she would write Charles and apologize for leaving upset and tell him that she could now see his views. Such was not the case with Dr. Cady and Lowell. They had a very warm relationship and he was always very appreciative of the articles she would write and send for Unity publications. Lowell never mentioned paying her for the articles. But in Dr. Cady's letters to Lowell she always mentioned the gift that Lowell would include in his letters to her. In her late years she continued to write articles for Unity magazines and she praised Lowell for his payments and told him that they were her only income. She was a great supporter of Unity and the Unity principles that the Fillmore's established.]

Unity News May 14, 1927, "Mrs. Hall is in charge of Casa de los Amigos, the hotel, where visitors will be made comfortable this summer. The stakes marking the sites for future business buildings of Unity City are all set. Ground for the second green house was broken this week."

Unity News May 21, 1927, "Coming out party for Unity Farm. For years we have been coming out to Unity Farm, but now Unity Farm is coming out! It is to be informally presented , oh, very informally. Everybody in Kansas City connected with or interested in Unity is invited. Date June 18, 1927. We'll have good music for the open air dance floor this summer, at the amphitheater location. Rex has installed an electrical device whereby we get good music loud enough to be heard almost all over the farm. Rick says that the new walks, the drive and the turn around back of the apartment house have been finished.

The dam for the new lake is now finished and a road will be built across the top of it. This will provide access to one of the most beautiful parts of the farm, which up to now has been closed to exploration. The concrete pouring tower, which has been used at the dam, will be moved to the new building sites and the new buildings will be started immediately. The swimming pool has been painted a beautiful blue and was filled this week. There will be no peaches at the farm this year, but plenty of cherries, apples, plums and grapes. The recently poured section of #50 highway completes the road to the farm from Kansas City without a detour."

Unity News May 28, 1927, "The apartment house and the hotel have not been officially named. Chateau de Lac is a name in jest given by someone. Rick is asking for suggestions for names for both."

Unity News June 4, 1927, "Howard Colby says that the week end visits to the farm, or what we now call the Unity Country Club and which will soon be Unity City, is always most refreshing and inspiring to him. The welfare and progress of Unity City can't be beaten and the most beautiful and radiant city in the world will be the outcome! The green houses have had a phone installed. Flowers and plants can now be ordered direct and will be delivered.

Seven building sites have been staked out for Unity City and construction will begin soon. Another green house is being built, the third. Ten-thousand carnations that will bloom next winter have been planted. The club house road is being paved with a new kind of material and will be known as the 'rawhide' road. The new truck garage which is being built is seventy-five feet long. A new gasoline roller will take the place of the old steam roller on the farm roads. The old rock quarry is to be converted into a volleyball court. The new amphitheater is nearing completion.

Unity News July 9, 1927, "Reunion of the Fillmore's. The Fourth of July was a big day for the Fillmore family. They were all present at the family reunion at the farm. There were four generations there: Grandmother Fillmore, Charles and Myrtle, Rick and Harriet, Charles Rickert and Rosemary plus Myrtle's family, the Pages."

[Myrtle was the eighth of nine children, several of her family members followed her to the Midwest. One sister lived in Nebraska, others lived in the Kansas City area. There is a Page area in the Kansas City Mount Washington cemetery where several of the Page family are buried. Also, in that Page area are the graves of Royal and his wife, Frances.]

<u>Unity News</u> July 16, 1927, " Poem by Francis Gable entitled:

Unity Farm

Nestling over hill and dale;
Giant rocks and lowly swale;
While the sturdy hardwood trees
Rustle 'neath each balmy breeze;
Like a velvet carpet green,
Rolling visitors may be seen,
Touched by shade spots, dark and cool,
All surrounding limpit pool;

Beauty framed by nature's plan,
Other joy nooks shaped by man;
Fairest spot to which to roam,
This is Unity's new home.

Did you know that there is a hay press at the farm and hay is being baled at the rate of two-hundred or more bales a day? That there are new horses at the Farm? Last week a team of horses, a team of 'hard tails' and a white horse were bought. That the dam is completed and that there is all ready a small lake behind it? That an eight-thousand gallon gas tank is being put in just south of the green houses? This tank will hold a carload of gasoline. That the concrete pouring tower has been erected on the Silent Unity building site? Work has began in earnest on this new construction. Unity dam: When it was found that sufficient water could not be obtained from wells Unity officials decided to construct a large dam to compound water adequate to provide for the new Unity City development and the present activities at the farm. This dam, when it is full will compound 75,000,000 gallons of water. The dam is 20 feet long, the lake covers about eighteen acres of land, the water is fifty feet deep in some places. Water mains are now being laid from the filter plant at the dam to the site of the new buildings being erected on the farm.

There are now two ponies, Prince and Black Cyclone, Charles Rickert's and Frances' and three others sent for the children to ride.

The new garage and stockroom are finished and the carpenter shop enlarged. Under these is the basement built for a mushroom cellar. An addition is being added to the bunkhouse and to Mrs. Buckley's dining room. The water works building is nearly completed and the pipe line is laid. The new entrance to the Farm is ready and the county is fixing all the road approaches to new 50 highway. Oat thrashing began this week. The new garage, storeroom and the electricians shop is complete. The new kitchenette apartment house for Unity employees has eight five room efficiency kitchenettes. Unity Tavern, previously referred to as the Tea Room, is on the ground floor, [basement] of the apartment house where meals and fountain service are offered.

<u>Then and now at Unity Farm</u>:

In April 1919 the first part of Unity Farm was purchased. The first tract comprised fifty-seven and thirty-eight hundredths acres. Today Unity Farm comprises 1,113.144 acres. This represents a total of twelve different farms that have been acquired by twelve different purchases. During the last eight years many improvements have been made at the farm for the comfort of Unity workers and their families. In fact, it seems hardly possible that only eight years have passed since what is now Unity Farm was country. Gas pipes, electric cables and a sewerage system serve the residents of the farm, making it modern in every respect. Several hard surfaced roads have been completed and more are in the process of construction.

Hundreds of acres are wooded and are excellent for hiking. A railroad siding on the Missouri-Pacific railway provided train transportation for construction materials. In addition to the conveniences provided for Unity workers, there are three green houses where fresh vegetables are grown the year round for Unity Inn and for residents of the farm, there are two machine shops, ten barns, three poultry houses, twenty-two wells the majority of which are furnishing either oil or gas for the farm, a rock crusher, a large excavator, sixteen autos, trucks and tractors, two filter houses, two well houses, one farm office building, one amphitheater and dance floor, six cottages, four of which are vacation cottages, fifteen farm employee homes, six other residences for employees of the school and an apartment house with eight apartments for the workers who wish to live at the farm.

Who's who at the farm: Some day Unity Farm will be the site of Unity headquarters. A corps of workers is busy continually at the farm preparing the new Unity home. It is time for all the headquarter's employees to learn who's who at Unity Farm. Rick Fillmore is the firm's representative at the farm. He has completed the ensemble of the completed city. There is nothing dinky about his plans. He visions an establishment of magnitude and beauty that is rather astounding. He and his family have lived at the farm for six years. His home and its' furnishing are things of beauty. By the way, not the least of these is Rosemary, Rick's little daughter.

May Harris is the hostess at the club house. Her's is a difficult task; to encourage the youngsters to have a good time in the club house yet to restrain them from tearing it down. The old place still stands.

Dan Andrews is manager of the farm. When he speaks of agriculture he says the word reverently. He went to an agricultural college and absorbed so much knowledge that his hair hasn't room to grow. He knows gobs of things about soils, fruits, livestock and bugs. The bugs are the most mysterious he says. He knows what makes the peaches blush, but claims that he has nothing to do with it.

Al Osenberg is the construction foreman. He sees to it that the various projects grow according to blue prints. While the dam was being built, Rick was telling Al one day about some ambitious plans for the future. 'Down there below the dam, on that hillside, we're going to build Italian villas,' said Rick. "Wouldn't you like to live in one of them?' 'No, no,' said Al, 'not by a dam site.'

Grandmother Fillmore is the patron saint of the farm. She dispenses cookies to the children and sheds her benign presence on all.

Mrs. Law is manager of Unity Farm tavern. Try her food. She needs no further recommendation.

Mrs. Hall is head of the hotel and if you want to see what a perfect hostess she is go over there and stay all night.

Sandy Mac Nabb is probably the best known character on the farm. Nominally he belongs to little Rick; actually he belongs to everybody who visits the farm. He is the ideal reception committee. He escorts every outgoing car exactly as far as the road that leads to the tennis courts, that far and no farther. Vegetarians will be shocked to hear that after Sandy has shown a few dozen cars the way out on a hot day, he becomes a 'hot dog'.

We should like to have you meet the rest of the farm folk; A.E. Anderson, green house attendant; William Bergen, mechanic; E.L. Boyer, poultry man; Thurman Carroll, general man and caretaker of the horses; George Cravens and his son Ward Cravens, landscape gardeners and tennis court attendants; Floyd Cummings, electrician; Frank Curtis, golf course attendant and tractor operator; Herman Da Costa, 'Sparky', handsome life guard when he isn't working in the orchard; Al Kinnaman, gardener and 'pony man', Dallas Kreigh, who has done general work at the farm since it was first bought; L.W. Law, general work; Warren McGaugh, landscape gardener; Max Michells, manager of the green houses; Claude Sager, utility man; Amos Schlaback, oil man; Rollin T. Slatcup, green house attendant; H.D. Stilley, golf course attendant; Oliver Wakeman, general farm work; Charlie Watson, milkman; J.D. Woods, stock clerk; Arthur Zebley, blacksmith, G.S. Beals, watchman at the dam; June Adams, helps May Harris with her hostessing and J.N. McLeod, keeps the greens green."

Unity News July 30, 1927, "On July 24, 1927 WOQ was one of fifty-three radio stations that comprised the largest hookup ever to broadcast the same program simultaneously and included stations in Hawaii, England and Australia. The program consisted of a musical concert from New York and a lecture by Judge Rutherford in Toronto, Ontario Canada."

Unity News August 6, 1927, "Band concert at the Farm. The first in a series of Sunday evening concerts by Unity band was given last Sunday evening in the amphitheater and drew an audience of between 250 and 300 people. The band leader is Mr. Carl Franghiser and the quartet that sang is made up of the following; soprano, Maxine Korfhage Frye, contralto, Maxine Martin Stoves, tenor, Robert Newton and bass, Howard Reynolds. After several numbers by the band, Charles Fillmore introduced Ella Pomeroy, who gave a short lesson, then the band played again. Following this Charles Fillmore addressed the audience on the general teachings of Unity school."

Unity News August 13, 1927, "On Sunday the Unity band will give its' second concert at the farm amphitheater. A special invitation is given to the farm workers."

Unity News August 20, 1927, poem by Ernest C. Wilson:

Magic

There is a magic word which gives,
To men a little glimpse of God
Which stirs the best in human breast,
And lifts men from the clod.

When someone speaks this magic word,
That should not be its' end;
Its' better used by two then one
That magic word is Friend.

Unity News August 27, 1927, Includes pictures of what Unity City will look like when completed.

Charles Rickert and Frances Fillmore have been enrolled in the first garde at Hazel Grove grade school.

Unity News September 17, 1927, "There are now seventeen goats at the farm. Charles and Myrtle prefer goat milk!"

Unity News September 24, 1927, "Rick promises that this winter at the farm will remind one of a winter in the Alps, with skating on the new lake, skiing, tobogganing, goats and Swiss cheese! There are two-thousand pullets at the farm laying eggs. The old rock quarry is to be made into a winter picnic ground with ovens. Unity has purchased drill rigs and will do all of its' own drilling now. The bunkhouse and Mrs. Buckley's house have been newly plastered."

Unity News October 1, 1927, "Rick announced that there are now dances held at the amphitheater each Wednesday and Saturday nights."

Unity News November 5, 1927, "The farm is to be equipped with its' own telephone service. Dial will be used and intercommunications will be easy. Lowell and Alice Fillmore have one of the apartments, now."

Unity News November 12, 1927, "Part of the club house road has been resurfaced with a coating of road asphalt. The road that leads by the boarding house and by the two, two-family houses is being regraded and widened."

Unity News December 3, 1927, "The fifth floor was added to the campanile, tower, this past week. The building of Lowell and Alice Fillmore's new home is progressing rapidly. The new home sits high on the hill to the east of the club house/swimming pool area."

Unity News December 17, 1927, "The farm folk are enjoying the radio that Mrs. J.C. Rodahaffer presented to the club house. The Sunday morning meetings are held in the club house and the regular Sunday morning services from Kansas City Unity auditorium come to them over Unity's radio station WOQ. Those persons that drive to the farm this Christmas season will be greeted by an immense Christmas tree, brightly lighted. The tree stands near the campanile and can be seen from the highway. The farm looks very Christmassy, with all its' decorations. The club house, hotel and apartment house are beautifully decorated. The farm folk extend a cordial invitation to the city folk to come and enjoy the sight."

Unity News December 31, 1927, "The Christmas party at the club house was a howling success! The workman are roofing Lowell and Alice's house, its' beginning to look like a house now. Several brave people skated on the big lake."

1928 - Unity News February 1, 1928, "Under the expert management of the Boyer family, the poultry department at the farm is coming into the limelight. A $500.00 imperial cockerel from Detaubard special stock has been bought to add to the Unity stock. There are two new calves at the dairy. The green house has a new double capacity boiler ready to be installed. The sweet peas are blooming to the tune of eight-thousand a week."

Unity News February 16, 1928, "Arthur Zebley, commonly known as 'Shorty', is a mender of everything from scrapers on the road rollers, to curling irons, all breakdowns and wrecks are sent over to him to be made new again. He sharpens ice skates, also and does all the iron work that beautifies the landscape at the farm, including all the hand rails, and old iron gas and electric light fixtures. His place of business is in the power house and he is just starting the first sixty antique lamps for the new buildings."

There are several new rolls for the player piano at the club house. A point of interest is the goat farm where there are three new kids. All the farm wagons and one truck have new paint jobs a sure sign of spring coming. The construction force has resumed work on the Silent Unity building on the farm."

Unity News April 2, 1928, "Rosemary wears the pants. The scene opens at Rick's home, Unity Farm. Early morning, Charles, age seven and Rosemary, two and one half years of age, dressing in the nursery. Loud, contentious voices float down to the living room. Papa Rick calls up, 'What's the matter with you kids? Why don't you come down to breakfast?' Charles in tears, 'Rosemary won't let me have my clothes.' Papa Rick, 'Take 'em away from her.' Charles, 'I can't. She's got 'em on. She says she's a boy and she's going to school in my clothes!'

All the concrete is poured and all the floors are finished for the first structure of Unity City, the campanile, up to where the water tower installs. The foundation for the Silent Unity building is nearly finished. Monday several flocks of geese were flying over the farm. The men were working in the new building and perhaps the light blinded the geese. At any rate they flew right through the opening of the fourth floor of the Tower!"

Unity News April 16, 1928, "Unity Farm livestock. Unity Farm is teeming with life. Not only are the orchards bearing fruit and the fields yielding bumper crops, the oil and gas wells overflowing, but the livestock is increasing as well. We now have a number of horses, a dairy, a goat farm and poultry.

The horses number sixteen and are all draft with exception of two saddle horses. Every day one may see eight of these sturdy workers hauling dirt form the excavation for the new buildings. The other eight horses are being used for general farm work. Of course, one must not overlook the three Shetland ponies. There is Black Cyclone, Charles Rickert's mount; Prince, who belongs to Frances and a third pony that is visiting at the farm indefinitely.

Heading the dairy herd is Glenwod's Sequel Boy, a pedigreed Guernsey bull that was given to Unity Farm last year by Mrs. Scott Durand of Crab Tree farm, Lake Bluff, Illinois. Mrs. Scott has a wonderful stock farm at Lake Bluff and wishing to share her success with Unity, she sent Sequel Boy to live at Unity Farm. The remainder of the herd consists of three pure blooded Jersey cows, seven Guernseys and two calves; one is a Jersey and the other is a Guernsey. Claude Sager, who has charge of the dairy, is marketing $150.00 worth of A1 dairy products each month.

Mr. Anderson has charge of the goat herd and we hope that he will not be like the lady who complained of the lack of butter fat in her goats milk. You remember, when she voiced her complaint in the presence of her herd, one of the goats instantly turned to butt 'er. We hope that Mr. Anderson may never have cause to complain of thin milk, but if he does we're hoping he will use diplomacy. Last year Mr. Layne, of Independence, Missouri gave us his herd of twenty-six goats, which included Nubia, who is fourteen years old. Who now has three generations of her own descendants with her. And later, a second herd of goats were purchased from Dickey farms, most of the animals being registered stock. Bill William, two does and three kids are Togginburgs; Billy Whiskers, three does and one kid are Saanens and the rest are Nubians. Nubian among goats means what Jersey does among milk cows. Imperial Winfred Mountaineer is the registered thoroughbred of the Nubian herd. He is pure white and quite distinguished in appearance. By the way, have you tasted any of the goats milk at the Inn? About thirteen quarts of this milk are obtained daily. Some of the milk is sold and the rest is given to the kids.

Our poultry farm is in charge of Mr. Bowyer and family. We now have about six-thousand chickens, most of them young ones. Each day Mr. Bowyer gathers an average of 550 eggs, which are sold to the Inn, to the farm folk and used to supply the incubators. All of this years hatching, nearly ten-thousand chicks, have been from farm eggs. The eggs, with a few exceptions, are sent to Lee's Summit for hatching and each egg is weighted separately and must measure up to a certain standard before being sent to the incubator. There are 3,250 eggs in the incubators now and the last setting of 3,500 eggs will go in today, April 16th. Lindbergh, or 'Lindy' the $500.00 rooster and his flock of blooded hens have a private run. The eggs from this flock are being hatched on the farm. All ready Lindy is the proud father of forty-five chicks and 250 eggs are now in the incubator. During April and May more of these eggs will be incubated and by summer time should be a large flock of thoroughbred chicks. An open air chicken house twenty feet by sixty feet is now being constructed for these chicks, so that when they are eight weeks old they can be turned out of doors for exercise.

Surely the farm is growing. Life everywhere. Even a new city springing up overnight and the Joy of the Lord is over all. The Sprague family have moved into the second house on the Stout farm, behind where the Zebley family lives. Mr. Sprague is the orchard man. In 1928 subscriptions to Unity magazine reached 589,000. Mr. & Mrs. Mason and family have moved into the upper floor of the house at the Daudna place. Mr. Mason takes care of the horses. We wish to present Mr. Pippitt, the new policeman and watchman at the farm. 'He will ride a horse,' Rick says, 'and wear a uniform.' The progress being made at the farm is remarkable. The new telephone system is automatic, has eighteen phones installed and is our own system that takes no outside operation. The workers at the green house have been setting out trees and shrubbery around the lake. A new overhead sprinkler system is being installed over the large garden on the farm. Two large bags of gladiolus bulbs were received from California. Next year approximately ten-thousand should be blooming on the farm.

Lowell and Alice Fillmore moved into their new house May 1, 1928. They took Frances, Royal's daughter, into their home to live with them until her 21st birthday.

<u>Unity News</u> May 1, 1928, "Out at Unity Farm by Frances Simmons.

'Have you seen an apple orchard in the spring? in the spring?
An English apple orchard in the spring?
When the pink cascades were falling and the silver brooklets brawling
and the cuckoo bird is calling, 'In the spring!'

If you have not, then you may feast your eyes and other senses on the beauties and wonders of a Unity apple orchard that contains 7,500 trees. There are 3,000 Jonathans, 1,500 Grimes Golden, 1,500 York Imperial, 750 Yellow Transparents and 750 Delicious and Winesaps. They're from three to eight years old and in about five years will reach maturity, when they should yield about 75,000 bushels a year. Each month, from April to October, the trees are sprayed with a mixture containing five different chemicals. The ground is cultivated during the spring and summer months and in the spring a commercial fertilizer is used on the grounds. The trees are pruned during the fall and winter months, when they are dormant. Mr. Sprague and Mr. Law are in charge of the orchards and Mr. Law supervises the making of the delicious cider that is served at the farm and at the Kansas City Inn. About 100 gallons are made each year.

Not only has Unity Farm an apple orchard, but it also boasts a peach orchard of 400 trees. Next year these trees will have to be thinned out, as they are now too close together. Cherry and plum trees are scattered over the farm and about thirty of each kind are bearing fruit. There is an acre of blackberry bushes and there are twelve acres of grapevines. The annual yield from this vineyard should be about sixty tons of grapes. Did you know that last year at the Sedalia State fair some of the Unity farm grapes were entered in the Jackson Country group which won the blue ribbon?

The fields too are giving forth a rich harvest. Sixty acres are planted in wheat, eighty-five in oats and one-hundred in corn and soy beans. Some of the grain is sold and some is fed to the livestock. Last year 1,200 bushels of soy beans were sold and recently 1,000 bushels of last years corn were marketed. A short time ago six carloads of Timothy hay were sold to the Kansas City market. This hay was cut and baled at the farm and the first two carloads were reported to be the best hay received on the Kansas City market.

The farm is engaging in a new venture this year. Fifteen acres are being planted in sorghum cane. Plans are underway to install an old fashion sorghum mill and to make 1,500 gallons of sorghum molasses.

The Unity Farm Sunday school wishes to thank the Fillmore's and Ralph Boileau for the love offerings they have sent at various times. Last Sunday there were forty-two persons in attendance. This is our largest attendance on record.

The white ants at the farm are not starving. Lately they have been living pretty high on practically all the main beams that support the floor of Ralph Boileau's living room. And not being satisfied with that, they have helped themselves to the floor of Earl Ackerman's office.

Mr. Hawkens, the new electrician, will do all the wiring and roughing-in on the Silent Unity building,"

Unity News May 8, 1928, "Out at Unity Farm, by Frances Simmons. Oil production at Unity Farm. Among the many activities at Unity farm, by no means the least, is that of oil production. At this time there are thirteen oil wells in operation, producing an average of thirteen barrels of oil daily. In 1922 Unity decided to drill for oil, although there had been several non-productive wells drilled near the Unity Farm. Unity was not daunted and its' faith was rewarded, for at the depth of 300 feet gas was struck. The drilling was continued for another 100 feet when more gas was struck. Oil was also struck. This well was shot on August 2nd. Later in the fall two more wells were drilled, each producing about the same amount of gas and oil. The first supply of gas was consumed by Grandmother Fillmore's cook stove.

Later, as the farm grew, other stoves were supplied with gas from wells on the farm. The production of oil and gas at Unity Farm has steadily increased. In 1925 alone, five wells were brought in. The oil is pumped by a big engine in the power house into a 500 barrel storage tank, next to which is a refinery. The crude oil is run into the refinery and is heated to a temperature of 400 degrees Fahrenheit, the heat separating from it a lighter liquid that is sent through cooled coils where it condenses into gasoline. This gasoline partially supplies the farm trucks and tractors. The crude oil runs about seven percent gasoline and the residue is used as fuel oil in the various buildings on the farm. Twenty-one wells have been drilled on the farm and only four of these have proved to be dry wells. Two wells were drilled to a depth of 1,500 feet and then were abandoned. Two other wells are producing gas only, no oil. Every three or four years, the wells must be cleaned out. A drilling machine has been purchased for this purpose and also for drilling more wells.

The powerhouse, besides housing the pumping engine, contains an electric welder and other equipment for repair work. Arthur Zebley is in charge of this work. He also makes all the iron fixtures that are used to beautify the buildings at the farm. And that is not all. Arthur mends anything from curling irons to tractors and does it with a smile and a cheery word, which is characteristic of all Unity workers. On April

30th, 755 sacks of cement were used in mixing the largest amount of concrete ever poured at Unity farm in one day."

From Weekly Unity May 19, 1928:

> **The Purpose of Unity**
>
> "Unity School is a school devoted to prayer and study of the methods used by Jesus Christ. Unity School does not wish to take men and women away from their regular churches. Its' purpose is to give them a better understanding of what all Christian churches teach. It bases its' teachings on the Old and New Testaments. Unity literature gives the reader a new appreciation of his religion, strengthens his faith in the teachings of the Bible and makes his religion acceptable not because he has inherited it, but because it appeals to his common sense. Protestants, Jews and Catholics alike commend Unity literature and declare that they find it wholesome and acceptable."

Unity News June 30, 1928, "All the concrete has been poured for the second floor of the Silent Unity building and the columns to support the roof are being set. Excavation has been started on the sewers for the next building."

Unity News July 14, 1928, "The Silent Unity building is now roofed. Mr. & Mrs. Flynn have moved into one of the apartments. He is now in charge of the construction at Unity Farm."

Unity News July 21, 1928, "Mr. Pippett has left the farm and Frank George is now the farm policeman."

Unity News August 18, 1928, "Preparations for this years convention are complete. The pool has been cleaned and filled, the roads have been widened and oiled, the tents are up, the camping ground is finished, the parking space is fixed, the building is ready and cafeteria equipment is set up on the first floor of the new Silent Unity building. If you haven't seen the new Silent Unity building come and go through it - its' great!

A booklet was published; Unity Convention souvenir program August 19th through 29th, 1928. The sixth annual Unity convention. Speakers included; H.B. Jeffery, Georgianna Tree West, May (Whitney) Rowland, Irwin Gregg, Douglas De Vorso, E.V. Ingraham, Charles H. Watts and Charles, Myrtle, Lowell and Rickert Fillmore. This up to date information was given in the program. There are now 432 Unity employees of which 90 are in Silent Unity. There are now 1,200 acres on the Unity Farm. There are about 1,300 Unity centers that carry a full line of Unity literature.

The souvenir program had many Unity pictures including, at the center of the booklet, a panorama view of Unity Farm. On August 26, 1928 the Silent Unity building was dedicated and consecrated to the work of Jesus Christ. On August 25, 1928 the Kansas City Star newspaper had a feature article about Unity Farm and its' convention. In it was stated that the new Unity Farm Silent Unity building will cost, when completed, approximately $250,000.00 and the nearby Tower $50,000.00 to $60,000.00. One-hundred tents were set up for the many Unity people coming to the convention to stay in. During the ten day conference it rained almost constantly, making the ground muddy. The building was just a shell at this time, but it was a haven out of the rain! Not only did it have the cafeteria serving meals it also had rest room facilities and showers set in that were temporary. But it was a joyful time for the 300 that attended."

Unity News September 1, 1928, "More than 6,000 names were sealed in the cornerstone of the Silent Unity building last Sunday."

Unity News September 29, 1928, "The newest thing at the farm is the new outdoor oven at the picnic grounds, it burns wood and was designed by Rick Fillmore."

Unity News October 28, 1928, "The lake is being emptied in order to mend leaks in the dam. It is estimated that it well take nine months for the lake to refill itself."

Unity News November 3, 1928, "A gas and oil combination furnace has been installed in the apartment building. More than 500 gallons of cider have been made at the farm this fall. The brick work on the campanile is finished and the tile roof is being put on the Silent Unity building."

Unity News November 17, 1928, "Unity School is granted new wave length. Beginning November 11th Unity's radio station WOQ is now licensed to use its full power of 1,000 watts at a frequency of 610 kilocycles. It now shares time with Kansas City radio station WDAF. New equipment has been ordered and will make Unity school four times more powerful than before."

Unity News November 23, 1928, "Will wonders never cease? We stated in the news that when the lake was drained it would take nine months to fill. However, during a recent rain the lake filled in less than twenty-four hours with the valves open and water running out of the dam all the time! The partitions are finished in the Silent Unity building and the workers will start stuccoing soon."

Charles Fillmore made the decision that plans should be made for a new Unity church in Kansas City. A search for finding land in an area of Kansas City that was being developed was chosen and a lot was selected in the Kansas City, Missouri Country Club District at 47th St. and Jefferson for a new Unity Temple. The implementation of the 'Unity Temple Covenant Plan' was accepted by the public and an outpouring of gifts followed. A chart showing the purchase of the property, for the Temple beginning January 1929 with yearly installment payments of $5,000.00 was found in the Unity files.

Beginning in 1923 when Rick Fillmore moved to Unity Farm and then in 1928 when Lowell moved to the farm, each paid rent for his house in accordance to rules. [Which still prevail today.]

[Rick Fillmore collaborated with the architectural firm of Boillot and Lauck of Kansas City, Missouri in designing all floor plans for the Silent Unity building and the campanile tower. Also, another of the joint efforts was the designing of the Terrace Tea Room. It was perhaps one of the most beautiful and uniquely designed buildings on Unity Farm and Rick had much to do with this creation! It was built to the north of the apartment house which is just north of the amphitheater.

The new Terrace Tea Room replaced the Tea Room, also referred to as the Unity Tavern, which was in the basement of the apartment house. The design of the building followed the lay of the land, which was a hill. The main entrance to this new Tea Room was reached by two sets of steps and a long walkway from the street below. There was no parking area planned for this new building. Most of those arriving by car parked in the large parking area at the amphitheater to the south. Much of the pedestrian traffic came from the hotel, homes, golf course and other sports activity areas or from the new Silent Unity and Tower buildings. They came east to the Terrace Tea Room through the comfort station area that also housed the lily ponds.

The new Tea Room had five levels tucked into the hill. The top level was on the same plane as the parking area behind the east side of the apartment house. At this level of the Tea Room was a large open air terrace with a one story building on the north side. It was the width of the dining room below, but shallow in depth. Multiple doors opened onto the terrace and the interior room was called the Banquet room and housed banquet tables, chairs and supplies for serving guests. There was no access from the terrace room to the dining room below, its' purpose was for storage, but also its' position shielded any cold wind from the north. It also was a haven for shelter when a summer rain would invade one of the many parties held under the stars.

This was especially a popular location for those that had enjoyed the band concerts or other events in the amphitheater to first come for dinner or after a concert for soda fountain treats. Sidewalks in front and behind the apartment house gave easy access to the Tea Room from the amphitheater. From the upper terrace two sets of stairways, one going south and the other west led to the lower terrace. Each terrace had stone walls on the exterior sides with heavy concrete wide caps that held several large wrought iron fixtures that had triple light bulbs in the center of the top of the fixture and single lighting on each side. At the bottom were metal receptacles for a large flower pot. These always held the most beautiful planted flowers from the Unity green houses. The walls supporting these beautiful useful flower baskets were designed in the wall theme as carried out in other low walls at the farm. Those included open areas housing multiple concrete spindles that were pre-cast, colored and with simulated distressed surfaces.

The upper terrace had a smooth concrete surface and the steps, walk-ways and lower terrace were of native stone. To the building side of the lower terrace was the entry to the large vestibule that housed a large soda fountain fully equipped! From this entry area patrons were greeted by a hostess and seated in a large single dining room. The walls were a silver grey and the ceiling sky blue. To support the ceiling and also the upper terrace, were large columns about three feet square and almost two stories in height. On each of the four sides of each support post were the most fantastic plaster of paris ornaments. They covered most of each side and all exactly the same. Rick Fillmore designed these to be similar to the hand painted art work on the smaller support posts, in the new Silent Unity Chapel. Just as Rick had all of his metalwork creations hand made by Arthur Zebley, so fell the task to cast these post coverings.

As with all plaster casts the artists work came first, then a sculptured section was prepared. There were many of these made of the different sections that were part of the total covering. From this point Zebley took each section, prepared a pouring box, inserted and attached the patterned piece. He then placed on his blacksmith's forge containers of a brown liquid to heat and then pour into each box, being sure that the proper thickness was attained and the top was level and smooth. After an overnight drying the liquid had hardened into a solid, yet pliable state, and was removed from the box. Each section of the total wall covering was handled in the same manner. Then the plaster of paris was prepared and poured properly into each mold until all of the sections for every post were completed. After all were cured and inspected they were taken to the Tea Room and installed by others. Then they were painted in a gold leaf similar to those in the Silent Unity building.

From the large dining room there were five steps up near the southeast corner up to the salad room. Here all the salads were prepared, breads and desserts readied for serving. Also, at this level was the storage for all the table service. From this level up another five steps up to the south was the kitchen where the meals were prepared, dishes and utensils washed and all the provisions stored. Also, there were large refrigerators at the back of the room with a back door and steps up to the outside. This room was directly under the southeast portion of the upper terrace and all the delivery of supplies came in from the east parking lot. The upper terrace, kitchen, salad room, dining room and fountain area covered four floors.

The fifth floor was a small basement directly under the soda fountain and on the street level at the bottom of the hill. It housed the carbonation tanks and fountain supplies including root beer extract from which the fountain worker mixed the root beer. To reach this level that person went outside, down the steps, unlocked the door to reach his supplies. Also, of Rick's design there were wrought iron light fixtures, tubular metal table bases and chairs that Zebley fabricated. The lower terrace had several sets of four chairs and one table base, which had a center housing to hold a large umbrella; these were welded together for a fixed unit. Each unit was attached to the stone floor, setting in a configuration that allowed the best movement, from the street level, across the steps to the upper terrace. There were a few of these table-chair units on the upper terrace above the soda fountain area. But most of the tables and chairs were loose so that they could be moved and stored while folding tables and chairs could be set up.

This large portion of the upper terrace became very popular for banquets. The tables were set up in rows running in a north-south direction, this allowed the bus boys, waitresses and waiters to move from the storage room easily and the bus boys up and down the stairways on the south bringing large trays of food. No one used the upper terrace more than Rick Fillmore. Not only was he the inspiration for the design of the buildings, ground and ornamentations, he was also the biggest booster of Unity Farm. He belonged to a number of Kansas City civic and service clubs, notably the Rotary Club and the Chamber of Commerce. Here on the upper terrace he entertained the business people from Kansas City and also conventions brought people from far away. Rick was the perfect host and at every opportunity he was professing Unity to all his guests.

When the Terrace Tea Room was opened it was a vegetarian cafeteria and served similar meals as the very popular Unity Cafeteria at 9th and Tracy in Kansas City. An efficient and well organized lady managed the Tea Room and of course, there were a number of managers over the years that this facility was operated which was basically during the 30's and 40's. Second in charge was the hostess, usually an elegant lady with lots of charm and especially talented to care for the patrons and oversee the tea room staff. Most of the cooks and salad ladies were farm women that lived near Unity. The waitresses, waiters, bus boys and soda fountain boys plus the kitchen help came from near by towns or from Kansas City.

Of course, the warm months of the years were the busy times. Young people would come to stay and work during the busy season and they woud live in the apartment house. The ladies all wore hair nets, starched neat uniforms, hose and white shoes. The men wore dark trousers, waiter white jackets and the typical male servers ice cream caps! The younger workers felt pretty well couped up during the week and the vegetarian diet didn't please most. When time came on Saturday night to close the facility and they received their weeks pay they were itching to party. They would pitch in and buy the gas and pay for a good meat meal for whoever had a car.[That was always me at fifteen years old in 1938. We would jam everybody in my 1932 Ford model B leave Unity Farm going west to Knobtown, north on Noland road to 40 highway where all the hot spots were. As I had no desire to drink the task fell to me to gather up those that were at capacity, load them up and get them back to the apartment house in the wee hours. It was not uncommon for one of the Kansas City fellows to get fed up with the bosses, walk out, without the pay due them, and catch the next bus for the city.

During the cold months of the year the staff was much smaller and more permanent. Since I lived at home on the farm, until 1939 when my father passed away and the family moved. I then lived in the bunk house. During my high school years the manger was Mrs. Louise Bynam. Her husband Charley ran the dairy. When a special Unity function was scheduled for a luncheon or early evening, Mrs. Bynam would call the Lee's Summit High School and ask to have me excused for the afternoon so there could be a bus boy to help the ladies serve the special event. For me the most interesting part of working at the Tea Room was the great people I met and served. When many of those attending classes or just visiting Unity Farm found out that I lived on the farm they asked many questions, which most I could answer. A number of those people left as friends and we kept in touch through letters. One of the bus boys was a farm boy from Higgensville, Missouri and we remained friends a long time.

There was an evening when Rick Fillmore was entertaining a number of guests for dinner on the upper terrace, when an event happened that was the talk of the Unity workers for quite a long while. A lady was staying at the apartment house for a few days. She had been taking her meals at the Tea Room and apparently was taking classes or on a vacation. As the Fillmore party was eating this lady came from the apartment house unclothed and became the first 'streaker' ever reported at Unity Farm. She dashed across the upper terrace and disappeared down the steps. Rick's party completed their meal and soon left.

It was a few weeks later that Rick came to Zebley's shop with a package. In it was a sculpture about ten inches tall of the naked lady in the classic pose often, in those days, seen as a radiator cap ornament. He swore my father to secrecy and then told that he was planning a banquet to be held on the upper terrace at the Tea Room and the date. He told Zebley he wanted him to cast an amount of these to be used at each table setting at the banquet. He gave a specific number to be cast and the date they were to be ready to be picked up for the banquet. He also told that there would not be any additional copies made. My father cast these in plaster-of-paris, they were white and not painted. Each was wrapped and packed in boxes.

This happened during the time that I worked at the Tea Room and it must have been about 1937 or 1938. After the tables were set up and just prior to when the guests were to arrive farm workers came carrying the boxes of the special table settings. Rick saw that the gifts were proper in number and at the last minute placed on the table. I can tell you truthfully that when the meeting was over and the guests, that must have been close to a hundred, had left there was not one statue left on the tables!

To me this was an example of the humor that Rick could display on occasion. Later we learned, that the lady, that was the inspiration for the unusual gifts, received special counseling from Unity School and had left the area prior to when the banquet was held. When I heard of the counseling I then realized that Mr. Fillmore not only displayed the humor of the streaking event, but also showed his compassion for one that came to Unity for help.]

1929 - Unity News January 19, 1929, "The rigging has been removed from oil well #24 and has been moved north of green #8 on the golf course where #25 will be drilled. The green houses sold more than 12,000 flower plants last month. A total of 33,998 eggs were collected from the farm hens in December. An old fashion square dance, called and coached by Frank Akers, was enjoyed by those who met at the club house Thursday evening. Art Zebley and his wife furnished the music."

Unity News January 26, 1929, "Claude Sager has left Unity, he ran the dairy. The new replacement is Charley Bynum."

Unity News February 2, 1929, "Ed Shrock, who is cutting, dressing and setting stone at the campanile, has struck oil on his farm near Knobtown. About the same time that new well #25 came in at Unity Farm."

Unity News February 16, 1929, "The auditorium (chapel) in the new Silent Unity building at the farm is ready for use. The Sunday school and the evening regular service of the Unity Community society will be held there. Charles Fillmore will be the speaker at the evening meeting. A saw mill is being built at the farm. When it is finished the timber that is cut on the farm will be sawed into lumber in our own mill. The farm is disposing of its' goat herd."

[I attended Sunday school in this new building. I remember that off each side of the chapel room were a series of glass doors that for large events could be placed open and folding chairs set up for extra seating. These two rooms were used for adult Sunday school classes. At the north end of the chapel was a stage. When the children performed on stage I remember that we had to go outside to go around to the north door to get up on the stage. The children's Sunday school classes were held in rooms to the south. We were prohibited and not allowed to go to the second floor of the building. The portion of the L-shaped building that went to the east had a basement with garage doors on the east end and the school buses were parked there. At that time the basement level was on the same level as the street to the east. Now the Village Chapel sits in that space.]

Unity News March 9, 1929, "Roller skating on the dance floor in the amphitheater is now the chief past time of the farm children. The orchard men pruned the fruit trees during the winter months, whenever the weather would permit. Now they are busy pruning the grape vines and the blackberry bushes."

Unity News March 23, 1929, "Charles Rickert and Vance Boileau are seen almost every evening urging the Shetland ponies to work off some of the surplus fat that the ponies accumulate during the winter months."

Unity News March 29, 1929, "Tulips, carnations and Easter lilies are the flowers that the green house has to offer for Easter. At the farm there are now 101 persons on the payroll. Spring has stirred up these activities at the farm: spraying the orchard trees, setting out 100 new trees on the lawns, planting oats and garden and harnessing the gas at the new well on the Meyer place. The permanent road past the club house is being extended around past the new saw mill location and back to tie in to the road that goes past the two duplex worker's homes and the bunk house."

Unity News May 10, 1929, "Silent Unity leaves Kansas City today for Unity Farm. Today is the big day for Silent Unity. The workers of that department have been looking forward to this day for more than two years. A new bus has been purchased and three buses will be going to the farm each morning and back to Kansas City each evening. By this time next week the new building will be transformed into a beautiful office. The new steel desks will be in place. A new desk lamp will set on each desk and will plug into the floor. The main letter writing room will be on the second floor. Each Charles and Myrtle Fillmore's offices on the second floor, the new chapel and the assembly rooms are ready to be occupied."

Unity News May 17, 1929, "The Filter plant by Earl Ackerman, the farm's superintendent. No doubt many of the workers who go to Unity Farm go over to the dam and see the beautiful body of water that we have there. But how many of them stop to think of all the equipment that had to be installed in order to prepare the water for use in the homes and in the farm buildings that are scattered over the farm? Just west of the dam stands the building that houses the filter plant proper, in which Unity School has invested about $25,000.00 in filtration equipment. In addition to this building 3,300 feet of eight inch cast iron water main and approximately 1,000 feet of four inch main has been laid from the filter plant to the 100,000 gallon storage tank in the campanile. Of course, the old water lines that were used when the farm was first started will have to be taken up and replaced by new lines, in order to take care of the additional load that is placed on the system by the new activities.

New and large fire lines will have to be laid in order to provide better fire protection. Standard city fire plugs are now located around the Silent Unity building. Fire lines for future buildings are all ready installed in the finished tunnels. Two pumps are used to pump the water to the storage tank, one pump being held for reserve in case of a breakdown. But, in case of fire both pumps can be used giving a capacity of 500 gallons a minute. The system is capable of furnishing pure water for 3,500 to 5,000 persons and accordingly the foundation must be planned as thoroughly as for a city of that number in inhabitants. As to the operation of the filter plant; no doubt you have noticed the tower in the lake just east of the dam proper. This is the intake well, through which the water is let into the main that leads to the filter plant. Six gates, or valves are located in this tower at various depths, so that the water may be taken from whatever depth it is the clearest governed by weather conditions. The water is pumped from the intake well through an aireator into the mixing chamber and thence to the settling basins. As the water passes through the aireator, it is exposed to the light and sun and the first step of purification takes place. Then lime and alum are fed into the mixing chamber. The lime and alum remove mud and other foreign matter by collecting small particles into large ones and then settling to the bottom of the basins. This process is known as coagulation and these basins are sometimes called coagulating basins.

In the mixing chamber are a series of baffle plates through which the water passes. The water stands in the settling basins for six hours, after which it passes through a flume, by gravity, to filters, composed of eighteen inches of gravel and thirty inches of sand. From the filters the water goes into the clear well, which is underneath the filter plant building. From the clear well the water is pumped through the eight inch main to the storage tank in the campanile at the rate of 250 gallons a minute. Chlorine is fed into the water as it is pumped from the clear well. The next time that you are at the farm go into the filter plant building and J.S. Beals, the man in charge, will be glad to show you the various operations.

Nell Etue is very proud of her miniature cafeteria or Unity Inn in the lower level of the apartment building at Unity Farm. She has a steam table and everything. The Silent Unity workers are fed in relays and are driven to the Tea Room in a bus. From the comments of the Silent Unity workers, Nell's cafeteria is proving most satisfactory. The food and the service have been excellent, in fact, the variety of food served is beyond the worker's expectations. Nell says that she is open to any constructive suggestions that the workers might wish to offer."

Unity News May 24, 1929, "To Rick Fillmore: Congratulations on the beauty of the Silent Unity building, especially Mr. & Mrs. Fillmore's offices. Wonder who will be the first to suggest that the worm holes in the woodwork and furniture should be puttied? Few persons have an idea of the extensive stock that is carried at the stock room for farm operations. A recent inventory listed 485 items. Glen Lucky is the efficient receiver and dispenser of the farm stock. It must have been his name that attracted the farm to him or him to the farm, for we think that anyone is lucky who lives on the farm!"

Unity News June 1, 1929, "Construction engineer W.E. Flynn has a large crew of men finishing the cement work around the formal flower garden above the new rock wall on the east side of the club house road. One of the most important activities this week in the development of the farm is the digging of more ditches for the laying of more underground telephone lines.

David Walter Pye of New York City was a guest at the hotel this week. He had just spent a few days with John D. Rockefeller. Mr. Pye says that the estate that he visited does not compare with Unity Farm. Makes us wonder if we are fully appreciating all that we have at hand! [David Pye was a very close friend of Royal Fillmore and was Royal's best man at his and Francis' wedding,]

If anyone wants to see an interesting sight, he should be at the lake any evening when Mr. Beals feeds the fish. The fish show evidence of intelligence, the way they expect the food and come for it".[My father took me to the lake, on occasion, in the evening, to watch the feeding of the fish. Mr. Beals would have wheelbarrows full of stale bread that he would dump off the side of the dam. Truthfully the fish were so plentiful and so eager for the food that the school they formed at the dam's edge literally blocked out the sight of the water!]

Unity News June 7, 1929, "Unity joins chain broadcasting. This week marks an epoch in WOQ's existence for WOQ hooked up with the American Broadcasting Company and will hereafter broadcast programs that come from Seattle, Washington where the main studio is located. The programs begin at 12:30 P.M. and continue until 2:00 A.M. Of course, WOQ is not broadcasting all the time, as the time is divided with WDAF."

Unity News June 15, 1929, "Have you been to the top of the ridge at the new addition, Unity Ridge and Gardens, across the highway from Unity Farm? A pleasant surprise awaits you. Alice Fillmore, wife of Lowell, instigated a picnic on the ridge and those in attendance are still talking about the beautiful view. The farm has purchased a new combine for the wheat crops. This machine cuts and thrashes the wheat and spreads the straw right back on the ground from whence it came."

Unity News June 28, 1929, "Spend the Fourth of July at Unity Farm. You can golf in the morning, play tennis in the afternoon and just before that picnic dinner you can take an invigorating swim. After you eat dinner you can go to the amphitheater and dance in the twilight and listen to the Carl Frangkiser band. As soon as it gets dark, about 9:00, the fireworks will begin! There are plenty of benches in the amphitheater for you and your friends. Meet you at the farm on the Fourth. A new elevator is being installed in the campanile. It undoubtedly will exert a very uplifting influence on the farm community!"

Unity News July 6, 1929, "Everyone enjoyed the concert Sunday and then the meeting in the open air after the concert. What is the campanile? According to Webster a campanile is a bell tower, especially one built separate from a church. According to Kenneth Jarman our campanile at the farm is the building that is to be used for broadcasting. According to Helen Neal it is used for part of the Silent Unity offices. If the rest of the workers do not know any more than this about this building, we doubt that they do, it is high time that we do some tall explaining. Plainly speaking it is just a water tower, camouflaged as a beautiful bell tower to fit in with the architecture of the whole building plan. The water tank for the farm had to be put that high and in order that it might not look like one of those western Kansas small water tank towers, the building was built around it to beautify it.

The campanile is 150 feet high, a height equal to almost any 16 story building. However it has only seven floors. Rick's plans for the campanile are very extensive. On the top there will be an observation platform with high powered glasses that one may see the whole farm and maybe someday Kansas City. Under this observation platform is the water tank. Under this, on the floor below, will be Rick's office and studio. Other floors will be occupied by Clint Bernard and Whitty, the field department and other small departments. On the lower floor will be the reception room, which according to Rick's plans, will be very beautiful and interesting. A hostess will be in charge and boys with cars will be available to take visitors around the farm. Rick plans to have the PAX telephone system inclosed in glass, so that all can see how calls are made electrically. He says that this will be much more interesting to watch than an aquarium of gold fish, which is the usual thing in a reception room! So this is what the campanile is and will be and the cause of it all is just a water tank!

"One of the most interesting things that has come to our attention recently is a copy of Silent Unity's A message to you from the Weekly Unity issue of January 26, 1929. Why should this be so especially interesting? Because it is printed in Japanese. As far as we know this is the first Unity article to be translated into the Japanese language, but we hope that it is the forerunner of many more. A.F. Cahusac, a good friend in Japan, was called in to visit a sick Japanese woman to try to help her through his understanding of Truth and he felt that if he but had some Unity literature printed in her language what a blessing it would be to leave it with her. So he put his idea into action and thus, Truth began its pilgrimage in another foreign land. Our hearts go out to Mr. Cahusac as he so faithfully serves the Master and we bless him, knowing that he who gives to his fellow man through love and a desire to serve is being replenished most bountifully with all good from the one Substance and one Power, God."

Unity News July 19, 1929, "The Silent Unity telephone workers moved to the farm this week. The new switchboard is working and 24 hour service will be maintained each day. The Silent Unity boys living on the farm will operate the switchboard at nights."

Unity News July 26, 1929, "In March 1920 Unity Farm contracted for electricity at $2.00 per month. Four years later the cost was $65.00 per month. Today the farm is paying an average of $500.00 a month. In nine years the expense increased from $24.00 to $6,000.00 a year."

Unity News August 2, 1929, "Included in the plan for the farm development are three large reflecting pools in the court that separates the existing buildings on the north and the planned buildings on the south. The construction crew is now making the cement structure for reflecting pool A. Last Sunday June Adams checked 136 persons in and out of the swimming pool. That's more than twice as many as the previous years same day."

Unity News August 9, 1929, "The Davey Tree experts are working on the trees around the pool. The pool is lovelier than ever this weekend. The new filters added last year make the water much cleaner."

Unity News September 6, 1929, "Lowell and Alice Fillmore have moved into their new home on the farm and say they are enjoying it very much. Their house is high on the hill east of the club house and north of the Terrace Tea Room. The stone wall on the east side of the road to the club house was laid from the amphitheater, past the Terrace Tea Room and north in front of Lowell's house.

[That special retaining wall was built around shelves of native stone that were cut off for the preparation of building the road. Across the street east of the club house is an arched depression in the wall with a specially designed wrought iron ornamental flower pot holder. In the summer months the pots are always full of flowers of vibrant colors. As all of the other ornamental wrought iron work on the farm this piece is the creation of Rick Fillmore and Arthur Zebley. A beautiful picture of this depression area in the wall is in the picture files at the Unity Library and it is dated 6-15-31.]

Unity News September 13, 1929, "After four years of cheerful service at the boarding house, Mrs. Buckley steps down for someone else. Mrs. Louise Bynum, the wife of Charley who runs the dairy, will take charge of the boarding house. Nell Etue resigned her position as manager of the Tea Room and Madeline Keathley is now in charge. The green house workers have been very busy the last couple of weeks. Dallas Kreigh, catering to the public on the highway, sold in one afternoon $120.20 worth of grapes and peaches."

Unity News September 20, 1929, "Max Michels, who is in charge of the green house, planted 10,000 carnations this year. They will be for sale soon. There are 2,400 chickens on the farm. Don McCafferty, who is watchman at the new buildings, states that we have more than 300 visitors on Saturday and Sunday. They are persons who are curious and interested in the Prayer Tower (campanile) and Silent Unity Building."

[Many pictures of the buildings along this street are in the library from this era. Additional pictures show the Power House and its' companion building, that is to the east, the Pump House. These pictures are dated 1923 and show the strong influence of the English Cotswold architecture that Rick used in some of the very early Unity Farm buildings. Other pictures of historical interest have to do with the oil wells. These have no dates, but history states they were taken in the early to mid twenties. One of particular interest shows the "shooter" (man) with two cans (fifty quarts) of nitroglycerine standing near the well next to a very old pickup truck with a fabric roof.

Another most interesting picture dated 1928 shows the Unity band at the dedication of the Tower, including Carl Franghiser, band leader. The band is on the ground floor and steel reinforcing rods rise up around as the band performs at this momentous occasion!]

A September 23, 1929 letter from Lowell to H. Emile Cady stated that the peaches this year have been marvelous, the Jonathan apples abundant and all picked and the Starks' Delicious are ripening. [Letters show their closeness and that she has been shifting some of her correspondence answers over to Silent Unity to help lighten her load. She had been told by Charles Fillmore that Unity would be pleased to receive articles for Unity magazine whenever she felt well enough to write. Her articles that appeared in Unity magazine were very popular and many readers wrote to her at the Unity address. Lowell would open, read them and then send them on to her with a copy of his answer to her admirers. She was very pleased to have this assistance as her health was failing and as she grew older her letters revealed that the income being received from Unity was her only income.]

Unity News October 4, 1929, "The new disposal plant is nearing completion. Machinery and equipment has been installed and the finishing touches made."

Unity News October 18, 1929, "The Unity farm is growing so fast that duties have been separated. Mr. W.E. Flynn will take care of the public utilities; gas, oil, lights, telephone, water and disposal plant, since these things fit in with the line of construction work that Mr. Flynn is managing at the farm. Dan Andrews will handle the agricultural end of the farm work. He will increase the orchards and will make general improvements and agricultural developments at the farm. Unity Farm has become well known for the excellent quality of fruit produced in its' orchards and vineyards. Dan has made all of this possible.

Last Sunday Grandmother Fillmore was surprised with a birthday party in her honor. One of the presents that she enjoyed most was an all-day sucker presented to her by her son Charles. She is now 97 years of age and is growing younger and better looking each day!"

Unity News November 22, 1929, "A new gas well has been brought in on the farm and is supplying the heat at the apartment house. Another well is being drilled and it is hoped that these two wells will produce enough gas to supply the farm needs."

Unity News December 13, 1929, "The tunnel on the east side of the Silent Unity building has been completed. The buses will be parked there when not in use. There is also some spare room for a few private cars."

[From December 1929 until January 18, 1933 there were no news publications during those depression years. A special edition of the Unity News was published January 18, 1933, then again nothing until April of 1942. The information written for those years have come from letters in the files of Lowell and Rick Fillmore plus other sources.]

In 1929 the Fillmore's decided to invite Mr. W.W. Thurston, the former owner of the fifty-eight acre farm that was the first ground purchased for Unity City. It was their desire to have Mr. Thurston visit and see the changes that had taken place in his farm over the past ten years. Mr. Thurston accepted the invitation and a car was sent for him. On his arrival Charles, Myrtle and Rick greeted him and they took a tour of the farm. He was shown the oil and gas wells, the new lake, swimming pool and club house, golf course, green houses, orchards, berry patches, amphitheater, Terrace Tea room, Tower and Silent Unity building. At the conclusion of the tour a very quiet Mr. Thurston said, "You sure have ruined a good corn field!"

In Lowell Fillmore's files were found letters from disgruntled workers. "A married couple that were co-editing a unity magazine named Youth wrote that they felt that they were grossly underpaid for their efforts and that they were resigning from their positions at Unity. A letter from a lady that said she thought Lowell felt second rate to his father and didn't understand what the employee was putting out in effort because he was born into the job and never had to get out and find a job and work for someone else and try to please them."

[In all of Lowell's answers to letters received he showed his kind and gentle nature, his love of his parents and brothers and he always represented Unity very beautifully.]

Myrtle Fillmore was very pleased with the New Silent Unity building, the campanile, her home and all of the other improvements at Unity Farm. During the years of the 20's she wrote articles for Unity publication and many letters to friends and to many of the subscribers telling about Unity City. She had so many requests for information that finally she wrote an article entitled,

Tour of Silent Unity, Unity City

"We shall start at the Arches, my fairy home. We shall pass the tennis courts and the golf links, cross the foot bridge over the swimming pool, past the club house and enter the driveway that gives us views at the left of Lowell's home, the apartment house, Tea Room, the amphitheater, the green houses and the homes of those who are helping us grow things and build homes. On the right we see, the pond, the hotel, the homes of Rick and Mr. Boileau and Mr. Gables.

Ah, you are right, the building we are approaching is the Silent Unity building, the south west corner of which Mr. Fillmore and I occupy. The tall structure is the campanile from which there is a tunnel to the Silent Unity building. The colorful foliage and flowers that border the winding walks about the building are from the green house on the farm. The pillars in the cloisters in the north wing of the building give just the right touch as one approaches the building. We'll look into the auditorium and then take a peep at the busy workers on the first floor, God's garden room, the division of the beginning Silent Unity letter writers and the files division.

Then we will make our happy way up the wide stairs to the second floor. We shall not stop to accept the invitation of the tempting chairs that are at the head of the stairway. There is a table there, too with literature placed attractively upon it, for visitors, but we will go into the healing room in its' quiet beauty and look into the telephone room on our way back through the north wing. Then we pass through the spacious room occupied by Silent Unity letter writers in the cloister, with its' arched ceiling supported by columns capped by Italian corbels, from which we enter my office on the left.

The door at the right leads to Mr. Fillmore's office. The two rooms in between are for our respective secretaries. Nothing seems to have been left undone that would add to the beauty and comfort of our surroundings. Each office has a fifteenth century fire place. The woodwork is of Wormy Chestnut. The furnishings are lovely, Mr. Fillmore's a bit more elaborate than mine, but not prettier. The bench in front of my fireplace is upholstered in tapestry as are the loveseat and arm chair. The colors in the tapestry blend with the tints in the frieze that borders the ceiling. Each office has an elegant Persian rug. There are most comfortable leather chairs at our hand carved desks. Leading from my office to the secretaries and the cloister are book coves. Our doors open out on tiny Romeo and Juliet balconies. Shall we open the glass doors and step out to view the sweep of the grounds and valley? We may enjoy the view from the west window, too and then have a heart-to-heart talk about this wonderful gift of love and the expansion of the work."

[In the late 20's a tunnel was being constructed from the tower to the Silent Unity building. A crew was working in one section of the tunnel when there was a cave in and one of the workers was buried alive. There has not been found a record of this death in the Unity history that I have studied. However, the day that the accident occurred my father told our family of this tragedy happening. As I was about five or six years old, I do not remember the person's name or any other information of the circumstances involved.]

[1929 is listed as the year that the Tower and the Silent Unity buildings were completed and occupied.]

1930 - Letter from Lowell to H. Emile Cady dated February 4, 1930 states that Francis Sleater Fillmore, Royal's daughter, that lived with Myrtle and Grandmother Fillmore, after the death of her mother was now living with he and Alice.

Letter dated February 28, 1930 tells Mrs. Cady about all of the beautiful flowers that are now being grown at the Unity Farm green houses.

Letter of April 8, 1930 tells that Rick has had hundreds of Lombardy Poplar trees planted. These were planted in close proximity to each other behind the stone wall that surrounds the amphitheater. As these grew they formed a perfect shield for the amphitheater against wind and made a very beautiful facility much more attractive.

Lowell wrote at length about the garden he has started on the south side of his new home and how much he enjoys working in it, the beautiful results and that he is now having a walkway added through the garden. Also, he is planting apple trees in the garden and has added a fish pond. Additionally, that he has vegetables in many varieties and had grown cucumbers over two feet long. He told that his niece Fran wanted only a puppy for Christmas and they got for her a wire haired terrier that she named Ripples!

[The stock market crash in 1929 and the depression that all of America was involved in did also affect the Unity School of Christianity. Contributions were down, subscriptions to Unity literature not renewed and the economy of the country was going down rapidly. It was necessary that Unity reduce its' work force and make other changes to lower the cost of operation.

By mid-July of 1930 the decision was made to move Silent Unity back to its' previous quarters on Tracy Avenue in Kansas City. Although Silent Unity was gone the Chapel in the new building was used for the Unity Farm church services and for the Unity Training School. It was fully maintained and cared for. The Tower became the hub of activities for Unity Farm and with Rick's new quarters in the Tower he directed the continuation of the farming operation, the completion of the building of the Terrace Tea Room and other limited building activities. Unity Farm was not closed and it was maintained and growth actually continued during the depression years.]

Charles Fillmore's fourth book The Twelve Powers of Man was published September 6, 1930.

December 1930, Lowell tells of Unity lessons being broadcast over WOQ radio.

1931 - January 4, 1931 letter to Lowell from Charles and Myrtle Fillmore. "To our beloved son, Lowell. I want you to realize what a joy and blessing you have been to us all these years you have spent with us in our close relationship of son. You came to us in the guise of a wee babe, a gift from the hand of the infinite Father. We welcomed you gladly, for we felt dimly what we now fully realize. You are a great soul in the making given unto our charge for a season for care and guidance in your unfoldment on this experimental plain we call living. You have been through it all with us and we have never had reason to regret. Lovingly yours, Myrtle Fillmore, Charles Fillmore."

From the Kansas City Star newspaper, "Mrs. Mary G. Fillmore, mother of Unity School founder Charles Fillmore, passed away at the age of 97 in March 1931."

Charles and Myrtle celebrated their 50th wedding anniversary on March 29, 1931.

Myrtle began talking to family and close friends about her time on Earth becoming short. "I have done all I can here on Earth and now I am tired. I can help more on the other side." She began putting everything in her personal life in order.

Letter from Lowell to H. Emile Cady August 7, 1931, states that the new tea room called Terrace Garden Inn has just been completed. "Rick's tea room terraces are beautiful. The wrought iron baskets on the terraces with their colored lights and fragrant petunias are a beautiful sight."

On October 6, 1931 Myrtle slipped away to the inner side of life she knew so well. Two weeks later, at the Sunday service at Unity 9th and Tracy, Charles took over the meditation that Myrtle had led for the past forty years. Before Charles spoke the congregation knew what was in his heart. He would speak of Myrtle and his message would be one of love. Only seven months earlier Grandmother Fillmore had passed on. Now Myrtle had gone and their leader's heart seemed almost too full for words.

Charles said, "Dear friends and co-workers in Christ. It is not our custom here at Unity ever to mention the visits of the last enemy whom we have resolved finally to overcome, as taught by Jesus. But there are certain conditions under which we should exchange sympathy and give thanks for that universal unity which these days of stress and strain have brought. I feel your sympathy and I thank you from the bottom of my heart for your expressions of comfort in thought and word.

This occasion is as pregnant with the absence and the presence of the one who has for years stood in my place at this point in our Sunday morning lesson that I am constrained to speak a few words of consolation and comfort, not only for you but for myself. Personality sorrows and grieves when the bodily presence is withdrawn, but the sense of absence can be overcome when we realize that there is a spiritual bond that cannot be broken. We who are following Jesus Christ in the resurrection know life as a spiritual thing, that we live spiritually if we understand the law of life and that we shall continue to live in Spirit whether in the body or out of the body! And we know that this spiritual bond is the only bond that will really endure." At her passing Myrtle was 86 years old.

Charles was always close to his sons. With the passing of Myrtle he came closer to Lowell and Rick. Lowell in his usual unassuming way took over as much of the administrative work as possible. Rick found many good reasons to take his father to the farm to discuss its' growth.

Letter from Charles to H. Emile Cady dated October 16, 1931, "Mrs. Fillmore passed into a new phase of expression. She decided several weeks ago that she wished to make the change and it was with this idea in her mind that she peacefully passed out of the body. Frequently to those nearest and dearest, Mrs. Fillmore spoke of feeling that she was ready to make the change. It was difficult for us to share her opinion, especially since she was in good health, radiantly happy and filled with life, energy and vitality. But nothing that we could say influenced her decision. We feel that since it was her wish, it would be wrong for us to mourn her going.

Your love for Mrs. Fillmore and the Unity work has been much appreciated by her and all of us. We want you to have a copy of the enclosed newspaper article." An earlier edition of the Kansas City Star stated that " Mrs. Fillmore never considered that in her work she was founding a personal service, but rather that she was teaching others and encouraging them to carry on the work in which she was a pioneer. Her all embracing love and devotion to this work can never leave us and her presence abides as a living force, to uplift, to inspire, to bless in all ways. Join us in knowing for our Myrtle Fillmore the joy and loving care of Spirit as she continues her journey toward the absolute."

Letter dated November 17, 1931 from Lowell to H. Emile Cady, "Your beautiful letter about mother made me very happy. We are not letting ourselves indulge in the thought of what we might term our personal loss, the loss of mother's dear physical presence. We want her pathway toward the absolute to be free from even the tiniest shadow of negative thought. Mother had spoken many times the past year of wishing to make the change in her life and two weeks before she left she mentioned it to several friends. Naturally, we tried to dissuade her. We told her how much we needed her here, how the Unity work needed her, but she said, 'How do you know I mightn't do better work from the other side?' You see, she had a vision of a greater work to be accomplished and we who may not fully grasp her spiritual outlook could but withdraw our argument and stand by with thoughts of love and strength and joy so that her beautiful soul may have freedom in Spirit to continue its' chosen work. We have lost her, dear friend and let her go.

Would you like to know about the service we had for her at the Chapel? It was beautiful, so unlike any other service I have ever attended. Mr. Ernest Wilson's address was a talk to her friends. The idea of love and joy was stressed. She was dressed in a dainty lavender dress which she had worn last May Day when she was crowned May Queen of Unity School. She was so radiantly happy that day and she loved her lavender dress. Those who looked upon her body as it lay in the casket can never doubt her joyousness in making the change in her expression of life. It was as though she had put her house in perfect order, had closed its lips with a sweet smile. About her face was a glow of happiness radiating and all who looked upon her there were glad that they had done so, for instead of causing them to mourn and grieve it stirred within them a corresponding flow of happiness."

Charles Fillmore started his book Prosperity in 1931 and continued writing it during the depression years.

[No record was found of a date that the blacksmith shop and Arthur Zebley were moved from the power house to the mushroom cellar, that was built in 1923. The upper floor, which faced north, was to house a tool house and repair shops. In 1931 at the age of eight years I can remember my father working in the cellar with a blacksmith building that was added on and faced south, a full story below the shops above. I am guessing that the year of the move was about 1931.]

In 1931 Charles Fillmore's fifth book, The Metaphysical Bible Dictionary was published. These words have been said about this book; " There is no other book of equal length or content, it has over 500 pages and is the most often used dictionary in the Metaphysical field." [This book is on view and for use in the Heritage Room at the Unity Village Library. The printing is small the contents staggering as surly was the time that Charles Fillmore spent on this effort !]

1932 - Letter from Lowell to H. Emile Cady dated June 9, 1932, "You asked about Grandmother whether she is still with us at the farm. No, dear friend, she left the farm a year ago last March (1931). You can imagine how very much we miss her, but we have such happy memories to fill our minds and thinking of them brings her very close to us in spirit."

[The severe drought throughout the Midwest during the early to mid years of the 30's killed or damaged the Oak and Walnut trees. Rick had the trees taken down and sawn into lumber. Walnut lumber totaling 50,000 board feet and several thousand board feet of Oak and Elm lumber were cut and stored. Unity had its' own saw mill which was located west of the creek and railroad tracks and to the east of the house on the hill where farm families lived. There was a narrow rock road going north past the bunkhouse, then east around the bottom of the hill, then north and west and finally south at the club house. The road nearly formed a complete circle. The saw mill was located to be as close to the timber source as possible.]

[The Arthur Zebley family was moved into the house on the hill in 1929 and lived there through May of 1939. In 1932 Zebley was sent to the saw mill with his acetelyn welding outfit. A portion of the mantrel, which held the 30" diameter saw blade, had broken and work was halted until it could be repaired. To do so a pulley was rigged and a rope attached to raise the upper part of the mantrel and blade. This was suspended in the air above where Zebley did the welding. The repair work was completed and Zebley was moving away from the saw when the man with the rope let it slip and the saw part came crashing down. One of my father's fingers was cut off at the second joint. At the assembly of this information the house on the hill is the residence of Christopher Jan Chenoweth the minister at the Unity Village Chapel. Years ago the saw mill was disassembled and moved away. The road around the bottom of the hill closed.

No records were located for a date that the railroad was moved to high ground, because of having to be closed at times, because of high water in the creek. This relocation of the railroad tracks eliminated the beautiful hill that was originally to the east of the house. Now the hill where I played, gathered wild strawberries and mother cut what I thought were weeds for her spring dish called greens is gone.

Rick had young Ash trees planted along the planned sidewalk near where the mirror pools are located between the Administration building location and the Silent Unity building.]

After Myrtle Fillmore's passing Charles encouraged the people on the Administrative staff to step up and take more responsibility and make decisions, telling them, "Go ahead and work out the problems, you can do it!"

Clipping from the Kansas City Star newspaper dated May 13, 1932 entitled The stroller visits Unity Farm. "A beautiful expanse of ground bordered by conventional Popular trees provides a classical effect and an ideal setting for the amphitheater (sketch of the amphitheater area). the training school building and the campanile (artists drawing). The Tower is 176 feet high and contains a reservoir holding 100,000 gallons of purified water from the lake. It is piped to all parts of the farm. Picture of Charles Fillmore. Picture of the swimming pool and ornamental arched bridge. Drawing of the Tea Room with wide terrace where refreshments are served. The employees and students club house picture. Along one of the winding paths in the sunken garden. There is a brook from a sparkling spring, lily pools and a pool of gold fish."

Unity Office Bulletin December 30, 1932. "Rick's New Studio. W. Rickert Fillmore is truly the man higher up. He now offices in the Tower just under the water storage level. He has to himself the entire fifth and one half of the sixth floor (or mezzanine to the editorial rooms). His studio allows him views in every direction. When he works, our artist has practically the whole Unity School behind him. His office contains everything that Rick could desire. He has a window seat with portfolio chest beneath, a clothes closet and lavatory room that grace the ivory den of Unity's Michelangelo!"

1933 - Youth magazine article January 1933 When to Disagree by Stella G. S. Perry.

> "Samson yielded to Delilah and told her the secret of his strength because, it is generally believed, he loved her so well. However, this view does not seem to be borne out in the narrative. The reason given there is less romantic, stating that Delilah 'urged him, that his soul was vexed unto death.' That would seem to indicate that Samson did it to stop Delilah's nagging. Anything for a quiet life! He told her his secret and was betrayed into the hands of the Philistines. From that bondage Samson had no escape except to die with his enemies.
>
> Any one who has both amiability and devotion to principle is confronted with Samson's problem. Will constant nagging wear away his strongest resolution? If those about him should ask only once that he surrender the thing that he holds to be right, he could resist them. If, once and for all, his associates begged him to conform to that which seemed to him unwise or unworthy, he could make a stand.
>
> But it is the steady disapproval, the insistent affectionate appeal, the constant air of injury, the very press of custom -- it is this that vexes a man's soul 'unto death.' So, after a few evasions, and a little temporizing like Samson's, he finally succumbs; with the strength of his position departed forever.
>
> In order to be amiable, you and I are tempted, often, seemingly to approve of theories and courses that we really oppose; apparently to admire that which we secretly distrust, or, still worse, to depreciate in chorus what, alone, we would have commended. Even in less important matters of conduct we have to be on guard. For a comfortable conformity, a normal desire for popularity, might betray us. We have to protect ourselves, too, against our will, those precious hours that we have designated for study, or for any other useful work. We have to protect our 'talent,' lest the spade of a weak desire to be a 'good fellow' should bury it.

It is only by a firm resistance that we can maintain the strength of our sincerity, of our personal integrity, and avoid being shorn like Samson by the shears of amiable surrender. This loss would cause the deterioration of our vision and our hopes, with no escape but to perish with the enemies within us.

We all know men and women who can keep firm and yet not give offense by their attitude. To be agreeable to others, yet honest and just to ourselves at the same time, requires character. Another essential is a sense of humor. And our compensations should be peace and the knowledge of accomplishment."

An advertisement in Youth magazine for Christian Business magazine.

"In a recent issue of Christian Business magazine this constructive creed was offered by Paul D. Marvin, and it seems a worthwhile one with which to begin the New Year. The thoughts suggested in this creed are typical of the message that Christian Business brings to its readers month by month. Why not subscribe for it, and make 1933 a richer, more successful year? It will come to you twelve months for $1.50. Unity School of Christianity, 917 Tracy, Kansas City, Missouri.

A New Business Creed

I believe in business as a means whereby each
member of society may render helpful service to others.

I believe that if any conflict arises between human
interests and business, human interest should be placed first.

I believe that the profits of a business should be shared
and that this is fundamental to sound business success.

I believe that business, to be of greatest value,
must take God into active partnership.

I believe that meditation and prayer are
essential to business and personal success.

I believe that business life should be a rich, expanding, abundant life, ever opening new channels of service.

I believe that partnership with God will give a joy, a satisfaction, a faith, and a courage in business that cannot otherwise be obtained."

Letter dated January 14th states that Alice, Lowell's wife, and Harriet, Rick's wife, each own a number of acres of property at Unity Ridge and that Alice had just sold part of hers for cash.

Unity News January 18, 1933, "The past few months several new 1932 model cars have appeared on the Farm. Charley Bynum, Arthur Zebley and Glen Lucky have their new Ford Model B high stepping automobiles! See the new banquet room on the upper terrace at the Terrace Tea Room. Mr. Arends has completed the decorating and it is going to be a wonderful place for your private parties this summer."

Unity News January 30, 1933, "A friend in Oklahoma gave us a cereal mill last fall as a love offering and since we had a great supply of wheat and corn raised on the farm, Rick set to work to mill the grain. Now we have whole wheat flour and fine cornmeal for sale."

Unity News April 10, 1933, "We expect our young apple orchard on 100 acres will bloom for the first time."

In July 1933 the name of the Unity publication Christian Business was changed to Good Business. Francis Gable, editor.

Articles from Good Business magazine July, 1933.

"My July Program: Today It Is Good Business To:

1. Start a new month of joyous activity.
2. Come close to God in true worship.
3. Find strength in the joy of the Lord.
4. Be free in spirit.
5. Rise above the limitations of past errors.
6. Deal with causes rather than with effects.
7. Be not content with less than my highest endeavor.
8. Hold myself aloof from negative influences.

9. Shape my life by a more spiritual mold.
10. Be just and tolerant toward all men.
11. Accent the joyous features of my work.
12. Carry on regardless of obstacles.
13. Pursue each task in the order of its importance.
14. Keep my mind charged with constructive ideas.
15. Watch my thoughts and my words.
16. Contribute in some way to spiritual activities.
17. Work more with mind than with hand.
18. Find a new meaning in my work.
19. Direct my faculties to closer cooperation.
20. Cultivate loyalty to my highest purpose.
21. Be frank, yet kind and considerate.
22. Be mindful of the need for recreation.
23. Give thanks to the one Source of good.
24. Qualify myself for greater responsibility.
25. Think through every activity.
26. Be alert, confident, vigorous.
27. Follow a straight course to success.
28. Simplify every task by careful thought.
29. Devote both heart and head to my work.
30. Become newly filled with the grace of God.
31. Accord perfectly with my highest surroundings."

"Everyday Religion by Godin V. Greene.

Some people think that because of our great progress scientifically, the young folks of today give little attention to their relationship with the divine power. This can hardly be accurate, however. In fact, during the past thirty-five years we have progressed spiritually in the same proportion as we have progressed scientifically. All is part of the one Mind. The very latest electrical discovery was a part of divine intelligence, cosmic intelligence, or universal intelligence, whichever you wish, before it became an idea in some physical brain. Friendly, confidential conversation with the successful young people of today will generally convince any thinking person of the important part that religion plays in their lives.

As spiritual development increases, we are more and more coming to realize our loss from giving attention to religion only one day out of seven, and that a day of rest, instead of recognizing our oneness with divine intelligence seven days a week. We are God's children on Sunday. We must also be children of the Father on the other days of the week, and, as such, have the same privilege of oneness with the Almighty, receiving the same guidance, protection, and blessings as we did on the Sabbath day.

I should like to give you the experience of a young man who has been out of school only a few years. His first job was as a helper in a bakery. Being an alert individual, he soon learned the bakery business thoroughly. Scores of formulas for pastry and breads were tucked away in his memory before he had spent many months in the shop.

Then business dropped off, and his employer was forced to let him go. By this time the young man, whom we shall call Bert for convenience, had decided that he liked the bakery business a great deal and wished to follow it as an occupation. 'Don't be foolish, Bert,' his older brother advised him. 'If those folks, in their good location, can't make it pay enough to keep a helper, it's no job for you. It's not a paying proposition.'

But Bert felt differently. Just because his employer had financial difficulties was no reason why he need have them, he thought. The young baker's assistant had an advantage of which even his own brother was ignorant, however, that of constant contact with the divine power; for Bert's religion was an everyday affair, and not something he held in reserve for Sundays only. As soon as his job was gone he asked his Creator to guide him to more work in which he could serve mankind as enjoyably as he had done in the bakery. After that he daily gave thanks that his prayer had been heard and that he was being led to his right work, under grace and in a perfect way.

Days slipped by. Bert visited every baker in the county, but none wanted to hire a helper. His brother attempted to persuade him to take other work and forget the bakery business. 'They're going to put on an outside contact man at Harper's Hardware Store,' the older boy said one morning. 'You know, talk to prospects for washing machines. A small salary and commission. Why don't you try to get that?'

'My desire to work in a bakery is too strong,' Bert replied. I .know I wouldn't be happy anywhere else.' He stopped for a moment and thought. 'It does seem like a waste of time, though, to try to get bakery work,' he mused. 'I've visited every shop, but no luck. I'm going to keep trying for just two more weeks; then if I don't get bakery work, I'll take anything that comes along.'

He continued his practice of daily thanking the Father for guidance in finding his right work, and his prayers were in secret. Ten days later the Father rewarded him openly, however, and in a most unusual manner. He received word that the baker in his own neighborhood wanted to see him. He had applied there for work, but there had been no opening. Wondering what the man wanted, Bert dropped in at the bakery the same day.

The owner seemed suddenly glad to see the young man and asked him to take a seat in the back room. 'You asked me for a job a few days ago,' the baker began, after the young man was seated, 'and I couldn't do anything for you. Nothing has changed since then, except that I have been working out an idea. Now that the idea has proved itself practical, another idea has come and this one concerns you. Do you see those?' He pointed to a stack of curly objects upon a nearby table.

'Yes,' Bert answered. 'They look like potato chips, only they're larger and whiter.' 'Well they're not potato chips,' the baker explained, 'and I think you'll agree with me that they taste even better than potato chips. I've been experimenting with various kinds of cheese flakes for some weeks now and this product is the result of my experiments.'

Bert accepted one of the flakes, ate it, and commented on its tastiness. 'Now the idea that concerns you is just this,' the baker continued. 'These can be put up in glassine bags the same as potato chips and sold through stores. If a demand is created for them I can hire some one to work in the bakery producing cheese flakes alone. If you're willing to invest your time for a week or two, giving out free samples, introducing them to stores, and so forth, and create a demand, I'll give you a job in the bakery and a half interest in the cheese flake business.'

Bert accepted the offer immediately. That day he gave thanks to the Father that his request for bakery work had been granted, and asked God to guide his steps in introducing the new product.

He made his county acquainted with 'D____'s Cheese Flakes,' was given the job of producing them in the bakery, and in less than a year the volume of business in this one new product was greater than in the other bakery goods combined.

Today these tasty flakes are being shipped into the neighboring counties, and even the brother who advised Bert to stay out of the bakery business because it was not a paying proposition, is engaged at a good wage in the work of hauling the new bakery product. Each time the flakes are introduced into new territory, a local representative is chosen to handle orders and collections. The business has grown so rapidly that Bert now has three helpers under him, and is using more than twice the original floor space, to say nothing of the very latest electrical cutters, mixers, and so forth.

'It certainly pays to recognize the Father's presence in our affairs,' the young baker said recently, 'and to accept His guidance. It was my faith in the Almighty within that gave me the feeling of certainty that I could have and be successful in whatever work I truly desired. I don't talk about these things very much, but I can truthfully say that I have a religion for every day in the week.' Then, noticing my puzzled expression, he laughed and went on, 'It's the same one I use on Sunday.'"

"Discouraged? Unless you are an exceptional individual you are like most of us, quite likely to have periods of discouragement. There comes a time to nearly all of us when the struggle seems hardly worth while, and because of this, I refer you to the following reflection which we have taken from the story of the Pantry Shelf by the Butterick Publishing Co.

> 'Charles Williams Post made the first Postum in a barn.'
>
> 'Messrs. Loose and Wiles were retail bakers and confectioners.'
>
> 'J.L. Draft was a grocery clerk who started with a capital of $65 to peddle cheese from a one-horse wagon.'
>
> 'Charles Hires ran a drug store in Philadelphia.'
>
> 'In 1869 H.J. Heinz planted a small plot of horseradish . . . he and two women and a boy grated and bottled the root.'
>
> 'Mr. Gordon worked in a cotton mill. He had a liking for fish and packed salt mackerel in his cellar after working hours.'

'Coca-Cola was first made in the kitchen of an old home adjoining Mr. Pemberton's Drug Store.'
'E.A. Stuart, president of Carnation Milk Products Company, drove a team of mules in a construction gang on the Santa Fe. Later, he ran a grocery store, and in 1899 bought a bankrupt condensary in Kent, Washington. -- Heinz '57 News.'"

Letter dated October 2, 1933 from Lowell to a friend. "We are having the amphitheater graded. It was a natural bowl shape, but we decided that there should be more of a slope towards the stage if large audiences were to have a good view of the speaker and performance."

Unity News October 27, 1933, "Rick is soon to put on the market preserves from Unity's fruit and berries."

During 1933 Charles Fillmore and Ernest Wilson went to Chicago where Charles was to address the World Fellowship of Faiths at a Century of Progress meeting. Charles talked about the scientific developments of the day that the other religious leaders knew nothing about. Then he told them, "My aim is to prove that in developing the unseen forces of the ether, science is merely revealing the mechanical side of that realm which Jesus called the Kingdom of the heavens."

Charles spoke of Jesus as if they had been friends. He stated that when we see that Jesus spoke of the basic energies and powers and forces of the universe, we now see those forces being made available to us by science. This was an unusual declaration at the time in history. Those that heard Charles speaking very clearly and simply with no rhetoric knew how old he was. He appeared to be much younger, but his age was often mentioned. Charles explained that his aim was to prove that the unseen forces of the either were the mechanical side of the Kingdom of the heavens.

In December Charles Fillmore retired from the pulpit in Kansas City and he delegated his ministry to Ernest Wilson. On December 31st Charles, then 79 years of age was married to Cora Genevia Dedrick, then 57 years of age, by Ernest Wilson in a quiet ceremony at Lowell's home on the farm. Cora had served both Charles and Myrtle as their secretary.

In December the Unity publication Youth was changed to Progress.

1934 - Charles Fillmore had never made a lecture tour of the country, he felt that now was the proper time. On January 1, 1934 he and Cora left for California where he would begin his extensive lecture tour. At each stop he turned the proceeds over to the sponsoring Unity Church. A Unity service featuring Charles Fillmore was held at the Shrine Auditorium in Los Angeles, California February 25, 1934. Attendance was 7,200 with 1,000 persons turned away. Later in the spring of 1934 Charles and Cora returned to Kansas City.

During the summer Charles spent his time writing and teaching students at the training school. As Charles Fillmore moved into his eighties he was a great observer of life and he could trust his sons. They had each found his place in Unity. Lowell was the manager and Secretary of the Unity School of Christianity. Rick was the artist, planner and dreamer for the Unity facilities. Rick had much to do with the planning and development of the Unity complex on Tracy Avenue from 9th to 10 Street. And then he was the vision for all of the Unity City that his father had dreamed of. Now in his 80's Charles felt it was time to organize all his material and to publish books that would cover his teachings. His invaluable aid in the work was Cora. On January 1, 1934 Ernest Wilson replaced Charles as the minister at the Unity Church at 9th and Tracy in Kansas City.

A new government law went into effect March 7, 1934. It is the NRA law that allows for a 40 hour work week and additional hours worked will receive time and one half per hour. When this law went into effect the workers at Unity headquarters in Kansas City had their hours per week reduced to 36, but received their usual pay for 40 hours. At Unity Farm the new law changed the worker from a ten hour day to an eight hour day and changed the week worked from six to five days. [In 1934 my father was paid 42 cents per hour and this rate of pay was still in effect the day he passed away January 29, 1939. Our family felt blessed that we had a home and father a regular job and income during those 1930's depression years.]

March 20, 1934 Unity purchased a 1930 Ford truck to be equipped and used as the first fire truck at Unity Farm.

A Kansas City Star article dated July 29, 1934 carried pictures of the Unity farm amphitheater and a full house attending the Heart of America Community Opera 'The Mikado' held July 14, 17 and 19th. Plus pictures, including three wide angle snapshots attached to each other, showing the amphitheater at full capacity.

Unity News September 13, 1934, "We are having the largest grape crop we've ever had! Rick will have had bottled two to three hundred gallons of grape juice. Also there will be cider when the apple harvest comes.

Rick supervised the making of a deep well at Unity Ridge. A vein of cold water was struck that was about 50 degrees in temperature. Now completing a well fifteen feet in diameter and fifty feet deep. They will pipe water to the houses on Unity Ridge and also pipe water to Unity Farm for domestic purposes. [Unity Ridge was not owned by Unity but many of the lots were owned by Unity employees and many had homes there. In recent years the area has been more densley developed.]

In the fall of 1934 Charles and Cora Fillmore made an automobile trip on a lecture tour through out the northeast part of the United States. They were chauffeured by a ministerial student. Cora was very dedicated to Charles and took good care of him.

During Charles and Cora's lecture tours a flow of letters from Charles to Lowell and Barney Rickerts kept them up to date on the Fillmore's trip costs and charges. Barney Rickerts was a long time Unity employee serving in various capacities including Unity's Treasurer.

1935 - Letter to Alice Fillmore from David W. Pye about Emmett Fox, his coming from England and being ordained in the Unity church in Denver dated January 26, 1935.

LOVE

A poem by Emmet Fox

There is no difficulty that enough love will not conquer;
No disease that enough love will not heal;
No door that enough love will not open;
No gulf that enough love will not bridge;
No wall that enough love will not throw down;
No sin that enough love will not redeem.

It makes no difference how deeply seated may be the trouble,
How hopeless the outlook,
How muddled the tangle,

How great the mistake,
A sufficient realization of love will dissolve it all.
If only you could love enough you would be
the happiest and most powerful being in the world.

Unity News March 25, 1935, "We cut down about 200 lovely Cedar trees recently because of cedar rust. Are now replacing them with 3,000 Spruce and Pine trees."

Unity News April 19, 1935, "During a cold snap Rick has 1,000 smudge pots burning in the peach orchard."

From Lowell Fillmore's diary August 7, 1935, "We have decided not to send out Unity lecturers into the field anymore. A new three year study course is now available beginning September 30, 1935 at Unity 917 Tracy Kansas City, Missouri."

September 1935, the Unity publication Daily Word was published for the first time in braille.[A Unity employee, Michael Beach, was very instrumental in preparing the needed translation. He had a unique interest and education in this field and he was extremely helpful in getting this new service prepared to be available to the public.]

[In the fall of 1935 a special event took place on Unity Farm that has not previously been recorded. Rick Fillmore came to my father's shop and told Arthur Zebley that a speical piece of equipment would be delivered to Unity Farm soon and it was to be unloaded and stored in the north bay of the service center. The service center was an L shaped building above Zebley's basement level blacksmith shop. The last opening on the upper level east side of the L had doors and Rick told that when the machine was inside to place a pad lock on the doors. He gave a padlock to Zebley, it had two keys, one that Rick would have and the other for Zebley.

When the equipment was to arrive Zebley was to anchor it to the concrete floor, with the front of the machine facing the doors. He was then to have the electrician on the farm to wire the machine and to see that it was in running condition. No one else was to be allowed in to see the machine.

Soon the machine arrived and several of the workers were called to help in the unloading and positioning of the machine inside the building. Of course, there were a lot of ideas floating around the farm on what the machine was for.

Again Rick came to my father's shop and told him the date and time that the machine would be operated. On that date, which was a Saturday, and I was not in school, I was there watching close by. Rick arrived in a four door large car with three men, all in suits and looking distinguished. Rick told my father to open the doors, then the four men went in the bay and looked over the machine. Soon several small Unity Farm trucks arrived with loads of bushell baskets with grain. He told Zebley to turn on the machine and then the farm workers from the trucks brought the grain and poured it in an opening on the side near the top of the machine.

The men and Rick stood at the door as the machine made lots of loud noises and emitted grain dust. I could see that everyone was at the front of the machine and soon out came the first ever vegetarian hot dogs, very similiar to what we had at home, each in a thin covering and continuously attached to each other

There was a dog that belonged to one of the families that lived near by and Rick whistled to him. When he came Rick fed the dog one of the hot dogs and the dog ate it and was ready for more.

The grain was soy beans, the three visitors were from Kansas State University and Rick had worked with them towards the experiment. Whatever else was inside the machine, that contributed to the assembly of the hot dog, must have been of the proper contents, for at least the dog at the service center seemed to have deemed the experiment a success!

Since all of the grain was used and a lot of hot dogs came out I am still wondering if some of those found their way to the Unity Inn in Kansas City!"

The Story of Unity's Spanish Magazine, El Sembrador. "For some time Unity's Spanish-speaking friends have shown a growing interest in Unity literature. Many of them have become deeply interested in our work, and we believe our teachings are particularly helpful to them at this time. For this reason we published several months ago an introductory issue of a magazine in Spanish called El Sembrador (The Sower), consisting of translations of material from various Unity publications and including a series of lessons form Daily Word for daily use."

"Now Being Published Regularly. Many letters of appreciation from Spanish-speaking friends testified to the helpfulness of El Sembrador. In response to requests we have decided to issue the magazine quarterly. No price has been set on it, but we are grateful for love offerings from friends who desire to support the magazine until it is possible to publish it monthly at an established subscription price.

It is our desire to reach and help all people everywhere who are interested in applying the principles of Christianity in their lives in a practical way. El Sembrador is dedicated to this purpose and will teach the use of prayer in demonstrating health, happiness, and prosperity as well as peace and joy.

If you know anyone who would be interested in El Sembrador we should like to have his name and address so that copies of this magazine may be sent to him. We shall be glad to send the two numbers already printed and also future copies as they are published. Unity School of Christianity 917 Tracy, Kansas City, Missouri."

Charles and Cora went on a lecture tour into Florida. They stopped at a tourist inn and stayed in a cottage with a large front porch. Charles liked it so well that he took its' measurements and decided he wanted a home with such a porch. He sat up late that night and drew plans for the home and in the morning sent the plans to a Lee's Summit, Missouri builder giving details and told the builder to build the house right away. The house was to be built on Cora's property in a pleasant wooded area on Unity Ridge a quarter of a mile from Unity Farm. There he spent the rest of his career. [That house stands today, at the assembly of this book. It is south of Bannister road and just west of the intersection with #350 highway. After Charles and Cora passed away the house was used as another home for Unity Farm employees. I was in that home many times visiting a high school friend who lived with her grandfather who was a carpenter for Unity.]

The purchase of the property for the new Unity Temple to be built in the Country Club Plaza area of Kansas City, Missouri was paid off in 1935. The total purchase price of the land was $40,000.00.

1936 - When Charles and Cora returned from their Florida lecture tour their new home was completed and ready for them to occupy.

From the Kansas City Star newspaper the following article appeared with pictures. An ice harvest at Unity, "Severe cold this winter brings first yield of ice blocks at Unity Farm. Not since the lake was formed eight years ago has it been cold enough to harvest ice for the farms big dairy on Colbern Road. The barns cellar was stuffed with 350 pound ice cakes. Al Sprague said it was as good ice as he's ever harvested and he has sawed ice in Montana and the Dakotas. Enoch Anderson, W.L. (red Bill) Roberts, Bill Fowler, B. Dodson, Bernard Barker and Walter Drake helped in the ice cutting project. Harry Guengerich is the farm manager."

[As the years of the Great Depression began to improve, the weather certainly did not. The summers were desperately hot with daily temperatures well over 100 degrees, the crops hardly grew, the orchards suffered with small or little fruit and there was hardly any grass on the golf course. The winters were just the opposite with temperatures just right for rain to turn to ice and although Unity Farm looked like a fairy wonderland it was near impossible to drive or walk around. I can remember that my father fashioned himself chains that he wore on his work shoes back and forth from our house on the hill to his shop just east of the old log house and under the farm's repair shops area.,

Some time after the ground was purchased that had the house on the hill, Rick had a small basement dug under the house. Installed was a concrete shower room about five foot square, a toilet room with sink and a dressing area with a hot water tank. At the end of this area was a door that led into a small room that was unfinished. Its' walls, on three sides, were the stone house foundation and open crawl space to the floor above. In the severe hot days my sister, Altina and I would spend lots of time sitting on the cool concrete floor and leaning against the stone wall. It wasn't a fancy place to be, but it was cooler than the house!

A lean-to back porch was added to the house with steps going down to the new basement. Right outside the back door was a cistern that stored run off rain water from the roof of the house. I remember the cistern as it was my job to carry water from it to our garden behind the house. Also, I remember the cistern, as many times during the summer months there would be 'hobos' jump off the train in the valley to the east, as the train slowed to make it up the steep grade and come to our back door asking for water from the cistern to drink and wet their head to cool off. Mother would call my sister and I from the basement to come up as she took out a cup for water, towel to dry off and some food for the man. Also, I guess that mother felt more secure with us by her side. But those days most of the men that rode the rails were just moving in search of a job and a new start in life.

The cistern also became part of a messy circumstance that happened to our father. He was sent with his acetylene welding outfit to go to a metal storage shed on the farm to cut apart a piece of machinery. Once in the shed he found himself not alone, he was sharing the shed with a skunk that was between he and the door. He tried to frighten the skunk out the door and succeeded, but not before he was sprayed. A short time later he came home and knocked on the back door. Mother wouldn't let him in the house. I went for towels, soap and clothing and he spent a lot of time taking a bath at the cistern!

Sunday night in the summer we always went to the band concerts at the amphitheater as did most of the farm families. We especially looked forward to the Sunday closest to the Fourth of July. Because on that night after the concert, Unity workers would set off fireworks outside at the back of the amphitheater in the peach orchard. That practice was stopped by Rick after one of the Roman candles was lit and it accidentally was knocked over and it zoomed down the center isle of the benches and hit the front of the stage. It didn't do any damage in the amphitheater, but it did light other fire works that set the grass on fire in the orchard. So much for fireworks on Unity Farm at a July fourth celebration!

A second Unity Farm worker died as a result of an accident. Unity's drilling rig was set up and operating in a field south of Colbern Road and just short of the east limits of the farm. A single worker was at the rig in the early afternoon. He was smoking a cigarette when the drill bit broke through into a natural gas pocket. The cigarette lit the rising charge of gas and there was an explosion that was heard by a nearby resident. Unity's fire department came soon. The grass in the field was on fire and the man was burned badly. He was taken by car to the Independence Missouri Sanitarium and passed away that night. No record of this death or the other in the 1920's or the names were found in Unity's existing history.

The Unity fire station that housed the 1930 model truck stands today just west of the old log house which was just west of Zebley's shop. When the fire department's phone number was called it rang in the parts department room and the clerk on duty turned on the fire siren. The closest workers to the fire station including the clerk ran to the fire truck. The first there was the driver and by the time he had the building's door opened the clerk was there to direct him to the fire's location. The other workers that arrived boarded the truck and were the fire department on that run. My father was on that trip and saw the injured man and helped put out the grass fire.

Unity hired a new orchard man in 1936. Clyde Corn and his wife Margaruite quickly became a very popular couple at Unity Farm. He was well educated and trained for his job and his abilities brought many awards to Unity for the splendid fruit that he was so responsible for. His wife also became a very popular and valued Unity servant as she excelled in both the piano and organ. She played for church services, retreats, special events and her music was loved by all. Their two children, son Roy and daughter Ann also were extremely talented and were strong supporters of the Unity Farm Chapel and the Youth of Unity.

[When the Corn famly came to Unity Farm they were given the home in which to live just south of Colbern Road on #50 highway. Once Marguerite told me, "How shocked we were to move into a home without indoor plumbing, after having had a modern home before. I was quick to tell her that was where we had also first lived at Unity Farm. We were there two years, then to the two story house on Colbern Road, next to the dairy barn for a year, which was also with the 'little house out back' and then moved in 1929 to the house on the hill that was modern. The Corn's were fortunate to move a year later to the modern farm house just east of the cold storage barn where they lived until Clyde retired.]

In 1936 Charles Fillmore's sixth book <u>Prosperity</u> was finally completed and published. He had started this book in 1929 when the Great Depression enveloped our country and he continued the writing during the years of recovery. Also, in 1936 Charles Fillmore's seventh book was published, <u>The Mysteries of Genesis</u>.

1937 - The following article dated October 25, 1937 was received at Unity School from Elwood C. Nance, minister of the First Christian Church in Seattle, Washington.

> "Unity School of Christianity. 'I am a child of God and therefore I do not inherit sickness', said a metaphysical lecturer to a small group of curious listeners, about fifty years ago. There was one person in that group who had been given only six months to live. That person was Mrs. Charles

Fillmore, who had tuberculosis of the lungs. She received the metaphysical idea with great joy and claimed she was healed and transformed by its' far reaching amplifications. Charles Fillmore, the husband, was also seriously crippled. He had been told that he had a disease in the hip. Furthermore, he was partially deaf and had curvature of the spine. On top of all of this he had just lost a fortune of $150,000.00 in the collapse of a real estate boom.

Mrs. Fillmore got him interested in the "I am a child of God" idea and he was soon healed of deafness and greatly strengthened mentally and physically according to the history of Unity. Almost incredible to those unfamiliar with miracles wrought by faith and prayers. So grateful were Mr. & Mrs. Fillmore that they conducted a spiritual clinic for others, who were healed and in turn healed others. The good news spread rapidly and a new religious movement was started. The Fillmore's decided to consecrate their life to this new healing ministry. They declared; 'Since the power of God is doing this healing, we have no right to set a price on it. We shall trust God to recompense us.' The new movement has long since been called the Unity School of Christianity and there are Unity centers all over the United States and in Canada, England and Scotland.

A training school for leaders headquarters and publishing house of the movement are located in Kansas City, Missouri. Like the New Thought, Christian Science and other modern cults, 'a friendly feeling is always expressed by Unity and its' workers toward all other religions. Unity is a school rather than a church.' The leaders say it is a non-sectarian, undenominational teaching a practical Christianity which applies to the individual of all churches and all religious organizations regardless of sect, race or color. Its' purpose is not to found a new church or sect, but to help and teach men and women of every church and also those who have no church affiliations to use and prove the eternal Truth taught by the Master.

Unity School of Christianity cooperates with, but does not exercise jurisdiction over the classes and Unity centers in America or elsewhere. Like the leaders of New Thought and

Christian Science the leaders of Unity say the strength of the movement should be judged by its' influence rather than by number of member organizations. Many Unity books and magazines are widely read. In almost every congregation located near a Unity center there are some who read Unity magazines or books. I have found their books very popular among shut-ins and hospital patients. Even Catholics and Jews have found Unity books inspiring and helpful. Unity, a monthly magazine teaches Christian healing and Christian metaphysics is the leading paper of the movement. There are many Unity books dealing with the application of their interpretation of Christianity to the everyday affairs of life. Unity teaches that God is the Spirit of life, love, intelligence, substance, omnipotence, omniscience, omnipresence. God is everywhere present. There can be no absence of His life, substance or intelligence anywhere. He is in the world about us and in the world within us. God is not reflected in man, but is manifest in and through him. Unity affirms with Paul that the body is the temple of God, not that it is a creation of mortal mind. Unity does not condemn the body as a being or mortal or unreal, but recognizes it as the servant of the mind and subject to thought both good and ill, 'as a man thinketh in his heart so is he.'

Unity teaches the healing ministry of Spirit, but does not claim to do the healing; that is done by the Father. The Father does the healing and knows what the compensation should be; therefore Unity proclaims Him as its' resource, making no fixed charges for its' ministry, letting the people give as they are moved.

The leaders of Unity claim that Unity is quite distinct from Christian Science, 'except in the fundamental concept of the being of God,' common to all religions. Unity departs for Theosophy in teaching that the law of karma (reincarnation) endures only as long as the ego submits to it and that to suffer much penance in many incarnations for the errors of the past is unnecessary. Through the Christ Power one may dissolve and redirect the thought energies that are carrying these errors and start anew. Concerning eternal life, Unity says, 'Even through to many the overcoming of death seems a fair goal, this should not deter us from pressing toward it. We should dwell in the consciousness of eternal life until death is swallowed up in victory. The last enemy to be over come is death. We reach past the fear of death.'

Unity urges its' students to practice certain affirmations and denials. These should become levers by which man lifts himself out of fear, ill health, destructive thinking. If you are sick, say you are well, 'as an ideal you desire to call forth in your life or well when apparently you are sick,' just as a builder speaks of his finished building, even in the face of debris and litter incidental to its' construction. Leaders of Unity frankly confirm; Unity can encourage you, it can inspire you, but the final result depends on you. Unity teaches today as Jesus taught 2,000 years ago, that thy faith hath made you whole; if you have the faith as a grain of mustard seed nothing shall be impossible to you. 'All things are possible to him that believeth.' Students of the Unity movement have been recruited from all walks of life and from all older churches.

An Episcopal minister recently told me that he often discovered in his parish visitations a Unity magazine on the table with the Bible and a prayer book. Traveling through the straits of Juan de Fuca this summer I met a robust Irishman and his wife. They were from New York. They were intelligent, successful business people. Being Irish and from New York City I thought they must be Catholic. But I discovered they were firm believers in Unity They were enthusiastic too. 'We found in Unity the peace, personal help and optimistic outlook on life that we never found elsewhere.' I have found that many Unity students and members of many of the modern cults, are diligent students of the fundamental concern about missions, evangelism or the social Gospel. Among many there is a happy freedom in dealing with the realistic views of life. Everything will turn out all right if we hold the right thought.

Many of the Unity students go into the deeper metaphysical teachings of their faith. They study and seek to demonstrate the spiritual teachings of Jesus. They seem to be happy in the simple, more practical promises of their creed which offers them health, success, happiness here and now.

They are great believers in prayer, in the power of prayer and affirmations in every realm of life. If you are not succeeding in business, in love, or in social affairs you are more than likely out of touch with God. You are disobeying or disregarding some spiritual law. They believe in the law of abundance. God owns everything, but you can have your share if you believe in God and yourself firmly enough.

Unity's metaphysical commentaries on the Bible are highly symbolical and as different from the accepted methods of biblical interpretations as one could imagine. Not leaders, but lay members of the movement make an effort to understand the metaphysical side of Unity. Any person who has a Bible has all the Truth there is in Unity which is a mixture of the new psychology, a certain brand of metaphysics and a considerable amount of Christianity. Unity stresses the assuring promises of Jesus. 'Ye shall know the truth and the truth shall set you free!'

In 1937 Ernest Wilson, who was serving Unity as the Editor in Chief of Unity publications, wrote a letter to Lowell asking to be relieved of his position, given a leave of absence for a year to rest and travel. Lowell tried to talk him out of leaving, but to no avail. Ernest was tired and needed a change.

On July 4, 1937 Lowell Fillmore gave a speech over the Columbia Broadcasting Company to a national audience entitled Freedom for Today.

Unity News November 18, 1937, "Rick had a cold storage plant installed in a barn on the north side of Colbern road just west of the Unity Farm's east property limits. Also, a modern kitchen to make preserves, cider, grape juice, jams and jellies to send to the Unity Inn and to sell at the road side stand."

[Not only did Rick take advantage of the natural resources that were on the farm ground, he saw a unique opportunity to use the big barn. For the cold storage area he had panels of cork put on the walls of the portion of the barn to be temperature controlled. He planned the thickness of the cork covering to be sufficient to insulate the area for the cold storage of apples, fruit juices and those fruits and berries that would be turned into preserves, jam and jellies in the kitchen area. For its' day the kitchen was very modern and efficient and with refrigerator and freezing equipment. At the assembly of this book that large barn still stands.]

1938 - [January 29, 1938 was Charles Rickert's seventeenth birthday. His father presented him with a brand new 1938 Ford V-8, royal blue, the most beautiful automobile most any of us had ever seen. All the boys in school were very envious and all the girls were hoping for a date to be seen in that dream of a car with Charley!]

June 25, 1938 hardback blue book entitled, Where these Rocky Bluffs meet. The story of the Ten Year Plan given to Rick for his assistance in development of the plan for Hazel Grove school. [Hazel Grove school was a typical rural one room framed school house. It set opposite of Unity's main entrance on the west side of highway 50. Altina Zebley and other Unity workers children attended Hazel Grove grade school in 1926 in the first grade. Charles Rickert Fillmore and Frances Sleater Fillmore began grade school in 1927.

Prior to the 1929 school year Rick Fillmore made the decision that the Unity Farm children would receive a superior education at the Lee's Summit, Missouri schools. He provided a school bus that was driven around the farm picking up students and the bus was at the school for the end of the days classes to bring the children home. Arthur Zebley (junior) started the first grade that school year and Rosemary Fillmore in 1931.]

February 4, 1938 a letter to Lowell from his father told of his enjoyment in his lecture tour in the New Orleans area.

In April 1938 Ernest Wilson chose to go to California to take up a new position as the west coast representative for Unity. He was replaced as the minister of the Unity society by Louis E. Meyer assisted by his wife also a Unity minister, Ethel G. Meyer. They were formerly the ministers at the Rochester New York Unity church.

Unity News October 5, 1938, "The farm produced an abundant crop of apples this year and Rick added apple butter to our many things we sell at the market across from the main gate."

In 1938 the Unity workers on Tracy avenue in Kansas City established a Credit Union. Lowell Fillmore was not a member, but was responsible for Unity backing the Unity workers Credit Union. The name chosen was Justus Credit Union. The word Justus came from the workers 'just us' and the credit union began on October 25, 1938.

When Charles Fillmore moved to Colorado, prior to his marriage to Myrtle he went to school to become an assayer. He loved the beautiful country in Colorado and returned for vacationing there when ever he could. He discussed his previous work as an assayer with his sons and it was Rick that took up the interest in ore and mining.

[During the 1920's and 1930's the farm operation at Unity Farm was an important part of the history of Unity School of Christianity. The farming area was south of Colbern road and east of the railroad. Crops raised were, oats, barley, rye, corn, wheat, soybeans, alfalfa and garden produce. Also, just east of the railroad was the dairy barn and pasture. On the south east corner of 50 highway and Colbern road was additional farm ground that in later years became an apple orchard. Where the Unity Villa housing area is today was the original grape vineyard.]

1939 - On January 29th Arthur Carey Zebley passed away. He had not been ill nor were there any signs of his impending death. He leaves his wife, Mary Meikel Zebley, Altina Marie Zebley, age 18, Arthur Zebley, junior, age 15 and Mary Anne Zebley, age 3 all of the home. Altina works at the Unity headquarters in Kansas City, Missouri as a junior letter writer. The beautiful iron work and plaster casts that he had crafted from Rick Fillmore's designs live on and much of those are still visible at Unity Village. Zebley was 51 years old. Within the next week Rick went to see Mrs. Zebley and told her that her family could stay in the house on the hill through the remainder of the school year.

In the spring of 1939 Charles Rickert Fillmore graduated from Lee's Summit High School. Also, Francis Fillmore received her diploma from the same school. However, her senior year was interrupted by an illness of typhoid fever that kept her out of school most of the first semester. She attended Southwest High School in Kansas City, Missouri the second semester, where she was also able to make up work for the first semester sufficiently enough to graduate.

In July 1939 the name of Unity Daily Word was changed to Daily Word.

In 1939 Charles Fillmore's eighth book was published, Jesus Christ Heals.

The Story of Unity's Fifty Golden Years 1889-1939 by Dana Gatlin was published. A copy is found in the Unity Heritage Room of the library. Following is a review:

"Lovingly Dedicated: To the founders of Unity, To Unity School of Christianity, To those workers whose generous collaboration made this book possible, To Truth workers and seekers everywhere, And to the great, loving, omnipresent Spirit of truth, in whom all men are brothers."

Dana Gatlin

A picture of Charles Fillmore and message. "Charles Fillmore, co-founder and president of the Unity School of Christianity. At 84 his body is strong and his mind active and alert. He is called 'Papa Charley' by many of the Unity workers, who love and admire him, and by his three grandchildren. His wit and keen sense of humor make him a welcome visitor and lecturer in the field and a favorite speaker at Unity headquarters."

A picture of Myrtle Fillmore and message. "Myrtle Fillmore, often called the 'Mother of Unity'; for it was through her desire to help others find health and prosperity that the Unity work was started. Beloved by Unity workers and students all over the world for her loving ministry and her cheery, helpful letters. One of her great desires was to share Truth with children, and she devoted much of her life to this phase of Unity work."

A page listing the officers of Unity School and pictures with names and functions: "Lowell Fillmore, Treasurer and Manager of Unity School and Editor of Weekly Unity; Clara May Rowland, Vice-President of Unity School, and Director of Silent Unity; Retta M. Chilcott, Office Manager and Personnel Director of Unity School; Rickert Fillmore, Secretary of Unity School and General Manager of Unity Farm."

An article entitled 'Confidentially' by Charles Fillmore' [the text of this complete article appears near the end of this book - Tributes to the Fillmore's - Charles Fillmore.]

Chapter One - Inception of the Unity Movement

Chapter Two - Silent Unity: The Society of Prayer

Chapter Three - Unity's First Publication: Unity "How beautiful upon the mountains are the feet of him that bringeth good tidings, that publisheth peace."

"When the idea of printing a magazine was conceived by Charles and Myrtle Fillmore to disseminate the Truth doctrine, in lieu of previous publishing and editing experience they relied with complete faith upon the guidance of Spirit. Besides they were students, and investigative. During the first years of the magazine its pages were open to all schools of metaphysical thought; but it is interesting to note how they never deviated from the one clear-cut purpose of their spiritual mission. Glancing through the early files of Unity's first periodical, one is struck by the freshness, clarity, consistency, and integrity of the editorial contents. What was then presented, if reprinted, would 'weigh up' essentially with what is being printed in the Unity publications today. Truth is eternal, unchanging.

In April, 1889, the first issue of Modern Thought was published. This first issue evidenced the fact that Charles Fillmore was making a serious study of contemporary thought, and under the heading 'Our Mission' he stated editorially: 'Modern Thought occupies an anomalous place and being somewhat of a pioneer in the field, it has to overcome the precedent and prejudice of generations of religious journalism. That a publication devoted to the development of man's spiritual nature could be liberal enough in its ideas to embrace the good in all sects and systems, has not heretofore been deemed a possibility.

We believe, however, that the spiritually progressive men and women of the age are desirous of coming into closer fellowship with all laborers in religious fields, and that this class has outgrown the creeds and dogmas of sect. The development of that principle of love and charity, so thoroughly taught and exemplified by Christ, just as certainly sweeps men into universal brotherhood as does the river its sands to the sea. When this Christ principle is freely developed in man, he sees good in all things, and he feels that it is presumptuous in him to assert that anything that God created is not good in its place.

The time has arrived in the evolution of man on this planet, when works and not words are the true measure of worth; and as man grows in intelligence he finds this to be the only correct gauge by which to test the innumerable sects and schools that make up the world's religion. 'By their fruits ye shall know them' is the unit of measure for the moral and spiritual universe.

The teaching of Christ rightly understood and applied will lead the human family back to Eden, but so long as men haggle over the meaning of the letter and overlook the spiritual import, so long will they distort and misinterpret the divine message.

It is for the independent Christian, or the independent thinker on any line of spiritual philosophy or science, that Modern Thought has a word. There is not a periodical in all the land devoted to this class. Papers and magazines there are by the thousands, the acknowledged exponents of this church and that society, each claiming to point out to man the true path; but where is there one that accords to its contemporaries the full measure of truth to which they are entitled?

Modern Thought hopes to perpetuate its existence by showing the good in all religions and philosophies, and by demonstrating to men and women that they can acceptably serve God without being bound hand and foot by creeds of church or beliefs of isms. All these have good within them, and are doing the work needed on their respective planes, but that any church or ism has a copyright on God's Truth is preposterous. Perfection, being the prerogative alone of divinity, can never be attained; hence more or less error inheres in all the inspirations of men. The gentle dew of heaven hangs in glistening beads from the heads of golden grain and sparkles in the meshes of the wily spider's web; but in either place the morning sun reflects His glowing face; so God has planted Truth in the hearts of all men, and the measure of the Truth is known by its reflection. Hence we have but one standard by which to estimate the truth or error in the beliefs and creeds of men, and it can be applied, successfully to them all. 'By their fruits ye shall know them.'

Thus clearly at the beginning Charles Fillmore expressed the tolerance, open-mindedness, integrity of spirit, and consecration of purpose that was to characterize his and

Myrtle Fillmore's lifework and the spreading tide of the whole Unity movement.

In Modern Thought for May 1889, a special department was given over to Christian Science, although on page 12 of the same issue an article by Charles Fillmore discussed several points on which he did not agree with the Christian Scientists. In another column, 'Notes and Comments,' the editor commented on certain typographical errors in this wise: 'We may not be able, outside a printing office, to convince our Christian Science brothers and sisters that matter really exists, but shall have no trouble in backing our position when once its portals are passed. What outside was a dream, a shimmering illusion, the Maya of the Buddhist, becomes cold, metallic fact within, endowed with a creative power that coins words and phrases, and plays such fantastic tricks before high heaven as makes the angels weep. In the face of such facts it were useless to beg our readers' pardon for the many typographical errors in our last issue.'

This printed admission and comment is illustrative of the poise and the strong vein of native humor that is so characteristic of Charles Fillmore and that runs through the entire Fillmore family. They are 'folks' true to their purpose and keen-witted but friendly and happy, and they understand, appreciate, and like other 'folks.' Perhaps it is these genuine qualities of the spirit, the likability, companionability, interest in others, tolerance, magnanimity, generosity, and ability to smile at all human foibles and absurdities, including their own, that has helped them to 'weather' the times when the externalities seemed difficult, as much as has the sterner stuff of courage and dauntless faith. Any one who has heard Charles Fillmore teach a class or preach a sermon is familiar with the flashes of humor that suddenly enliven the air; in his writings likewise this humor flashes out unexpectedly from time to time. This trait helps to make life happier and more enjoyable for both the possessor of it and for the people around him. Charles Fillmore keenly enjoys a good joke, and is not averse to telling one that is on himself. So perhaps it is not out of order here to take a little 'time out' from weightier themes to relate an anecdote or so that reveals this salient characteristic in the co-founder of Unity.

Lowell Fillmore tells this one on his father in connection with a little colored boy who appeared in the neighborhood where Lowell and his brother Rick played as small children. They played with the little boy all day, and at dinner time, when they came in to eat, the little boy didn't seem to remember where he lived. They mentioned this at the dinner table, so Myrtle Fillmore sent her husband out to find him. Mr. Fillmore brought the little colored boy back with him and they fed him, but he still couldn't remember where he lived.

After dinner, when it looked as though he would have to stay the night, Myrtle Fillmore went into the kitchen, took down the tin tub, heated the water, and commenced to scrub the little boy. As she washed him she talked to him and told him about God. She said, 'You know God is always with you; wherever you go, you can't get away from God.' Just then Charles Fillmore walked into the kitchen, and the little boy pointed to him and said, 'Is that God?'

The next morning Charles Fillmore took the little boy into the colored district and went from door to door with him until he found his home."

Poem by Myrtle Page Fillmore:

My Love to Thee

The hours I've spent with Thee, dear Lord,
Are pearls of priceless worth to me.
My soul, my being merge in sweet accord,
In love for Thee; in love for Thee.

Each hour a pearl, each pearl a prayer,
Binding Thy presence close to me;
I only know that Thou art there, and I
Am lost in Thee.

Oh, glorious joys, that thrill and bless!
Oh, visions sweet of love divine!

My soul its rapturous bliss can ill express
That Thou art mine, O Lord!
That Thou art mine!

Chapter Four - Contribution of H. Emile Cady to the Unity Movement
Chapter Five - Wee Wisdom: A Truth Magazine for Boys and Girls
Chapter Six - Unity School: Faith and Works

Poem by Hannah More Kohaus:

The Prayer of Faith

God is my help in every need;
God does my every hunger feed;
God walks beside me, guides my way
Through every moment of the day.
I now am wise, I now am true,
Patient, kind, and loving, too.
All things I am, can do, and be,
Through Christ, the Truth that is in me.

God is my health, I can't be sick;
God is my strength, unfailing, quick;
God is my all; I know no fear,
Since God and love and Truth are here.

Chapter Seven - Further Works of Unity School
Chapter Eight - Later Unity Periodicals
Chapter Nine - Unity Farm: Unity Community Center
Chapter Ten - Unity Centers World Over

Poem by Grace Noll Crowell:

Fifty Years

Fifty years of service to our King!
Fifty years of high ideals that climb
Forever in the heart's remembering!
Beyond the borderland of space and time

Clean words have flown; clean actions that endure
And hope and faith held high that all may see
Have borne rich fruitage; and reward is sure
To those who labor for humanity.

Fifty years of service! Looking back,
We pray Thee, Lord, where we have failed, forgive.
Looking ahead, we see the shining track
Left by Thy sandaled footsteps. As we live
Help us to follow where those footprints lead;
help us to serve Thee daily as we should.
We pray for years to meet the human need;
And, Lord, we kneel to Thee in gratitude.

Weekly Unity December 23, 1939 article entitled Help from Silent Unity, "The workers in this prayer group, whose lives are consecrated to service to others, stand ready to extend their ministry to everyone who has faith in the power of God to heal, to prosper and bless. Their help is given without charge, but the expense of the Silent Unity work is met by the freewill offerings of those who receive help."

1940 - "January 11, 1940 Mrs. Harriet Collins Fillmore passed away, at the age of 49 years, at her home at Unity Farm where she had lived the past 18 years. She was the wife of W. Rickert Fillmore, Secretary of Unity School of Christianity and manager of the farm. They were married on August 5, 1920 in Kansas City, Missouri. Mrs. Fillmore contributed much to the success of the farm and the religious movement. She had been ill for two years. Mrs. Fillmore was the daughter of Mr. & Mrs. John L. Collins, Johnson County Kansas, pioneers. She was reared in Johnson County. She was a member of the Kansas City Art Institute, the Unity Country Club, the Woman's City club and was organizer of the Jackson County Community society at Unity Farm.

Besides her husband she leaves a son, Charles Rickert Fillmore, a student at Missouri University, a daughter Miss Rosemary Fillmore, of the home, three sisters and one brother. More than 350 persons attended the funeral services at the Newcomer chapel, Brush Creek boulevard and the Paseo. Dr. Ernest C. Wilson, formerly minister of the Kansas City Unity Society was in charge. Dr. Wilson flew here from Los Angeles, where he is the Pacific Coast representative of the Unity School of Christianity. The Unity quartet sang." Note: this is copied from the Kansas City Star newspaper.

January 6, 1940 Weekly Unity, "The Purpose of Unity. The purpose of Unity School of Christianity is not to found another sect, but to show Christians their aim and their common brotherhood; not to separate them or to emphasize their differences, but to bind them together more closely. Through helping church goers to apply to their daily living principles taught by Jesus Christ, Unity makes any church affiliation even more practical. Unity spreads its' teachings the Scriptures metaphysically and explains the action of the mind, the connecting link between God and man. How the mind affects the body, producing discord or harmony, sickness or health here and now is made clear in the Unity publications. Unity centers and study classes are places of religious research for all people, regardless of creed and places where helpful instruction in Christian living may be received." [The Weekly Unity was a publication to anyone that wished to subscribe at a low cost. It was first published in May of 1909 and Lowell Fillmore was the editor.]

[In 1940 Jackson County, Missouri R-7 school district made the decision to build a new Hazel Grove Grade School to replace the old single room school that was across 50 highway west from the Unity Farm main entry. Rick Fillmore discussed the need for the new school with the R-7 school district board. He offered 6.5 acres of Unity's ground at the corner of 50 highway and Rhinehart road as a gift from Unity providing that he could have an input into the architecture of the school and that its' exterior would resemble the nearby Unity buildings. The new school was built a short distance north and west of the Arches and the golf course.

Unity Training School 1940 pamphlet. This message printed on the inside of the front cover, "The Jesus Christ teaching as interpreted by Unity solves all problems, educates, heals, prospers, adjusts all inharmonies and can be easily learned by anyone who will apply himself." Forward, "Unity Training School is one of the departments of the Unity School of Christianity, of Kansas City, Missouri. Its' purpose is to offer intensive instructions in the Jesus Christ way of life for center leaders, prospective leaders and students during the summer months. It gives those who have been studying the correspondence course an opportunity to learn how the principles they have learned are taught under actual classroom conditions. It also enables those who have studied in the local centers to make direct contact with the headquarters of the Unity movement and get a broader view of the whole work."

In recent years the Training School has had an increasing attendance of those who are not especially preparing for leadership, but who wish to develop their own spiritual understanding and at the same time enjoy a Unity vacation. On the school grounds are a large outdoor swimming pool, golf links, tennis courts and a splendid dining room for their service and enjoyment. Those interested only in their own spiritual development are not required to register in each class or to turn in written work. They are encouraged to come and to sit in on any or all of the classes. Some of the classes meet three times each week, Monday, Wednesday and Friday, which means a total of twelve lessons for a course that is completed in four weeks. Other classes meet on Tuesday and Thursday, the course thus comprising eight lessons.

Board of Governors: Charles Fillmore, President; W. Rickert Fillmore, Chancellor; Lowell Fillmore, Manager; Clara May Rowland; Francis J. Gable; Celia Ayers; Elsie W. Shaw; Louis E. Meyer; G. Le Roy Dale. The Faculty: Charles Fillmore, President of Unity School; Lowell Fillmore, General Manager of Unity School; Louis E. Meyer, Minister of Unity Society of Kansas City, Missouri; Francis J. Gable, Editor of Good Business and Field Lecturer; Richard Lynch, Author and Lecturer; Ralph O'Day, Leader Unity Society of St. Joseph, Missouri; Ralph E. Johnson, Silent Unity Department; Ernest C. Wilson, Editor of Progress magazine; Clara May Rowland, Director of Silent Unity; Elsie W. Shaw, Director of Field Department; Celia C. Ayers, Dean of Unity Correspondence School; Ida Palmer, Minister South side Unity Kansas City, Missouri; Ethel Meyer, Assistant Minister Unity Society of Kansas City, Missouri; Hilda Walter, Secretary to Mr. & Mrs. Charles Fillmore; Cleda Reyner, Silent Unity Department; Jane Palmer, Editor of Wee Wisdom magazine; and G. Le Roy Dale, Registrar and Director of Recreation.

1941 - In the spring of 1941 Miss Frances Fillmore, a niece of Mr. and Mrs. Lowell Fillmore, was graduated from Stephens College in Columbia, Missouri (a two year college). She was Vice-President of the Honorary Dramatic Club, Theta Alpha Epsilon Sorority and recipient of the Stephens college drama award. A newspaper article, with her picture, stated, 'Frances Fillmore has left for Iowa City, Iowa where she will be a Junior at the University of Iowa this fall.'

Unity Training School 1941 pamphlet. On the back of the front page is a picture of Christ with this statement, "Jesus Christ is the head of this school. We are now open to His instructions and guidances." This constitutes the opening prayer at each class. The Board of Governors and faculty basically the same as 1940. Guest teachers; Norma Knight Jones, Associate Leader of Christ Church, Unity Los Angeles, California; Rose Emery, Associate Leader of Oakland Unity Truth Center Oakland, California; Raymond Barker, Leader of Unity Church of Truth Rochester, New York; Georgiana Tree West, Leader of Unity Center of Practical Christianity New York City; Margaret Norwood, Leader of Unity Center Cincinnati, Ohio; Maeble Carrell, Leader of Unity Truth Center Louisville, Kentucky.

Tuition or compensation for spiritual instruction. No price can be set on a love offering basis. Yet there is definitely a tuition cost, for the expense incidental to classroom must be met. Each student feels a responsibility and sets his own tuition fee, paying as he feels he has received. The fees charged for rooms and meals are a separate account and in no way cover any of the cost of instruction.

Women's dormitory. Its' rooms are located in the training school building convenient to classrooms, study hall, library and office. They offer the convenience of indoor activities, with the exception of meals, under the same roof. All meals are served in the Terrace Tea Room. Dormitory rooms are semiprivate and simple furnished with shower baths, lockers, laundry and all other facilities located in the building.

Men's dormitory is in another building, a short walk from both the classrooms and the Terrace Tea Room.

Hotel - For those desiring more commodious living quarters there is a lovely English-type house of seven rooms that has been made available for hotel purposes. Near it is another lovely house of five rooms called the Hotel annex.

Apartments - There is an eight-unit apartment building adjoining the Terrace Tea Room located at the heart of the farm activities. Those renting apartments can buy meal tickets at the Tea Room.

Terrace Tea Room - The Terrace Tea Room is modern and placed in a lovely setting. Meals are served both in the main dining room and on the terraces out of doors. It is mainly vegetarian, but fish meals are served. Most of the fresh fruits and vegetables served are grown right on the farm. The dairy products come from Unity Farm's fine herd of Jersey cows. Fountain service is available at the Terrace Tea room throughout the day and evening and on Saturdays and Sundays.

[When Pearl Harbor came on December 7, 1941 operation of Unity Farm was reduced. One section of the ground was set aside for a "Victory Garden" for members and staff to plant gardens. Rick Fillmore kept his workers busy. From the quarries on the grounds he had stone excavated and cut into building blocks. Much was of limestone, which was being prepared for the next building projects. A casting building was built next to the railroad spur where sections of concrete were poured. Most of the stone trims were made from concrete and molded with color and distressing added to recreate the Italian Renaissance architecture. From the lumber cut from the trees that were killed in the drought years much of the fine furniture pieces that remain today were hand crafted in the carpenter shop. Perhaps the most unusual chairs ever designed came from Rick's ideas and were made of Walnut. Those magnificent chairs can be seen on the stage at the Activities center and elsewhere.]

[On Sunday evening December 7, 1941 the Youth of Unity was having its usual Sunday night meeting at the clubhouse. During the meeting the clubhouse hostess, June Adams, interrupted the meeting with the news, that had just come over her radio, and told of the bombing of Pearl Harbor. The Unity Farm Chapel's Youth of Unity coordinator was Dorthy (Dot) O'Conner, she lead the group in a special prayer for the military personnel and the people living in the Pearl Harbor area. Arthur Zebley, Junior was one of the several young male members present that served in the military during the war years. Dot O'Conner was later ordained as a Unity minister.]

In 1941 Charles Fillmore's ninth book, Teach Us To Pray, was published. The title page reads, "By Charles and Cora Fillmore." Later Cora indicated that this book was an amplification of stenographic notes which she made during Charles lectures and discussions on prayer.

1942 - The Unity News was printed again this year, from April through December.

Unity News April 1942, "The Justus club is really what its' name implies. It is a financial organization for the purpose of helping 'Just Us', the workers at Unity School. If you want to borrow money, save money or both, you will find the Justus club convenient, friendly and always ready to serve you.

Unity Training School, by Dr. G. Le Roy Dale. "On April 27, 1942 the Unity Training School begins its' eleventh year at Unity Farm. the first session of the school was conducted from May 4th to October 16, 1931 and consisted of four terms of six weeks each. In those days the teachers were Charles and Cora Fillmore, Francis J. Gable, Celia C. Ayers, Edith Kinley, W.G. Miller, Ernest C. Wilson, E.V. Ingraham, H.B. Jeffery and William Stack. The standard text books used were Lessons in Truth, Christian Healing and Twelve Powers of Man. This years training school will consist of six terms of four weeks each and the twenty subjects offered will be presented by thirty-five teachers.

[A library has existed at Unity as far back as the turn of the century when Jenny Croft was the Librarian. There is no record available to document the transition from Croft's librarianship to that of E. Pharaby Boileau. In May of 1942 E. Pharaby Boileau started the Worker's Reference and Research Library.]

Unity News June 1942, "The Terrace Tea Room is serving meals family style to the Training School students this year. This has proved to be very popular with everyone and has done much to stimulate fellowship and good cheer."

Unity News July 1942, "Altina Zebley and Leroy Siler were united in marriage June 20th at the home of Mr. and Mrs. William Fields Lee's Summit, Missouri in the presence of relatives and a few close friends. Reverend Lewis E. Meyer conducted the service. Before the ceremony Mrs. Rena Bergen played 'Liebestiaum' and then accompanied Eric Butterworth who sang 'At Dawning. The bride was given away in marriage by her brother, Arthur Zebley and Mary Anne Zebley, sister of the bride was the flower girl. Lucille Trappe was matron of honor and Pat McGlynn was best man.

A reception was held following the wedding and Mrs. Mary Zebley, mother of the bride, and Mr. and Mrs. Norman Siler, parents of the groom received with the couple. Ruth Hackett, Catherine

Butterworth, Jean Lynch and La Verne McNabb served at the reception. Mr. and Mrs. Siler are now at home at 1004 E. 43rd Street Kansas City, Missouri.

1943 - Charles Rickert Fillmore graduated form the University of Missouri in 1943 with a degree in journalism. He entered military service following graduation from college, and served as executive officer aboard a U.S. Navy mine-sweeper during World War II.

[In the Unity Library Hertiage room is a poster with this heading; Unity Boys in Service. Below the heading is a colored drawing of an American flag and below that the following verse: "Be strong and of good courage; be not afraid, neither be thou dismayed; for the Lord thy God is with thee whither-soever thou goest."

Leroy Cummins
Eric W. Butterworth
Dean McCollum
Richard Henry Vernold
Otto Arni
Lawrence E. Browning
Victor A. Boyer
Ross C. Peeler
John E. Manola
Joe F. Koggie
John M. Abbott
Hugh Clark
James E. Sweaney
Charles Rickert Fillmore
Clifford H. Jones
George E. Moore
James Parker Stokes
Lewis Davis
Calvin M. Lakin
Harry H. Cloverdyke
Asa N. Pinkerton
Richard A. Rowland
James Vann
Glen E. Miller
George E. Shores

Alva F. Will
Warren E. Meyer, Jr.
Gorden J. May, Jr.
Theodore Carroll
Fayne Boesch
James Thomas Coffey
Jack Conkin
John E. Simons
Claborn Brants
Richard S. Kirbendall
James J. Hackleman
Barney S. Ricketts, Jr.
Virgil Henry Bates
Herbert M. Thomas
Marshall Hull
John J. Hinkle
William C. Johnson
Marion B. Hanway
Frank Cravens
William D. Weeks
Ralph Jarles Alberg
Allie L. Cook
Earl McLannan
Milton Kramer
RayM. Loek

Roger C. Frangkiser	Robert D. Bearss
Mitchel C. Taylor	James R. Vaughan
Charley Bunch	Tom W. Butterworth
Robert W. Gray	Robert Dodson
Henry Keller, Jr.	Alun Williams
William L. Schille	Burton Whitworth
Chester Rich	Frank G. Exter
Arthur Beall	Arthur W. Johnson
Ralph Perry	Richard Brummell
George Joslin	Alden R. Hembree
Roy J. Howard	Lyle S. Hulen

This list of Unity men in the service dated 1943. There are two gold stars placed before the names of Lawrence E. Browning and Chester Rick.]

1944 - [This information about the Unity Temple to be constructed on the Country Club Plaza in Kansas City, Missouri came from records found. By the end of 1944 the new Unity Temple building fund had grown to $91,966.12. In December 1945 additional ground for the Unity Temple was purchased. The contract for the building was awarded to the Swenson Contracting Company of Kansas City, Missouri to be the general contractor. Construction began.

In the files were found copies of the Unity Temple News; a paper issued by Unity from 913 Tracy for the sole purpose of keeping friends of the church up to date on the building of the Unity Temple, its' costs, debts, payments and progress of construction. Often it was stated that the incoming love offerings were offsetting the bills of the construction.

In 1943 Rick Fillmore kept a construction diary with daily remarks concerning the construction of the printing building and the shop buildings at Unity Farm. He also noted the weather of the day and was somewhat meticulous in precisely what craft was working and the progress of their work. The diary ran into 1948 when the basic construction of the buildings were complete.]

1945 - February 6, 1945 publication of news about Unity resumed again with a new name, Unity Office Bulletin. It continued under this name until March of 1952.

In 1945 the Unity Librarian, E. Pharaby Boileau, made the distinction between Unity Library and the Worker's Reference and

Research Library. 'Unity Library, located in the Chapel building at 913 Tracy, sold Unity literature, accepted Prosperity Bank receipts, took subscription orders, no reference room or information files. Worker's Reference and Research Library, located on 4th floor of Unity Office five steps from the Editorial Department, information and reference."

Through the years 1898 to 1945 there has been some history recorded of a functioning Woman's Auxiliary organization. In 1945 articles of association were printed as follows:

Articles of Association of the Ladies Auxiliary of Unity Farm Chapel

First: Name - The name of this organization shall be the Ladies Auxiliary of the Unity Farm Chapel

Second: Object - The object of the auxiliary shall be to promote Unity of Purpose, Fellowship, Service and the application of Truth Principles to our daily lives, and to help with improvement of the club house and send Love Offerings to the Unity Farm Chapel.

The Ladies Auxiliary was organized - 1945

The aim and purpose of the Ladies Auxiliary is to express the Spirit of Truth in Love and Service to the Unity Ministry and to promote fellowship in that service among Unity people and their friends.

The Ladies Auxiliary of Unity School of Christianity seeks to maintain in all its programs, contacts, fellowship activities and service, the high ideal of Christian Womanhood. It welcomes all women in the realization that each one is eager to learn through Unity the truth as taught by Jesus Christ, and to express that Truth in Love, Service, Fellowship, and Peace.

By Laws

Membership: All women who are interested in Truth teachings as interpreted by Unity in cooperation with Unity School and in the object and purpose of the Ladies Auxiliary shall be eligible to membership.

Powers and Members: All members of the Auxiliary shall be entitled to vote. Members may, at any time offer such suggestions to the president or her officers, in their opinion, seem advisable for the good of the Auxiliary.

Meetings: Regular meetings of the Ladies Auxiliary shall be held the second Wednesday in each month through the year. The meetings shall take place at 12:30 p.m., with a covered dish luncheon. The lesson will begin at 2:00 p.m., proceeded by a short business meeting.

Article II.

1. The officers of the ladies Auxiliary shall consist of a President, Vice President, Recording Secretary and Treasurer.

2. Term of Office - Two years, except the office of treasurer.

3. Duties of Officers - President

a. The president shall preside at all meetings and shall be a member ex-Officio of all the committees except the nominating committee.

b. The president shall appoint all special committees as Historian and Corresponding secretary.

Vice President

a. Shall in the absence of the president, perform all duties of that office.

b. Shall be chairman of the Social Committee supervising the Luncheons and seeing that there are at least three hostess each month.

c. Over-seeing the kitchen, that all is left tidy and everything in its proper place.

Recording Secretary

a. The recording Secretary shall keep an accurate record of transactions of the meetings held by the Ladies Auxiliary.

Treasurer

a. The treasurer shall be custodian of all funds of the Ladies Auxiliary disbursing payments upon recommendation of the membership, or in an emergency as requested by the President. Funds shall be placed in a bank or the Justus Credit Union.

b. The Treasurer shall give a financial report at the regular meetings.

c. Shall be responsible for the $20.00 love offering given to person or persons who give the lesson each month.

d. She will order plates, cups and place mats as needed.

Hostess Responsibilities

a. Hostesses shall supply napkins, bread, butter, tea, coffee, cream and sugar. Also, any decorations if desired (not necessary).

Corresponding Secretary

a. The corresponding secretary shall handle all official correspondence and letters or cards of sympathy or condolence. She shall send cards or letters to members who are hospitalized. All cards and postage shall be furnished by the club. (No flowers are to be sent in the name of the club).

Historian

a. To record all past and future events pertaining to the Ladies Auxiliary.

1946 - Unity Office Bulletin January 28, 1946, "The Challenge of Unity" words spoken by Lowell Fillmore emphasizing several points in connection with Unity's place in the world that we believe will interest all. "One of our strongest points," he said, "should be tolerance, of other religious groups, tolerance of the other fellow's view point and way of doing things. Our main objective is to be helpful. We want to put out the truth regardless of what we get back. We are advertising an idea; we aren't advertising to get any visible results for our selves. But when we do reap results which loving service always seems to attract we should accept them graciously and thankfully.

Our main concern as we go about our work must be to improve ourselves, not to worry about what another group or individual is or is not doing. We cannot succeed in what we are trying to do by tearing down anybody or anything. Nor is it necessary for us to use any high pressure method or disparage another in order to go forward. We are offering something to the world that is based on proven fact. Unity teaching is not a theory. It is a practical tried way of effective living, the Christ way and Unity is continuing to grow because it is constantly demonstrating what it is teaching."

Charles Rickert Fillmore completed his service in the United States Navy and returned to Unity Village in 1946. He again became involved in the Unity work because of a "personal commitment to the Unity teachings and a conviction that Unity can help people live more successfully." He is now working in the printing department.

A single sheet press release from the Johnson County, Kansas newspaper about Dr. Ernest C. Wilson, minister of the Christ Church Unity of Los Angeles who will speak at the Unity service to be held at the Plaza Theater on June 16, 1946.

A sheet of information concerning dedicating the new organ for the Unity Temple in the honor of Charles Fillmore. That it will be ready when the building is ready for it and that its' cost will be $25,000.00.

In 1946 the book Mysteries of John was published from the writings of Charles Fillmore.

Here is an outline for a folder for the Triumphant Sunday school class entitled, How to make friends with influential people by Rick Fillmore. "Perhaps we should start off with a little explanation of what we are trying to accomplish through this folder. You see, we want to make friends mostly because we're friendly people. And of course, when anyone decides to make friends or to do anything systematically he usually gives a little thought to the matter as we have done in this case. So, we decided that in making friends we should of course, try to make friends with people of influence, one of whom we have on our list as you.

And while we're making explanations let us say that while we know a little flattery is a mighty good thing, we're not trying to employ this devise in inviting you to become our friend, for the truth is that one of our number has named you as the kind of influential person we should know better. Sales talk on ourselves. We are members of one of the best and one of the most up and coming Sunday school classes in this part of the universe. Composed of men and women, married and unmarried, between the ages of twenty and forty, named the Triumphant class, we are a part of the Unity Sunday school and we meet each Sunday morning at 9:30 in the Unity building at 9th and Tracy.

Our teacher is Mr. Ralph Rhea of whom we think so much that we are devoting a special panel to him on the back page of this folder because we want you to be sure to know him. We're friendly and we like fun, but we're deadly serious about the principles of Truth we're endeavoring to put into practice as a result of our Sunday school lesson.

Our invitation to you. From past experiences we have discovered an important thing about inviting people to parties or meetings or Sunday school classes. We have found that the person invited nearly always says, 'Who's going to be there?' So that this question will be properly answered in your case and because we're rather proud of all the good folks who are all ready members of our class, we are printing our roster of members right here. We hope you find many of your friends listed. Why not check it and see? And then why not accept our invitation to be one of us? We would like that very much.

Meet our teacher. Our teacher is Mr. Ralph Rhea. Ralph is the kind of fellow you like to be around. He's young enough not to be too serious and old enough not to be anything but serious about important things. He's a veteran, he walked from one end of Europe to the other, along with a lot of our other good American boys. To hear him tell it, his experience in the Army was considerably like the Sad Sack's. He has been a favorite teacher in the Unity Sunday school for a good many years and he is employed by Unity School of Christianity where he is preparing for the ministry. He's a good speaker and he knows the theory and practice of successful and plausible living."

Unity Office Bulletin September 6, 1946, "Columnist likes Unity Viewpoint. You'll be interested in knowing what one Canadian newspaper columnist recently wrote commenting on merits of various religions programs in Canada. He stated, 'I must confess I had to wait for a little radio station in Toronto to give me what I really wanted. Station CHUM introduced Donald O'Connor in the Unity Viewpoint. Here I found good clear thinking. Here I found no unction, no condescension. Here was Christianity without dogma. Here was simplicity I could understand. Here was an early broadcast that will start my day off right. Here was my radio program.'

1947 - Unity Office Bulletin February 7, 1947, "Unity featured in American magazine. Workers will be interested to know that the March issue of the American magazine will feature an article on Unity. So that everyone who wishes may get this issue of the magazine, copies will be on sale beginning February 7th at the Information desk and at the Chapel library for the regular newsstand price of 25 cents and five mills.

Printing department and Unity Farm. Now that the printing department will soon be moving to its' new building at Unity Farm, this is a good opportunity to tell you something about the work of the printing department and to give you information about Unity Farm, the future home of all Unity School. The printing department, which now employees 93 persons, is well equipped to handle the tremendous job of printing Unity literature. It has seven cylinder presses, three job presses, one offset press and an array of folders, stitchers, trimmers and other bindery equipment sufficient to complete all our work. More equipment has been purchased for use in the new building. The printing department turns out a vast quantity of work. Each year Unity prints about 40,000,000 pieces of printing. Just for the month of December, of last year over 4,200,000 finished pieces of printing were turned out. Unity is one of the largest paper users in this area, using about 1,400,000 pounds of paper each year.

Unity School will have ample working space at Unity Farm. The farm itself covers 1,100 acres, including an eighteen acre lake. It normally employs 100 workers, but during seasonal rushes there are over 150 workers. The new printing building contains 33,000 square feet of floor space. Almost half of the total space in the present building at Unity headquarters. The Silent Unity building at Unity Farm has 32,000 square feet of floor space.

Unity Farm has its' own facilities for water, gas and electricity. Each year the water stations pump about 13,780,000 gallons of water. Unity Farm is well known for its' many products. Its' apple orchard is considered one of the largest and finest in the middlewest. Besides regular farm crops, Unity Farm grows peaches, nursery stock, grapes and vegetables of all kinds. It has a dairy, a cold storage plant, a grinding mill and many other kinds of specialized equipment for processing its' products into the finished form. In the summer the farm is the home of Unity Training school, attended by students from all parts of the country.

Coming soon - 1. A new pamphlet entitled Meat Hater. A reprint from an article in PM, the pamphlet will be distributed by Unity Inn. 2. New free edition of The Golden Key by Emmet Fox. 3. A new Easter greeting booklet, Be At Peace, by Ethel M. Hosmer. It will be ready this week. 4. Three new radio stations will broadcast Unity Viewpoint. Unity's first radio program in Spanish will begin soon. Complete details later.

Unity Office Bulletin March 6, 1947, "The printing department is slated to begin its' move to Unity Farm on April 1st. The complete move should be over and the full department in operation at the farm by June 1st. The building for the future home of the publishing department is now under construction.

Just for fun. During a Sunday school session the teacher called upon one of the pupils to recite some parables, 'Do you know the parables Johnny?' she asked. 'Yes ma'am.' 'Well, I want you to tell us about the one you like best.' 'That's easy, ma'am. I like the one where somebody loafs and fishes.'

The Kansas City offices and facilities began their move to Unity Farm. The Printing Department was the first moving in April 1947. The Bindery Department was next on July 1, 1947.

[Engraved prints of the Unity Temple on the Plaza were found in the files and a letter from Charles Fillmore on the anticipation of the completion of the building of the Unity Temple. Letter came from California where Charles was living in 1947.]

The Unity Temple News reported that contributions have been keeping up with incoming bills on the construction.

A letter was received from Winnipeg, Manatoba dated June 16, 1947 in which the writer told of purchasing a building to house a Unity church for $29,100.00 with only $2,100.00 down payment. the first Unity church in Canada to own its' own building.

Charles and Cora Fillmore spent the summers at Unity Farm and the winters in California. In his nineties he wrote one of his best known affirmations in clear, strong script, "I fairly sizzle with zeal and enthusiasm and I spring forth with a mighty faith to do the things that ought to be done by me."

Printed article in the Kansas City Star newspaper dated March 6, 1947 entitled, Unity Movement. Started in Kansas City, Missouri now has five million members around the world. Phenomenal success of the religious organization with headquarters here in Kansas City is described in the American magazine. Business promotional methods used in building up a million dollar downtown plant and the 1,200 acre Unity Farm.

1948 - January 1948 article News of 'Unity City' "For more than a quarter of a century to millions of people all over the world Unity has been identified with the address '917 Tracy, Kansas City, Missouri.' Some time next year Unity's new address will be Unity Farm.

The Farm is located on U.S. Highway No. 50 and is seventeen miles southeast of Kansas City. Almost thirty years ago the first sixty acres of this now thirteen-hundred-acre tract was purchased by men with the vision of a great spiritual center, from which the word of Truth would radiate around the world and to which Truth students would turn for instruction and prayer. This was to be 'Unity City.'

Since then the work of making the vision a reality has gone slowly but persistently forward. Slowly the Farm has been made into a place of 'green pastures' and 'still waters' and the needed buildings are being erected. In 1947 our printing department moved into its building at the Farm. It is expected that Silent Unity will move into its building next spring. A building to house the general offices of Unity School, including the administrative, subscription, and a number of other departments is under construction now.

Much more construction work is necessary before 'Unity City' will be completely prepared to fill all the demands that will be made on it, but the moving of headquarters to the site chosen for it so many years ago will mark a milestone in Unity's progress.

This move to 'Unity City' means much to us, because it increases our ability to serve more people; and we want you to know that we appreciate what you have done to make it possible. The growth of this work has been made possible because you have loved Unity and have expressed this love by your blessings and your offerings. As the buildings rise in usefulness and beauty we bear in mind that there is not a stone lifted into place but what God through you has provided. You may think of your gift as small. Yet perhaps a rose in one of the gardens of prayer is there because of you, and someone walking there, in need and seeing it, may be lifted up in heart. A gift that is large in love and faith can never be small in the sight of God.

Unity City means the opportunity to render more effective service in spreading Truth. This is the sole purpose of Unity, of Silent Unity, of all our publications, of all the buildings we are building, and of all the equipment in them, to serve God through serving you."

Charles ended his lectures in California in February 1948. He and his wife Cora returned to their home near Unity Farm in April because Charles was not well. He spent most of his time in bed, sleeping a lot and when awake, talking to his family and friends. Cora was constantly by his side caring for him. Often Charles would ask her to read to him. Much of the time she read from her stenographic notes of his talks or from his writings. On the morning of July 5, 1948 Charles awoke and saw Lowell, who was constantly by his side, smiled and passed on.. Rosemary Fillmore Rhea, Charles' granddaughter, said, "In everything I say about Charles Fillmore I must make it clear that I looked upon him as my grandfather and not as a metaphysican. He was one of the most delightful people I have ever known. To me he was a nice, warm, human person."

[With the passing of first Myrtle and then Charles Fillmore it is realized that their vision of building a bridge between religion and science is becoming a reality! And how wonderful it is that two sons, Lowell and Rickert, are equally dedicated to carry forward the message of Jesus Christ!]

March 31, 1948 at 1:05 A.M. a baby daughter was born. She was named Constance by her parents Charles Rickert and Ann Fillmore.

May 1948 article, "Unity Farm. At Unity Farm recently a party of visitors was viewing the new buildings and the construction work. At the beautiful entrance to the printing building one of the visitors remarked, 'Stucco, trimmed with stone!' 'No,' replied Rick Fillmore, 'there is only one piece of stone in that building, the round piece just over the center of the doorway with the word 'Unity' carved on it. The rest is concrete stained to match that piece.'

W. Rickert (Rick) Fillmore, manager of Unity Farm, is developing a new precasting process that is revolutionary in building operations. Concrete sections are cast for walls, floors, and other parts of the building. These concrete sections are treated in many ways, according to their position and use. Some of the interior sections are being covered with plastic enamel that will last indefinitely, thus cutting the maintenance cost considerably. What appears to be a piece of beautiful tiling is actually 'dressed-up' concrete. The cost is small, the material durable, the effect rich indeed. Precast concrete blocks are used for outside trimming and are made to look like stone, even to the 'worm-eaten' effect, which is gained just by tossing bits of mud on the form before the concrete is poured, and then washing it out afterward.

It is in this manner that the new office building on Unity Farm is being constructed. As soon as this building is completed, Unity headquarters will leave 917 Tracy, Kansas City, Missouri, its location for over 42 years, and move to beautiful Unity Farm. It is hoped that the move can be made in 1949.

The ever-enlarging Unity work evidencing urgent need for larger quarters is not the work of one person or of a few persons; it is the work of the millions who during the past sixty years have affiliated themselves with the ministry begun by Charles and Myrtle Fillmore and who have helped to increase the power of the healing word by reading the Unity literature and passing the word of hope and comfort on to others.

To each of you who has helped, who is now helping, and who will continue to help us in our ministry of Truth with your prayers, your loving thoughts, and your offerings and manifest expressions of good will, we say: 'God bless you everyone, and may you receive abundantly of His joy, peace, and plenty.'

Consecration services for the Myrtle Fillmore prayer chapel Tuesday June 29, 1948 at 1:15 P.M. conducted by the Unity Farm Chapel Women's Auxiliary. In the files a beautiful rodevaguere picture of Myrtle is included.

Letter to Lowell Fillmore dated September 17, 1948 post marked at Covington, Indiana, "During this lessons in truth week, I have felt so strongly that never before has this special week of study inspired, enlightened and given hope to so many over the world as it is giving this year. Of course, I am only one of many who are conscious of this. This week I have sensed that Unity headquarters is under a special, more direct and greater flow of divine inspiration than ever before.

As if the beloved spirit of Charles Fillmore is closer, greater and more able to help his people in his new and advanced work than he could when physically present. As much as he loved life here, how much happier he must be now, in this greater capacity that is his, to help you, his physical son, and his beloved Unity headquarters and all his Unity people. God bless and guide you, Lowell Fillmore and make easy the way when great responsibilities seem to pile upon you. With gratitude to God and the Fillmore's, A friend in Truth." Not signed.

1949 - Unity Office Bulletin January 7th, "Unity Farm building goes on. The basement, ground floor and main floor of the new general office building at Unity Farm has now been inclosed and the ground floor is being painted. All efforts are being directed next toward the installation of the freight elevator so that it can be utilized in the construction work during the cold winter months. As yet the winter weather has not interfered with the construction work and much progress is being made toward the final completion of the building."

"Move to Unity Farm. Much information concerns the movement of Unity workers from Kansas City to the farm and an arrangement with the Missouri Public Transportation Company. They have agreed to provide the service from locations in Kansas City to Unity Farm providing two buses with morning out and evening in arrangements. A price of 28 cents per ride was given, statements were made that it was less expensive than other quotes and less than Unity could purchase and operate its' own buses." This information came from a letter dated May 27, 1949.

Unity Office Bulletin June 7, 1949, "Unity Farm activities. The summer band concert series of 1949 will open on Sunday evening, June 19th, in the amphitheater at 8:00. Carl Frangkiser will direct. Pauline Deniston, of the Unity radio department, this year replaces Maxine Korfhage Frye as the soprano with the Unity Quartet. Square dances are held every Saturday evening beginning at 8:00 in the amphitheater. Spectators as well as square dancers are invited."

The move from Kansas City to Unity Farm again began in 1949. By July 13th the Shipping and Stock Room move was completed. By October 22nd Accounting, Graphotype, Mail Opening, Order, Publicity, Radio, Readers and Checkers and Sales Departments were moved, followed on the 23rd by the Adjustment, Addressograph, Circulation Files, Letter Files, Front Office (Field, Purchasing, Retta Chilcott and her secretary and Lowell Fillmore and his secretary). On October 26th the Form Letter, Letter Mailing and Multigraph had been moved. By October 29th the P.D. Letter Writers, Silent-70, Silent Unity (except phone room), and Correspondence School were moved. The Silent Unity Phone Room, Information Desk were moved on November 7th and that is the date the switchboard at 917 Tracy was discontinued. By November 26th the Editorial Department (except Good Business which moved 7-8-49), and the Reference Library were moved. On November 28th five pianos were moved. A receiving desk and a receiving clerk, service car and truck were left at 917 Tracy until the Receiving Desk was the last department moved on December 6, 1949.

In 1949 the eleventh book, Atom - Smashing Power of Mind, was published from the writings of Charles Fillmore.

In the Unity library there is a bound booklet entitled; Unity Society of Practical Christianity 913 Tracy Kansas City 6, Missouri. It contains the following information on the new Unity Temple: "One of the largest church edifice in Kansas City. It has a large sanctuary seating 1,450 persons; two prayer chapels; fellowship hall, seating 450 persons; kitchen facilities; stage and accommodations for entertainment, and it serves as Sunday school assembly hall. It has 12 large Sunday school rooms, seating over 1,100 persons; 6 consultation rooms for the Society's healing ministry; office quarters for ministers and staff; library; 8 room apartment for minister; bus service to the door and ample free parking space, through the courtesy of nearby Sears Roebuck and Company.

Architects, Charles A. Smith Company 1009 Baltimore, Kansas City, Missouri; Contractor, Swenson Construction Company 3305 Terrace, Kansas City, Missouri. The location is on the southwest corner of 47th street and Jefferson; mailing address 707 W. 47th Street. The ground was acquired in two purchases, lot A in 1929 for $40,000.00, lot B in 1940 for $2,500.00. Architecture and construction; the new Unity Temple follows a modified Spanish design in keeping with the architecture of the Country Club Plaza area of Kansas City, Missouri; the structure is 194 feet long by 94 feet wide, the bell tower is 102 feet in height. The building provides 50,000 square feet of floor space. The construction is structural steel and concrete."

December 6, 1949. Construction began in late 1945 on the new Unity Temple to be located in the Country Club Plaza district of Kansas City. This new building was planned to serve the ever growing membership of the Unity followers in the area and to eventually replace the church facilities on Tracy avenue at 10th street when the headquarters of Unity is moved to the new Jackson Country, Missouri Unity Farm location.

After construction of the new Temple was completed in the late 40's and the building was occupied a group of faithful male Unity supporters formed a special Unity men's organization. Adopted December 6, 1949 were the Articles of Association of the Men of Unity, Unity Society of Practical Christianity 707 West 47th street, Kansas City 12, Missouri.

<u>Preamble</u>: We, the undersigned men, members of the Unity Society of Practical Christianity, desiring to further and exalt the spirit of love and friendship in the world and to strengthen the brotherhood that unites all men in the spirit of God, do hereby associate ourselves together in the Men of Unity.

<u>Association Statement</u>: "I set God before me this day. He guides, governs, protects, heals and prospers me."

<u>Name</u>: The name of this association shall be Men of Unity.

<u>Purpose</u>: The purpose of this association is to search out and apply the laws of God in all relations between ourselves and all other men, to establish fellowship with those who seek to exalt the spirit of love and friendship in the world, and to know and apply the teachings of Practical Christianity as interpreted by Unity School of Christianity, in order not only to live and let live, but also to live and help live.

Membership: Membership in this association is open to all men, but by applying for membership a man therefore signifies his belief in the principles and purposes of the association, as set forth in the preamble and purpose of these articles, and his desire to abide by them. New members may be admitted as provided in the bylaws of the association.

In witness whereof, the undersigned officers, on behalf of the membership and by authority of said membership duly voted, have herunto signed their names: Harry Roark - President, Irvin Barker - Vice President, Robert Garvin - Secretary, Gustav Vollmer - Treasurer.

The Men of Unity is a department of the Unity Society of Practical Christianity and in accordance with the bylaws of the Society.

Effect of Bylaws: These bylaws shall take effect immediately upon there adoption by the membership. Adopted November 23, 1948. Amended and adopted December 6, 1949. Alex J. Alberg, President, Herbert S. Shue, Secretary.

1950 - Office Bulletin February 22, 1950, "Editorial to move. The fifth and sixth floor of the Administration building are nearly complete and the Editorial department will be moved into its' permanent offices soon. New cottages rising. Under construction at Unity Farm are four new style dwelling units, composed of four cottages each. The floor plan is in the form of a Greek Cross, each cottage or apartment occupying an arm of the cross. Each cottage has a private entrance with bath and shower, a kitchenette, two bedrooms and living room. There is no connection between units. The cottages, located along the old orchard road, are protected by 2" of cellotex insulation to insure comfort during extremes of weather. Sixteen units are planned."

Office Bulletin August 22, 1950, "Administration building nearing completion. The Administration building is receiving its' final grooming. Alvin Miller, construction foreman, said that the roof tiling will be completed soon as the painting and guttering is finished. The final touches on the ground between the Administration and Silent Unity buildings and the Tower are also being added in the form of new walks and a bridge over the mirror pools. The attractive bridge will be flanked on each end by a pavilion and the bridge itself will have loud speakers through which organ music will be amplified. Colored lights and flowers will enhance the beauty of the structure.

Broad new concrete walks are being laid connecting the three buildings. A walk will lead to the Silent Unity parking lot and two others will run on either side of the mirror pool to the entrance gates on highway 50. These walks will be surfaced with multicolored concrete like used on the walk between the Administration and Silent Unity buildings. The bridge has been chosen as a structure to commemorate the lives of Charles and Myrtle Fillmore. During the days of their spiritual work they built a veritable bridge of faith from old race beliefs to a new comprehension and demonstration of Truth. Mindful of this symbolism, Unity will dedicate the bridge to their accomplishments and to the innumerable ways in which their example has helped others."

Unity Office Bulletin November 1950, "Work Progresses On New Building. The new east wing will extend approximately 300 feet toward the roadway east of the Administration building and will be 48 feet wide. It will house a worker's cafeteria and provide expansion room for several departments. The first 64 feet of the extension will be three stories high. A breezeway will connect this with the cafeteria. The new cafeteria will seat 386 persons and will have three outside entrances. On the 2nd floor of the cafeterial there will be a soda fountain. In all probability, when the worker's cafeteria is ready for use, the Terrace Tea room will be operated only during the summer months to accomodate Training School students and visitors."

In November of 1950 the Unity publication Progress had a name change to You.

1951 - January 1951 article, "A Bridge of Faith. Visitors to the new home of Unity School at Unity Farm are impressed by the beautiful bridge, now under construction, which will span the mirror pool and connect the Silent Unity building and the Unity Tower with the Administration building.

The bridge combines beauty and utility and, like the other structures at Unity, it was inspired by spiritual vision and is being built for practical use. Of flowing Venetian design, the bridge is of concrete, roughened and weathered by a special process to harmonize with the nearby buildings. Inside the bridge structure are filter chambers, through which water from the pool will pass as a part of the air conditioning for the Unity buildings. Thus an added utilitarian purpose of the bridge will be accomplished.

Loud speakers through which organ music will be amplified will be installed upon the bridge. The organ console will be on the balcony of the Administration building. Organ music for vespers, concerts and inspirational services will add to the peaceful atmosphere of Unity's new home. Comfortable seats will offer sanctuary to those who wish to rest and meditate.

The bridge has been chosen as a structure to commemorate the lives of Charles and Myrtle Fillmore, founders of the Unity School of Christianity. During the days of their spiritual work they built a veritable bridge of faith from the old race beliefs to a new comprehension and demonstration of Truth. Mindful of this symbolism, Unity will dedicate the bridge to their accomplishments and to the innumerable ways in which their example has helped countless others.

Many friends of Unity have expressed a desire to have a part in the expanded building program constantly in progress at Unity School. Therefore, a Building Fund has been established to which all friends of Unity may send love offerings if they feel led to do so. Each offering received is considered to be the individual's part in the Unity building project.

At the dedication ceremony of the bridge, which will be held next June during the annual conference of the Unity Ministers' Association, a metal chest containing the names of the persons who have made love offerings will be sealed and placed in one end of the bridge balustrade. All who wish to have a part in Unity's building program and to have their names included in the dedication ceremonies may do so. Love offerings may be sent to the Unity Building Fund, c/o Bridge Committee, Lee's Summit, Missouri.

Poem written by Grace C. Huntington of Chestertown, Maryland for the dedication of Unity Fillmore Bridge on June 27, 1951, Lee's Summit, Missouri:

This Bridge a Symbol is to me,
To Stand for all eternity;
A structure built by loving deeds,
By answered prayers for all our needs.

A concrete thing, yet made with love,
To walk o'er water, safe above,
As Jesus walked across the sea -
A pathway to serenity.

I lose my burdens as I go,
The pool dissolves them all, I know.
My human mind can be at peace,
From trouble I shall have surcease.

Now is the time to drop the past,
And face the future, courage fast.
I dedicate my life, anew,
With God to guide in all I do.

The name inspires, enriches, too,
A sixty year old dream come true.
'Fillmore' my heart with Love that's fine,
'Fillmore' my mind with thoughts Divine.

This is my Bridge, let each one say -
It takes me toward the Perfect Way.
The Bridge belongs to everyone,
We share with joy a job well done.

Here as we cross, new blessings pour
Into our lives, forevermore.
We now are led by Truth and Grace,
We now behold His smiling Face.

For Unity has helped us see
How God's Word truly sets one free;
And so, with grateful heart and mind,
I bless this Bridge for all mankind.

Poem by Dove Ellis:

The Bridge of Faith

It has a grandeur all it's own,
This masterpiece of art,
Etched there against an azure sky,
It's purpose to impart.

A living thing with heart and soul,
Holds out it's arms to man,
To bridge him over human fears,
Across it's golden span.

A span conceived by hearts who knew,
Truth's everlasting light,
And made it clear to all mankind,
Their pathway could be bright.

Now it stands majestic, strong,
In true commemoration,
To those who gave this bridge of faith,
To every man and nation.

<u>Office Bulletin</u> June 1951, "The Unity dairy, under the direction of Robert Thompson, is one of the busiest places on the farm. Twenty - seven cows have to be fed, cared for and milked. Approximately 95 gallons of milk are produced each day and a great deal of it is sold to Unity workers. Gilbert Greenwood and Guy Marshall assist Mr. Thompson in the work. Greenhouses - a place of beauty. Here are many flowers and shrubs and vegetable garden plants attractively arranged. William Parker is in charge of the staff and the work there."

Unity broadcasts on station WHB. A series of weekly broadcasts on radio station WHB began Monday June 4, 1951 from 1:45 to 2:00 P.M., which will explain the history of Unity and tell points of interest about the farm. Scripts are prepared by Rosemary Fillmore Grace and are in the form of round table discussions. Also participating in the program with Mrs. Grace are Carl Frangkiser, Pauline Deinston and Roland Rexroth.

Lowell Fillmore, in a letter to a friend, told of the dedication service to be held on June 27, 1951 for the Charles and Myrtle bridge that spans the mirror pool. Later the name of the bridge was changed to the Bridge of Faith.

[In the Unity Library Facilities department file box 5 was found this Historical information: Southeastern Jackson County Mental Health Association has offices and counciling rooms at Unity. Also, 'Stepping Stones,' a remotivation and resocialization group uses facilities. Also housed are the headquarters of the Association of Unity Churches and the Omega, a center for the development of human potential.]

No records of meeting minutes for the Ladies Auxiliary of the Unity Farm Center from 1945 until October 10, 1951. "The Women's Auxiliary met at the club house for the monthly meeting and luncheon. Della White, club president, called the meeting to order. Frances Seymore, Mary Clark, and Mrs. Van Horn were the hostesses. A motion was made to give $5.00 toward playground equipment for the school in District No. 7. A gift was presented to our president, Della White, for her good work as president of the Auxiliary. Helen Davis, club treasurer, presented the Mustard Seed lavalier, to our President whom we all love. The November meeting will be a day spent at the Unity Retreat. Plans were made for our Christmas party in December and we will have an exchange of gifts. The collection was $14.85 and Mrs. Osla Jones was presented with $7.40. Mrs. Jones' subject for the lesson for today was the 4th chapter of Genesis."

1952 - Letter from Charles Rickert to Uncle Lowell dated February 8, 1952, thanking him for the raise in pay and that he and wife Ann are settling in their beautiful new home. During the construction they lived in the Arches. The new home was built by the Alton Blosser Construction Company that also built the Unity Village Villa Apartment Complex.

Unity News has been resumed, May 12th, "Dallas Kreigh, the first resident of Unity Farm. Dallas Kreigh, who keeps Silent Unity offices spic and span, says he is going to retire in July and go away. But he is not sure it will be for long. 'Unity has been the only home I ever had,' he declares, 'and I may not be able to leave for good.' It was a cold morning in February of 1913 when Dallas came to work for Unity. His job was firing the first general heating plant at 917 Tracy Avenue.

He had met Charles and Myrtle Fillmore in 1906 and became interested in Unity and had attended Unity services since 1910. Dallas was working for the Strobel Steel Construction Company in 1913, then engaged in helping to erect the present Union Station, when Lowell Fillmore offered him a job at Unity. 'I decided that was where I wanted to work and since then have been with Unity.' he says, 'and every day of it has been wonderful.' Dallas was suffering with tuberculosis and the physicians had told him he had but a short time to live. 'But I knew that was wrong,' he says, 'and when I explained it to Myrtle Fillmore she prayed for me and I was healed.'

When the first 58 acres of Unity Farm was purchased in 1919, Dallas came out here and lived in a tent. He just looked after things in general and has watched the farm grow from the almost barren spot it was to one of the most attractive places in the world. Dallas was the first resident of Unity Farm. 'Soon after I came out here,' he says, 'Unity folks began to come out for picnics and I was always glad because they brought so many good things to eat which they shared with me.

I remember the day the deed was signed for the first 59 acres of the farm. The land was purchased from Warren Thurston and I was present in Independence when the deal was closed. After the deed was fixed up, Charles Fillmore bought all of us ice cream sodas and a silk dress for Mrs. Thurston. It was a great day.' Dallas saw the first oil well come in and he helped on every job on the farm in the old days and he is not through yet even if he does plan to retire and go away. Dallas has seen the Unity movement grow. He has seen and helped in the development of Unity Farm and is one of the proudest persons in the work of Unity. When he talks about his years here and recalls incidents, some comic and some seemingly tragic, his eyes alternately sparkle and cloud with tears. One can understand what Unity has meant to him and what he has meant to Unity Farm. Dallas retired on October 20, 1952."

Unity News October 20, 1952, "Unity Apple Harvest Near An End. Have you noticed the fine flavor and quality of our apples this year? Our apples have always seemed good, but this year they seem better than ever. Harvest from the 5,000 trees this year will run an estimated

12,000 bushels, according to Clyde Corn, our orchard manager. Last week the apple shed was full of the sixteen varieties and workers were busy grading and packing, while other workers were processing the fruit into jelly and this week they will be making apple butter. The cider mill is running full capacity. There will be about 14,000 gallons of cider. An interesting feature at the storage plant is that all the apples are used. The choice apples are packed in peck, half bushel and bushel baskets. Many of these are sold at the sales stand on Highway 50 across from the Administration building. One customer always takes about 300 boxes of the fanciest kind to send to his friends during the Christmas season. The apples that are made into cider, apple butter and other products are good too. Not one apple is used for any other purpose before being inspected. If there is a bruise or blemish, it is cut away and cut so deeply that there is not a chance of a piece of bad apple in any product.

The huge storage rooms are refrigerated to a few degrees above freezing, so that the apples are kept firm. Cider is also kept at an even temperature just above freezing and the rooms where the fruit is processed are spotlessly clean. A trip through the orchard last week revealed that many trees were already stripped of fruit, while the ones still to be picked were loaded with bright red or yellow apples. A sight well worth beholding. Of the sixteen varieties in the orchard five are regarded as the choice. They are Jonathan, Golden Delicious, Grimes Golden, Red Delicious and York Imperial. There are at least two new varieties that have not been named.

Unity apples have always been in demand because buyers know that they get only the best from Unity Farm. They are picked by men who know apples and Clyde Corn says that a good picker will harvest around 100 bushels a day when the trees are loaded. The bearing life of an apple tree is approximately twenty years. Here at Unity when a tree has been badly damaged by the weather or has passed the peak of productivity it is replaced, thereby keeping the orchard in full production year after year.

In the cooking room last week grape jelly was being made. There is a big demand for jelly, apple butter, pickles and other Unity products. All these may be had at the sales stand. It has been suggested that Unity workers who desire the fancy fruit should put in their orders as early as possible, because the demand for fruit from now until Christmas will be brisk. Those at Unity who are not entirely acquainted with our farm products would do well to visit the sales stand. There are many products appropriate for gifts during the holiday season or to give to friends and relatives at any time.

Charles Rickert Fillmore spent the weekend fishing in the Ozarks region. He says he got no response from the fish, but enjoyed the outing. Mary Moore of Silent Unity was another who couldn't resist the call of the hills last weekend. She crossed the state line into Arkansas and is enthusiastic about the splash of color that decorates the trees in the Ozarks."

November 1952, Precast Units - Backbone of Unity Housing, article by Tip Brown:

> "Folks who have entertained doubts about further expansion of the market for concrete in any of its monolithic, masonry, or precast forms would instantly find doubts changing to optimism if they could see what goes on, concrete-wise, at Unity Farm, 16 miles east of Kansas City on Highway 50. It is the international headquarters of the Unity School of Christianity and consists of 1,300 acres of highly developed farm property and a group of all-concrete buildings which house the executive and administration offices, an immense printing plant, besides facilities for housing employees, guests, and students. Between 700 and 800 people are employed in the religious, construction, and farming activities at the center.
>
> For many years the construction program has been under the personal direction of W. Rickert Fillmore, secretary of the school, who with great consistency has designed precast concrete buildings of challenging Italian architecture, flanked by cloisters, fountains, mirror pool, and campanile. Flower gardens, orchards, outdoor theatre, swimming pool, golf course, dairy and packing plant complete a development that is unique in its entirety.
>
> Mr. Fillmore has pioneered his concrete way with ever bolder invasions of new fields and with an end result of structure of sound construction, initial low cost, unlimited life, remarkably free of maintenance, and of a uniformity and beauty that is a revelation in this rural section of Midwest America. A central mixing plant, casting plant, carpenter and metal shops and modern mechanical equipment in shop and

field have been indispensable factors in carrying out the program plus dependable people laboring on building projects.

As a simple illustration of the concrete possibilities in American life, let's take a look at the way concrete houses are being built at Unity. Four units have been already erected, particularly designed for temporary student use, and accommodating 36 people. Each unit has four complete apartments with separate entrances, together with concrete terrace, and a lawn and hedge. Two bedrooms, dining room-kitchen, and wall-separated bath room facilities to accommodate four people at the same time complete the apartment layout. Built-in closets, thermostatic control of heat and air conditioning, running ice water, rubber based carpets glued to the concrete floor or square panels of pressed wood also glued to the concrete floor are among the many refinements of the living quarters.

A central section of the unit, 12 x 12', and extending slightly in height above the rest of the roof line, contains the plumbing, combination gas heating and air conditioning plant, water line, 50 gallon hot water tank, gas and electric meters, and even a small amount of storage space. Gas heat is conveyed through overhead ducts, 12" x 30" and 22' long, with individually controlled vents usually placed above the entrance to the several rooms. In reverse action, cool air is blown through the ducts and returned through outlets in the floor area. Thermostats regulate the room temperature to suit individual needs.

Exterior walls are precast concrete panels with sections joined by male and female joints with 'dum-dum' filler to take up any shock of unusual temperature changes. Cornices are an integral part of the panels at the time of casting. Window openings are made complete with concrete casings and trim and fully equipped steel frame, panes, and connections that are interchangeable for screens and storm sash. This casting method eliminates all sills, aprons and trim to window installation. A similar practice in casting is followed on multiple-story buildings where glass blocks are used, the installation being completed on the casting floor.

A standard inside height of 8' is used for wall panels; lengths and openings may vary. The panel is cast with 2" of concrete on the exposed side and 5" of vermiculite-concrete mixture on the inner wall, with a later application of a facing coat of vermiculite plaster. Decorations are applied direct to this coating without furring.

The roof section is made up of 2" x 4" dimension lumber formed into trusses in jigs, and an over-all application of 5" of vermiculite plaster on expanded metal lath overlaid with asphalt shingles.

The cost exclusive of land has been $20,000 per unit to 4,000 square feet or $5,000 for each individual apartment of 1,000 square feet.

The construction process of these houses may well illustrate the possibility of making precast concrete distribution yards a common necessity of cities and towns along with the bank, post-office, grocery store, and let's not forget the beauty shop.

The casting plant at Unity occupies a large concrete block and steel building, 176' long and 64' wide. An overhead 5 ton travelling crane handles precast members from the floor. A flat panel casting bed on the floor is of concrete and is 112' long, capable of holding numerous wall panels which do not exceed 16' in length. A paraffin wax treatment of the concrete base smoothed out by a gas burner acts as a separating medium, with no discoloration of the green concrete. On the upperside of the panel exposed handling hooks of 3/8" reinforcing steel are placed in the concrete. Dowels of similar size of reinforcing steel are anchored into the mesh reinforcement of the panel and left exposed for later electric welding to other panels. This method has met all full requirements for stability and strength of walls, and carries the additional advantage of providing for expansion and contraction of the steel and concrete in the panels.

The usual weight of a standard wall panel is about one ton. When the wet concrete has gained sufficient set, the overhead crane picks it up and sets it upright in a section of the casting building set aside for steam curing. The panels are covered with canvas and have a 32 hour steam bath.

When needed on the job, the panel is again moved by the overhead crane to a waiting four-wheel steel wagon attached to an industrial tractor. It is thus transported to the building site and placed in position upon a previously poured concrete foundation and floor with 1" offset, upon which the concrete portion of the panel is set. A mobile gasoline-electric crane with a five ton lift sets the panel in place and ready for welding. The small mobile crane in use at Unity has drawn unusual attention from visitors. It was developed for use in World War II and is equipped with a 8' hoist, which is supplemented by a 10' crane on the front. By reason of mobility, the crane is used on upper stories of buildings.

The next stage of house building at Unity will be a street of standardized precast one story apartments in which utilities will be carried in a tunnel some 6' square with end entrances for repairs or changes. Further economies in the use of living space will include newly designed storage features and disappearing beds. Open and covered garage space will be provided for the needs of occupants.

An outstanding feature of the heavy construction at the farm is the ease of adding additions simply by extending the precast sections in the desired direction. Mr. Fillmore believes the application of this principle to home building will ease the burden of original cost and provide additional facilities according to individual family needs. Standardized precast wall sections fit in well with the rapid changeover to modular designing in the architectural field."

Unity News December 15, 1952, "A petition was filed with the Jackson County Court asking that the area comprising all of Unity Farm be incorporated as a town with the name Unity Village. The above action was taken as the results of a meeting of the residents of Unity Farm. More than thirty-three years ago the first parcel of Unity Farm was purchased and at that time Charles Fillmore predicted that some day the community which would be built here would become the core of the worldwide center of the Unity movement. Now the orderly development of Unity Farm as the worldwide center of the Unity movement is fast becoming a reality and the incorporation of Unity Village is another step in this direction."

Unity News December 29, 1952, "Harry Guengerich was the manager of Unity Farm for a period of time then he went to work for Stark Nurseries in Louisiana, Missouri."

In 1952 the magazine You was first published in braille.

Following is a summary of the monthly meeting reports for the year 1952 of the Ladies Auxiliary. Officers for 1952; Della White, president; Mrs. Pitner, vice president; Florence Hill, secretary; Helen Davis, treasurer.

February: Silverware was purchased for the club house.

April: A gift of $25.00 was given to the Unity Village Center (Chapel) for Easter.

May: A gift of $5.00 was given for childrens playground equipment.

September: A thank you letter was sent to Rick Fillmore for his donating black walnut lumber for a new club house lectern. An electric clock was purchased for the club house.

1953 - Unity News February 2, 1953, "Unity Village will soon be a reality, if plans progress as well as expected. The county planning commission recommended that the county court approve the petition, signed by 86 taxable inhabitants of Unity Farm, to incorporate as the town of Unity Village. John Moberly, one of Unity's attorneys, told the planning commission, 'With all the people living there it is time for the dream of the founders to be complete. That is for a community of Unity.'

Rosemary Grace interviews Mrs. Caspari. Rosemary Fillmore Grace, who is making a name for herself as one of Kansas City's top radio commentators, presents her program 'Young Ideas' each Sunday at 12:30 P.M. over station WHB. Last Sunday she interviewed Mrs. Caspari about the Montessori system of child training. Mrs. Caspari uses this system in conducting 'Wee Wisdom Gardens' the kindergarten for children of Unity folks."

Unity News March 16, 1953, "Unity Village wins court approval. The incorporation of Unity Village was unanimously approved at a session of the Jackson County Court in Independence, Missouri last Monday afternoon. Certain surveys will now be made to determine the exact limits of the new town. When these are completed we will have the distinction of coming to work each morning in Missouri's newest town. The board of trustees for Unity Village consists of Lowell Fillmore,

Rickert Fillmore, Charles R. Fillmore, Dr. G. Leroy Dale and Jessie Gable. Official blue book Jackson County, Missouri Unity Village incorporated March 16, 1953."

Unity News March 23, 1953, "Unity Village was described in the Independence Examiner newspaper last week as the only incorporation of its' kind in the United States except for Boys Town, Nebraska. Unity Village is humming with activity as the weather improves. Work has started on the paving on the east parking lot, adjacent to the bindery and shipping department. On the opposite end of the Administration building, materials are being stockpiled for the extension of the west wing of the building. Two floors will be built, the roof of the second floor being about level with the floor of the front office. The basement of the new addition will house air conditioning equipment, while the floor above will provide added space for the bindery operation. In the area between the Silent Unity and Administration buildings more lovely roses are being set out. These added to the many roses already growing around the mirror pool will contribute to the color and beauty of the farm this summer."

Unity News March 30, 1953, "Unity tours prove popular. Only those who have taken conducted tours of the Unity buildings can realize the significance of the work that is going on. Unity's guides and hosts to visitors give complete tours of the Administration building, Silent Unity building and the Tower that takes about an hour and one half. The tours are prefaced with a short amount of history of the Unity movement, to give guests a background for what they will see and of course answer lots of questions. To many of our guests, visiting Unity is the culmination of long cherished amibitions. And whether guests are old friends of Unity or strangers, nearly all are amazed at the scope of the Unity work as evidenced by the size of the buildings, the number of employees, the amount of equipment, etc."

Unity News April 6, 1953, "Interest in Unity constantly spreading. Sometimes we are so engrossed in the routine work that we do that we lose sight of the fact that Unity School of Christianity is becoming more and more everyday a focal point for the prayers, hopes and interests of hundreds of thousands of people. Letters from world famous figures find there way to Lowell Fillmore's desk almost every day. On one day this week, Lowell received personal letters from General Mark Clark, Commander in Chief of United States Forces in the near east; Dr. Norman Vincent Peale, well known radio speaker and minister at Marble Collegiate Church in New York City; and Hudson Strode, author of several popular books and prominent member of the faculty of a southern university. In his letter to Lowell Dr. Peale added this postscript, 'No person is doing more good for more people than you.'

April 13, 1953 the Unity Village Board of Trustees met. Glen Lucky was appointed Village Clerk and Bill Bergen Fire Chief.

Unity News April 13, 1953, "Ralph Rhea's television appearance. Ralph Rhea returned home from California at 3:00 A.M. last Sunday in time to prepare for his regular morning worship service at Unity Village Chapel. Then he had a few hours of relaxation before his appearance on WDAF-TV's 'Pulpit Portraits' at 6:00 P.M. For the benefit of those who weren't able to hear and see Ralph on television this is what he said. 'For a few moments I would like for you to consider with me something that is essentially very simple and yet something that I feel can have a profound effect upon the lives of those who practice it. If you wanted to give it a title I suppose you could call it 'The Place of Silence'.

This is a busy, noisy world in which we live. Airplanes roar overhead, trains, buses and automobiles roar through the streets, sirens scream their warnings and as though to add to the mechanical noises we hear, we sometimes talk loud and long and so quietness is something we rarely experience. We do not have to look far to see the results of this noise and hurry and bustle on the minds and bodies of men and women everywhere. It comes as increased tension mentally and physically from which there must be found some release. There is a way in which we can find release. It is to find the place of silence within ourselves where our faith and confidence is renewed.

A few days ago I visited Forest Lawn in California. It was early in the morning. I walked around the grounds in silence. As no other visitors had yet arrived there was not even the noise of others' voices. I went into the chapel of one of the churches and sat alone, observing the sunlight filtering through the stained glass windows and listening to the soft organ music. It was a wonderful time of spiritual renewal. It is not always possible to withdraw to such a beautiful place for quiet meditation and so we have to learn to find this place of quietness within ourselves no matter what is going on around us. It cannot be done by mere mental gymnastics. It must be accomplished through learning to trust in God.

Long ago the author of the 23rd Psalm gave us the beautiful thought, 'He leadeth me beside the still waters, he restoreth my soul.' A bus ride to work, a few minutes before the office or store opens, standing on a street corner waiting for a friend, can be turned into this time of 'walking beside the still waters' and having the soul restored. Learn to take some simple thought such as 'I trust in God to guide me at all times,' or simply, 'God is my help in every need.' Say the words and then quietly and confidently realize that God is working with you every moment of the day. You will find the results so constructive that you will wonder how you ever got along without it. And may I now say this blessing for you? May each day bring you new strength and inspiration in the knowledge that God is your help in every need and you are tremendously important to Him!"

Unity News June 1, 1953, "Congratulations Doctor Rick! At commencement exercises on May 29, 1953 the Kansas City Art Institute and School of Design conferred the degree of Doctor of Fine Arts on W. Rickert Fillmore and four others. It is an honor that has been awarded previously to only six persons. The official citation reads as follows, 'W. Rickert Fillmore, member of the Board of Trustees and Board of Governors for nearly a quarter of a century, former president of the board, cultural and civic leader, chairman of membership campaign for the Institute, Christian statesman, designer of church buildings, the Kansas City Art Institute has benefited greatly not only from your own experiences as an art student in our neighboring school, the school of the Art Institute of Chicago, but also from your high ideals of the role of art in society.' Also 1953 brought Rick another honor, he became the first Mayor of Unity Village!"

Unity News July 6, 1953, "To satisfy the curiosity of many, we'll tell that the beautiful trees lining the sidewalks along the Mirror Pool are Green Ash, a rather unusual variety, distinct from the common Mountain Ash. Most were purchased in Tennessee. They are trimmed every other year or so to control their growth, so they will probably remain at their present size."

The Lone Star Cement News August 1953. A colored brochure showing Unity Village on the front page and containing this written information: "Distinguished construction featured by imaginative use of pre-cast 'incor' concrete. Covering about 1,400 acres, Unity Village is practically self-contained with its' own water system, disposal plant, central heating plant and electrical system. The Tower, Silent Unity building, the Administration building with printing wing contains a total of 250,000 square feet of floor space. Designer and supervision - Rick Fillmore; Construction superintendent - Alvin Miller; Precast superintendent - Harold Brummel."

[Pictures in the Unity Library files show the inside of the new buildings in a mailing folder. It shows the precasting methods used for wall sections, stairway sections shaped like a key and the methods of forming in large sections then raising those and then welding the units together. Aerial views show that the two buildings south of the administration and printing wing were constructed about the same time. The maintenance building, on the east, and the power house building with heating plant and high stack on the west are visible in these photographs. The maintenance building was first used as the casting building.]

Manual for Unity workers - Publishing; Silent Unity printing: "Dear Unity workers, We are happy to have you with us in the Unity household and we pray that you will find joy and satisfaction in your work. It was not by chance that you came to Unity School, but for a divine purpose. We feel that you came to receive a blessing and to give a blessing. The work of Unity School is one of service to God and we daily acknowledge Jesus Christ as the head of this work. Upon entering the work in any capacity you express your desire to work for God and to promote His good. The more you dedicate yourself to God and make yourself a channel through which mankind is blessed the more satisfying and rewarding will be your service.

As a Unity worker you have many opportunities that contribute to your spiritual growth and progress. There is no limit to the health, happiness and success that you may bring into your life and affairs as you endeavor to apply the Truth principles in every activity of your life and your work. As you enter into our working days and into our meetings and meditation periods each day, do so with an open mind and heart and watch yourself grow in spiritual understanding. Always remember that when you work for God you receive an inner satisfaction and as you promote His good. He rewards you abundantly. Every effort you make to use the Jesus Christ teachings means joy and satisfaction in your work, in your life and in all your affairs. We bless you as you each go forward to serve in the name of the Father. Blessings, Unity School of Christianity.

What Unity School is and its' origin: The Unity School of Christianity is a religious, educational institution devoted to demonstrating that the Jesus Christ teachings is a practical seven days a week way of life. Because Unity is entirely undenominational and nonsectarian, its' message is acceptable to men and woman of every church and even to those who have no church affiliation.

Purpose of Unity work: The purpose of Unity teachings is to help all who are seeking, regardless of race, creed or church affiliation to find peace, joy, prosperity through day by day practice of Christian principles. Unity is in perfect agreement and harmony with that which is good and true in the teachings of every church and school of thought. In Unity we stress likenesses, not differences, and we are interested not so much in creed and doctrine as in meeting human needs. Unity School of Christianity is a non-profit organization and is a school rather than a church, prepared through its' activities to promote the teachings of Jesus Christ. The expense of carrying on the work of Unity School is met by love offerings from those that have been helped by the Unity ministry and who wish to see it bless and benefit others. In most cases the charge made for Unity publications does not fully cover the cost of publishing and distributing them.

What Unity teaches: Unity teaches that through faithful practice of the presence of God anyone can be healed of illness, lack, or any other inharmonious condition. Unity teaches that the Spirit of God dwells within every person and that mind is the connecting link between God and man. Unity teachings explain how mind affects body, how it brings man into an understanding of his oneness with God. Through right thinking, faith replaces doubt and new courage, new hope, new health and happiness are brought into manifestation. We believe that God is not separate or far away, but that he is in each of us. God is a part of you, as you are a part of Him and He is right where you are at all times.

Unity is strong in the belief that the healing principles of Jesus Christ is as practical and as powerful today as when Jesus taught and demonstrated it during His ministry on earth. We stress the value of affirmative prayer. We believe that God is our loving Father and that it is His will for everyone of His children to be well, happy and prosperous. Therefore, we affirm the Truth for ourselves that we are true spiritual beings and we deny the power of evil in any condition. We affirm good through daily prayer and meditation and we declare the omnipresence of God at all times and in all places.

The day at Unity School is started with a period of meditation. Our form of prayer is to repeat an affirmation and meditate upon it in quietness and stillness. This we interpret as "entering the silence", which is merely the stilling of our human thoughts and forces in order that God's divine wisdom and inspiration may come through us. There is no more important experience than that of observing the silence, which is in reality the practice of the presence of God.

Ways in which Unity serves: There are many ways in which Unity School serves in addition to the printed word. We think of our ministry of prayer as proceeding our ministry of teaching. Undoubtedly prayer was the foundation upon which Unity was conceived and started and continues to function. By means of letters, study classes, correspondence courses, radio and television programs, affiliated local Unity centers, lectures, personal interviews, Unity has become a means of help and strength and enlightenment throughout the world.

Organization and scope: Unity School publishes many books, booklets, pamphlets, cards and other printed material in addition to its' periodicals. A brief description of each magazine, that is being printed at the publication of this book: Daily Word is recommended for new readers and contains an affirmation and Bible quotation with each days lesson. It is a wonderfully practical magazine for the beginner. The magazine helps all people to tune up their consciousness at the beginning of the day, which is of tremendous importance in the life of every person. Unity Magazine was the first of the Unity periodicals to be published. It was founded in 1889 by Charles Fillmore and continues to carry an article each month from his writings. Unity Magazine endeavors to teach the reader to understand and use his spiritual powers to demonstrate a healthy, happy, harmonious and successful life.

Departments of Unity School: Silent Unity; This group of consecrated workers renders a twenty-four hour a day service in response to calls for prayer that come by letter, telephone or telegraph. No request is too small or too great to take to God in the quietness of prayer. There are thousands of persons turning to God through Silent Unity every hour of the day asking for prayer help and the ministry of Silent Unity encircles the globe. Many of our readers unite with us in prayer as they look to God for healing and seek His light and guidance in handling their problems.

Silent Unity maintains a constant prayer service day and night and its' work is wholly supported by free will offerings. Silent Unity responds whenever it will be helpful. The Daily Word is edited in Silent Unity. The Ministerial Education Program is also a department of the Silent Unity work. Mail sent to Silent Unity is first sorted in the Silent Unity files. There a record card is attached and letters are prepared for Silent Unity letter writers. A card is kept for each correspondence giving a coded record of each request, our answer and literature sent. All Silent Unity letters are filed and retained for six months for any needed reference.

Prosperity Bank Plan: The idea of the Prosperity Bank Plan, which came to Lowell Fillmore, was born of his earnest desire to offer Unity readers the best possible service. Its' prime purpose is to give spiritual help to those that are seeking greater prosperity or more good in any form. It is to help people build into their consciousness the truth that God is the source of all supply and that there is no lack of any good thing. It teaches one how to make contact with God and thus bring good into manifestation. The bank plan also offers a convenient method of obtaining Unity literature for oneself and others. The plan consists of a daily drill in right thinking and an opportunity to share blessings. When a request is made for a bank, the users name is entered with Silent Unity for prayers for propriety and success. A folder of instructions accompanies the bank and includes a prayer to be repeated and held in silent meditation when depositing a coin in the bank.

Silent-70: Through this department of Unity books and periodicals are distributed free of charge to hospitals, prisons, industrial homes, orphanages, homes for the aged, school for the blind, veterans hospitals and leper colonies. Many Unity publications find their way to the folks in these groups, bringing them fresh hope and the desire and determination to build their life anew. More than ten-thousand institutions in thirty-five countries are served by Silent-70. Literature is also sent to military camps. This service is made possible through love offerings to Silent-70 and to our Good Neighbor Fund.

Braille: The Daily Word is published in braille. The love offerings of interested friends help to maintain the braille services. When a letter in braille is received, a specially trained Unity worker transcribes the letter on a conventional typewriter. The request is then filled and the answer is put into braille on a braille writer.

Editorial department: The editors select and edit the material for the various Unity publications and with the help of their editorial staff, prepare all for publication.

Reference Library: The Unity Reference and Research Library is a specialized library adapted for use by every department of the Unity work. The editorial workers and ministerial students make frequent use of the library facilities. The library is located in the east wing of the Education Building. The library on the first floor checks out books that may be taken from the library. The Heritage Room on the second floor is a repository for all the historical material pertaining to the Unity movement. Also in this area are replicas of the offices of Charles and Myrtle Fillmore that may be viewed by the public. Books and material may be viewed in this room, but not removed or checked out for outside use.

The Association of Unity Churches: Unity School serves the Unity centers and ministers in the field, this includes U.S. and foreign countries. This organization places Unity ministers and authorizes the establishment of new Unity classes and centers. While the centers are governed and financed in their local district, they are affiliated with Unity School where all ministers are trained. Some of the centers are called churches though most Unity ministers make their centers more a religious school than a church, emphasizing a teaching and healing program. There is a close spiritual bond between the centers and Unity School.

Unity Village: Unity Village is an incorporated municipality, having a Mayor and other village officials. Prior to its' incorporation it was called Unity Farm. The architecture of Unity buildings was designed and construction supervised by W. Rickert Fillmore and are of a modified Italian Renaissance period. Natural raw materials were quarried on the grounds. From the early 20's Unity had its' own saw mill, cold storage facility, canning department, cider mill, dairy, green houses, orchards, vineyard, berry patches, grain products and milling equipment, chickens, goats, horses, gardens, rock quarry, carpenter shop with its' talented wood carvers, furniture and cabinet makers, blacksmith and welding shop where all of the early wrought iron lamps, gates, flower basket fixtures and ornamental iron work plus the wood slat benches with special metal frames were manufactured. Also from that shop the beautiful plaster cast ornaments were poured and finished.

Following is a summary of the monthly meeting reports for this year of the Ladies Auxiliary. Officers for 1953; Della White, president; Mrs. Pitner, vice president; Florence Hill, secretary; Helen Davis, treasurer.

February: "Misters Rick and Lowell Fillmore attended the club meeting and dedicated our new lectern. Mr. Rick told us about the Walnut trees they found on Unity Farm and in 1919 he had them cut down and made into 50,000 square feet of lumber to season and in time the beautiful desks and lecterns at Unity Farm were made from this lumber. Ivan Lee, was the cabinetmaker of all these fine pieces. Mr. Lowell gave a very good blessing for our new lectern."

March: The subject of buying new tables for the club house and using paper plates was discussed and motion approved to purchase the tables and to use paper plates.

June: The new tables recently purchased were used and enjoyed. Mrs. Osla Jones gave lessons from the Bible monthly.

1954 - Unity News January 4, 1954, "They like Unity viewpoint. Carl Frangkiser, of the radio department, has received a letter from the manager of WNOE in New Orleans, a new outlet for our radio program Unity Viewpoint, which says in part, 'I think the Unity Viewpoint program is one of the finest programs of its' type I have ever heard. Actually, we feel that it is a plus to our programming, instead of thinking of it in terms of being a religious program which would lose audience for us.' The program is presented over WNOE by Bill Stanley, a young announcer who is well known in New Orleans for his 'Happiness Exchange' program."

Unity News January 11, 1954, "A letter from Dallas. Dallas Kreigh, formerly in the maintenance department and conceded to be the first 'settler' at Unity Farm, has written from Socorro, New Mexico as follows, 'It seems to me that I am back at Unity at times. Anyway my spirit is there. I learn at time the changes that are made and I'll say you are making a lot of improvements. They all tell me that the rose garden is wonderful. Perhaps I won't know the place. My prayers are for Unity Village to be completed. I am getting along fine, improving by the aid of my Unity friends. I wish to send my best regards and good luck to all!'"

Unity News February 1, 1954, "To publish writings of Charles Fillmore. The American Vegetarian, only English language vegetarian newspaper in the world, published at Santa Barbara, California, in its' February number announces that it will present the early writings of Charles Fillmore, co-founder of Unity. The first article, taken from Weekly Unity, appears on the front page of the publication with the explanation that the articles will be a regular feature. In connection with the article a two column picture of Charles Fillmore appears. The editor's note preceding the feature says in part, 'The writings of Charles Fillmore, vegetarian, founder of Unity, remains today among the greatest on the subject of vegetarianism.'

New Lake Being Built. To provide water for vineyards and orchards, a new lake is being constructed on the land in the southeast part of Unity Village. The lake will lie near the railroad tracks, north of Colbern road. Also to be constructed in the same general area is a road which will make it possible to drive to Unity's 'natural bridge'. Not many folks here know of this wonder of nature. It is thought to be one of the few natural bridges in this part of the country. It is a natural stone formation situated north and east of the old trailer campsite.

Unity Work Forges Ahead In Japan. Lowell recently received a letter from Shigeharu Ushida, of Tokyo, Japan, inclosing a Unity pamphlet that he had translated and printed for the benefit of his Unity class. Mr. Ushida is a teacher and has been interested in Unity for a long time. His wife also teaches a Unity class. All this goes to show that Unity is reaching more and more people every year."

Unity News February 8, 1954, "Swing magazine carries article about Unity. The magazine Swing, published by radio station WHB in Kansas City, carries in its' current issue a well written comprehensive story about Unity Village written by Tip Brown. The article tells of the founding of Unity, the establishment of Unity Farm, changing the name to Unity Village, the building program and Unity's importance to greater Kansas City.

The last paragraph of the article reads as follows, 'The benign influence that moves out from this tiny dot of earthly space goes far beyond the physical properties and creative comforts that have been so adequately developed. Unity's welcome carries no hollow sound and there are no 'keep off the grass' signs anywhere to bewilder the stranger. There is no bar to any creed. People of varying religious affiliation find soul-refreshment in the shelter, food, recreation, music or meditation according to their individual desires. Thousands have a deep attachment for this bit of heaven brought down to earth and perhaps never better expressed for them than in the words of an old beloved hymn, 'For the joy of ear and eye, For the heart and minds delight, For the mystic harmony, Linking sense to sound and sight, Lord of all, to thee we raise, This our hymn of grateful praise.'

The New Lake And Our Water Supply. Concern has been felt for the water supply at Unity Village, because of the lack of rain the past several months and the heavy drain on our lake. However, there is a lot of water in the lake now and there is no immediate danger of a shortage. The lake, which now covers twenty-one acres is about seven feet below it's normal level. Work began last week on the new lake in the southeast part of the Village area. It lies east of the old trailer park and near the Missouri-Pacific railroad tracks, although not on the right of way. The new lake will cover a six acre area and drain a sixty acre area. It will be approximately twenty-three feet deep and will hold 20,000,000 gallons of water when filled to capacity. It is expected that it will be ready to take water in a few days. The water will be used for the orchards and vineyards, thus taking a big load off the old lake that has been our only water source in the past."

<u>Unity News</u> February 22, 1954, "Unity Village center is growing. Services are to be held from now on in our Assembly Hall on the third floor of the Administration building. The new quarters have been made necessary by the growing crowds who attend the Village center's Sunday services in the chapel of the Silent Unity building. A 1,000 seat auditorium is planned to be constructed at the east end of the Administration building and we know that the interest and prayers of each worker are behind this planning."

<u>Unity News</u> March 26, 1954, "Lowell's writing is in good company. A recent edition of the Carl Holmes column <u>Mental Stimulators,</u>

published in the Elizabeth New Jersey Daily Journal started off with this, 'Winston Churchhill once said, 'Courage is the first of human qualities because it is the quality which guarantees all the others.' After commenting on the Churchhill quotation the columnist wound up with a quotation from one of our favorite authors. 'Lowell Fillmore gives us much encouragement in his statement on courage. He says, 'God has given you courage commensurate with your every need, courage to stand firm in the truth that you know, courage to step out on the faith that you have, courage to live for the Christ even as the Christ lives in you, courage to face life cheerfully and valiantly.'"

Unity News May 21, 1954, "The Charles Rickert Fillmore's home was the scene of a birthday celebration Tuesday evening, May 11th, in honor of Alice Fillmore's birthday. Bob Lakin of Birmingham, Michigan was also a guest of honor. Bob, who is with the Delco Division of General Motors, is to be transferred back to Dayton, Ohio and will move his family there soon. Bob is the husband of the former Frances Fillmore, Lowell's niece."

Unity News October 15, 1954, "Unity Village population increases. The newcomers are Pixie and Target, two Mexican burros that Rick Fillmore bought. Target's new owners are Connie and Harriet Fillmore and Pixie belong to Rickey and Rosalind Grace. However, the children will not be able to ride their new pets for a while as the burros are still very young."

Unity News October 22, 1954, "Inspect new utility house. On October 12th the Board of Trustees of Unity Village made an inspection tour of the new utility house under Rick Fillmore's able guidance. This new building is being constructed across the road from the student cottages. When completed it will house a laundry room, fully equipped, additional showers, bathing and sanitary facilities, a five room cottage for a year round caretaker and a community study room that may be used for meetings of forty to fifty people.

Rick explained the new type construction in detail, pointing out the different steps in the process at the casting building. No wood is used, window and door casing are built right in the wall section. Perlite insulation, mixed and poured in the molds on the concrete is also being used. The roof is cast in sections complete with ceiling, sheeting, metal joists, roofing, plastering and insulation. After being assembled, the roof will be painted red to simulate tile roofing."

A public hearing November 22, 1954 before the Board of Trustees of Unity Village was held. Present were board members and town officials; Rick and Charles R. Fillmore, Bill Bergen, Hub Whiting, Otto Arni and Jessie Gable plus Frances Poindexter, who owns land adjacent to Unity. The meeting regarded a slight change in zoning.

Unity News December 3, 1954, "Zoning Ordinance Unity Village. Specific legal description of all the land governing by a Board of Trustees. Dated December 3, 1954 signed, W. Rickert Fillmore, chairman of the board and A. Glen Lucky, Village Clerk.

Our Ten-thousandth Visitor. A careful check has been kept of the number of visitors registering at the Tower this year. Last Sunday Robert Jacobs, a ministerial student at National College Lincoln, Nebraska, registered as our 10,000th guest. He was presented with a copy of The Story of Unity in recognition of his status. Then he and his wife toured the Unity buildings."

A movie film entitled A View of Unity Village was produced and was narrated by Rosemary Fillmore Grace as follows.

> "I really have been associated with Unity all of my life. I was the only child ever born on Unity Farm, as it was called then. My grandfather wanted to name me Unity Farm Fillmore in honor of the occasion, but fortunately, from my point of view, my father and brother dissuaded him. The Arches was one of the first homes erected on the farm. The clubhouse and pool also were completed in the early twenties. In 1920-1930 the Silent Unity building and Tower were completed.
>
> Then came the years of depression and building construction was stopped at Unity Farm for ten years. However, landscaping, gardening and plantings continued. In the forties building resumed and Rick Fillmore introduced a new conception in building, a method of making pre-cast concrete sections and linking them together into buildings. Not only the forms for the buildings were cast from concrete, but ornamental stonework was made by special coloring and casting. Columns, cornices, balustrades, urns, and fountains

all made of concrete. Even great door frames were cast and swung into place. Gradually Unity Village began to take its' present day shape at a great savings in cost, but with no loss of beauty. Limestone quarried on the grounds was used for roads and retaining walls.

Oak and Walnut trees, killed by the drought of the thirties, were turned into blessings when the lumber was salvaged and made into beautiful doors, panels and cabinet work for the new buildings. In front of the Administration building was placed a Mirror Pool and the fountains in this serve not only as a note of cool beauty in the summer, but as aerators for the air-conditioning system.

In 1951 a bridge was erected across the Mirror Pools, now referred to as the Bridge of Faith, in honor of Charles and Myrtle Fillmore. It has always seemed fitting to me that my grandparents memorial should be a bridge for their lives were devoted to building bridges of understanding between person and person and between man and God. Here are words spoken long ago by Charles Fillmore, 'The joy of the Lord is here. Whoever enters here will be conscious of the presence of radiant joy. Only love dwells here. This house is filled with the presence of love. God is love and love is here. All anger, hatred and revenge are cast out. Whoever enters here will be conscious of the pure, the holy presence of love. We are thankful to Thee, O' Father, that this house is filled with Thy presence. We are thankful that we live in Thy light, Thy truth, Thy health, Thy prosperity, Thy peace, Thy wisdom, Thy joy, and Thy love. Amen."

Following is a summary of the monthly meeting reports for the year 1954 of the Ladies Auxiliary. Officers for 1954; Della White, president; Laura Meyer, vice president; Ella Le Mieux, secretary; Helen Davis, treasurer.

February: A project to provide new slip covers for the club house divans was approved. It was agreed to spend $25.00 from the treasury to purchase the needed materials. Mrs. Meyer volunteered to make the slip covers.

April: A motion passed to send an Easter gift of $25.00 to the Unity Village Center (Chapel).

June: The Auxiliary met at the Unity Inn for lunch and then went to the Tower, held their business meeting and attended a class, by Osla Sekit Jones, on Talks on Truth.

1955 - Unity News January 28, 1955, " New Lake In Prospect. Plans are underway to build a new lake, our third, just below the swimming pool. It will be used to take care of the overflow from the pool and will thus provide additional water for the lawns surrounding the pools, the greens on the golf course and other purposes. A road is to be built across the dam to connect with the picnic grounds and provide additional parking space for those using the pool. The old road across the golf course will be closed when the new road is opened. The new road will be a convenience for those using the picnic grounds. There is a substantial watershed around the swimming pool, as well as a spring, that will feed the new lake."

Article about the death of Mrs. Cora Fillmore. "Widow Of Unity School Founder Dies At Age of 78. For many years she was a secretary at Unity and later became the second wife of Charles Fillmore in 1933. Mrs. Cora Dedrick Fillmore, 78 years old, widow of Charles Fillmore, a founder of the Unity School of Christianity, died today at the home on Bannister road just west of Unity farm in Jackson County. She married Mr. Fillmore two years after the death of his first wife, Mrs. Myrtle Page Fillmore, who also was a founder of Unity and suggested the doctrine upon which Unity is based.

Started in 1910. Mrs. Cora Dedrick Fillmore became interested in the Unity movement in about 1910, and for twenty years, as Miss Cora Dedrick, she was secretary to Mrs. Myrtle Fillmore. She later became Mr. Fillmore's secretary. Fillmore died at the age of 94 in 1948. For many years, Mrs. Fillmore was a worker in Silent Unity. This is a prayer service. Telephoned and telegraphed requests for prayer are accepted day and night at Unity and Mrs. Fillmore was one who provided the prayers. Another of her interests was the unpublished manuscripts left by the late Mr. Fillmore. She edited these, and they still are being published about once a week.

Recent Trip to California. Mrs. Fillmore had not been ill long. She returned several weeks ago from a trip to California. Mrs. Fillmore was a native of Beagle, Kansas. She leaves two step-sons, Lowell

Fillmore, president of the Unity School of Christianity, and W. Rickert Fillmore, secretary of the school, both of Unity farm; two brothers, Max Dedrick, Osawatomie, Kansas, and Floyd Dedrick and three sisters, Mrs. Margaret Giles, Osawatomie; Mrs. Mary Darland, Pueblo, Colorado; and Mrs. Maude Masters."

Memorial service announcement. "Memorial Services for Mrs. Cora Dedrick Fillmore. Departed January 29, 1955. Services held at D.W. Newcomer's Sons Chapel. Date February 1, 1955 at 4:00 p.m. Officiant The Reverend Louis E. Meyer, Unity Society of Practical Christianity. Music The Newcomer Quartet, Mabel Moreman, Organist. Entombment Newcomer's vaults."

Unity News March 4, 1955, "You might be interested to know when Ernest Wilson conducted the Christmas candle lighting service on the Betty White show some 60,000 candles with blessings were sent out in response from television viewers. Moo-Sical notes. We all know that Unity dairy produces fine milk, but how many of us know the fine fellows behind the scenes? Bob Thompson is the manager of the dairy. He has been with Unity for eighteen years. He is ably assisted by Gilbert Greenwood, who has been here for ten years and Guy Marshall, a Unity employee for eight years. The dairy has about 80 head of cows, of which some 40 are being milked, producing close to 500 quarts of milk a day. Unity milk is rich because the herd includes Jersey, Guernsey and Holstein cows."

Unity News April 1, 1955, "A new vineyard is being planted on Unity property south of Colbern road. That explains the posts that have been placed there during the past week."

[From Rick Fillmore's files dated April 6, 1955 was found a notebook of Modern Thought - Editorial Excerpts of Charles Fillmore. There are seventy pages of most interesting reading, heavily expounding the Christian Science beliefs, but noting its' deficiencies. On page ten is an article entitled The Savior, which is a description of Jesus by Publius Lentulus, president of Judea in the reign of Liberus Caesar text ending. This description was found in an excavated city, on stone, in hieroglyphics and was written up by an uninterested party. First Charles and then Myrtle Fillmore's writings are told including instruction from Myrtle for children concerning the sexual part of learning about life.]

Unity News July 15, 1955, "Soldiers like Unity Village. Officers in charge of the transfer of troops from Fort Leonard Wood in Missouri to Fort Riley in Kansas have been making Unity Inn the luncheon stop for some time. Many of the soldiers who have stopped have gone up in the Tower and otherwise spent what time they could in looking over Unity Village. Last Saturday three boys who had been here in one of the earlier groups obtained weekend passes from Fort Riley to spend a few days here at Unity Village. In commenting, the boys stated that Unity Village is one of the most wonderful places they have ever visited and believe other buddies feel the same.

A special fund was set up by the Association of Unity Churches to help new churches get established and to help other churches in expansion needs. The funds to come to the association from the Unity Emeritus Fund.

The Midwestern Beekeepers Association held its' monthly meeting at the cold storage plant last Sunday afternoon with Clyde Corn as host. There were some fifty persons present from three states. After conducting a business meeting in the cool apple packing shed, members were taken on a tour of the bee yard, located in the young cherry orchard just north of the dairy. From there they went to the rose garden. Clyde says everyone had a wonderful time and without exception they were interested in the information he was able to give them concerning the Unity work.

Unity Village Center chapel services are held in the workers assembly room on the third floor of the Administration building. Ralph Rhea continues to serve from the original Unity Farm chapel.

Charles Rickert Fillmore has worked in all major departments of Unity School. He was first employed as an assistant in the bindery, advancing within a few years to the position of production control manager of the Publishing Department. In 1955 he was named Director of Public Relations of the school and was instrumental in developing Unity's retreat program which hosts more than 2,000 visitors to the Village each year. During this time, he successfully completed the requirements of Unity's ministerial training program.

New visitors record in 1955. A total of 11,571 persons registered as visitors to Unity Village during 1955. An interesting comment heard from many visitors was that they had been urged by friends to stop and see Unity, because the friends found it to be one of the most interesting places in the country."

Much information about the Sunday school material that Unity publishes and has available for distribution is found in Rick Fillmore's files in the library.

In mid 1950 Unity was considering changing from a loose leaf type of study material for boys and girls to a booklet form. A letter was sent asking the Sunday school departments of each of the Unity churches to respond to this anticipated change. Most of the return letters opposed the change and there were many good reasons given in supporting the continuation of the loose leaf sheets.

The review of the information Unity has prepared for the teaching of the young children included song sheets, stories, the use of the magazine Wee Wisdom and outlines for special occasions such as the true meaning of Christmas. Also the study material was programmed for the various age groups. Included in the information reviewed were instruction sheets and folders for officers and teachers of Unity Sunday schools.

[The young people's information also included a 'Good Words Booster Club Pledge' card. This small card had on one side, this information, 'We are happy to announce that (space for name) is now a member of the The Good Words Booster Club. (Space for the signature of the club secretary.) Also on this side of the card is a sketch of three monkeys (speak no evil, see no evil, and hear no evil). On the reverse side of the card is the following, 'Good Words Booster Club Pledge. I pledge myself to try to think and say and do only that which is loving, joyous, happy, truthful, kind, cheerful, encouraging and helpful. I will try to think only good thoughts at all times toward all people. I will try to let my words and actions express these good thoughts. I know that God is my help in every need. Because He loves me, He guides and protects me. I am happy and I radiate joy to all the world."]

[The following form letter has the heading, Unity School of Christianity 917 Tracy Avenue Kansas City 6, Missouri.] "Dear Co-workers in Truth: Day by day more Unity leaders are recognizing that the Sunday school has a very important part in keeping our Unity centers alive and growing. In view of this, we are making renewed effort to furnish well rounded material for your use and to aid you in promoting the Sunday school."

The Unity Graded Sunday school course is composed of the following:

Beginners Course - 26 lessons explaining to children under 5 years of age 'what God is.' These lessons are designed to be repeated several times in order to impress their truths on young minds.
Primary Lessons - a three-year course with 13 lessons to the quarter, four quarters a year, for children 5 to 8. These are based entirely on Unity's textbook 'Lessons in Truth' and are, in effect, lessons in Truth for young people.
Unity Junior Bible Lessons - a three-year course with 13 lessons to the quarter, four quarters a year, for children 8 to 11. These lessons acquaint the child with historical Bible background and give their practical application to his own life and affairs.
The Unity Sunday School Leaflet - flexible lesson material, 52 issues a year, with teacher helps, for children 11 to 13 and over.

The Unity Sunday school committee is now studying and revising our Sunday school material. You have seen the new Unity Sunday school Leaflet and it is being received enthusiastically wherever it is used. Other lesson material has also been in the process of revision for many months and we are now happy to report that the first of the new lesson books to be revised, the Unity Junior Bible Lessons, Second Year, Second Quarter, will soon be available for distribution in the Unity Sunday schools. A sample lesson book is being forwarded to you under separate cover so that you may see what a great improvement is being made.

You will notice that the lesson books will no longer be of the loose-leaf type, but will be in bound book form. Covers will be sturdy, colorful, and attractively designed to interest the pupil. The back cover furnishes space for recording the pupil's name and address, teacher's name, and attendance record. Of interest to the teacher is that each quarter's lesson books will be of a different color to make them more easily and quickly identified. A table of contents, giving the title of each lesson to be studied and the Bible chapters and verses from which they are taken, is a feature of the new style books. Each of the lessons have been revised and rewritten with respect to the age group of the pupils. Accompanying each lesson is an illustration that brings out the main point of the story. These illustrations are planned so that they may be colored with pencils or crayons by the pupils. The center spread of each lesson book is devoted to short prayers which may be repeated by the class at the opening or closing of the lesson period, or memorized by the pupils if they so desire.

Inasmuch as there are over 300 lessons yet to be revised, and it will be a tremendous task in its entirety, we are adhering to the plan of printing the lessons in the new style not in sequence but whenever the present supply of a particular quarter's lesson sheets is exhausted. In this way we hope to gradually replace the present style lesson sheets with the new style books.

We feel sure that you will find the new lesson books more interesting and easier to use in your Sunday school classes and will appreciate your comments and suggestions on the sample book being sent to you. Our blessings go with you in the wonderful work of presenting Truth to tomorrow's citizens of the world."

In the same file is a form letter dated April 30, 1965 as follows:

> "Dear Friend, It is again time to give consideration to the Unity Vacation School Course. This course lasts from one to two weeks, as determined by each center. This is a special time when the children come each day, Monday through Friday, for a period of two to three hours of spiritual instructions, handicraft and other activities.
>
> The weekly Sunday school hour is always a joyous hour. Often the time is too short to accomplish the great good desired. The longer period offered in the vacation school each day gives opportunity to present a living Truth lesson in a clear, easy way and to repeat the lesson objective through songs, stories, handiwork, plays and projects.
>
> The theme of the Unity Vacation School Course outline that we have prepared for your use this year is 'God Is Everywhere.' Also available for your use are two other outlined themes, 'The Sunday School Story' and 'The Golden Rule,' that we have prepared for use by the teachers and adult workers only.
>
> Our love and blessings are with you always. We rejoice that God's presence and power are ever with you, loving and guiding you in your service to His children. Joyfully, lovingly, thankfully, Unity Sunday School Department."

Following is a summary of the monthly meeting reports for the year 1955 of the Ladies Auxiliary. Officers for 1955; Della White, president; Laura Meyer, vice president, Ella Le Mieux, secretary; Helen Davis, treasurer.

February: A discussion was held concerning the purchasing of a new cook stove for the club house kitchen. It was agreed that Helen Davis would contact Jessie Gable and ask her opinion of what kind of stove to consider.

May: Helen Davis reported on the purchase of the new kitchen stove, that it was installed and in use. Helen also reported that love offerings for the stove purchase amounted to $110.00 and only $28.21 had come from the treasury.

July: A period of silence was held in honor of club vice president Laura Lee Meyer who recently had her transition. Discussion was held concerning a suggestion that the auxiliary could obtain a coffee-maker free from the sale of vanilla. A motion passed to adopt this new club project and the treasurer to order a supply of vanilla.

August: The treasurer called attention to the beautiful new coffee-maker which was on display. Following the meeting there was a brisk sale of the vanilla. Nominations were called to fill the vacated seat of the club's vice president. Dulsie Stockton was elected.

October: A discussion was held concerning the purchase of a new refrigerator for the club house. Mrs. Jessie Gable reported that the Unity Village management would be willing to make any necessary changes in the club house kitchen to accommodate a refrigerator. A motion by Alice Fillmore carried to set aside $25.00 from the club treasury to start a fund for the purchase of a refrigerator.

November: The treasurer reported that a $5.00 gift for the refrigerator purchase had been received. The club president suggested that all those present consider themselves a member of the committee to bring back a report on refrigerator types, sizes and costs. It was announced that club member, Mary Clark, who donates cakes and cookies to veterans in hospitals would appreciate any donations for this good cause.

1956 - Unity News January 20, 1956, "What the Unity wings stand for. Lowell Fillmore explained the wings in this way, 'It is an ancient Egyptian symbol, but it is found in various forms in the religions of other races. It represents the relation existing between spirit, soul and body. Soul gives wings to the body. Spirit is the enveloping principle, like the atmosphere in which both soul and body exist and from which they draw their original inspiration.' The winged globe is also a symbol of the earth and its' soul. The earth has soul as have its' products of every description. All exist in the either, the anima mundi, the Divine Mother. When the people of the earth lift up their thoughts to God and the animus dei or directive Spirit then the planet takes wings into a higher radiation of universal life.

As man develops spiritual consciousness, he attains the realization of the soul as the wings of the body. Back of the soul is spirit which quickens and energizes the soul, that is, gives the soul wings. Artists paint their angels with wings, representing in this way their freedom from physical fetters. But the soul does not have wings like a bird. The life activity of the soul is quickened by spirit until it rises above the thought of matter and floats free in the either of the fourth dimension which Jesus called the 'kingdom of the heavens.'

Unity News January 27, 1956, "Dr. and Mrs. G. Leroy Dale accompanied Nina Wright to Lansing, Kansas Sunday, where they conducted morning chapel services at the Kansas State Penitentiary and the Kansas State Industrial Farm for women."

Unity News February 10, 1956, "It is not unusual to receive letters of appreciation for the writings of Lowell Fillmore, but the one received recently was so outstanding that we want to share it. Referring to his column in Weekly Unity, Things to be remembers, the writer said, 'The joy of the Lord is my strength and it is. I am thankful for Mr. Fillmore. Everything he writes has that deep spiritual quality that his father, Charles Fillmore, had with a light hearted brightness added.'

The beautiful hand carved identical cabinets in the Conference Room just off the Reference Library and a matching table were designed by Rick Fillmore in 1934. The work of constructing and carving them were done by Ivan Lee, a worker in the cabinet making shop. For several years they were kept on the first floor of the Tower. Then transferred to the foyer just outside the Library. The cabinets now house six volumes of a rare edition of the Bible, of which only 150 copies were made.

Dallas Kreigh, who for long years was a faithful and zealous employee of Unity, passed away recently at the age of 80. He worked for Unity from March 1, 1913 until his retirement. Dallas was a general handyman and fixer. Soon after Unity bought its' first tract that make up Unity Farm Dallas came here from Kansas City Unity to work. He was the first Unity worker to live on the farm and for some time lived in a tent. He related that one morning he awoke and saw a cow standing over him, gazing down at him gravely. Dallas loved the farm and worked on it until his retirement.

Beginning March 1, 1956 and through June 6, 1957 Lowell wrote twice monthly articles entitled Viewpoint On Life for the Canadian newspaper, The Saskatchewan Farmer.

Unity News March 30, 1956, "Unity in the World Book Encyclopedia. The new edition of the World Book Encyclopedia contains the following entry about Unity; 'Unity School of Christianity is a religious educational institution which aims to give practical application to the teachings of Jesus Christ in daily living. It emphasizes constructive thinking, affirmative prayer and spiritual healing. It says that the will of God is to give all men health, peace, happiness and plenty. Unity is not a denomination.

But Unity teachers have formed independent organizations for study in the United States and foreign countries. These groups called centers, societies and churches are part of the Unity fellowship. Persons who attend Unity are free to belong to other religious organizations. This movement was founded by Charles and Myrtle Fillmore in 1889 in Kansas City, Missouri. Unity maintains a prayer and healing department known as Silent Unity. It also publishes books and magazines. Headquarters are at Unity Village, Lee's Summit, Missouri.'

T.V. Timetable November 1956. Rosemary for the first time went on television 'live' over KMBC-TV. Her program was continued through November of 1957, when she began a filmed T.V. series."

Unity News December 14, 1956, "New Unity lake is taking form. A big new lake for Unity Village is being constructed about one half mile north of the present lake. Work is now underway by A.G. Aldridge, one of the contractors who built a large section of the Kansas turnpike. The new lake will cover 35 to 44 acres and will have a capacity of 182,000,000 gallons of water.

[Mr. C.W. Ferguson, council and director of the Department of Rail Transportation Salem, Oregon came to Unity in December to discuss with Rick Fillmore concerning Rick's desire to have a railroad siding for receiving box car loads of paper for the printing department and other materials for Unity Village. The agreement was discussed that the railroad would build the siding, but Unity would have to agree to let the railroad alter its tracks and install a new raised rail system to move the tracks to higher ground to avoid flooding from the creek that at times floods the tracks. To do this much of the beautiful grassy hill to the east of the 'house on the hill' was sheared off which changed the beauty of the yard at the house.]

Following is a summary of the monthly meeting reports for the year 1956 for the Ladies Auxiliary. Officers for 1956; Della White, president; Laura Meyer, vice president; Ella Le Mieux, secretary; Helen Davis, treasurer.

March: A motion was approved to send an Easter love offering to the Unity Village Center (Chapel).

May: The president appointed Alice Fillmore and Helen Davis to contact Mrs. Jessie Gable regarding the purchase of a refrigerator for the club house. Helen Davis moved and Mary Clark seconded to take $100.00 from the treasury to apply to the refrigerator purchase fund, motion carried.

June: The treasurer gave her report, then read a wonderful letter of appreciation from Lowell Fillmore thanking the club for contributions to the refrigerator purchase. The new refrigerator is a Frigidare and there is a balance due of $50.00. New curtains and drapes were up and many expressions of admiration were given.

July: Because of extreme heat the luncheon was held at the Unity Inn and the meeting in the lounge.

October: The following letter dated October 4, 1965 was sent to Mrs. Jessie Gable: "The ladies of the Auxiliary of the Unity Village Center voted at their last meeting that a letter of appreciation be written to you expressing their joy at the beautiful appearance of the club house. The newly finished floor, the drapes the new furniture, and the beautiful new finish on the piano all combine to make this a most beautiful and restful room. Many compliments are constantly heard regarding it, especially comments on the lovely lamps. The ladies thought you would like to know how much it is being enjoyed and they also want to express their appreciation at having such a lovely place to hold their monthly meetings. Sincerely yours, Ella Le Mieux, secretary."

November: Helen Davis explained the Building Fund for a new chapel at the Village. A motion by Mrs. Alice Fillmore that the auxiliary give $50.00 to this fund, carried. A report was given

concerning a sink for the club house kitchen and that Unity School will pay for the installation. Mr. Otto Arni will build cabinets.
Mrs. Osla Sehit Jones again gave the monthly lessons at each meeting this year.

1957 - Unity News January 11, 1957, "Unity television program a hit. In the words of show business, the new Unity television program on KMBC-TV is a 'smash hit'. So say all who have been watching the daily program, which features Rosemary Fillmore Grace reading from the Daily Word, the Bible and other Unity literature. Rosemary's presentation is entirely sincere and has strong appeal. In five minutes she manages to convey the warmth, kindness and helpfulness that is at the heart of the Unity teachings. We are proud of Rosemary's efforts in presenting a pioneer series of Unity television programs."

[On March 22, 1957 a flag and flag pole were given to Unity by Mary Howard Moore of Lee's Summit, Missouri as a memorial to her father, Brigadier General Harold Palmer Howard, United States Army. Mary is a worker in Silent Unity. The flag pole was installed near the front entry of Unity Village. The beautiful gift of a very tall pole and the United States flag and the state of Missouri flag stands as a welcome to all who come to Unity. It is a fitting memorial for one who served our country and the flags close proximity to the Unity 'Beacon of Light', that shines from the Silent Unity Building together reminds all who enter Unity Village that freedom of government and freedom of religion are among our most treasured blessings!]

A full page advertisement, that appeared in the May 17, 1957 issue of the Sponser, a top trade magazine in the television and radio field, contained information about Unity. It was written by Don Davis of KMBC-TV, who interested the editors of Sponser in the Daily Word program. They were so impressed with the program that they ran the ad gratis. The advertisement information follows; "Daily Word, non-denominational religious program now available to T.V. stations everywhere and on transcriptions for radio! Featuring Rosemary Grace, granddaughter of the founders of Unity Charles and Myrtle Fillmore. Trained in the Pasadena playhouse in Hollywood radio, Rosemary Grace brings a fresh, sparkling, vivid new personality to religious programing on films made especially for television and transcriptions for radio. Each daily program times out at four minutes, thirty seconds and the series is dated to be scheduled Mondays through Fridays. A different program every day, made to play day and date, with special inspiration messages for every holiday, not just the major ones, for each season of the year, including Lent, vacations, back to school time and anniversaries of important world events. Daily Word is now hailed by television executives and audiences as the 'find' of the year in religious programing. Says one station manager, 'It is meticulously produced, simple, straight forward and in the best of taste.' Because of these very qualities, Daily Word answers television's need for a daily non-denominational religious featurette which can be programmed at any time day or night and attract audience on merit. Daily Word magazine is published in seven languages and braille and goes all over the world where it is read by persons of every race and faith and also by many who belong to no specific faith. Rosemary Grace includes in each program a passage from the Bible applying to that day's dated message in Daily Word and closes with an inspirational thought for the day. The text is stimulating, thought providing and helpful in an intimately personal way. Listeners comments run like a refrain, 'It gives me a real lift for the day.' 'I need just that kind of starter-upper every morning.' 'I feel better, work better and get along better with people because of the message I receive from Daily Word.'"

Unity News July 19, 1957, "New building going up. You've heard of a house of cards. Well, Unity will soon have a paper house, but there will be nothing insubstantial about it. The foundation and pillars of the building are now being erected below the bluff, east of the green houses. The Missouri-Pacific railroad has constructed a new spur from its' main line, a distance of 1,100 feet, so that carloads of paper for Unity can be switched to the doors of the new building. The 6,000 square feet of space in the building will accommodate ten carloads of paper, a three months supply for our printing plant. The building will resemble the motel from the outside, with concrete roof and overhanging eaves. It will be entirely pre-cast."

Unity News August 16, 1957, "Salute To Our Unity Band. This year marks the thirtieth continuous year that the Unity Band has been playing summer concerts, and this summer's seventy-piece band is one of the finest we have ever had. Musicians from the surrounding territory practice through the winter months, under the direction of Carl Frangkiser, so that we may enjoy their fine music every Sunday evening during June, July, and August.

Merle Turner and Harry Cloverdyke (Printing) and Rod Friend (Publicity) have been with the band almost from the beginning. Roland Rexroth (Editorial) has served fifteen years, and Ann Corn and her father, Clyde (Orchardist), have played several years, as has Bill Thurman (Multigraph).

The music that the band plays is of the 'pop concert' type and one of the highlights of each concert is the quartet, composed of Pauline Deniston, Maxine Stover, Morris Walker, and Harold Reynolds. Another outstanding feature is the rendition of several numbers by Eugene Sorflaten at the console of the Conn Classic organ. The acoustical qualities of the amphitheater are probably the best in this area, and add a great deal to the pleasure of the concerts that are so carefully planned and produced by Dr. Frangkiser.

Only two more concerts remain this season. Why not make it a point to come out, around 7:30 next Sunday evening, or the next. (Incidentally, the grass has been 'de-chiggered.')"

Unity News December 27, 1957, "After the Terrace Tea Room was closed it was used for an art class and later as a commissary for student ministers. Unity workers could donate furniture items for the students to use."

Following is a summary of the monthly meeting reports for the year 1957 of the Ladies Auxiliary.

January: The weather was quite unfavorable and attendance was only 14. It was decided to hold the election of officers at the next meeting. The new sink has been purchased at a cost of $49.00. Love offerings of $35.00 had been received. A motion was approved to pay the due balance from the club treasury. Helen Davis reported that the club had given president Mrs. White a Sunbeam electric skillet for her service to the club which pleased her very much and for which she was very grateful.

February: The president Mrs. White could not attend the meeting so it was decided to hold the election of officers next month.

March: An Easter donation of $25.00 was voted on and passed to send to the Unity Village Center. The president appointed the club secretary to conduct the election of officers for 1957. It was moved and passed that the previous years officers serve again. Officers for 1957: Della White, president; Laura Meyers, vice president; Ella Le Miex, secretary; Helen Davis, treasurer.

April: A motion carried to purchase an exhaust fan for the kitchen.

May: A rising vote of thanks was given to Mrs. Alice Fillmore, Helen Davis and the Unity Village Club committee for the installation of the sink and fan in the kitchen.

November: It was moved and approved to send a $10.00 donation to the new Unity Chapel building fund in honor of club member Mrs. Frances Seymour, who had her transition recently. A motion carried to send a $25.00 Christmas donation to the Unity Village Center.

December: A Christmas reading by Mrs. Florence Jones, 'Lady Yardly's Guest' was beautifully given and much enjoyed. Mrs. Osla Sehit Jones gave the message, 'Peculiar People In The Bible' and she wove it into the Christmas story.

Mrs. Jones again gave the lessons at all the auxiliary meetings for 1957.

1958 - Unity News January 31, 1958, "Information. There is now 250,000 square feet of office and industrial space at Unity Village. Glen Lucky is in charge of all clean up in the six main buildings. Beauty and facility are features of the 54 water fountains in front of the Administration building. The 300,000 gallons of water in the fountains is carried through the cooling system in the summer, thus getting two-fold result of providing cool in the offices and lending to the beauty of the landscape with the spraying fountains. In the cold weather months, hot water is carried through the same pipes for heating the plant. About 200 acres of the area that Unity covers (1,400 acres) are covered with spacious lawns."

Unity News February 21, 1958, "Don and Dot O'Connor served six years at Seattle, then came back to Unity Village as the Directors of Education in October 1955. They have now accepted the Seattle Unity Church to go back into the field ministry again. The old log cabin south of the motel and cottages is believed that the Missouri-Pacific railroad built this cabin about 1865. When this portion of the farm was purchased the cabin was included. It was used as Unity's farm office in the early years. Another old building still sets on the golf course. It was erected in the early 1920's by Unity. It was built to cover a well located there and to serve as a pump house for the farm water supply."

Unity News May 23, 1958, "Because there are so many interesting spots around Unity Village that Unity workers seldom see, Unity News will endeavor to bring you stories about these places from time to time.

Here we will tell about the building referred to as the powerhouse, because it was built for the purpose of housing the engine that pumped the oil wells on Unity Farm. The engine was fired with natural gas and it operated a huge wheel, approximately thirty feet in diameter and mounted flat, that pulled the cables that pumped the wells. The tower of the building housed a large water tank, because the engine had to be cooled by water.

In those days the oil that was not sold was used to fire the boilers for the heating plants in the Silent Unity building and Tower. It was also used to heat the green houses, the apartment building and other buildings on the farm. Since the oil and gas wells no longer produce the former powerhouse has been converted into a maintenance shop for the orchard. Spray materials are mixed here and the water that goes into the large spray rigs comes from the water tank that sits to the south of the powerhouse. Ladders and various other types of picking equipment are stored in the building. Oil is kept in the former water tank and from the windows at the top of the tower one gets a good view of the orchards. At this time of year the former powerhouse is a busy place. Men are spraying the apple and peach orchards and in a few months people will be coming from miles around to make purchases at the sales stand."

Unity News August 15, 1958, "The west wing of the Administration building is now in the process of being extended to make room for more office space and to provide larger quarters for Unity Village Center."

In September of 1958 the name of the Unity publication You was changed back to Progress.

Unity News November 21, 1958, "Unity's fruit packing and cold storage plant. The plant is located on Colburn road about half a mile east of the Unity office buildings. Lets take a tour of the apple packing shed, cold storage and fruit processing rooms. First we visit a large room 40 x 60 feet which houses an apple washer, apple grader, bottle washing equipment and repair room. It is on this floor that apples, peaches and grapes are packed. Peaches and grapes are sorted by hand. Apples are unloaded from trailers at the receiving dock, then fed into a polisher that has a capacity of 50 bushels or more per hour. This polisher was made in our own maintenance shop. Next the apples are sized by dropping them through rubber belts with holes in them, then they are further sorted by hand into the fancy, number one and utility grades. The apples are then packed for the sales stand or put in cold storage.

There are two cold storage rooms. The one on the ground floor will hold two thousand bushels and the one above will accommodate five thousand bushels. Apples may be kept in cold storage from harvest until spring. Cider pressing takes place in a large well lighted room just outside the lower cold storage room. The mill has a capacity of more than 600 gallons per day. After the apples are ground into fine pulp, the juice is pressed and pumped into large barrels inside the cold storage. Cider bottles are washed and sterilized upstairs. Fruit butters, jellies and other products, including honey and pickles, are made in the fruit processing kitchen, which is on the west side of the building. The steam boiler is in an adjoining room.

This year a new apple product is being made from apple cider. After precipitation the pectin from the cider is removed to prevent the juice from jelling, it is concentrated to one-fourth its original volume by means of steam heat evaporation. A small quantity of brown and white sugar is also added. The apple-flavored syrup is delicious on breakfast pancakes, etc. The attic above the cold storage is where the thousands of half-peck and peck pasteboard boxes are stored and assembled. Gift boxes and other packing supplies are also stored along side beekeeping equipment for the apiaries. The entire building is used to grade, pack, process and store the harvest of fruit and honey produced at Unity Farm."

Statistics/Facts about Unity in 1958. Disposition of land. One-hundred acres landscaped, 500 acres crops and pasture, 58 acres lakes, 100 acres apples, 20 acres peaches, 2 acres plums, 2 acres cherries, 10 acres grapes, 5 acres nursery stock, 300 acres natural woodland and parks. Seven miles of hedge and rose garden with 1,000 bushes of some 50 varieties.

Following is a summary of the monthly meeting reports for the year 1958 of the Ladies Auxiliary. Officers for 1958; Della White, president; Laura Meyer, vice president; Ella Le Mieux, secretary; and Helen Davis, treasurer.

March: It was approved to send the usual Easter love offering of $25.00 to the Unity Village Center.

June: A motion carried to send a $25.00 contribution to the Daily Word T.V. program.

August: A motion carried to send a $50.00 contribution to the Building Fund for the new Unity Village Chapel.

November: A motion carried to send a $25.00 contribution to the Unity Village Center.

Mrs. Osla Sehit Jones gave the lessons at each meeting during 1958.

1959 - A letter to Unity dated April 10, 1959 was received from a lady that wrote, "I have found an article in a 1958 Boston newspaper and I am anxious to know if you know all about this wonderful boy. I can't help thinking he must be a reincarnation of your wonderful Charles Fillmore as no ordinary boy could possibly do the wonderful things he has been doing since he was three years old." She enclosed the following article, "Preacher, age nine, talked to 80 million. Little Marjoe Gortner has been billed as the miracle boy' with an excellent vocabulary, there is no overlapping of his sermons. The thoughts and ideas in his sermons are far above the average of a grown preacher." Lowell Fillmore responded to the letter writer as follows, "It is interesting, but I know that the child is not a reincarnation of my father. Those who have made a study of reincarnation say that the soul rests for a period of years before taking a new body and my father passed only nine years ago. Also, from the account of Marjoe's preaching I would say that his manner and ideas are certainly not in accord with those of Charles Fillmore, however stirring they may be."

Unity News July 24, 1959, "The building that houses the farm shop and maintenance department and the casting building are being completed."

Unity News August 14, 1959, "The old saw mill, which originally was housed west of the railroad and east of the 'house on the hill was moved to just south of the casting building. There are only a few of these saws in existence anymore, so this one is something of a museum piece. In July 1959 it was being used in sawing up native Walnut and Oak logs that were cut down when the new lake was recently built.. The logs have been air drying for sometime and are now being cut into huge beams and dimension lumber. Some of this material will be used for repair work on Rick and Lowell Fillmore's houses and some of the older cottages built in the mid to late 1920's. This is just one of many instances where Unity's natural resources are being put to good use. We are indeed grateful for God's supply that is always available to us when we use wisely the good that is at hand."

Following is a summary of the monthly meeting reports for the year 1959 of the Ladies Auxiliary.

March: A motion carried to send the usual Easter gift of $25.00 to the Unity Village Center.

April: Meeting cancelled because of a very severe snow storm.

December: A Christmas offering of $25.00 was sent to the Unity Village Center and a $25.00 gift to the Wee Wisdom Garden School for a puppet stage that is needed.

There was no election of officers in 1959. The president Mrs. White was away most of the year with illness. Again Mrs. Osla Sehit Jones gave the lessons monthly. She is a teacher at the Unity Training School.

1960 - A letter was received at Unity dated April 6, 1960 from Dr. Juan A. Orta, Executive Director of the office of the Prime Minister, Havana, Cuba. He states, "Thank you very much, on behalf of our Prime Minister, Dr. Fidel Castro, for the copy of the Daily Word May magazine."

A letter from Lowell to a friend dated May 11, 1960 tells that the Terrace Tea Room is undergoing a conversion into an apartment building. [The dining room conversion to apartment units includes covering the beautiful plaster cast ornamentation on each side of the columns supporting the roof and upper terrace. Each column was covered over with plywood sheets and banded with bailing wire prior to boxing around each post in the reconstruction of the large room. On the upper terrace the equally beautiful banquet room was also converted and the upper terrace built over for more apartment space. Only the lower terrace and walkways remain.]

A letter to Lowell dated July 19, 1960 from the Church World Press, Inc. suggested that Unity offer for sale the booklet by Marcus Back, Faith to Live By.

Unity News July 22, 1960, "On July 1, Bill Bergen, farm shop, started his 35th year at Unity. When Bill began work here one of his first jobs was farm mechanic and chauffeur for Grandmother Fillmore. Whenever she wanted to go to Kansas City Bill dropped what ever he was doing and took her. Since 1926, Bill has served faithfully in many capacities on the farm. At present, he is Chief of the Fire Department of Unity Village and performs his duties for the fire department in addition to his regular job. His wife Rena works in Silent Unity and is a regular organist for Unity Village center. Bill and Rena built a new home on Unity ridge in 1956, but previous to that they had lived 29 years on Unity Farm at the last house to the south west from the 'house on the hill'."

Following is a summary of the monthly meeting reports for the year 1960 of the Ladies Auxiliary.

March: The puppet table gift given by the auxiliary to Wee Wisdom School was on display at the club house.

April: A motion carried to give a gift for Easter of $50.00 to the Unity Village Center.

August: Two new tables for the club house were purchased and in use at the meeting.

There was no election of officers for 1960. Mrs. White was ill and Dulca Stockton, vice president presided for much of the year. Ella Le Mieux, secretary resigned in mid-year and various members filled in. Mrs. Osla Sehit Jones gave the lessons each month and her continued service to the auxiliary was appreciated.

1961 - Unity News August 25, 1961, "Ralph and Helen Rhea leaving Unity Village. Ralph will be the new minister of the Unity Center of Practical Christianity, Miami, Florida. Ralph first came to Unity in 1928 and Helen in 1946."

Unity News November 3, 1961, "J. Sig Paulson has served Unity churches in St. Louis, Missouri and New York City. He and his wife Jane are now returning to Unity. Sig will be the co-director of the Unity Field Department and leader of the Unity Village Center."

1962 - Unity News February 16, 1962, "Harriet Fillmore chooses Duke University. The daughter of Charles and Ann Fillmore, has been accepted as a 1963 freshman at Duke University at Durham, North Carolina."

A fall-out shelter license has been issued to Unity Village, dated May 14, 1962.

Unity News August 24, 1962, "The Unity Band. The band started with twelve pieces in 1926 and the players were all Unity workers. It has evolved into an 80 piece symphonic band. Carl Frangkiser, the conductor, soon found that it was necessary to augment the band with other musicians. Consequently a number of members of the Pinto Pony band joined the Unity band in 1927. The Pinto Pony band was the brainchild of W. Rickert Fillmore and the late Lou Holland. It was organized and directed by Carl Frangkiser and appeared for two weeks in Madison Square Garden in New York City.

Through Carl's association with local high school and college students, a goodly number of fine music supervisors, college music majors and excellent high school student musicians joined the band. Carl received his bachelor, master and doctor of music degrees from Capitol College of Oratory and Music at Columbus, Ohio. He has written a large number of compositions for band and voice as attested to in Who's Who In Music. Carl is one of three men from the state of Missouri listed in that volume. He is a man of many accomplishments, whose name has also appeared in leading musical publications."

There were no Ladics Auxiliary mceting minutes found from January 1961 through February 1962. Following is a summary of the monthly meeting reports held for 1962.

May: A thank you note from the Unity Village Center was read thanking the auxiliary for the $50.00 Easter love offering. "Our former president Della White was with us for this meeting."

June: A motion carried to purchase spoons and cups for the club house. It was decided to hold the next two meetings at the Unity Inn because of the severe heat.

September: A suggestion was made that the auxiliary work toward purchasing an air-conditioner for the club house next spring.

November: A motion carried to purchase a new coffee-maker for the club house.

December: A motion carried to send $50.00 Christmas love offering to the Unity Village Center.
Dulca Stockton, president and Helen Davis, treasurer were the only officers identified. The secretary did not sign the minutes. Mrs. Osla Sehit Jones gave the monthly lessons.

1963 - Unity News January 25, 1963, "By Charles Fillmore. 'Do not hold yourself in poverty by the fear of lack by practicing a pinching economy. If you believe that all that the Father has is yours, then there is no reason for skimping. When you realize the boundlessness of your spiritual inheritance, nothing shall be lacking in all your world. See with the bountiful eye for 'he that hath a bountiful eye shall be blessed.' This passage states an exact law, the law of increase."

Unity News February 8, 1963, "Seeking God. within changes our whole mental viewpoint. We find ourselves right in the presence of creative mind and seeking to cooperate with the Mind, we receive spiritual inspiration and are guided in even the most minute detail of life. The ability and courage to press forward makes a great soul of us. Charles Fillmore"

Unity News April 12, 1963, "Catholic Radio Station In Brazil Broadcasts Daily Word. The publisher of Daily Word and other Unity literature in Portuguese wrote recently from Brazil, 'I received a letter the other day from a Roman Catholic priest, a friend of mine, who informed me that he maintains a program called God's parable at 12:00 each day on his radio station. The station is in the heart of the jungle! He reads a page from Daily Word each day!'"

Unity News July 26, 1963, "Poem by Francis Gable.

Friendship

I want the man I meet each day
Where ever I may be,
To know that joy and happiness
Just radiates from me.

I want to put so much into

The handclasp I extend
That every man I meet will say,
'I know he'll be a friend.'

I want to greet my fellow man
With such a hearty smile
That it will banish all their care
And make life seem worthwhile.

I want to understand their need
And such assistance lend
That every man I know will feel,
'I'm glad he is my friend.'

I ask not honor or reward
For anything I do;
I just would open wide my heart
And let the love shine through.

Though I but meet a brother once,
And touch, one smile I'd send,
And cause that man to sing for aye,
'I'm glad he is my friend.'

Unity News August 16, 1963, "Tribute To Lowell Fillmore. The following poem by Jane Traux expresses our appreciation for the very wonderful way in which Lowell Fillmore guides the Unity workers and for the inspiration he gives each Monday morning. Lowell, all the Unity workers love you and bless you and agree with Jane that you are:

The Perfect Boss

Unity is busy, working with God's plan,
Every single worker doing what he can.
We feel the joy and order, happiness and peace,
That always here surrounds us and never seems to cease.
If our work is blessed, we know what makes it so,
We've a presiding genius who makes the whole thing go.
We work in the Christ Spirit, the strength that is inside,

But always in the outer, Lowell is our guide.

In that Christmas workshop up at the North Pole,
They have elves aplenty, each one with his role.
Hammering, painting, fitting with a happy noise,
Making dolls and playthings for good girls and boys.
The elves are glad and busy in this pleasant place,
But they need Saint Nicholas to set their tone and pace.

So we work together, we take our leaf from you,
Every Monday morning in thoughts so good and true.
The every day and all day in our working week,
We see your faith expressing in all you do or speak.
Your consciousness is our guide in our times of prayer,
Helping us to lift our thoughts, to have faith and to dare.
You are our good example in everything we do,
And we are blessed in service as we follow you."

Unity News October 18, 1963, "Rick And Rosemary Off To Europe. W. Rickert Fillmore and his daughter Rosemary Grace left October 8th on a tour of southern Europe. They will be visiting some exciting and fascinating places. Madrid, Spain, Majorca, the island where Chopin once lived, Rome, the eternal city, Capri, Italy, where the famous Blue Brotto is located, Sorento, Florence, Venice, and Paris, France. When they return we can expect to hear some wonderful things about what they saw. Although Rick will probably see only the beautiful architecture which is his chief interest. Rick first saw Europe in 1910."

Following is a summary of the monthly meeting reports of the Ladies Auxiliary for the year 1963.

February: A discussion was held concerning the purchase of an air-conditioner for the club house. Helen Davis was to ask Unity to get a report of what the cost would be.

April: A motion carried to send an Easter love offering to the Unity Village Center for $25.00.

May: A motion was carried to purchase an air-conditioner for the club house. Helen Davis, treasurer was appointed to make arrangements for the purchase with Unity School's purchasing agent.

June: The air-conditioner for the club house was installed and operating at the June meeting.

November: A motion carried to send a love offering of $50.00 to the Unity Village Center as a Christmas gift.

December: The opening prayer for Mrs. Jones' lesson was given by the Center's minister J. Sig Paulson.

No mention was given in the meeting minutes concerning the officers. Mrs. Osla Sehit Jones again gave the lesson each month.

1964 - Unity News March 6, 1964, "Under construction for three years a four-story Italian Renaissance style addition to the main lobby of the Unity School of Christianity headquarters building is nearing completion, to be dedicated in June, will house offices of the international secretarist which are now scattered throughout other buildings. Unity craftsmen are doing the fabrication and construction."

Unity News April 17, 1964, "Unity's 75th Anniversary. An open letter to all Unity workers. As you all know, 1964 is Unity's 75th anniversary year. At this important milestone in our history I am proud to announce a great 'Vision' that our Board of Trustees has outlined for our next 25 years of growth. By 1989, our 100th anniversary, we plan to have established here at Unity Village a great educational center. We plan to build a preschool, elementary school, high school, college and post-graduate school. Our goal for these Unity schools is that they offer the highest possible levels of academic instruction while being conducted in a spiritual climate of Unity ideals. Here the student will be given the best possible opportunity to develop his own unlimited potential. Here he will learn, not only to think, but more importantly the love of thinking.

Here he will learn, not only to know about God, but to know God as the guiding principle of his everyday life. As a first step of the program, Unity has arranged to take over the sponsorship of the Wee Wisdom Preschool and Madam Elizabeth Caspari has graciously accepted the appointment as school superintendent. On September 1st the children will begin classes in adequate though temporary quarters in the western most motel building.

On June 7, 1964 to open our anniversary celebrations, we shall break ground for our first new building, the new Wee Wisdom Garden School building. The ground-breaking ceremony will begin a historic week of celebration here at the Village. We anticipate that large crowds of people will visit Unity during this time to hear Norman Vincent Peale, Marcus Back, John Payne and other interesting speakers who will be taking part in our evening meetings at the amphitheater. During these meetings, we shall announce a number of exciting changes in our Educational and Field Service Departments.

We want you to know about these plans, besides we feel that every single worker in Unity Village has a vital contribution to make toward their fulfillment. These are stirring times. Unity is on the move, knowing the sacred trust of our founders, Charles and Myrtle Fillmore. The world needs an answer to the mighty challenges of our century. We believe that Unity has that answer and with your loving help and guidance we shall send that answer ringing round the world. 'Christ in you' is your hope of glory.' God bless you all Charles R. Fillmore."

Letter dated April 27, 1964 from the Board of Directors. Resolved, Charles R. Fillmore be appointed to the new position of Executive Vice President of the corporation, Unity, signed by the board members, Lowell Fillmore, May Rowland, W. Rickert Fillmore, Barney S. Ricketts and Charles Rickert Fillmore.

Mr. Fillmore served in this capacity during a time of innovative and progressive change in the school's history. His concern for both the spiritual and educational needs of mankind prompted him to lead Unity School into an educational expansion and development program. Out of this program evolved a comprehensive adult education curriculum and, later, the Unity School for Religious Studies, which serves a growing number of people each year.

Unity News May 15, 1964, "Thank You Lowell. A comment from a reader about Lowell's book, The Prayer Way to Health, Wealth and Happiness. However, one of the letters that Lowell has received expresses how readers feel about the book in this way, 'This book read through once and I have started going through again. I am not skimming through it lightly it isn't that kind of a book. Sometimes I read one section, sometimes only a page or two, occasionally only a few paragraphs. I am trying to let the full meaning sink in. This book is simply and beautifully written. I think anyone could understand it and apply the inspired teachings."

Unity News May 22, 1964, "Bridge Of Faith. Faith is the inexplicable quality binding the past to the future. Today is the bridge upon which man walks in faith to achieve his desires of the past and hopes for the future. Alice and Lowell Fillmore stride surely and confidently upon a bridge of faith. Because of their faith and vision many good things have come to pass at Unity School, Unity Temple and in the hearts of friends and co-workers. Unity Society will honor Alice and Lowell with a reception following the Sunday morning service May 24th at Unity Temple. All society members, Unity workers and other Unity friends are urged to attend this reception honoring two of Unity's longest proved and approved friends. Alice and Lowell are richly blessed by being a blessing."

A memorandum, dated May 29, 1964 was written concerning a proposal to encompass Wee Wisdom Preschool into the Unity School of Christianity.

Unity News June 12, 1964, "Vision And Expansion. Ground was broken on Sunday June 7th for the Wee Wisdom School for preschool children. This is the first step in an expansion program to provide educational facilities from preschool to the college level. Only 75 years old, flexible and growing, Unity is a vision of further horizons. Unity sees no limits to what man may achieve, except the limits of thinking. Unity is a way of helping men change their thinking. Unity believes that truth is as timeless as God, but needs to be constantly restated in terms of the times. Unity leaves people free to determine for themselves what truth they will accept. Unity is more interested in meeting needs than in writing creeds. More an attitude than a doctrine, more a call to prayer than a church, Unity stands for Unity. 'Ye shall know the truth, and the truth shall make you free.'

Unity News June 19, 1964, "Something New. The new wing of the Administration building was dedicated last week as part of the 75th anniversary observation. The speaker was W. Rickert Fillmore, Secretary of Unity, Mayor of Unity Village and architect of the Unity buildings. The new area will house the International offices, supervising Unity centers in Nigeria, Australia, Europe, Japan and other countries throughout the world. The new wing is a work of art in design and appearance. When you visit this area, look up and you will see the words, 'Ye shall know the truth and the truth will make you free.'

The letters are set on the wall and illumined by concealed lights. The beautiful woodwork, be sure to see the door leading to the outside, was done by Ivan Lee, shop and the floors were laid by Hollis Spainhour, casting building.

A card printed by Unity in 1964 entitled, 'Shining Words'. These affirmations were chosen for display in the lobby of the administration building at Unity headquarters because they were favorite affirmations of Charles Fillmore. "The joy of the Lord is your strength.- God in me is infinite wisdom. He shows me what to do. - In all ways acknowledge him and he will direct thy path. - I can do all things through Christ which strengtheneth me. - Naught can disturb me, for Christ is my peace and my poise. - All things work together for good. - In quietness and in confidence shall be your strength. - Faith is the strength of the souls inside and lost is the man without it. - The greatest teaching ever given is Christ in you, the hope of glory. - God is my help in every need."

Rosemary has now been on television for eight years and made 88,974 T.V. appearances equivalent of 26,100,000 feet of film or 5,000 miles. Her programs are now seen on 71 stations including Alaska, Hawaii and Trinidad. In 1961 Rosemary traveled around the world and filmed her special color movie, Around the World in Search of Faith."

A letter dated November 2, 1964 tells about the dedication of the Unity church of Hawaii. Co-ministers are Phillip and Dorthy Pierson.

Following is a summary of the monthly meeting reports of the Ladies Auxiliary for 1964.

February: A motion carried to purchase new coffee servers for the club house.

March: A motion carried to send an Easter love offering to the Unity Village Center for $50.00.

July: A motion carried to give a love offering of $50.00 to the Unity Village Center.

November: A motion carried to send a Thanksigiving love offering of $75.00 to the Unity Village Center.

No mention was given to officers for the club except Dulsa Stockton as president. Mrs. Osla Sehit Jones gave the monthly lessons.

1965 - Unity News January 29, 1965, "Another Step Forward. The trustees of the Fillmore Foundation, Charles Rickert Fillmore, May Rowland, Barney Ricketts, Dale Batesole, Eric Butterworth and Hal Rosencrans, met in a joint session with the Board of Trustees of Unity School. Commenting on this eventful week Mr. Fillmore said, 'This has been a week of prayerful discussion and progressive planning. Our meetings have been conducted in an atmosphere of Unity; a Unity of Spirit and a Unity of purpose. In June 1964, we outlined our Great Vision, now in January 1965 we take this small, but significant step toward its' realization.' Dale Batesole, Director of the Fillmore Foundation, presented a check for $30,550.00 to Lowell Fillmore. This is the first grant made by the Fillmore Foundation toward the establishment of Unity's new education program. The money will be used to provide preschool equipment, graduate library equipment and research facilities."

Newspaper article dated April 24, 1965 states that Ernest Wilson will return to this area and become the Minister of the Unity Temple on the Plaza.

Unity News April 30, 1965, "Ground-breaking Held For New Apartment Complex. Ground was broken at Unity Village on Tuesday afternoon, April 20th, for a new five-building apartment complex, being built by the Blosser Building Company of Topeka, Kansas, on ground leased from Unity for a 75 year period. The two story colonial-style buildings will stand on the south side of Colburn road where part of the old apple orchard has been cleared for their construction. Forty-four units will be included. Sixteen with one bedroom and twenty-eight with two bedrooms. They will rent on a yearly lease basis and Unity workers will be given preference.

The buildings will be completed about August 15th, weather permitting and occupancy date will be announced later. The five buildings will be grouped in a H-shape around a central court, with separate carports at the sides. Laundry facilities will also be offered. All utilities, including electricity, will be underground. The design is one that has been tested for beauty, comfort and practicality in Indianapolis and other cities. At the ground breaking shovels of earth were turned by Lowell Fillmore, President of Unity, W. Rickert Fillmore, Secretary and Architect of Unity, and by Alton Blosser,

Chairman of the Blosser Building Company. The site was blessed by Lowell and also by May Rowland.

Name Contest With $25 Prize! Unity workers are invited to name the new apartment complex. Mr. Blosser has offered a $25 prize for the best name submitted. So get your suggestions into May Rowland or Charles R. Fillmore by May 14th. They will be contest judges along with Mr. Blosser."

Alton Blosser has been a long time Unity supporter and close friend of Charles Fillmore. He enjoys telling the story of visiting Charles and Cora in their home one winter evening. Charles was relating a story when Alton's attention was interrupted when a field mouse came across the living room floor. Alton tells that he was taking off a shoe to eliminate the mouse when Charles said, "No, Alton, leave the mouse alone, he is my friend!"

Lee's Summit, Missouri Centennial Celebration 1965. Unity participated in the celebration with a float in the Lee's Summit parade and an open house tour of Unity Village.

Unity News May 7, 1965, "New Chapel In Silent Unity Building. There is now a new meditation and prayer room which is open to the public 24 hours a day, everyday of the week, in the Silent Unity building. What was formally a class room, on the west side of the Silent Unity Visitors Chapel, has been remodeled and is now know as the Peace Chapel. Anyone may use this room anytime and a PAX, phone, is available to contact Silent Unity to ask for their help.

Moved Education Offices. The Education Department now coordinates not only the former Training School work, but also the completely new Science of Living School, the Resident Ministerial Program, the Silent Unity Staff Training Program, the Correspondence School and Wee Wisdom School. All of these various activities are under one administration for the first time.

Unity's New School For Teachers And Counselors. This new summer school program enables dedicated students to prepare themselves to help the many people who are seeking a greater awareness of God's good in their lives. The graduates of the School for Teachers and Counselors will provide trained staffs for Unity centers and churches all over the world and they will assist in expanding the Unity work in many ways. It is expected that this program will eventually develop leadership to take such positions as Sunday School

Superintendent, Hospital Ministry Director, Church Librarian, Director of Music, Prayer Panel Director, Youth of Unity sponsor, Director of Education, teacher, counselor, Publicity Director and Administrative assistant to minister. It is hoped that the various Unity centers and churches will use this program to build their center staff."

June 1965, Harold Whaley named Library Director; Unity School Library is located above the Unity Inn where the student lounge was; there is now a major commitment to build a fine circulating (lending) library.

Letter from Unity School of Christianity October 11, 1965. "Dear Friend, Our beloved Rickert Fillmore passed on to his next assignment in the Father's House on Friday, October 8, 1965. All of us in Unity bless Rick as he goes on into a larger expression of life. Certainly no one had a deeper faith in eternal life than Rick, and he was looking forward confidently to continuing his growth and unfoldment.

Unity Village is a living memorial to Rick's genius and inspiration. The beauty that all who visit Unity Village enjoy, came through his inspired mind and heart. A private family service was held for Rick on Saturday afternoon, October 9th. A public Memorial Service, conducted by Sig Paulson, was held on the 'Bridge of Faith' on Sunday, October 10th, at 3 p.m.

We felt that you would like to have a copy of the Friday morning Devotional Service presented to the Unity workers, which is enclosed. We know that you join us in a spirit of loving remembrance and deep appreciation for all that Rick has shared with us through the years. Together we go forward in the Unity work to carry out the high ideals and vision he has held for us. Faithfully and lovingly, Unity School of Christianity."

Copy of devotional service for Rick Fillmore given by Sig Paulson, October 8, 1965.

> "This morning I had planned to talk with you about the recent trip we took to Europe. However, I have to discuss with you briefly another type of journey. Our good friend Rick Fillmore passed away this morning. So a familiar figure has gone from our midst, but we know he is active on that pathway of eternal life that continues forever.
>
> Rick, of course, is intimately identified with the development of our Unity work throughout the world. His particular field of endeavor has been here at Unity Village. He

is responsible for all of the buildings and the beauty that we live in and work in and grow together in. He is also one of the spiritual giants of the Unity movement.

Many of you have know Rick much longer than I have. He has always been closely identified with the interests of the workers; he felt that he was one of us, and he did many many things that perhaps we are not conscious of to make this a pleasant and inspiring place to work. One of his co-workers of many years told me just this morning that the light used to burn late at night up in the Tower as Rick planned the buildings and the beauty that surrounds us here at Unity Village. He loved to have people get together and do things and, I guess, if he had had his way we would have had a picnic for the employees about every other week. He thought that this would have been a wonderful thing to do!

The buildings were designed for our comfort and, of course, Rick looked years ahead. Many of you have seen the model of Unity Village. He had a great vision; he planned the Rose Gardens, for example, in such a way that we couldn't miss them as we go from one building to another. He was also interested in establishing facilities here for recreation; the swimming pool, the golf course, and one of the first things that he had built was our clubhouse. He was intimately identified with everything that we do here, everything that we will be doing in the future.

All of you who have been working here remember how Rick used to move around through the buildings. He would come into my office quite often, sometimes he rapped on the door and sometimes he didn't. It didn't really matter whether anyone was in the office with me or not, Rick would just come in and join in the conversation. Rick was a man who made a lasting impression on everyone he met.

I know of no man who believed more firmly and more completely in eternal life than Rick did. I recall one of the last times I saw him before we left for Europe. He said, 'Well, Sig, I'll see you here or in our next experience.' He always had this feeling of the eternal quality of life, that he was going to go on, and he was interested in life. He had a scientist's interest, and an artist's interest in life. It was an inspiration just to know Rick, to be with him. Of course, we might not always agree with what he said or what he believed, but there was never any doubt as to what he believed. He stood for what he believed.

I read the Daily Word lesson this morning, and I thought how striking it is that today's subject is 'Decision.' 'All of my decisions are made from the Christ center of light and wisdom within me.' Certainly this is the source from which Rick drew his decisions. During his illness he was taken into the hospital and there was some question about whether his leg should be amputated. When I went in to see him, he said that he had prayed and released everything to God the Father. The word that came to him was that he was not to have the operation. He said, 'I'm not going to leave this life experience piece by piece. I came into it a whole man and I'm going out the same way.' He certainly had the ability to reach a decision and to stick by it.

I know that we all drew much inspiration and strength from having known Rick Fillmore, and having had the opportunity of watching the Spirit move in and through him. This really is not a time of sadness. Certainly we are going to miss Rick, perhaps a great deal more than we realize right now. But this is not a time of sadness, because he felt the eternal character of life so deeply that he was looking forward to the next assignment as part of an eternally unfolding adventure.

Life has many chapters in it. The chapters seemingly come to an end, but the book of life never ends. Life continues to grow and to unfold in wonderful ways, and we can draw strength and faith for ourselves from the recognition and the realization that here was a man who believed in the eternality of life and in its basic goodness. He said once that our problem was that we study the Truth rather than practice it, that we spend too much time studying and not enough time practicing.

So we have an opportunity together here this morning to practice the Truth, to go to this inner Source of all wisdom, and to reach the decision by which we will meet this experience, not only for Rick but for ourselves. We can search within ourselves and find this assurance that life is eternal, that it is greater than anything we have to meet in our living experience; and then we can release Rick as he would wish to have us release him.

We are going to have a memorial service for Rick on the Bridge of Faith at 3:00, Sunday afternoon. I'm certain that this is the way Rick would have wanted it. He loved this place. He loved all of the people who work here, and he loved all those who came and will come, so this is a fitting tribute to Rick Fillmore, to release him officially here in the midst of the beauty that he loved so much and which was brought into being through him.

I think the best thing we can do this morning is to have a time of prayer together, just a time of opening our minds and our hearts to God's inner presence, to the eternal quality of life, and consciously setting Rick free, not with a sense of separation, but with a sense of his ongoing, his moving ahead, his moving forward and upward. Then we can rededicate ourselves, too, to these principles of Unity, of the indwelling presence of God in all mankind. We can set Rick free, and set ourselves free, to give ever greater expression to these qualities of the Spirit.

Let us just become quiet. Father, we give thanks that we have known Rick Fillmore and that we will continue to know his spirit. We share in the spirit of adventure, the spirit of life, the spirit of love and joy. We give thanks, Father, for the assurance that life is eternal, that we are all the children of life, that our experience continues to grow and to unfold. We give thanks, Father, that your Spirit is the shepherd of the visible and the invisible. We are firmly anchored in the consciousness of your Spirit.

Father, we give thanks for the assurance that life is greater than any of its experiences, that we have caught the vision of the eternal quality of life. We give thanks for the privilege of sharing in this Unity movement, for the privilege of accepting and giving expression to the powerful ideas of life and love, of joy and strength. Father, we give thanks for Rick Fillmore, for what he stands for, for what he did and for what he tried to do, and for what he will continue to do. We give thanks for the realization that we are more than flesh and blood, that we are eternal Spirit, made in Your image.

Now for just a few moments, let us each one in his own way bid a farewell and a blessing to Rick Fillmore. He is something special to each one of us. So, deep in that secret place where mind and heart meet, let's breathe a prayer of blessing, of release, of Godspeed for Rick. Rick Fillmore, son of God and son of man, we bless you and we give thanks for the privilege of sharing with you an eternal life.

For just a few moments, let us consciously bless the members of the Fillmore family; Charles, Rosemary, Lowell and Alice, all those near and dear to Rick. Let's know confidently that they have the strength, the inspiration, the comfort, and the guidance that they need.

Father, we give thanks for life, for life eternal that keeps us through all its experience. In the name and through the power of Jesus Christ, amen."

On December 17, 1965 the last Unity News was printed and on January 15, 1966 the name of Unity's news publication was changed to Voice of Unity. The name was changed again on February 15, 1967 to The Unity Newsletter. On May 1, 1968 the name changed to Unity Village News and that name has continued for the remainder of this book.

Following is a summary of the monthly meeting reports of the Ladies Auxiliary for 1965.

January: Officers were elected. Delsa Stockton, president; Charolette Rheams, vice president; Dorthy Snodgrass, secretary; Helen Davis, treasurer.

April: A motion carried to send a love offering of $50.00 to the Unity Village Center as an Easter gift. A motion carried to purchase a new refrigerator for the club house.

May: The new refrigerator was in use at the May meeting.

November: A motion carried to send a Thanksgiving love offering to the Unity Village Center of $25.00. It was voted to pool the usual Christmas money, for a present exchange, and send it instead to a worthy cause.

Mrs. Osla Sehit Jones gave the monthly lessons.

1966 - Unity News January 1, 1966, "Sale. The Unity Dairy will be sold on January 8, 1966, beginning at 10:00 A.M. Also on sale will be a large number of plastic dishes, including about 400 divided plates. Glasses, china dishes, pots and pans and other items too numerous to mention."

January 18, 1966, Unity Ministers Association. "A graphic study of lessons in truth. Long range goals and charts planning for Unity Ministers Association. The results: A new proposed corporate entity to be called the Association of Unity Churches, to assume the responsibilities formerly performed by the Field Department of Unity School. Charles Rickert Fillmore stated, 'We welcome this new association to stand with Unity school and the Fillmore Foundation as mutual partners in spiritual service to humanity.'"

As Dr. Sue put it. An inspiring expression of the meaning of today's stirring events was given by Dr. Sue Sikking, Unity by the sea, Santa Monica, when she spoke to Unity School workers on January 18, 1966. Here is a digest of her talk:

> "Unity is in the process of growing. It is moving forward; this is progress that is happening to each and every one of us. And when I say Unity, you are Unity, and I am Unity. We are all together in it. Charles Fillmore thought that Unity would be the spiritual center of the world, and I feel that we should all think that too, and feel that we are a part of it.
>
> Now we have been for years speaking words, praying prayers, saying affirmations, thinking along these lines to build the consciousness that we have right here. And there is a tremendous consciousness here. If you come here from out in the world you surely know that. I think that sometimes when we get a long way away that we gain a full realization of what we have. So I'd like to be an ambassador to you this morning to tell you how wonderful you are and how tremendous this place is. I don't think we are completely aware of what is happening to us, because what is happening to us is in the inner realm, and we are capable only of being aware of what is happening to us in the outer.
>
> Now, this is not happening just to Unity. The whole world is being swayed at this time, and we interpret it as confusion, as uncertainty, as indecision. People without a belief in prayer may interpret it as panic, or as some evil thing that is coming

upon this earth. But it is not evil at all. What we are experiencing is the end of an old state of consciousness that has ruled in the world, and the labor pains of a new state of being. We are all being ushered into it. It is being felt throughout the churches, throughout government, throughout business. It is everywhere, on every level of consciousness. Our first inclination is to be frightened, to wonder about ourselves and about our position and our part in what is happening. If this were just something that was happening in Unity, we might have a problem. But this isn't just happening in Unity. It is part of the taking over of man's consciousness by a greater power.

Charles Fillmore says, in the first printing of Mysteries of Genesis, that we ask and we pray, we say, 'God is in me and I want to know God,' and then if we feel God in us we become frightened. But he also says that once you start on the path, never turn back no matter what happens to you, never turn back. In a sense, whether we know it or not, we are all committed to this. We cannot turn back because we are on our way. It is an untried way, a way that we haven't walked in before, but nevertheless it lies before us and it is ours, and there isn't anything we can do but walk in it.

One of the reactions we have at a time like this is mistrust, not only of ourselves but of our ability. We feel that maybe we are not capable, or maybe we are fearful about others and their motives, what they might do to us and what could happen to us. I think we are all in the same boat, because exactly what is happening to us is not yet made clear. But if we know anything on earth, we must know that what is happening to us is for our highest good. It is the next step forward.

When a family grows up, there is often a feeling of emptiness and fear that comes with the growth, both on the part of the parents and on the part of the children who are growing up. But we wouldn't have it otherwise. If you have a child, you certainly want the child to grow up. The last thing on earth you would do is to keep him as he is.

I think that God is a great chess player and I think He is making the moves nowadays. We are all moving in to the Kingdom whatever that may mean. I don't know and perhaps you don't know. The only thing we know is that it is good. You have to remember, too, that you cannot have the new heaven and the new earth without letting the old ones go. It is sometimes difficult to stand and see the things that are happening and know that they are for good, when we cannot see. In the Gospel of Thomas this is called 'to know without knowing.'

We are being ushered into a new dimension of life. All the world is not just Unity, not just you individually or some group or some government or some countries. This is something that is happening to mankind at this particular time and if you have studied a good deal you know that it has been prophesied for thousands of years that this time would come. We are moving into a new way of life; we know that from the outer, and we must also know it from the inner. It is an awakening of our own soul and our own being, and an awakening of all of mankind's soul and being.

You ask, 'What's going to happen to me?' All right, I'll tell you. If you are free to move, if you are fearless in the place where you stand, you will be moved into a better position and everything will work together for good. Because that's the only way God can work. The only way we can interfere in any way with the law of God's good is in ourselves, and it still works for good, even though we fight sometimes. So we must be aware that what is happening to us is the action of Spirit, because that is the only movement in the world. This is the truth in every religion, the only movement in the world is the movement of the Spirit. We may interpret this movement and say that it is good or bad, but nevertheless, it is a movement of Spirit.

Where we are, right now we have the greatest opportunity on earth, because we have the power. If one with God is a majority, then certainly everyone who is holding his thoughts toward the highest is a great power today. I believe with all my mind and heart that Unity is one of the greatest powers on earth at this time. When we have a child who grows up and comes into some place of responsibility, we say, 'Well, the child has been prepared for that.' All right, we in Unity certainly have been prepared.

I think that the thing we should do is 'gird up our loins.' In Bible times everyone wore a long robe, with a girdle, or belt. When a man was going to work he tucked the robe up under his girdle. Here, and everywhere in the world today, we are 'girding up our loins' and getting ready for action. And let us know that this power that is at work is the activity of Spirit that is moving into this place. I'm not going to call it change, because I don't know and if we know it, everything changes.

Someone asked me if I thought that we could lose the Jesus Christ teaching. I don't think there is anybody in this place, any group of people in the world, who could possibly lose the Jesus Christ message. That message is the message of life. And that's what Unity's message is, the message of life. This is the offering that we have to give to people, life. 'I came that they may have life, and may have it abundantly.'

Jesus always taught in terms of life. He didn't talk about the shallows of life, or the lack of life, but about the fullness of life. If there is any place on the face of the earth that should believe and accept the fullness of life, it is right here where we are, because this is the fullness of life. This is what our healing department represents, life. This is what the magazines represent; they are life blood, they go out , they circulate.

It is very hard for us, when we are in the midst of a difficult challenge, or when we are filled with fear and our human consciousness testifies to what seems to be, to realize that at this moment the greatest Power of all is at work for us. Sometimes we can see it afterward, but it is difficult to understand it at a certain time.

We are in the process of changing, or learning a new technique, a new way of living, a new expression , for all mankind. All those who have gone before us have established a state of consciousness, and we are committed to it. Charles Fillmore wrote, 'Unity is the truth that is taught in all religions, simplified and systematized so that anyone can understand and apply it.' A woman from my center went to another metaphysical teacher, after she had been to our service and she asked what was the difference between Unity and the other teaching. The other teacher said, 'Unity is simpler.' Simplicity is the movement of life.

Charles Fillmore also said, 'We want a better and purer Truth to go out into the world under the name of Unity.' That is all we want today, a purer and more wonderful Truth. This Truth was meant for all men always, so Unity has to open its' gates to let all people in. We can no longer feel that we have a little invisible wall around this great, great Truth. Now that we have nourished it, as one nourishes a child, we have to send it out into the world. We must send it out into the world and let it do its' perfect work. What we really want is to send out a more wonderful, a more tremendous, a more powerful brand of Unity than ever before. And we want it for all men, always. As the angel said in the Christmas story, 'these good tidings are for all men.' So our next step is to be sure that we share with all people this great Truth.

There must be a blending of all that we have with all religions. What this means is that we must open our gates, to every religion. It is our function to open the gate of our consciousness and the Truth we know, and share it with all mankind.

So this ferment is started. We didn't start it, but we are in it. The fire is kindled and it is spreading. While we may have been just a queer little group in the beginning, the invisible walls are thinning, and the people of the world are coming to us. Why are they coming to us? Because the time is ready for us to open the door and let them in. We are strong enough. We have grown strong enough to now be able to share what we have with all mankind. And this is what is happening, we are making a new beginning. We are starting the activity of opening the doors of Unity to let all mankind in. This is our divine heritage from God, and this is the part we have to play in this particular time."

Letter dated February 7, 1966 to Lowell from Charles R. Fillmore (letter in part). "The executive committee has instituted a definite retirement program for Unity employees. When each reach their 70th birthday they will retire and will receive annuity payments to supplement their social security and savings. This plan to begin on March 1966. List of names include these of note: Pharaby Boileau -

79, Retta Chilcott and Tom Conkin - 74, Le Roy Dale - 72 and Elsie Page - 77."

Unity News February 25, 1966, "Unity Personalities Head Northwest For Health Rally. Guests at the second Northwest Unity Healing Rally, February 27, 28 and March 1 will find three distinguished Unity personalities on the program held at the Olympic Hotel in Seattle. James Dillet Freeman, who probably enjoys the widest readership of any contemporary Unity writer, is given top billing on the program. Jim has done most of his work at Unity headquarters where he now holds the title of Director of Spiritual Research. Largely identified with his writing skills in prose and inspirational poetry, Jim was a favorite lecturer in the Science of Living classes last summer.

May Rowland, the Director of Silent Unity, who has prayed with so many correspondents, will see many friends as she appears on the program. It will be a fine experience for all at the healing rally to pray 'in person' with May Rowland. Ed Rable, Unity minister, known to many persons here from his training days, appeared at the first Northwest Unity Healing Rally, lecturing on metaphysical Bible interpretation. He was a great success, so they've asked him back. He will do a series of lessons from the Old Testament titled, Forerunners of Jesus Christ.

Unity Caribbean Retreat. The Retreats office is now releasing information on a November retreat and tour of the beautiful islands of Puerto Rico, Jamaica and Trinidad. They are planning a regular retreat program that will include special speakers, prayer times and personal counseling in addition to the opportunity for seeing the beauty and variety of the islands.

They Brighten The Corners Where They Are. Unity is blessed with guides, for tours of the buildings, whose attitudes and thoughtfulness have changed peoples lives. This is attested to by letters which Unity receives and by letters sent to the guides themselves. Last week a letter was received by one of the guides from a woman who had been taken to the top of the Tower two years ago. This woman had taken a taxi from Kansas City to Unity and the cab was kept waiting while she went to the top of the Tower. On the way to the top she started crying and the guide asked her if she was being affected by the height. However, the woman assured her that she was all right. She said that she was just overcome, because she had recently lost her husband and was finding it difficult to pick up the pieces of her life. When she returned to the ground level she wanted to buy some apple butter, but explained that she had come to Kansas City by plane and that her luggage weighed the maximum allowed.

The guide found herself thinking about the woman from time to time, so at Christmas time she sent her a jar of apple butter as a gift and enclosed some helpful literature. The following letter is a thank you note, sent two years later. 'I am very much ashamed for my rudeness in not writing you two years ago after your extreme kindness to me when I stopped at Lee's Summit and your generous thoughtfulness in sending me the delicious apple butter that I so thoroughly enjoyed. You meet and correspond with so many thousands of people that I know you cannot possibly remember me, but I went to Kansas City to attend a national convention of the American Association of University Women. About six months before I had lost my husband to whom I was devoted and I just could not seem to gather up the pieces of my life. I had written Unity many times during the years and when I reached Kansas City I felt I must visit Unity. I was only there for a short time but you took me up on the Tower and talked to me. I cannot seem to get used to life without my husband, but because of you and your help and understanding, I have picked up the pieces and am living a busy and useful life.

The governor of New Jersey appointed me a member of his cabinet in charge of civil service over 130,000 employees. I drive seventy miles to Trenton in the morning and seventy miles back at night. Thought you might be interested because you really put me on my feet again.' Sometimes we little realize the effect things we say and do may have on the lives of others, the needs a few words can fill. The guide felt that the things she said were insignificant, but her words changed a woman's life. We bless all of our sincere guides and wish we could share with you some of the wonderful letters we get praising them."

For a short period of time, beginning on April 1, 1966, the Unity News was replaced by The Voice of Unity issued from the office of Charles Rickert Fillmore in bulletin form.

Bulletin #4 - Announced the framework of a proposed plan under which the activities of the Unity Ministers Association would be handled independently of Unity School activities. This transition to take place over a two year period. "In many ways we have been standing on each others feet. The time has come for each to stand on his own feet as important partners in the Unity structure. Those who are active in the Field Ministry are best equipped to see its' needs and potentials. Those who are active at Unity School are best equipped to do their job. As we work together, we shall see a new niche and productive relationship established between the Field Ministers and Unity School."

Bulletin #6 - Announced the appointment of a Unity book editor, who will supervise the selection, styling, editing, promotion, etc. of all books, new and reprint.

Unity News February 1, 1966, "Unity Ministers Association President Ralph Rhea described the meeting just completed as 'one of the most important meetings that we have ever had. It produced a remarkable demonstration of unity, divine order and enthusiasm. Everything took place in an atmosphere of love and we go forward now with even greater enthusiasm and determination toward the establishment of the Association of Unity Churches.' Bob Sikking has been named as Executive Director of this new group and will assume this position in April."

Bulletin #9 - Announced the establishment of The Voice of Unity as a regular channel of communing news, ideas and progress reports to Unity School employees, leaders and teachers in the field and all other friends of Unity.

Bulletin #10 - Presented a vital and far reaching statement of the Purpose of the Unity Movement. Emphasizing the fact that Unity is an open system for teaching and demonstrating the spiritual potential of man. The statement points out that while we avoid strict creeds, we recognize the necessity for dedication to desired objectives and the need to gather our forces for good around a fundamental Statement of Purpose.

> "The Statement of Purpose lists four fundamental purposes of the Unity movement. Prayer and Healing, Education and Publication, Professional Preparation and Research and Study. The fundament thesis of the movement upon which our teaching rests, are named as: (A) The essential unity of Universal Mind and individual mind. (B) The interdependence of all mankind and all nature, giving expression to the essential

unity. (C) The practical unity of principle and expression. The fact that knowledge based in trust can be demonstrated in the material world. (D) The free will conscience of man, by which the individual accepts or denies Universal Mind in his conscious life. (E) The healing power of the Spirit, mind, body and affairs that follows upon communion with Universal Mind. (F) The abundance of supply, health, fellowship, compassion, peace and creativity that follow upon man's awareness of unity.

In light of these purposes and thesis the Unity movement has dedicated its' self to these eight resolutions: (A) That such teachings, being spiritual, should never be submerged in organized religion, dogmatic creed, ritual or ceremony, or personal ambition. (B) That the movement, which is based on its' conception as an integrative educational program with a spiritual origin, is institutionally centered in Unity School of Christianity. (C) That all acts of students, ministers, administrators and affiliates should be centered in love, prayer and unity of purpose. (D) That no spiritual service, such as healing activities, should be identified with a sum of money, but will be supported by the gifts of those who want to help expand this service. (E) That no form of racial, religious, or economic prejudice or discrimination is consonant with Unity teachings. (F) That while we appreciate the contribution that other religious teachings are making to humanities progress, we stand firm in the light of universal truth, differing where we must from conventional and popular creeds. (G) That the movement as a non-profit, educational work, must be guided by high awareness of public trust. (H) That the movement should not officially affiliate with any other movement whose purposes would alter or dilute our own. (I) That the governance of the Unity Movement should rest in democratic Spirit of Truth, rather than authoritative and hierarchical processes."

UMA President Speaks To Workers. Addressing Unity School workers on January 21, 1966 UMA President Ralph Rhea said in part:

"It turned out that God knew, even though I did not, that we were coming here for one of the most important meetings that we have ever had. This was truly an hour of destiny for our Unity field work, and I think for Unity School. The steps that have been taken here, all in an atmosphere of harmony and order and mutual respect, put us months ahead of the schedule that we had set up.

We had no static, we had no friction, we had honest discussions, there were no egos sticking out. In an atmosphere of mutual respect for Unity School and for the ministers, this forward step has been taken. We voted to become a corporate body, an Association of Unity Churches.

What does this do to our relationship to Unity School? I think that it will make us closer than ever, because it has caused us to grow up. It will cause us increasingly to accept our own responsibility.

What does this do to the unity field? Well, I think it will make little difference as far as what we represent is concerned. The ministers have a very deep love for the teachings of Charles Fillmore and nothing as far as I can see in the years to come could possibly take the place of these teachings. I have heard people in scientific positions say, 'If you just changed a few words here and there in Charles Fillmore's writings, it would be obvious to any scientist or physicist, or anyone else reading his teachings that he was precognitive, that he had a vision, that he was a prophet, that he had revelation and that he gave to the world a great teaching.' This will continue to be what the ministers in the field will teach.

In the few years that I have been in field, when I came back here for UMA conferences I felt a sense of frustration and I wasn't exactly sure what it was that frustrated me. But now I know. We were trying to be an organization and we were not one. We didn't even act like an organization. Now I am positive that we will be an organization and I am excited about it. I think it will be good for the school and good for us. We will not be stepping on each other's toes. We will be working for a larger vision of Unity in the world with a capital 'U' and with a small 'u'. And this means a great deal.

I cannot tell you anything as to Unity School, because no one in authority has given me any authority to speak on this subject. But I do feel this, things in these times move rapidly and where Unity as a movement is concerned, I think there is no difference. We have a unique and wonderful thing to give to the world and we will be very busy giving it. We can certainly improve the techniques that we have for giving it from day to day and week to week, but the world needs it desperately and we will be giving it. I cannot deny feeling that some pieces of a rather complex puzzle have all fallen into place and about this I am extremely happy."

News Notes. David McClure and his wife Barby plan to leave February 4, 1966 on their return trip to Australia. After stops enroute at Phoenix, Honolulu and the Fiji Islands the McClures will resume their ministry in Sydney, developing a branch there of Unity School of Christianity. Our warmest blessings go with Dave and Barby. There are still a few vacancies in Bill Fischer's Lenten Pilgrimage to the Holy Land. A twenty-one day tour from New York City with visits to Egypt, Lebanon, Jordan, Israel and Greece. For information write to Bill at 1075 W. Market, Akron, Ohio. Dr. Ernest Wilson's 'master class' lessons at Kansas City's Unity Temple drew a registration of 970 students.

Dr. Sue Sikking was scheduled to speak to regional managers of the Encyclopedia Britannica Corporation at a meeting in Freeport, Grand Bahamas last week. Sue treasures a letter that her son an EB executive received from William Benton, distinguished president of the corporation and a former Senator, commenting in detail on Sue's book. Incidentally, A Letter of Adam is one of the best selling Unity books in many years. More than twelve thousand copies were sold in the first three months of publication, resulting in a second printing order in record time.

Interesting statistics from the Field Department's recently released survey of center activities: One center which monitored its' Dial-a-Prayer telephone found that 50,000 calls were handled in 1964. Center membership ranges from fifty or less to as many as four thousand. Sunday attendance ranges from that of fifty or less at fifty-two centers to a weekly figure of from a thousand to sixteen hundred at one center.

Bulletin #11 - Announces the appointment of James Dillet Freeman as Director of Spiritual Research for Unity School. This promotion frees Jim for creative assignments in writing, teaching and spiritual research for Silent Unity and other departments of the school.

The bulletin also acknowledges with great gratitude Jim's many contributions to the spiritual resources of Silent Unity the Ministerial Training Program and counseling work as well as his invaluable creative contribution including The Household of Faith and immeasurable contributions to Daily Word through the years.

June 1966, the Unity Library was moved to a larger area above the classrooms of the School for Ministerial and Religious Studies on the third floor of the Administration building. The Reference and Research Library were combined with the Lending Library.

October 1, 1966 article about the Unity Inn announces that a meat dish has been added to each days menu. This is the first serving of meat at Unity Inn. In October the name of the Unity publication Good Business was changed to New Magazine. In December the Unity School Leaflet was discontinued.

Following is a summary of the monthly meeting reports of the Ladies Auxiliary for 1966.

January: A motion carried to send a love offering of $50.00 to the Unity Village Center for Christmas and the New Year. In the absence of beloved Osla Jones, a splendid lesson was given by Jane Paulson.

March: A motion carried to send a love offering for Easter of $25.00 to the Unity Village Center.

July: A $50.00 donation was sent to Silent Unity, in the name of the boys in service of our country, to be applied for sending the Daily Word monthly to those in Vietnam.

December: A motion carried to send a $50.00 love offering to the Unity Village Center for Christmas.

From February through the balance of the year Mrs. Jones gave the monthly lessons.

1967 - Unity Newsletter February 15, 1967, "Transition. Carl Frangkiser, who for many years conducted the band concerts at Unity Village and directed the Unity radio department, passed on January 17, 1967."

Unity Newsletter March 11, 1967, "Carillon To Be Dedicated. A 111 bell carillon will be installed in the Unity Tower. This fine instrument can be played manually from a console or automatically. Unity's new corillon will be a memorial to W. Rickert Fillmore. A dedication recital is planned for Sunday, June 4th. Rick's birthday was June 1st. A Unity

Village wedding. Miss Harriet Fillmore, daughter of Charles Rickert and Ann Fillmore, became the bride of Richard Allen De Bauge of Parsons, Kansas at a ceremony at Unity Village on April 14th. Reverend J. Sig Paulson conducted the ceremony. They will make their home in Parsons, Kansas. J. Sig Paulson is the Director of the Department of World Unity while also the minister of the Unity Village Chapel.

Farm Survey. Preliminary plan for long range development. The town of Unity Village, Missouri. Runnells, Wintrollz & Associates 910 Penn Kansas City, Missouri dated 1967. "Unity's 1,400 approximate acres include 400 acres of natural wooded areas. Unity Villa Apartments; 16 one bedroom units and 28 two bedroom units. Twelve additional units include eight studios and 4 one bedroom units. All of these are open to the general public. The land is leased, the developer is a 'Friend of Unity.'

The institutional headquarters for Unity occupy approximately 45 acres. The nine hole golf course 50 acres and also 50 acres for hotel and cottages. Unity Lake #1 is the primary water supply. Unity Lake #2 is a supplementary water supply, but its' present use is primarily recreational. An 8" water line connects the lake to the water Tower. Lake #2 is approximately 1/2 mile north of #1. Kansas City has a 10" water line along the right of way of Highway 50. It was tapped with a 6" line to serve Unity Villa. Sanitary sewer utilizes the main trunk line built by Lee's Summit, a 21" line parallels the Little Cedar Creek and connecting to a 25 acre sewage lagoon adjacent to the Little Blue River one mile north of Unity.

Electricity comes from the Missouri Public Service Company. Distributions within Unity are owned and maintained by Unity. Telephone service by Southwestern Bell. Public schools Hazel Grove School is part of the Lee's Summit district. It occupies 6.5 acres within Unity Village. It was built in 1940. Fire station; Unity maintains a volunteer fire department. Pumper truck is housed in the basement of the Silent Unity building. Police; Unity does not have an official police department, but maintains a patrol car for policing surveillance. Preliminary plan represents a new town development on approximately 2,800 acres, the existing 1,400 and adjacent properties owned by the Unity School of Christianity."

New magazine, April 1967, articles, "Stir Up The Gift Of God. All things are possible, yes, 'But we have this treasure in earthen vessels.' Paul says, 'The exceeding greatness of the power may be of God and not from ourselves.' A number of psychologists have agreed that man is not so much a receptacle as a channel of energy; that power flows through him for the enrichment of humanity. Many years ago the Teacher of Nazareth knew and understood this, which He called the mystery of the kingdom. So clearly did he see this truth and use it in His life that miracles resulted.

How many of us are accomplishing the miraculous today? Comparatively few. And why? Many people go to church and hear lectures and sermons; other read books and discuss the subject of religion. But applying it as a motive power in their daily lives is a consideration which has never occurred to them.

Nature is an economic giver, prodigal in her bounty to those who use her largess, but withholding from those who will not expend it. We may not receive and hoard, and at the same time, expect constant replenishment. An open channel blesses and enriches all it contacts; lacking an outlet it becomes stagnant and deadly. Many of natures species have deteriorated and become extinct. Through inactivity others have lost their functions. Science tells us that barnacles and oysters once had heads, and snakes had limbs. That ostriches and penguins could fly. Through lack of use man might just as easily lose his intelligence.

On the other hand, we have a wonderful picture of man taking his own evolution in hand and so amplifying his powers as to make his future progress boundless. His possibilities are unlimited. He may be free from poverty, disease, and death; he may think and write, compose and paint, discover and invent as greatly as the masterminds of our age. Incapable of hatred, ignorant of fear, living by the law of love, he may reach his goal of immortality.

'Neglect not, then, the gift that is in thee; be diligent in these things, giving thyself wholly to them, that thy progress may be made manifest unto all. Guard that which is committed unto thee, and stir up the gift of God which is in thee.' By Richard Lynch.

Petals Of Truth. A number of years ago a student from one of the Spanish-speaking countries came to me with a problem. He had come to the United States with high hopes, and things had been going very well for him until all at once a series of unpleasant things had happened. A friend had not been completely honest with him, a teacher had been inconsiderate, and his offer to do some free translating had not been acknowledged.

'I am sorry it happened, Roberto,' I told him. 'We are selfish and thoughtless and inconsiderate at times, as you have discovered, but more often you will find us to be generous and thoughtful and easy to live among. You will need to give your attention to our virtues rather than to our flaws, in order to be happy with us. Is it not that way in your country too?' He was thoughtful for a moment and then he said, 'Why should I expect perfection? When I look into the mirror, what do I see, an angel? No,' he said with a sad shake of his head, 'no angel, just Roberto.'

I think of Roberto on those days when the world seems to be in one of its selfish, thoughtless, unkind moods. 'But how can I expect others to be perfect?' I ask myself. When I look into the mirror I see no angel, though I searchingly look; then a feeling of tolerance comes over me. A look into the mirror is a therapeutic measure that I recommend to everyone. By Cleda Reyner."

Fillmore Festival April 3-8, 1967. Unity-By-The-Sea Santa Monica, California. Opening statement: "Welcome! Unity-By-The-Sea welcomes you to the first Fillmore Festival. The purpose of these special days is to return, as Charles and Myrtle Fillmore did in the beginning, to the great reservoir of Truth from whense all Truth proceeds. This is the great God-Presence in everyone of us, that Paul called, 'Christ in you, your hope of glory.'

We have been challenged that we have drawn our beliefs from Theosophy, Christianity, Hinduism, Rosicrucianism, Buddhism and other religious systems and so we have. We have reached for the golden thread, the Truth in all religions and we have found it, for we have found Spirit. Our world is suffering from spiritual starvation, so our doctor-science tells us. All the world is seeking and searching for spirit. Unity's destiny is to follow in the footsteps of Jesus Christ who was truly the first to demonstrate universality. He pointed out 'the way'. A way broad enough and true enough that every soul might walk upon it, regardless of their religious background or affiliation. Unity penetrates the invisible walls that separate man from man and man from God. We are moving across the threshold of the new age. We are here to review and rededicate ourselves to pure, unchangeable, unadulterated Truth, God in man and man in God."

Kansas City Star article dated May 23, 1967, "Unity Receives Roses In Celebration Of Canadian Centennial. A new rose bed in the world-famous Unity rose garden now has 24 rose bushes commemorating the Canadian Centennial. They are the gift of Mr. Jack MacIntyre through the Unity Center at Montreal, Quebec, Canada. The orange coral floribunda rose was developed and grown especially to be a memorial for Canada's Centennial this year.

It was in October, 1964 that the Reverend May Duncan, minister of the Montreal Unity Center, notified W. Rickert Fillmore, a son of the founders of Unity, that Unity's world headquarters in Lee's Summit was to receive the gift of rose bushes. Mr. Fillmore, who died in October 1965, laid out the plans for the rose garden with its beautiful fountains and winding paths. He was architect for the complex of Unity buildings. His brother, Mr. Lowell Fillmore, president of Unity, officially accepted the roses when they arrived last fall.

Harry H. Bowers of Lee's Summit, who has tended the rose garden for the past five years, said the spring freezes set the roses back and they would not bloom until June, but they were all healthy plants. The Rose Festival Retreat begins May 27th at Unity."

New magazine article June 1967, "A Letter From May Rowland, Director Of Silent Unity. Dear Friend, It makes no difference where, in this great world, you live, our love reaches out to you, and as you have opened your heart to read these words, you have opened your heart to the love of Christ that moves through Silent Unity. So I feel that I know you, for we are all one in God's love.

We think of Silent Unity not as a group of people or a department of Unity School but as a consciousness. The word consciousness means the sum total of all that one thinks, feels, and believes. Our consciousness in Silent Unity is based on prayer and love; a consciousness that, we can gratefully say, has blessed the lives of untold thousands.

I believe that the words of Charles Fillmore express well the truth about Silent Unity: 'A company of persons gathered in the name of Jesus Christ can build a place in the ether and make it a continuous spiritual battery, from which rays of energy and spiritual substance can be radiated to believing minds anywhere on earth. The Christ Mind will take up its abode in such a center of spiritual energy and cooperate with the minds in it in broadcasting health, wealth, and spiritual understanding everywhere.'

The perfect expression of God was fulfilled in Jesus Christ. In Silent Unity we teach a way of life built upon the teachings of Jesus Christ, who perfectly expressed the fullness of God. In order to maintain the high standard in which we hold ourselves and in which others who look to us for help hold us, we have developed, through prayer, a high degree of spiritual value to the world. This we call the Christ consciousness. It is this consciousness of which Jesus spoke when He said, 'The Father that dwelleth in me, he doeth the works.'

We recognize that it is not because of personal effort that the Silent Unity ministry is successful. Rather, the Christ consciousness, the Father within does the work. In order to maintain this high Christ standard, we in Silent Unity pray many times a day; and we know that 'I, if I be lifted up, will draw all men unto me.'

In this consciousness there is a feeling of love for all people, for you. This is not a sanctimonious feeling but one which leads us to do something, and to want to do more, about the needs of humanity.

We invite you to invite our prayer consciousness into your life. Call us, drop us a letter, or just 'tune in' in prayer with us now. In so doing you will open yourself, not just to us, but to the Christ of God which already lives within you, and which will guide you to the health and harmony that is rightfully yours as a child of God."

<u>New</u> magazine article by Jane Truax, July 1967, "Gift Of Freedom. In the United States, July means Independence Day, the 'Glorious Fourth', when we celebrate freedom with special programs and speeches and with the embroidery of fireworks on the night sky. But July brings a freedom day to several other countries too. July 1st is Dominion Day in Canada. July 14th is Bastille Day in France, commemorating the beginning of the French Revolution. Freedom is not the special property of any country or any person. It is the gift of God to all His children, and equally desired by each one of them.

Perhaps we are too prone to think of freedom in terms of history and world affairs. The place where it is needed most is in family relationships, for it is when we love people the most that we are most likely to place binding thoughts upon them. It is so easy to feel that we must 'help others along'; so hard to let them alone to follow their own way of development, especially when that way happens to be a slow or strange one, at least from our point of view.

We would certainly think of Jack Benny as a successful man, not only from a monetary standpoint but in his ability to give delight to others. Yet a biographer says that Benny has never been convinced that being a comedian is a worthwhile career. His parents set such a high valuation on playing the violin and such a low valuation on acting that, for all the success he has achieved, Jack Benny still tends to feel guilty inside because he is not a concert violinist. Psychologists say that this is not uncommon, when a person has a talent that his parents do not respect, appreciate, or encourage, but which grows in spite of their opposition.

Another case in point is that of Paul Morphy, the great American chess champion and one of the most brilliant strategists in the history of the game. He had little respect for the art he had mastered, even though it is a tremendously difficult one, because his mother had brought him up to think that chess was a game for the lazy and shiftless. She wanted him to be a lawyer. All his life, Paul Morphy's great triumphs in chess tournaments were bitter and unsatisfying; and all his life he envied lawyers. Eventually he became an alcoholic and died in poverty. What a pity it is that he should have had so little happiness from so wonderful a talent!

Those we love need to be free, to be loosed from the obligation to please us and do what we think is best for their life's development. And as we free them, we ourself are freed from the heavy burden of directing their lives. In all our dealings with those dear to us, we need as our watchword the prayer of the prophet Hosea: 'I will love them freely.'

Letter to Charles R. Fillmore, September 1, 1967. "Dear Mr. Fillmore: In compliance with the terms of Part I of our contract, we are pleased to submit, herewith, twenty copies of the Preliminary Comprehensive Plan report for The Town of Unity Village.

On the basis of our previous discussions and progress reports to the Advisory Planning Committee, we believe that this report will meet your initial needs both directly and indirectly by bringing into focus and helping to resolve some of the basic goals and objectives of Unity pertaining to the potential growth and development of land within the incorporated limits. Each particular step in daily decisions should, of course, be related to the overall concept. From a planning standpoint, it is not so important that the total scheme be achieved within an estimated time period, but rather that each practical day-to-day decision be made in accordance with the total concept, in order that the long-range objectives might be achieved over a period of years. A basic consensus on these points is essential toward continuing with the more detailed report as outlined under Part II of the above contract.

This particular planning project has been unique in our experience, and we would like to add that it has been a most enjoyable one. It is our considered opinion that Unity has a unique opportunity to point the way in many fields of need, not only within this particular metropolitan area, but with ramifications into World Unity.

If there are any points which require further clarification, or that you may have need to discuss in more detail, please feel free to contact us at your convenience. Sincerely, David B. Runnells"

New magazine article by Ernest C. Wilson, October 1967, "A Minority Of. 'You don't know what it feels like to be poor, to be without work, not to know where the next meal is coming from!' is an accusation that sometimes used to be directed at me in a prosperity class that I taught. This never bothered me. I could take it with composure, and stand smiling until the speaker had finished. Then I would answer, 'Thank you for such a good affirmation. I'm glad you picture me as being needed, as well-fed and prosperous. But, as a mater of fact, I have known from personal experience the very things you've described.'

It has been a long time since that particular accusation has come my way, but another has followed it, 'You don't know what it is like to be a member of a minority, the embarrassments and misconceptions and rejections that this can mean!' True, I do not experience what it must mean to belong to a racial minority. And I remember reading the account of a white man who had his skin treated medically so that he could pass for a Negro and what tremendous adjustments he had to undergo almost overnight!

But I am a member of a minority in many ways, and most everybody is in some way. For one thing, I represent a minority viewpoint in religion. I am a Unity student, and almost every Unity student, proud though he is to be one, is nevertheless often asked, 'Is that the same as Christian Science?' or 'Is that the same as Unitarian?' or 'Do you people believe in Jesus Christ? Do you believe in the shed blood? Have you accepted Jesus Christ as your Savior?'.To the first two questions I would say, 'No, but we have some things in common.'

To the last three, 'Yes, but possibly not in exactly the same way that you do.'

More frequently, people do not even ask, but make their own often-mistaken estimate of Unity by some chance contact with our publications, or even by reading tracts published by other minority religious groups who feel, and probably sincerely, that we are leading people astray.

There isn't as much prejudice against us now as there used to be in the beginning of Unity before and at the turn of the century. We are in fact becoming 'respectable.' The fact that many Unity congregations have prospered, obtained valuable properties, and built handsome churches has contributed to this. Better educational standards for our ministers has been a factor too. A growing number of clergymen in many denominations subscribe for Unity publications, even ask the prayers of Silent Unity, read Unity textbooks, and in some instances recommend these to members of their congregations.

Some Unity ministers have served people high in government, in the realms of entertainment, the arts, and business, in matters of health, or prosperity, or bereavement. Some of our ministers are prominent in fraternal orders, in civic projects, or have become popular in mass communication such as radio, television, and the printed word. All these things have helped our 'public image.'

But I am not trying to justify people's approval of Unity so much as to offer some practical approaches as to how to meet the issue of being a member of a minority. For in some degree at least we all are minorities.

If you are left-handed, you are a member of a minority, so you may look a little odd, by which I mean simply different from most persons, in the way you handle knife and fork at the dining table. (You don't have to be different. You can learn to use eating implements the same as right-handers do, if you want to enough.)

You may look peculiar to some people as you sign a check with your left hand. But if the check is in their favor and is honored at the bank, they will accept it pretty readily. Or if you are a baseball pitcher and can win more games than some of the right-handed ones, there will be no complaints, except from the opposing teams.

Most people respect a job well done and appreciate your help in time of need, regardless of whether you are a Catholic or a Jew or a Hottentot, and whether your skin is dark or fair, or whether you have a physical handicap and do not measure up to their notion of physical beauty. If your house is burning down, or your child needs artificial respiration, you will not be choosy about who comes to your aid. So, if you are a member of a minority, what can you do to be more acceptable to other people, and hence happier and better adjusted? Because nobody lives to himself alone, however it may seem to be.

I asked a good friend of mine, who from the majority viewpoint has several counts against him, how to meet the issue. This is what he told me, 'As you know, I am in a profession where almost every prominent member is a college graduate and has one or more degrees. Financial pressure in an impoverished family, and a physical handicap that I had to meet, kept me from much college education. The only degrees I have are two honorary ones. In a time when every red-blooded American was expected to serve his country in the armed forces, I was rejected as a 4-F. I tried to learn to speak in public, and the first time I did so I got stage fright so bad that I had to rush off the platform and lose my breakfast, then go back and finish the talk. (I knew that if I didn't, I'd never have the courage to try to speak in public again.) I got a job where I had to talk on the telephone a great deal, and was so panicky over the technical terms of an unfamiliar business that my ears seemed to close and I couldn't hear. I quit the job and it took me months to prove to myself that it was not my ears, but my fears, that kept me from hearing.'

'So what have I done? I think I have overcompensated to some degree. Some of the greatest men have had handicaps, and there's a theory that on occasion these have been blessings in disguise. Steinmetz was hunchback. He withdrew from the world into a laboratory where he outdid other scientists in discovery and invention. George Washington Carver was the son of Negro slaves. He devoted his energies to devising manifold uses for peanuts, the basic product of the area where he was born. He was offered many inducements to go North and work under more favorable conditions. Glenn Clark, who wrote Carver's biography and brought him to worldwide attention, quotes him as saying, 'No, the good Lord put me in the South and in the South I'll stay!' His dedication, his humility, and his service to others, black and white alike, have made his name revered by millions. Edison was deaf, Beethoven was deaf, Byron was lame, Charles Fillmore was a cripple.'

'Me? I'm not a Steinmetz, a Carver, a Fillmore, but I've tried perhaps a little harder than most to excel in the things I do. I have deliberately taken on jobs that seemed beyond me and then tried to live up to them. I've cultivated people who knew more than I about things that would enrich my life and thereby give me more to share with other people. I've tried for some attainments that have eluded me, but I have had more opportunities offered me than I could have aspired to. I have hobnobbed with the humble and the great and have loved both equally. I've received more love and appreciation than any one man could expect from life. I'm still working hard. I'm still trying to improve my mind. I still read more books in a month than I am told the average person reads in a year. I still have an inferiority complex, but now I can grin over it. And since I am one with the majority in this, it helps to balance some of the other differences.'

'How should we deal with minorities, racial, political, religious, or any other kind? I think we have to deal with them as individuals. The saying that putting men in uniform does not make uniform men has many applications. Putting men into categories doesn't make them the same either. And besides, people rise out of the categories that may have characterized them at some time. People, praise God, just will not stay in the pigeonholes in which dogmatists in religion or science or art, or just plain people, tend to put them. Now that I think of it, I don't much mind being a minority. PS. I'm left-handed too.' I agreed with him; I don't much mind being in a minority either."

Following is a summary of the monthly meeting reports of the Ladies Auxiliary for 1967

March: A motion carried that the auxiliary give $100.00 to the Unity Village Center to be applied to the Chapel Building Fund. This gift was presented to the Chapel at Easter.

June: A motion carried to give a love offering, in the amount of $75.00, to Unity School for the new Carillon in the Tower dedicated to W. Rickert Fillmore.

October: A motion carried to give a love offering of $50.00 to Unity School for the Carillon Bells. The offering was presented to Charles R. Fillmore, executive vice president. Jane Paulson gave the lesson on Joy. A motion carried that the club members exchange gifts at the December meeting. Jane Paulson gave the lesson, her topic was "Revelation of Truth."

December: The lesson was given by Jane Paulson and it was followed by the Christmas gift exchange.

1968 - New magazine article by David Williamson, Director of Education, Unity School of Christianity, January 1968, "Flower Power. The other day I was having a conversation with another minister about the 'hippies.' We discussed their ideas and way of life, and particularly their more noticeable rejection of accepted social values. I found myself in the position of trying to explain the good I see in many of the hippies.

I said, 'I question their use of psychedelic drugs. I wonder about their sense of responsibility to the society which makes it possible for them to live as they do. But I am convinced that many hippies are sincerely seeking to apply love in a world that so desperately needs more love expressed by all human beings.'

To the hippie, the symbol for love is a flower. Many call themselves 'flower people.' Have you ever had a hippie give you a flower? I did. Let me tell you what happened: I was standing in the Denver, Colorado, air terminal on the day following my conversation about the hippies. A group of them came into the terminal building on their way from San Francisco. One came across the waiting room toward me, and with a sincere smile said, 'Here is a flower; it represents love.' I expressed my thanks.

I stood there with the flower in my hand for a few minutes, reflecting on the meaning of that moment when two strangers encountered each other, and one had a way of communicating his faith that love in essence really is important. Then I walked over to a woman who was traveling in our group and said, 'Here, I want you to have this flower; it represents love.' She pinned the flower on her dress and beamed radiantly.

Our group went to the dining room to get lunch before taking the plane to Kansas City. We needed to get our food quickly and be on our way; but our waitress was slow, and she was sharp with us when we ordered. She brought the wrong food and acted as if it was our fault. I turned to the woman with the flower and said, 'Give her the flower and tell her it represents love.' When the waitress returned, our friend handed the waitress the flower saying, 'Here is a flower for you.'

The waitress hesitated a moment, unsure of what was happening. She said, 'Why are you giving me that?' The flower-giver replied, 'It represents our love; we want to see you smile.' The waitress broke out in a relieved smile. She said, 'Oh, it has been such a hard day and I've been so tense and upset! Thank you very much.'

She took the flower and put it in a tall glass on her station. She was a transformed person. She was friendly and expressed good cheer to us. Something had touched her. It was the power that love has to change us. The hippies call it, 'flower power.'"

Unity Newsletter, "J. Sig Paulson officiated at the marriage of Rosemary Fillmore Grace and Ralph Rhea on March 29, 1968. May 1st Keith House will again conduct the Unity band as it prepares for its' 42nd consecutive season of weekly concerts on June 9th. Keith is the director of Music for the Lee's Summit School District, having replaced Carl Frangkiser who retired after the 1965 season. Connie Fillmore, daughter of Charles Rickert and Ann Fillmore, began work at Unity in the Editorial Department on June 10th. In May the Unity publication Progress was discontinued."

New magazine article by Harold B. Whaley, Librarian February 1968, "Unity School Library, A Ministry. Of course, I have time to pray and counsel with you. For as our librarian says, 'We are ministers first, and then librarians.' This remark, made by the assistant librarian of Unity School Library to a student seeking guidance, gave the day a new dimension of meaning. Two of the staff of five in the new Library are ordained ministers; yet all of us look upon our work as a special ministry.

As well as being the intellectual heartbeat of an institution of learning, the Library stands in an opportune position to strengthen the spiritual growth of those 'seekers of the light.' Many visitors gravitate naturally to the sanctuary of a library; students, teachers, and workers, all of whom find something special here. A library means many things to as many people. There are varied blessings within its walls, as varied as those found in nature. William Cullen Bryant expressed this experience in 'Thanatopsis,' 'For his gayer hours, She has a voice of gladness, and a smile, And eloquence of beauty, and she glides, Into his darker musings with a mild, And healing sympathy that steals away, Their sharpness ere he is aware.'

Experiences in spiritual healing reveal that many persons have become whole through the reading of a book, an author's inspired conviction or viewpoint that brought healing long sought for but not found in other areas. Realizing this avenue to health as being a proved and valid one, in the Unity School Library we are seeking to concentrate on books that heal and inspire. The core of the collection is metaphysical, including both old and new approaches to the goal of health and wholeness. From Quimby to Clinebell are more than 2,000 books pertaining to the healing of the person. The Library mirrors the personality, purpose and goals of the Unity Movement and serves the needs of a wide reading public that includes workers, visitors, and students living on the grounds and those from the greater Kansas City area.

The new Library had its beginning in June 1965 in an empty room. To begin the accessions faculty members and friends generously gave several hundred metaphysical volumes from their own libraries, many out of print; and the acquisition of carefully selected books was begun. Faculty members, students, retreatants, visitors friends of Unity all converged to help set up the furniture and to process the books, so they could be made available for immediate check-out by the students coming to the July sessions of the School for Teachers and Counsellors.

A year later, Library shelves were bulging with books and periodicals; consequently the Library was moved to a larger area above the classrooms of the School for Ministerial and Religious Studies. This spacious area has allowed for additional tables, chairs, and student carrels as well as an activity area that includes typewriters, microfilm reader, tape recorder, and record player. Students in this area may listen through earphones to a large selection of sermons, plays, lectures, and music. More room has been made available for periodicals, and 250 magazines are now displayed for easy access. A Xerox 914 is provided so that portions of books, magazines, or articles that are of interest can be copied.

Seminaries in the greater Kansas City area have contributed ideas and suggestions, and one seminary donated 150 books, including the Education Index, an expensive reference tool. With the inclusion of approximately 6,000 books from the former Reference and Research Library, the book holdings of Unity School Library now total 15,000.

A library consultant from Yale University suggested that a staff of five catalog 2,000 books per year. However, over 9,000 books were cataloged in the first two years of operation, doubling the estimated acquisitions. Certainly the kindness of those who gave of their time and talents to supplement an industrious staff has contributed to the successful beginning of the Library. Many needed volumes and furnishings have come from Unity centers, individuals, and students, as well as from friends of Unity. At least 2,000 of the above figure were sent to the library as gift books. Ministerial students continue to give several hours of their time each week to help process books and file cards. It is gratifying to be told by someone who has driven through the city and out to Unity Village, 'I knew that you surely would have the book I needed and couldn't locate in other local libraries.'

A rich heritage was already waiting to be linked with the development of a new and larger library, for at the request of Lowell Fillmore, Pharaby Boileau began, in 1942, to draw together an orderly record of that material which Unity had printed. When this library was actually begun to attract other metaphysical material, until under Pharaby Boileau's guiding hand Unity had one of the finest metaphysical libraries in the midwest, containing over 6,000 volumes. The historical room of the library maintains all the historical records and writings of the Unity Movement, and copies of all printed materials, books, and periodicals published by Unity.

I feel Charles Fillmore would agree with the concept that a library is a ministry. These words from Atom-Smashing Power of Mind are relevant for our endeavor here, 'The great and most important issue before the people today is the development of man's spiritual mind and through it unity with God, the taproot of all this confusion is our failure to use our minds intelligently.' To the end of ministering to others mentally and spiritually, the new Unity School Library is dedicated. It is an adventure in faith that has been gratifying, and which continues to bless all who are engaged in the quest for Truth."

March 1968, "A note of thanks from Unity School Library. As the last section of the bibliography of out-of-print metaphysical books goes to print in the Unity Newsletter, our librarian, Harold Whaley, has submitted a report of the response to the published lists.

The original desiderate list contained approximately 1,200 books. To date we have received from donors over 300 of the books listed. An additional 300 have been purchased as a result of reasonable offers from used-book dealers.

We give thanks for the generosity and thoughtfulness of those who have responded. Books have come in from Australia, Canada,

England, as well as from Unity Centers in the USA and from ministers, laymen and friends of Unity.

As expressed in the article, Unity School Library - A Ministry, in February New, the purpose of the library is to minister to need, whether it be healing, inspiration, research or resource. A library of metaphysical books at one location is a blessing for the serious student of Truth and for scholars of researching this area.

Dr. Charles Braden, author of Spirits In Rebellion, a history of the New thought movement, recently wrote to the librarian, 'For the better part of a decade I have been hoping that someone would do what you at Unity are setting out to do, to build a comprehensive metaphysical library that will bring together in one place as complete as possible a collection of the very considerable literature that the metaphysical movement of the 19th and 20th centuries have produced. Only one who has attempted to make studies of one or more of the separate movements, to say nothing of the whole field, can know how comparatively little material can be found and how much travel and expense is required to get anything like a complete story of the development in this area.'

The excellent response to these lists have helped in the realization of this dream. For those who wish to pursue further the adventure of locating these books, a new list is in preparation, and will be mailed on request."

July 1968, Unity historical collection has moved from former quaters in the Reference and Research Library to a walnut paneled room just west of the Library.
Unity Villlage News July 15, 1968, "Unity Heritage Room Named."

Following is a summary of the monthly meeting reports of the Ladies Auxiliary of 1968.

January: A motion was carried to give a $50.00 love offering to the Unity Village Chapel building fund. Jane Paulson gave the lesson on "Your New Year."

April: A motion carried to send an Easter love offering to the Unity Village Center, the amount was not in the records. Discussion was held concerning the purchase of a portable dishwasher for the club house kitchen. Jane Paulson gave the lesson entitled, "We Are Gods."

June: A motion carried to purchase the new portable dishwasher for the club house as soon as funds are available.

August: A report was made that the new dishwasher was purchased and a letter of thanks was read from the secretary and treasurer of the Unity School for the fine gift form the Ladies Auxiliary.

December: A thank you was given to Mr. and Mrs. Dwight Jagger for the gift of their time in making new draperies for the sun proch at the club house.

Jane Paulson gave all of the monthly lessons this year.

1969 - New magazine article by J. Sig Paulson, January 1969, "A Way To Effective Prayer. Sometimes we get into the habit of sloppy praying, and nothing much happens, as a result. We just repeat our old complaints, desires, or problems, and return to our world pretty much as we left it. We rehearse old attitudes and even reinforce them, rather than getting rid of restrictive mental and emotional patterns. The purpose of prayer is to produce a miracle, and the miracle is always the one who prays!

Following is a course of prayer action that will produce permanent results for the better. Adopt the attitude that when you turn to God in prayer, wonderful things always happen immediately, even while you are praying. Decree that your mind is open, free, and relaxed, and that the power of God lifts you, consciously and subconsciously, into inspired courses of mental, emotional,and physical action. Affirm that the change for the better in your inner system of thought and feeling is prompt, powerful, and permanent. then rejoice and give thanks for the miracle-working power that prayer makes available to and through you.

Prayer is the most profitable and powerful process in the universe when we expect it to be, let it be, and rejoice and give thanks that it is! Prove it for yourself by entering joyously and confidently into the course of action outlined in the following affirmative statements: When I pray, and while I pray, I expect wonderful things to happen, and they do. When I pray, I give thanks that the change for the better in my inner system of thought and feeling is prompt, powerful, and permanent."

New magazine article by William L. Fischer, March 1969, "How To Escape Anxiety. 'Anxiety!' This is a term found more and more frequently in our modern vocabulary. To be anxious, is highly in keeping with the trend of our times. The thing chiefly behind anxiety is worry. There is quite a tendency to worry over bills, over health, over position, over any number of things, and worry is a real killer. It is now known that worry can kill by causing mental illness, heart disease, and many other disturbances of the human mind, body, and emotions. Obviously, if a person wants to be healthy, he must overcome his anxiety or worry.

There is no drug to treat worry. The barbiturates, bromides, and other sedatives, the great variety of tranquilizers, merely mask the source of anxiety and have a temporary quieting influence on the nervous system. However, there is an effective treatment to conquer anxiety, and that treatment comes under the banner known as Truth. Truth is a constructive way of life, based on the teachings of Jesus Christ and on other compatible philosophies.

If you have ever been overwhelmed with anxiety, you know that it is almost as if your life were a ship sinking in a terrible storm. It is a feeling of being hopeless and lost and perhaps going down for the last time. Such a thing was happening in actual experience one time to the apostles of Jesus. He was with them at the time in a small boat on the Sea of Galilee. A storm came up quickly, as storms often do there, and the apostles were in fear of their very lives. Jesus was resting in the boat, and the apostles awakened Him and asked His help, for they feared for their lives. Jesus stood up in the craft, and looked out upon the storm-tossed sea and said, 'Peace! Be still!' and the sea became calm, and they were saved.

It was not by chance that Jesus Christ was able to do this. This dramatic act was based on the sound knowledge that He had the element of peace at His disposal and obedient to His command. The question here is: Was this power the exclusive property of Jesus Christ, or is it available to us as well?

Jesus Himself gave us the answer to that question. Remember how He said: 'Peace I leave with you; my peace I give to you; not as the world gives do I give to you.' He also said: 'I say to you, he who believes in me will also do the works that I do; and greater works than these will he do.' So there you have it! You have assurance of peace at your command that enables you to do the same kind of works Jesus did and even greater works, if the occasion demands it. The mechanics of this are not difficult to understand.

You can also use the technique and power of affirmation in any situation in your life. There are, however, several things about the mechanics of this process that you must keep in mind. First, you must know that you have a vast reserve of peace within yourself. You must know beyond a shadow of doubt that unlimited peace is at your disposal, because you have the Spirit of God within you. Second, you must use the power of affirmation in complete confidence that it works. It worked for the Master. It will work for you; He is the one who said so. Third, when you affirm peace in your life, you must not outline the specific way in which that peace is going to be carried out. It is herein that we often get into difficulty.

The reason the technique of affirmation is so effective is that it produces a permanent attitude and character change, which in turn reflects itself as a permanent change in your life. Affirmation conditions your mind so that God may have fuller and more adequate expression through your mind and your life and affairs. When you affirm peace for yourself and your life, you throw your mind into neutral, so to speak, and let the actual peace of God work through your mind and come into expression in your life. The effect of this channel of peace through you has an exciting and transforming effect. In the process it touches every cell, tissue, and organ of your body, and thereby produces wholeness as well as serenity. In a very real sense, it produces a new you.

In eliminating anxiety, it is important to learn the art of living one day at a time. It is even important to go further than that, and live one moment at a time. Actually, all you can live is one heartbeat at a time. Remember the Master taught: 'Do not be anxious about tomorrow. Let the day's own trouble be sufficient for the day.' There is nothing you can really do about the past, except to have learned its lessons so that you do not repeat its mistakes. How can you prepare for the future, except through the quality of living you are doing in the present? You have the eternal now. There is nothing else in time. If you try to live in an era of time that doesn't exist, you can live in turmoil, and anxiety will be your constant companion.

Everyone needs to have an enthusiasm and zest for living. Once again, you can apply the power of affirmation here. When you face each dawn, take up an ancient biblical challenge, and declare: 'This is the day which the Lord has made; let us rejoice and be glad in it.' Anticipate the fullness that each day has to offer. Get excited about its possibilities. Inculcate this enthusiasm into your subconscious mind, and it will become a part of your very life.

All of this is designed to get the demon worry out of your mind and emotions. But you can't just evict worry, leaving a vacuum there. The deadly thought and emotion of worry must be replaced with the power of affirmation. Constructive thinking, optimism, inward certainty, and the gleaming upward look, all assure you of peaceful and progressive living. There is a blessing in every experience. Granted, it is sometimes deeply hidden, but it is there; just to know that is often conducive to greater peace of mind.

Along this line, I like a thought that Dale Carnegie once put forth. He said, 'When fate hands you a lemon, make lemonade.' This is precisely what you must do. Then your spirit will never be broken. You will know that the Spirit of God lives through you, the great Spirit of peace. You will accept that peace as your gift from God, and let it find beautiful and significant expression in and through you."

New magazine article, May 1969, "As A Butterfly Must Struggle out of its Cocoon, So Must A Teen-Ager Struggle Out Of Childhood. Some time ago I received a call from a young lady in my congregation, asking for an appointment for consultation. Her name was Jan; she was fifteen years old. When Jan arrived and began talking, she related a rather standard, teen-age kind of story (trouble between herself and her mother). When it came to the place where she sighed, as if to rest her case, I said to her, 'Jan, has it occurred to you that you are perhaps a bit difficult in your relationship with your mother?' To this she replied, 'Well, why not, I'm at the difficult age!'

This young lady knew she was going through a trying time in her life, and apparently she had determined to get as much mileage out of it as possible. Well, she is grown now, and has recently married. As most people do, Jan went through her difficult years and turned out quite well. But while these years of adolescence are indeed difficult, they do not have to be so much that way, if only they can be understood more fully by both young people and parents and then approached in a constructive way.

What makes these years difficult? Well, the years of adolescence represent a bridge between the time when one is a dependent child and when he becomes an independent adult. These are the years of ego development. These are crucial years, because it is during this time that character is molded, goals are more precisely defined, and much of the thrust and ambition are generated that will propel a person through his most creative and productive years. During this time of unfoldment, some rebellion is natural. As a butterfly must struggle out of its cocoon and the chick must burst from its shell, so must the teen-ager struggle out of and burst from the confines of childhood into the freedoms of maturity. This does not come without a measure of effort in chipping away at the old molds, that they may be revised and enlarged. And this exertion frequently takes on the characteristics of a contest between the teen-ager and the rest of the world. It all carries the label of rebellion.

If both the teen-ager and the parent could understand this, those difficult years could be made less difficult. The young person could know that what is happening to him are really the emotional growing pains which occur with the onset of maturity. He could know that all the rest of the world really isn't wrong, nor against him. Just as his legs hurt when they were growing, now his attitudes and emotions and feelings are in pain as the exciting growth toward maturity takes place. Pain is always difficult, whether it be pain in one's body or one's soul. And if a teen-ager reacts to this emotional pain in a spirit of rebellion, he is not to be condemned for it. Rather, he is to be understood.

As for the parent, he must know that, during the time when his youngster is being difficult, there are reasons. It is usually not just rebellion for the sake of rebellion, though it sometimes seems to be. It is rebellion with a cause, the cause of growth. After all, you had to come through those difficult years in your own life. And because the world was simpler a generation ago, those years were no doubt less difficult for you than they are for your children. If a youngster needs anything during his personal era of adolescence, he needs understanding. If you will temper your inclination to retaliate against his rebellion, and instead give him such understanding, the constructive effects will be of long range.

Young people today are edgy, and they have good reason to be. During most of their lifetime there have been wars and rumors of wars. These youngsters do not want to be killed before they have had an opportunity to live. Neither would I! The wrongness of war is not debatable. neither should valid objection to war be debated."

Unity Village News September 15, 1969, "Post Office Puts Unity Village On Map! A ribbon cutting ceremony officially opened the contract branch post office at Unity Village on August 18th. The new facility is on the first floor of the Unity Tower. 'It is significant that we have reached another plateau of service during the 80th anniversary of the founding of Unity.' stated Charles Rickert Fillmore, Executive Vice President.

Following is a summary of the monthly meeting reports of the Ladies Auxiliary for 1969.

January: A motion carried to give a $50.00 love offering to the Unity Village Chapel building fund. The draperies for the club house sun room donated by the auxiliary and lovingly made by Mr. and Mrs. Jagger were dedicated in memory of our beloved teacher, Mrs. Osla Sehit Jones.

March: A motion carried to send a $100.00 gift as an Easter offering to the Unity Village Chapel building fund.

April: In the absence of Delsa Stockton the vice president presided. A motin carried to send a $10.00 gift to Delsa. Beautiful organ and piano numbers were performed by Jeanette Allen, Bernice Collins and Marguerite Corn.

May: In the absence of the president, Mildred Hawthorne presided. It was suggested that an organ fund, for the purchase of an organ for the club house, be started. Currently have $30.00 for the fund.

July: In the absence of Jane Paulson our regular monthly speaker, Mary Rowe, associate editor of Weekly Unity, was the guest speaker.

November: A motion carried to give a $50.00 love offering to the Unity Village Chapel building fund.

December: A motion carried to give all the money remaining in our treasury to the Unity Village Chapel building fund. A Christmas love offering of $100.00 was sent.

Jane Paulson gave the lessons at the club meetings, other than the one exception.

1970 - Unity Village News January 1970, "Mutual Broadcasting Company To Broadcast Unity's 'The Word' Over 600 Stations. Ralph and Rosemary Rhea flew to New York to talk with officials of the Mutual Broadcasting Company at the companies request to discuss details for broadcasting 'The Word' over the Mutual radio system. As of February 2, 1970 'The Word' will be broadcast three times daily by all Mutual stations. This is approximately 600 stations and will be in addition to some of the stations already using 'The Word.' After meeting with the President of Mutual and other officials, a plan was worked out, Rosemary said, which was agreeable to all concerned. She said they seem to be very happy with the program and said they are proud to include it in their news broadcasts daily. Since so much of the world news is not of an inspiring nature, we should all give thanks for this opportunity of giving so many people a note of uplift."

New magazine article, January 1970, "The Unity Way Of Life: The Silence. The silence is not a great mystery known only to mystics and occultists, and difficult to you. It is the resting place within your soul where, with the simple trust of a child, you let go of self and learn to lean on Him who said, 'Come to me all who labor and are heavy laden, and I will give you rest. Take my yoke upon you, and learn from me; for I am gentle and lowly in heart, and you will find rest for your souls.'

The time it takes you to enter the silence or the ease with which you do so depends on your willingness to let go of self. The benefits that you receive from it depend on your compliance, in every detail of your life, with the principles of Truth that are revealed to you when you are quiet before God. In the silence you develop a consciousness of abiding quietness and peace.

When in the beginning you may have had to make some effort to enter the silence, later you find that you are encompassed by it, and no matter how great the need or turmoil of the outer may appear, you are constantly attuned to God. His unfailing love, power, and counsel are instantly available to you. The silence is not a passive, lethargic state of mind in which to sleep, dream, build air castles, or fidget. Rather it is an a wakening to the power of the inner man, where you give up your will that the will of God may be done.

Relaxation. During the period of meditation take a comfortable position and relax the body, because such a posture releases the mind from the necessity of giving attention to strained and aching muscles. A body trained for years to constant activity, eyes accustomed to be ever watchful, and ears that are alert to every outer sound may need faithful, loving, patient teaching before they will learn to relax.

Relaxation is poised and balanced control of the body. It reveals a willingness and a readiness to receive. The mind thus undiverted by the discomfort of the body can grow quiet. It is free to take an affirmation or a prayer and to feed on its words of Truth until even these are silenced by the opening of the inner door of consciousness that leads to the secret place of the Most High.

The first step in prayer is to direct your attention Godward. The second is to shut the door of your inner chamber. To aid in this close your eyes and your ears to everything in the outer that your attention may be fully centered in God., His wholeness, peace, and substance.

Your inner chamber may be likened to a radio studio, which in order to broadcast its programs successfully must be protected from the noise of the outside world. When you close the door of your mind and heart to the turmoil of the world that you may commune with God and learn of Him, your consciousness becomes a microphone through which God speaks His word of life, love, power, and wisdom.

Bless Your Thoughts. The only requisite needed to enable you to be still and know God as omnipresent and omnipotent good, is a willingness on your part to enter your inner sanctuary, to close the door of your heart to the thoughts that drown out the voice of love, faith, and Truth. You do not have to fight, resist, or condemn your thoughts. Neither do you have to give way to them, but you do have to train and direct, love and bless them. This you can do through frequent resort to the place of inner stillness where you are consciously unified with God and your mind is renewed with thoughts of Truth. These quiet moments of outer rest and inner communion will fortify you against adversity, and enable you to gain dominion in mind, body, and affairs.

Set Aside Every Obstacle. If you feel that you have neither the time nor the place for quiet meditation and prayer or communion with God, quietly speak to God, saying, 'Father, I come to Thee. Teach me to use my time aright.' God will definitely answer your prayer and make plain your way. In the meantime, as you go about your work, seek to feel and to practice an inner sense of stillness before God.

If you have ample time for meditation, but are unable to relax or concentrate because your nerves are tense, or because your thoughts are distracted by other things, or because anxiety or pain forces itself on your attention, do not struggle against yourself. Ask God to teach you how to be still and receptive.

The benefits of your silent hour go forward with you and brighten every moment of the day. They form the foundation of an eternal structure of Truth within you. The inspiration that comes to you in the silence will enable you to surmount any difficulty. Your body is rebuilt, your work is improved, your burdens are lifted, and your job is increased as your mind is renewed."

New magazine article by J. Sig Paulson January 1970, "What Is Your Image? This is the beginning of a new year, and unless you want to continue doing business at the same old stand of thought, feeling, and experience, now is the time to take a new look at yourself and your living potential. You might check out the pictures of yourself that are stored in your imagination chamber and see how they measure up against those that the Good Book, our Bible, proclaims are true of you. Here are words that describe some of these accurate images: 'The image and glory of God,' 'the light of the world,' 'sons of the Most High,' 'a life-giving spirit.'

What is your habitual image of yourself? This self-image is a god you worship, and you serve it consciously and unconsciously. It is an inner blueprint that shapes your thoughts and feelings, your actions and reactions, your experiences and your relationships with others. It is the cause of most of your difficulties and failures, your achievements and successes.

For a good exercise in mind stretching, take one of the accurate images listed above and think about it, meditate on it, get the measure and 'feel' of it. Just as a suggestion, getting a picture of yourself as a life-giving Spirit can stretch your mind to new dimensions. Following is a Mind Stretcher in words for a little practice: 'I am life-giving Spirit, and I give life to the beliefs, attitudes, habits, thoughts, and feelings that govern my being and experience.'

If you will go beyond these words to the truth they describe and the course of action they suggest, you will soon find a marked change taking place in your living experience. You will stop giving life to the limited concepts that have victimized you in the past and begin animating a new living style and pattern of action. You may wish to stretch your mind even further by embarking on the course of action outlined in the following Mind Stretcher: 'I am life-giving Spirit, and I joyously stop supporting all inferior images.'

If you are like most of humanity, you will find that you have plenty of inferior images on hand, and as they come to the surface of your mind, eject them from your imagination chamber permanently. Tell them frankly and gratefully that they can no longer depend on you for support and watch with growing delight as they dissolve and lose all power to enslave you. Then start laying a firm foundation for a new course of living by following the activity described in the following Mind Stretchers: 'I am life-giving Spirit, and beginning right now, I think, feel and speak like Spirit.' 'I am life-giving Spirit, and the universe treats me like Spirit.'

You are life-giving Spirit, not because of what you have done, but because of the way you are made, in the image of your Creator. Keep on stretching your mind, and your world will find that something new, namely a new you, has been added."

New magazine article February 1970, "Help Keep The Light Shining. Unity is supported mainly by the modest offerings of countless persons who have been helped through its ministry. The workers at Unity feel grateful for every offering that is sent in. They know that it is not the size of the gift that counts, but the love in the heart from which it comes. One time early in the history of Unity, a subscriber sent in one-hundred dollars for a hundred-year subscription to Unity. It is hard to imagine the gratitude to God that the one-hundred dollars evoked in the Unity office.

We believe, as the founders of Unity believed, that one's financial support of any movement should be based on one's own evaluation of the movement's worth. Charles and Myrtle Fillmore once wrote: 'The Spirit moves members to contribute, and it is observed that those who manifest gratefulness either in money, in love, or in works are helped more rapidly than those who are neglectful.'

We are often asked how Unity students may have a part in the expansion and growth of the Unity movement. While we do not believe in asking for money, we do believe in extending the privilege of giving to all who wish to share their abundance. If you would like to have a concrete share in today's Unity work, we would be glad to tell you of specific areas of service in which your gift would do the most good.

We realize that there are also many who would like to make sure that part of their substance will serve as a living memorial, in the form of a legacy. If you have questions along this line, we would welcome your inquiry, which will be held in strict confidence.

Writing of the Fillmore's in the early days of Unity, James Dillet Freeman said, 'Had they always waited until the funds materialized to do the things they needed to do, they would have been able to do little. They took a step, praying all the while in faith, and the supply came to meet the need.' We in Unity today hold this same faith, and we are always grateful for the sharing love of our friends who help us to meet the world's needs day by day."

Love Is Our Human Rose
By James Dillet Freeman

Many flowers grow in many gardens,
but none more beautiful than roses.
And in our soul-soil, flowers grow too,
but none more beautiful than love --
love is our human rose.
When I have love in me,
I am a garden of roses,
and when I am loved,
it is as if I have been given a rose bouquet.
With love, even a weed-patch life
becomes a fragrant garden.
O God of love,
let this rose, love,
bloom in me now!

Unity Village News June 15, 1970, "The beautiful outdoor amphitheater at Unity Village will be the focal point for activities climaxing the 1970 Unity International convention on Sunday, June 28th. The days events will begin with two services in the amphitheater at 9 and 11 A.M. and conclude with a lively band concert beginning at 8 P.M. A huge colorful tent will be set up in the parking lot south of the amphitheater where an expected six-thousand persons will be served a barbecue picnic lunch from 11 A.M. until 1.30 P.M. All workers and students and their families are invited and lunch tickets at $2.00 are available at the Tower until Friday noon, June 26th. Many conveniences are planned for the comfort of our visitors.

Attendants will park cars in the lot east of Unity Inn. Busses will transport persons from the convention headquarters in Kansas City. 'Are you ready for Unity?' is the subject J. Sig Paulson will use at both services held in the amphitheater instead of Unity Village Chapel to accommodate the large crowd. Janie Paulson will give the meditation and music will be by Rena Bergen, organist and Pauline Deinston, soprano soloist. From the lofty Unity Tower the 111 bell carillon will ring out a delightful concert in the afternoon at 2:30. Harold Whaley, Unity Librarian, is the able canilloneur."

The 1970 Library staff included E. Pharaby Boileau, Librarian; Dorthea Lauritzen, Assistant Librarian; Mary Culler, Book Processing; Virginia Berry, Metaphysical Collection; and Jill Breese, Volunteer.

Following is a summary of the monthly meeting reports of the Ladies Auxiliary for 1970.

March: A motion carried that the auxiliary send a $50.00 love offering to the Unity Village Chapel building fund. The treasurer reported that there is now $547.37 in the organ fund.

August: A motion carried to send a $100.00 love offering to the Unity Village Chapel building fund, in the memory of beloved vice president and wonderful friend, Charlotte Reames. The organ fund balance was reported at $617.37.

October: A motion carried to buy some artificial greenery to be placed on the mantle of the fireplace in the club house. In the absence of Jane Paulson, our teacher, Paula McClellan graciously presented the lesson.

December: A motion carried to give $50.00 to the Unity Village Chapel building fund. A second motion passed to give $25.00 to the Unity Village Choir.
Jane Paulson gave the lessons this year except two months when Paula McClellan substituted.

1971 - New magazine article by Jeane Dixon, "Your Unique Gift. From the very moment we are conceived and receive life, we become a part of God and from that instant God enriches our tiny spark of 'being' with specific talents and qualities that make each one of us unique. Every new conception is a privileged creation, and He watches over each one of us from that moment of life through eternity.

Receiving life is a blessing in itself; receiving a talent of rare and unique quality is a privilege granted only by God, and no man can choose or exchange it. Only God can take it from us. He gave each one of us a talent according to our needs and His wisdom. Only He knows what is needed in a given century, and when He gives life, He creates it with a talent the world needs at that particular time.

With this talent, however, comes the power of free will. God allows us to choose the extent to which we will develop our God-given talents. When we choose to use what He has given us, we strengthen our channels of communication with our fellowmen and with our Creator.

Only when we recognize and accept life as a unique gift, a special gift, and employ our individual talents to the fullest measure of our capabilities will we find harmony with ourselves, with Him and the universe. It is this balance within that determines our stature before God and among men.

When, on the other hand, we recognize but neglect our talents and turn away from our appointed places in life, perhaps we desire to be someone we are not, we resist His purpose and become frustrated and lost. We prevent our inner selves from being made manifest. Discontent and frustration become our daily companion. Are you in tune with your Creator?"

New magazine article by J. Sig Paulson February 1971, "The Love Commandments. Most leaders in the spiritual and psychological fields would probably agree that the finest guidelines for human behavior are to be found in the two 'love' commandments: 'You shall love the Lord your God with all your heart, and with all your soul, and with all your strength, and with all your mind,' and 'You shall love your neighbor as yourself.'

Why are these commandments so often overlooked and generally ignored? One of the reasons could be that they are presented as rules of conduct or regulations that we should live up to, and there is a natural resistance in us against being told what we should do. I find that a mind-stretching and refreshing way to consider the love commandments is to look at them as prophecy rather than law, as a prescription, rather than as rules of conduct.

These commandments tell us that the point comes in our spiritual growth when we can really begin to exercise the greatest talent, the most tremendous energy in the self-expression equipment of humanity, our ability to love! Any talent, whether it is of the mind, heart, or muscle is developed through one activity, exercise! Our ability to love is no exception. It grows through exercise, exercise, exercise!

Often, rather than exercise our ability to love, we exercise our ability to question; we demand to know the answers to ancient queries like these: What is love? Who is the Lord my God? Who is my neighbor? Who am I? Do I have to love those whom I don't like?

Our ability to love is as real as our biceps. If we decide to develop a muscle, we know what to do, not ask questions such as: What is muscle? What is exercise? What is this and what is that? No, if we really want to develop that muscle, we simply start to use it, to exercise it. Many of the questions we have asked will be answered as we exercise! Your ability to love, then, is your greatest talent, your richest asset. Exercise it with growing confidence, joy, and enthusiasm.

Following are some mind stretchers in words to develop your ability to love: "I accept the love commandments as a prophecy and prescription for my own growth and unfoldment. I am ready to exercise my greatest talent, my highest potential, my growing ability to love. I am willing to set aside my questions, knowing that they will be answered as I exercise. I rejoice and give thanks for my growing ability to love the Lord my God with all my heart, with all my soul, with all my mind, and with all my strength. Even if these exercises seem to be mostly words and vague thoughts right now, I keep exercising, knowing that at least part of my verbal and mental equipment is getting into the act of loving and that the rest of me will follow inevitably."

Unity Village News July 1971, "Thirty years ago, Ivan Lee, a man with a special talent, came to work in Unity's carpentry shop. To him we are indebted for much of the beauty which is our heritage. Ivan Lee is not just another carpenter, but a true artist working with wood as his medium. He has had no special training or lessons in this field and considers his natural talent a God given gift.

His works include the lectern in the Village Chapel, the beautiful library table and the two heavily carved cabinets located in the hall outside the Heritage Room, a dozen or more Roman type chairs and thirty ornate doors. Worthy of special notice are the doors in the west lobby of the Administration building. Each door was six months in the making and is decorated with twelve hand carved medallions. Each medallion is of a different design. The lectern in the Village Chapel is made of hand carved Walnut and took four months of hand rubbing to complete after it was carved. Ivan used no special tools for this work, just ordinary tools found in any carpenter shop.

The most intricate carving is to be found on the two cabinets near the Heritage Room. These cabinets hold the six volume Macklin Bible, a valuable gift from a friend of Unity. For all his work Ivan has used choice Walnut lumber selected from trees cut many years ago on the railroad right of way at Unity. This lumber was milled, kiln dried in Ivan's own kiln and stored for future use. As the Unity Village building program got under way, Ivan's skilled hands were busy. He remembers, with joy, his association with W. Rickert Fillmore who designed Unity's buildings and under whose direction he worked. For his valuable contribution to Unity we say, Thank you and bless you, Ivan Lee!"

Following is a summary of the monthly meeting reports of the Ladies Auxiliary for 1971.

January: The president requested a report from the nominating committee for officers for the new year. Elected were Katie Earl, president; Dulsa Stockton, vice president; Myrt Clevenger, secretary; Helen Davis, treasurer. Sig Paulson conducted a very interesting discussion on "Freedom of Consciousness."

February: Jane Paulson asked for new sponsors for the birthday club for the Highview School for Boys. Mary Erickson volunteered to be chairman with Dwight and Marion Jagger, Mildred Hawthorne and Hester Nickelson assisting. Jane also said that sponsors are needed for those on parole from the Jackson Country Probate Court and that Red Cross volunteers are needed.

March: Club president Katie Earl turned the meeting over to Sig Paulson for the dedication ceremony for the new organ that the auxiliary had purchased for the club house. Sig first introduced Lowell and Alice Fillmore, Charles R. Fillmore, executive vice president of the Unity School, Barney Ricketts, treasurer, Hazel Jay, 'Barney's right hand', Hugh Horne from Weekly Unity, Chuck Beech, student minister and Marguerite Corn. Katie Earl then in behalf of the auxiliary presented the organ to Charles Fillmore who graciously accepted it for Unity School.

April: A motion carried to send a love offering to the Unity Village Chapel of $100.00 for the building fund. Bernice Collins played the new organ in keeping with the slide picture presentation by Jane Paulson on her trip to Switzerland and Germany and the Passion Play. The slides were shown in lieu of a lesson.

May: A motion was carried to purchase a new table for the club house to replace a broken one.

September: Katie Earl, president announced that a new furnace is to be installed in the club house that will accommodate central air. Alberta Willard made a motion that only necessary expenses be used and the remaining balance in the regular fund be donated toward the air conditioning unit until it is paid in full, motion carried. It was suggested that persons bring a recipe to the October meeting. A cookbook could possibly be compiled for sale.

November: The meeting was called to order by president Katie Earl who asked for a silent prayer of thanksgiving for the beauty of the day and all the blessings we are able to share. Phoebe Brown announced that she would welcome cookies, candy (wrapped) and games for the Hill Top Home for Boys. Jane Paulson advised that the architect's plans are ready to be submitted for review on the new Chapel. A special blessing was given for the new club house furnace and future air conditioning unit.

Jane and Sig Paulson gave the lessons monthly for the auxiliary meetings.

1972 New magazine article by Eric Butterworth, "The Beauty Of Being Ordinary. Recently I heard someone exclaim, referring to a person of decency and largeness of spirit, 'What an extraordinary person!' Though I shared the feeling of admiration, I found myself wondering: 'Is he really extraordinary? Or is he an evidence of the truly ordinary?'

We have tended to think of 'ordinary' as below average, somewhat inferior. Actually the word ordinary is more accurately defined as 'normal, natural.' Possibly we have been influenced by Hollywood's use of superlatives. When things are referred to as 'superior, colossal, stupendous,' who wants to see an 'ordinary' movie? Or, for that matter, who wants to be an 'ordinary' person.

The person who is confident and yet humble, loving and yet wise, successful and still interested in others is usually referred to as an 'extraordinary' human being. But it seems to me that this downgrades mankind as a whole. It implies that man is an inferior product which only occasionally turns out good. This has been the traditional religious view, but I don't think it was Jesus' view. It certainly isn't my view.

If ever there was a person who qualified for the 'extraordinary' label it would be Jesus. Yet He always rejected such accolades: 'Why do you call me good? He who believes in me will also do the works that I do.' Jesus glorified the common man, implying that common to all men is a God potential for all-sufficiency. It follows that he who releases this potential is the normal person, the ordinary person. The extraordinary person is he who frustrates his God-potential and thus fails to express the divinely natural qualities of love and justice and wisdom.

Consider the 'common' cold. It is never natural to have a cold or any kind of sickness. For the human organism, a cold is a unusual thing, an abnormal thing, an 'extraordinary' thing, if you will. If a person were truly and wholly himself at the time, if he were what he is meant to be, he would never be sick.

Because we have accepted the cold as common, and only a few people never have a cold, we call them extraordinary. In point of fact, they are ordinary, normal, and natural, while the millions who get the colds are abnormal, unnatural, and 'extraordinary.' It is not a matter of numbers or statistics, but of departure from a norm. Sickness is always abnormal. The body is always biased on the side of health. It is never natural to be sick, and even the medical report of 'death by natural causes' is no longer considered accurate.

Too often we lose sight of the fact that the moral and psychic and emotional norm for man is not to express selfishness, hatred, or destructive and even criminal tendencies. When man acts in all the antisocial ways that we come to accept as common in our urban society, we must remember that these ways are not the norm, they are abnormal, unnatural, extraordinary.

So, when we see those occasional evidences of graciousness, honesty, integrity, and love, they represent what we all ought to be, are meant to be, and can be. They represent the natural man, somehow uncontaminated by the infections of negativity that plague so much of society. They demonstrate what it is like not to have a cold in the head or a block in the consciousness.

It is vital to our healthy-mindedness to believe in the norm of goodness (which essentially means to have faith in the inherent goodness in people), to know that all the vanities and lusts and pettiness and piques are simply the frustration of this basic goodness. The goal for every person should be to erase these frustrations, 'Opening out a way/Whence the imprisoned splendor may escape.' And when one person succeeds, even in a small way, he ennobles us all. He is not the extraordinary person but the ordinary one, the normal one. For he has demonstrated the true nature of man."

<u>New</u> magazine article by J. Sig Paulson, May 1971, "The Gift Of Giving Thanks. Thanking is a special kind of thinking that comes from adding gratitude to our thoughts. Thanking is the most delightful,

refreshing, mind-stretching, productive form of thinking we can practice because it opens our whole being to the good we naturally desire to experience and express. Thanking is the state of joyous receptivity that attracts every good in the visible and invisible universe. Thanking is the activity that converts us from beggars forever seeking handouts to full-fledged sons and daughters of the Infinite!

The Psalmist indicated that the best way through the gates and into the courts of the Almighty is praise and thanksgiving; Jesus constantly gave thanks to the Father who always heard Him and who knows our needs before we ask; others urge us to move boldly into the throne of grace and to make our desires known with praise and thanksgiving. Just thinking about giving thanks can stretch our mind and expand our receptivity to good! Moving into the activity of thanking works miracles.

Following are a few warm-up exercises to help move you into the activity of thanking: I praise and give thanks to the Almighty for the gift of gratitude. I am grateful for my growing ability to be grateful. I joyously practice the grace of grateful thinking. I am alive with gratitude. My thinking expands into thanking.

Following is a formula in words that can be used to improve our thanking ability as we add the thing for which we are grateful: With my whole being, I am grateful for______. This formula can be applied in all areas of living with splendid results. For example: With my whole being, I am grateful for the Fatherhood of God and the brotherhood of man.

Once we accept the Fatherhood of God and the brotherhood of man in gratitude, the whole nature of our thinking and feeling changes. We start to think from the reality of Being rather than toward it. We have opened ourselves to Truth, and it immediately begins to set us free from limited concepts and prejudices. With my whole being, I am grateful for the kingdom of God within.

If it is our Father's good pleasure to give us the kingdom, the least we can do is to receive it gratefully, graciously, and gracefully. Here, again, our thanking sets the stage for a whole new mental and emotional activity. With my whole being, I am grateful for my growing ability to be a delightful, stimulating, wholesome, total human being, the image of God, the light of the world, a life-giving spirit.

Even the greatest revelations of Truth can be received and made a part of us through the thanking process, also the simplest, most practical daily activities can be transformed by it: With my whole being, I am grateful for the food I eat and the marvelous way my body coverts it into living flesh and blood. Let thanking rejuvenate your whole living experience."

New magazine article by Mary Rowe, June 1972, "God Knows What I Need! I had been living on Long Island and commuting to Manhattan, where I was working. This strap-hanging start to my day didn't much appeal to me, so I decided to move into town.

A friend of mine was on a trip around the world, and she kindly lent me her apartment while she was gone; I was to look for my own home during this time. I relaxed in the atmosphere of this high-up apartment, and enjoyed the beautiful Manhattan lights each evening. One night before going to sleep, I thought to myself, I'd better do something about finding an apartment. Margaret won't be gone forever, and I must be out of here by the time she gets back.

I began forming a mental picture of what I felt my needs to be. 'All right. I need (or would like) a roomy, airy, apartment. I would like large closets...' and then I stopped. I suddenly felt this was a child's game. 'God knows much better than I do what I need' was the realization that came to me. And I turned over and went to sleep.

Earlier that month I had visited a friend in an apartment building. I liked the building, but barely acknowledged the thought that went through my mind: I wouldn't mind living here. Still, I had a reservation. My friend's apartment was small and dark, flush with the wall of the next-door building. And so I didn't think much more about it.

Now, however, the day after my realization that God knew just what I wanted, my friend sought me out. 'Would you like an apartment in my building?' she asked. (She didn't know I was apartment-hunting!) I said I would like to see it, at least, and so during my lunch hour I went down to Fifteenth Street. I didn't know what to expect.

A genial superintendent came with me to show me the apartment. This was on the ninth floor of a ten-story building. The wall that blocked the light and air from my friend's apartment ended at the eighth floor. My apartment was light and airy. Huge windows in every room, and closets right down the length of a hallway. High ceilings and plenty of room for me. And a rent almost unheard of in Manhattan. God surely did know what I would like!

Although this was several years ago, there were already lon_ waiting lists for moderately-priced apartments, but for me there was no list, no waiting. The apartment was mine that same day. Just what I had wanted, and more than I could have asked for. I lived contentedly in this apartment, made wonderful friends, and had some very happy times. I was within walking distance of almost any place I wanted to go. I walked to and from my work, window-shopping, discovering interesting buildings. This home was just exactly what I needed, and when I let go of my human planning and let God direct me, I was swiftly pointed in the right direction.

I don't think it does any harm to think about what we would like to have, and to get a clear mental picture of some aspects of it. But I do believe we must know that God already is aware of our needs. We don't have to outline to Him! When we can say, and believe, 'You know, Father, what I need,' then our way is prepared for us.

So, next time you have a longing, outline it if you want to, but do remember to give God credit for knowing already what is in your heart and what is for your highest good. God does know what we need! That is the miracle."

August Weekly Unity and New magazine incorporated into Unity.

E. Pharaby Boileau retired from the Heritage Room.

Biographical information of Charles Rickert Fillmore. Unity School of Christianity Public Relations Department. "Charles R. Fillmore was elected president of Unity School of Christianity 1972. In commenting on the purpose of Unity, he states, 'Unity exists to be of service to those seeking a practical approach to spiritual growth and unfoldment. We feel Unity has some insights that can help people live happier, healthier, more productive lives, and it is our sincere desire to communicate these ideas to all who express an interest.'

Mr. Fillmore has contributed significantly to the Unity message through the written word. His articles have been published in Daily Word and Unity magazine, and he has authored several pamphlets including, The Adventure Called Unity, in which he describes Unity as 'a religious philosophy with an 'open end', seeking to find God's truth in all of life, wherever it may be. I believe Unity can make one's life an adventure, because Unity arouses man's interest in his spiritual nature.'

Mr. Fillmore is active in several civic and service organizations in the community. He is a past chairman of the Greater Kansas City

Chapter of the American Red Cross and former member of the coordinating council of Lee's Summit school district. Mr. Fillmore is a former member of the citizens' advisory committee for the Missouri Conservation Commission and former co-chairman of the Jackson County Citizens' Committee for Conservation. The Committee successfully sponsored a petition drive which helped pass legislation for the conservation of Missouri's wildlife.

An avid naturalist, his hobbies take him out-of-doors where he enjoys fishing and golf.

Mr. Fillmore and his wife, Anne, reside in Unity Village. They have two grown daughters, Harriet and Connie. Harriet (Mrs. Richard DeBauge) is a graduate of Duke University. She and her husband live in Parsons, Kansas. Their two daughters are in college. An ordained Unity minister, Connie is a graduate of Pomona College, Claremont, California, and Unity's ministerial training program."

The Unity Correspondence School, that was created in 1909, was discontinued in 1972.

Following is a summary of the monthly meeting reports of the Ladies Auxiliary for 1972.

January: A thank you note was read from Bill Hunt of the Highview School for Boys for the Christmas party and gifts from the group. Mary Rowe gave the lesson based on Martha Smock's book Halfway Up the Mountain.

February: Jane Paulson told of the many worthwhile projects of the Youth of Unity. The group recently donated toys to the Cerebral Palsy Unit of the Harry S. Truman Children's Neurological Center and helped the youngsters assemble them. This group is very busy with projects to raise money like pancake breakfasts and chili suppers and need to be supported.

March: Jane Paulson introduced Pam Moore, president of the Village Center Youth of Unity, and Dick Savoy their sponsor. Pam on behalf of the Y.O.U. presented a check in the amount of $75.00 to the auxiliary for the air conditioning fund.

June: Helen Davis, treasurer reported a fund balance of $595.90. She had talked to Mr. Arni of Unity School and he told her that the air conditioning unit has been approved by Unity School and should be installed soon.

July: Katie Earl, president, thanked all that helped with the INTA Conference. It was a very meaningful experience for all who served.

August: In the absence of Jane Paulson, Wilma Powell told of her trip to the Holy Land. She had the trip outlined city to city and it felt as if we traveled with her to the Garden of Gethsamie, The Wailing Wall and many other points of interest.

December: Mr. Arni, Unity School treasurer, was a speical guest and he was presented with a check for $1,000.00 to pay for the air conditioning unit for the club house. Only one year and two months was required to obtain the goal.

"From The Beginning - Unity" continues in Volume II